MAN UP

Man Up

THE NEW MISOGYNY AND THE RISE
OF VIOLENT EXTREMISM

CYNTHIA MILLER-IDRISS

PRINCETON UNIVERSITY PRESS

PRINCETON & OXFORD

Requests for permission to reproduce material from this work should be sent to permissions@press.princeton.edu

Published by Princeton University Press
41 William Street, Princeton, New Jersey 08540
99 Banbury Road, Oxford OX2 6JX

press.princeton.edu

GPSR Authorized Representative: Easy Access System Europe - Mustamäe tee 50, 10621 Tallinn, Estonia, gpsr.requests@easproject.com

All Rights Reserved

ISBN 9780691257549
ISBN (e-book) 9780691257600

British Library Cataloging-in-Publication Data is available

Editorial: Rachael Levay, Erik Beranek, and Tara Dugan
Production Editorial: Theresa Liu
Jacket/Cover Design: Heather Hansen
Production: Erin Suydam
Publicity: Julia Haav and Kathryn Stevens
Copyeditor: Karen Verde

Jacket image: Brady Rogers / Unsplash

This book has been composed in Arno

Printed in the United States of America

10 9 8 7 6 5 4 3 2 1

For everyone who has been held down,
for anyone working toward change,
and for Zee,
who deserves this and so much more.

CONTENTS

A Woman's Place

"For a long time," Simone de Beauvoir wrote in *The Second Sex*, "I have hesitated to write a book on woman. The subject is irritating, especially to women; and it is not new." De Beauvoir eventually wrote what became a radical treatise on patriarchy after conceding that prior writing on the issue of women over the past century had "done little to illuminate the problem." It had even created the illusion, she suggests, that there might not be a problem at all.[1]

I find myself in much the same position. For years, I have been asked to comment on the intersection of gender and extremism, even though it wasn't the primary focus of my research. I did comment—in keynotes and op-eds, in congressional testimony, in global intelligence briefings and legal analyses. But in those explanations, gender was almost always a footnote—a momentary mention of toxic masculinity, rising women's engagement, or increases in attacks on trans people—while my main arguments about the reasons behind the exponential growth of far-right extremism were centered on other issues. In part, I have hesitated to shine a lens directly on gender for intellectual reasons: I worried that separating gender from the rest of my analyses would somehow marginalize it—as if readers could then say: Aha, here is where we learn about gender, but then afterward return to the rest of the analysis where they no longer need to consider it. When pressed by a reviewer to add a chapter on gender to my last book, *Hate in the Homeland*, I declined, instead rewriting the book's introduction to include this explanation: "There is no dedicated chapter related to gender in this book, in part because I see issues of gender and misogyny as central to all of them." I described the ways that each chapter in that book took up questions of gender in specific ways, such as through messages to men about manhood, brotherhood, and being a warrior, soldier, or protector. "In each of the new, mainstream spaces and places where the far right is recruiting and radicalizing young people today," I wrote, "gender, misogyny, and masculinity play a foundational role."

Not long after I published that book, though, the story broke about the arrests of fourteen men in a foiled 2020 antigovernment militia kidnapping plot targeting Michigan governor Gretchen Whitmer. I was stunned to find little discussion about the deeply misogynistic language the men used, including the call to "just grab the bitch."[2] The plot itself horrified the nation, and the world, with extensive global media coverage focused on the highly developed and violent nature of the plan—which included livestreaming a "trial" that would result in her public execution. But there was little discussion of the gendered or misogynistic aspects of the plot.

I had already watched as Trump rallies were peppered with misogynistic phrases like "Lock Her Up" or "Send Them Back" in reference to Hillary Clinton and several congresswomen of color. I had listened to the recording of Trump describing how he can physically grab women wherever he wants to, while #MeToo scandals, the Jeffrey Epstein sex trafficking case, and the resignation of the New York governor following sexual harassment allegations populated the news cycle. I saw calls for bans on LGBTQ+ themed books at libraries and schools across the country, and watched as dozens of anti-LGBTQ+ bills were proposed in state legislatures. All the while, I analyzed and commented professionally on violent hate attacks in Christchurch, El Paso, Pittsburgh, and Buffalo, among scores of others.

Those attacks rightfully launched a flurry of attention to the root causes of and potential strategies to interrupt and prevent the violence. They brought about dozens of US congressional hearings, a new national strategy on countering domestic violent extremism, a White House summit on hate-fueled violence, and untold numbers of policy reports and scholarly analyses about these trends in violence. Almost none of these analyses have attended to the gendered dimensions of violent extremism.

My aim here is to remedy this flaw—in my own work, first and foremost—by showing how gender and misogyny are foundational to the extreme right and its violent outcomes. I hope that readers will find this book in conversation with my previous work in specific ways. While I have previously focused primarily on the ordinary spaces and places where young people encounter extremist ideas in their everyday lives, *Man Up* argues that each of those spaces and places are fundamentally gendered in ways that shape violent outcomes. *Man Up* is also developed with an aim toward a more intersectional approach to exclusionary ideas, looking at how gender-based bigotry and misogyny underpins but also amplifies other forms of harm and hate—including racism, xenophobia, and discrimination related to disability.

In centering men and the violence some of them enact, I lean into Jared Yates Sexton's argument that the problem is not immigrants or women or minorities who seek fairness or a better life—rather, we have to look at the "men trying to hold them down."[3] At the same time, though, I emphasize not only the violent or misogynistic actions that men may take, but also the cultural norms and messages that boys and men constantly receive that too often police the boundaries of what it is to be a man. Those messages often insist that men eschew vulnerability and connection in the name of stoicism, aggression, and a view of manhood as determined by strength, power, and a willingness to be violent. Even very young boys learn to reject femininity and modify their behavior in public to hide their softness and sensitivity and to project toughness.[4] This book's title, *Man Up*, is a nod to one of these messages—that boys and men need to be tougher, or stronger, or less vulnerable or weak, and that those qualities of strength and bravery and toughness are inherently linked to manhood and being a real man. As Jean Guerrero recently wrote about the epidemic of men's loneliness, the message that boys often get is to "man up and shut up."[5]

Writing this at a moment when a Black, South Asian candidate was running for President—against a candidate known for his misogynistic and racist statements—brings a timeliness to this book that I could not have anticipated. Throughout the campaign and post-election period, misogyny frequently appeared in the news headlines—including through the sexist abuse directed at women Secret Service agents in the wake of the July 2024 assassination attempt on then former President Trump.[6] In a 24-hour period after US Election Day, the Institute for Strategic Dialogue recorded a 4600% increase in the terms "Your body, my choice" and "Get back in the kitchen" on the social media platform X.[7] As I continue to observe Kamala Harris be assailed with racist and misogynistic comments online, I am forced to admit that in truth, my reluctance to focus on gender and misogyny is not just intellectual. It's personal. I have resented having to look at the issue as closely as we all need to—at least not with the closeness that a book like this will require—because it feels like we should be beyond it. Clearly, we are not beyond it. This book begs the question of my own place—of anyone's place—in ways that I hope will spark reflection and recognition among its readers. Looking directly at the everyday misogyny that underpins mass violence and rising far-right extremism is painful. It unearths a lot of things I have had to look past to get the work done—by which I mean not only the gross rape threats on my office voicemail, but also the occasional sexist and sexualized comments from colleagues that have run through my career in big and small ways.

The stories of misogyny, harassment, and sexual and gender-based violence I listened to and wrote about—and the fact that so many of the victims will never get justice—haunt me. Once those stories were in my head, there was no other way for me to process them than to write about them and ideally to raise awareness of how ubiquitous and central gender-based violence is to the mobilization of extremist violence. Like de Beauvoir, I now see that my own reluctance to focus on gender may have helped create the illusion that there is no problem at all. Worse, it may have disguised the fact that the threats I receive and the occasional sexualized comment at work are connected—in ways that hold true for all gendered violence and the feedback loop between ordinary and violent misogyny.

After spending much of my career detailing ways the extreme has gone mainstream, this book takes the opposite starting point, arguing that the mobilization of violence on the extreme right is enabled by rising misogyny in the mainstream. The narrative arc of this book asks:

What happens if we approach sex and gender as a primary organizing framework that mobilizes extreme violence? Across five empirical chapters, *Man Up* articulates how gendered understandings of the world—including male entitlement to women's bodies, hierarchies of superiority and inferiority based on sex; a rigid and relentlessly narrow definition of manhood and permissible expressions of masculinity; patriarchal beliefs about power and leadership; the valorization of women's roles as mothers, wives, and caregivers; and sexist, homophobic, and transphobic ideas about purity, contamination, protection, and defense—establish cognitive footholds for violent extremism to take root and grow. I argue that these gendered understandings—and the patriarchy they seek to maintain—create a kind of mental scaffolding that enables greater receptivity to widely circulating propaganda, disinformation, conspiracy theories, and racist and misogynist ideas that originate on the fringes. I also show the many ways that gendered understandings are baked into that same content.

To make these arguments, I focus on cases that primarily draw on incidents of violence, sexism, and misogyny—and their intersections with racism and anti-LGBTQ+ movements—in the so-called West as defined by the Global Terrorism Database—Western Europe, North America, and Oceania. These regions are the parts of the world identified as facing the greatest rise in far-right extremism. I heavily situate examples in the United States, which bears a disproportionate share of both far-right terrorist attacks and lethality and exports much of the white supremacist propaganda that circulates globally online.[8] This is not meant to minimize the fact that people across the world experience virulent misogyny and structural forms of violence and exclusion, including state-sponsored ones—in ways that are often far worse than the forms I discuss here. I can't write this book without acknowledging these broader struggles and making it clear that there is no equivalency here: This book cannot do justice to the wide swaths of oppression, violent discrimination, and misogyny experienced globally by millions. Nor does this book address the rise of the far right in places like India and Brazil, which have seen disturbing spikes in antidemocratic and hate-fueled violence.

The cases I analyze here, and the examples I cite, draw heavily from the countries where I have spent my entire professional career. This is partly an effort to restrain any sense of hubris about what a book like this can accomplish, and what an author like me can contribute given the shortcomings my own lens and experiences bring to this work. I may not be able to challenge the worst kinds of gendered violence globally, but I can try to illuminate and address how misogyny and gender-based bigotry underpin extremist violence in the national and regional contexts I know best. I hope I have done this task some measure of justice.

The content of this book, I know, will be hard for readers. Misogyny is uncomfortable, both affectively and intellectually, and discussing it can be especially hard for men.[9] I dove into the writing and research for this book while being keenly aware of, and sensitive to, my own identity and positionality as a white, heterosexual woman. The book is conceived, written, and edited with ongoing intentionality and awareness of my own gaps and a concerted effort to see past them, including through invited feedback and conversations with activists and scholars who live the realities of intersectional forms of misogyny, racism, anti-LGBTQ+ hate, transmisogyny, and ableism every day. I am indebted to these experts for their critical and invaluable feedback, which has much improved the nuances of this book.

I also purposely spent time debating and discussing the arguments herein with people who disagree with me—about specific concepts like "biblical patriarchy" and about broader, foundational issues like the ubiquitous violence that is also enacted on men and boys, the fear men sometimes feel in regard to other men, and the pressures that patriarchal norms and expectations put on men to be stoic, strong, and reliable providers, protectors, and defenders in ways that affect their emotional and physical well-being. The book is infinitely better because of these discussions, which also helped me think more seriously about how to make sure this book engages people who disagree with me or who are skeptical about the arguments I make. I invite those readers to engage with this book knowing that I welcome constructive criticism and dialogue across a wide variety of opinions, experiences, and political lines.

Changing the trajectory of rising extremist violence—and the role that misogyny plays in it—will require nothing less. Despite their thoughtful and challenging advice, none of these experts, friends, or colleagues deserves criticism for what I write here. I take full responsibility for my inevitable failure to get it completely right.

One final note about nomenclature: As part of my commitment to center victims and survivors rather than perpetrators in the analysis and retelling of horrific acts of violence, I do not include the names of the men who carried out the acts of terror and mass violence I reference throughout this book. I refer to them instead by their act ("the shooter," "the attacker," etc.) in the hopes that their names will not carry the recognition they so desperately seek. In the smallest of symbolic ways, I do this to move those men out of view, clearing the way for us to see how they got there to begin with.

ACKNOWLEDGMENTS

IF THERE IS ONE THING I have learned across two decades of professional writing, it is that book-writing poses a tremendous burden for anyone living, loving, or working with the author, whose constrained time and intellectual energy can frustrate the balance of other priorities. Among the people who shouldered this burden disproportionately are my research colleagues in the Polarization and Extremism Research and Innovation Lab (PERIL). My PERIL team has been a constant source of patience, inspiration, and partnership, and I am grateful to each one of them.

I shared advance drafts of this manuscript (or portions of it) with more than a dozen people, who offered deeply substantive feedback, critique, and suggestions that have immensely improved the manuscript, especially related to how misogyny and gender interact with issues of racism, intimate partner violence, disability, and masculinity, as well as the role that misogyny plays in the online gaming world, and how we might grapple with legal barriers to addressing the intersection of misogyny and violent extremism. For this I am indebted to Lydia Bates, Jan Nolting Carter, Pasha Dashtgard, Alex DiBranco, Sahar Fathi, Jordan Green, Brian Hughes, Shamil Idriss, Galen Lamphere-Englund, Eviane Leidig, Esther Lehnert, Jean O'Barr, Alexandra Onuoha, Jane Palmer, Tara Palmore, Julie Rawe, Bess Rothenberg, JJ West, and Jessica White. The book was infinitely improved by the sharp eyes of two stellar research assistants who supported literature reviews, formatting, and proofreading and provided generative reflection about their own experiences, and I am so grateful to Anne-Joy Cahill-Swenson and Sydney Worrell for this support.

I am indebted to the many places I was able to workshop these ideas, including as part of the 2022 Alexander von Humboldt Foundation Berlin summer residency program, where Angela Saini and Mala Pandurang offered especially generative insights on gender, as a Stavros Niarchos Foundation (SNF) Ithaca fellow at the University of Delaware in spring 2023, at Penn State University's Mellon Foundation Sawyer Seminar in January 2024, and at Central European University (CEU) in Vienna, Austria during my time there as a visiting professor for a master class in spring 2024.

Closer to home, my thinking about male supremacy, misogyny, and its intersections with other forms of hate have been indelibly shaped by Pasha Dashtgard, Brian Hughes, Seth Limmer, and JJ West in PERIL. Lydia Bates deserves a special callout as the first reader of the manuscript and as one of the biggest champions in the field of the issues of misogyny and male supremacy. This book likely would never have happened were it not for her persistence in raising the issue. She introduced me to the investigative journalist Jordan Green, to whom I am indebted for sharing his research on sex trafficking and abuses by white supremacist groups. My colleague TaLisa Carter raised key questions about Black feminist scholarship in a department presentation that helped me see gaps in my own work—so did Alexandra Onuoha's thoughtful review of my previous book, *Hate in the Homeland* and our subsequent conversations about intersectionality, which were essential to my thinking about racism and misogyny in *Man Up*.[1] I am indebted to them both. My coauthors on our joint PERIL-Southern Poverty Law Center guide on gender-based bigotry have likewise deeply influenced my analysis and writing: Lydia Bates, Maya Carey, R. G. Cravens, Aaron Flanagan, Cassie Miller, and Rachael Fugardi. I am equally grateful to Beth Goldberg at Jigsaw for earlier discussions related to our prebunking and wolfeinoculation videos against male supremacism.

The book itself would not have seen the light of day were it not for a small army of people who helped shepherd it from idea to proposal to production. This includes my literary agent Farley Chase, my editors Meagan Levinson and Rachael Levay, and the broader team at Princeton University Press, especially Christie Henry, Katie Stileman, Molly Grote,

Erik Beranek, Theresa Liu, Karen Verde, James Schneider, and Kathryn Stevens. Two anonymous reviewers for Princeton University Press gave generously rich, insightful, and detailed feedback that inspired me and drove my revisions in a focused and extremely helpful way.

I received permission to include three epigraphs in this book and express my gratitude and acknowledgment here. I include a quote from George Orwell's *1984* with credit to US publisher HarperCollins and the estate of the late Sonia Brownell Orwell. I am grateful to Yale University Press and the poet Ansel Elkins for permission to quote the poem "Autobiography of Eve" from her collection *Blue Yodel*. And I express my gratitude to Sara Meger for permission to quote an essay originally available through the Gender and War Project.

This book raises a lot of difficult issues about men, masculinity, and manhood, and so I am compelled to say this: I have lived with and loved men my entire life—my father and grandfathers and brother and uncles, my coaches, my housemates from college and beyond, my husband, and many of my closest friends, neighbors, classmates, and colleagues from childhood through adulthood. These relationships have been the most meaningful, generative, and restorative parts of my life. I could never have written a book like this were it not for the constant and steady presence in my life of men who embody a different way of being in the world, who have struggled and worked to change when needed, and who have challenged me to remember the ways that they are affected by and suffer from patriarchal norms and expectations, the violence enacted by other boys and men, and the fear and shame that results. Each one of them has my love and gratitude.

Writing this book took a bigger toll than anything else I have written. I am forever grateful to the friends and family who tolerate and celebrate me in all my messiness, and whose patience and support in tangible and intangible ways made writing it possible. They gave me quiet places to write, in summer cabins and guest rooms, in housesitting arrangements and borrowed basement rooms and apartments. They read drafts, sent feedback, and talked with me for hours and hours about the ideas as I developed and worked on them. And above all, they offered me a safe and loving place to land when things were bleak. To Gary, Barb, Jon,

Zee, Milas, Bess, Traci, Jan, Julie, Andrew, Brian, Katie, Aaron, Lydia, Joan, Tara, Eileen, Sonja, Erin, Laurel, and all the Batters: thank you, thank you, thank you. Most importantly and closest to home, I am ever thankful for my children's patience and grace with their mama and their unquestioned faith in the possibilities for change, including on the very issues at the core of this book. As always, my most ineffable gratitude goes to Shamil, who has been my best friend, my unswerving champion, and my sanctuary for thirty years. This book, like everything, would be impossible without him.

LIST OF ABBREVIATIONS

AAP American Academy of Pediatrics

AAPI Asian American and Pacific Islander

ADL Anti-Defamation League

AI Artificial intelligence

ACLU American Civil Liberties Union

CDC Centers for Disease Control and Prevention

CELL Counterterrorism Education Learning Lab

CSAM child sexual abuse material

DEA US Drug Enforcement Administration

DEI Diversity, Equity and Inclusion

DHS US Department of Homeland Security

DOTR "Day of the Rope"

EGRN Extremism and Gaming Research Network

ERA Equal Rights Amendment

FBI US Federal Bureau of Investigation

GLAAD Gay and Lesbian Alliance Against Defamation

HRC Human Rights Campaign

ISIL Islamic State in Iraq and the Levant

KKK Ku Klux Klan

LGBTQ+ Lesbian, Gay, Bisexual, Transgender, Queer

LMR "last-minute resistance"

MAGA Make America Great Again

MGTOW Men Going Their Own Way

MLM Men's Liberation Movement

MRA Men's Rights Activist

MRM Men's Rights Movement

NAACP National Association for the Advancement of Colored People

NGO Non-Governmental Organization

ODNI US Office of the Director of National Intelligence

O9A Order of Nine Angles

PERIL Polarization and Extremism Research and Innovation Lab

PUA Pick Up Artist

SMV Sexual Market Value

STOP W.O.K.E. Stop Wrongs to Our Kids and Employees

TERF Trans-Exclusionary Radical Feminist

UN United Nations

UNOCT United Nations Office of Counterterrorism

VR virtual reality

This book contains data, stories, and analysis that may be triggering for victims and survivors of gender- and sexual abuse. Please consult the resource list at the back of this book for help. If you are in crisis in the United States, please call, text, or chat with the Suicide and Crisis Lifeline at 988, or contact the Crisis Text Line by texting TALK to 741741.

PART I

Othering Gender

Introduction

OTHERING GENDER

> When is terrorism not terrorism? When the political motivations are misogyny.
>
> —SARA MEGER, "WHEN IS TERRORISM NOT TERRORISM"

AFTER A COLLEAGUE followed me into a conference elevator some years ago and tried to kiss me, murmuring "What kind of games are you playing?" as I pushed away and ducked out the door, the first thing I did was call my sister.[1] How could I have possibly sent signals I wasn't aware of, I wondered? She sighed. "Your problem is that you're too nice," she admonished. "You have to be more of a bitch."

God forbid you are more of a bitch, though, because some men get unpredictably, viciously aggressive when you say no, or don't reply to their texts, or reject their advances.[2] This isn't all men, of course, but as I write, the news is filled with story after story of men who react violently when women or girls reject them.[3] Some of these stories are sensational—like that of a California man who made national news in January 2023 for repeatedly slamming a dump truck into his wife's home during their divorce proceedings, after he learned she had filed a restraining order against him. More often, the stories are so banal they barely register. Thousands of videos and threads on social media document women's everyday experiences of street harassment, catcalling, and stalking, including the reactive anger of men when their response (or lack thereof) is not pleasing enough. For these enraged men, women who say no are breaking the rules. For some men (and which men it might be is so unpredictable that women must act as if it is all men), rejection violates an unquestioned sense of entitlement to women's time, attention, smiles, and adoration. It can spiral into shame-fueled rage at the sheer audacity, lack of gratitude, and arrogance of women who reject them.[4] Women who say no are often called derogatory slurs, threatened with violence, or assaulted. Still others lose career opportunities. In the worst cases, women are murdered by men they reject.

Girls and women have been killed for "offenses" like saying no to a potential prom date, or for ignoring catcalling.[5] A Wisconsin girl recently was shot in the head multiple times by a 14-year-old boy after his "fit of rage" over their breakup.[6] In fact, 34% of the nearly five thousand women who were killed in the United States in 2021 died at the hands of their own intimate partner—a rate of almost five women per day and a statistic that is a certain undercount, given that it is based on only 63% reporting from US law enforcement agencies.[7] In case after case, these men kill not only their partners but also their children, bystanders, or others they target with their rage. In late 2022, a Utah man killed his wife and five children after his wife filed for divorce,[8] tragically illustrating what the data have consistently shown: The most dangerous time for a woman in an abusive relationship is when she leaves.

It's not that being a Nice Girl—or ignoring men altogether—is necessarily safer.[9] Around the same time as I was being cornered in that elevator, a 14-year-old girl standing on a Florida sidewalk refused a driver's offer to pay her for sex; the man pulled her into his car by her hair, choked her, threw her back onto the street and then ran over her several times.[10] Even online rejection between people who haven't met in person can make men angry. In one study of online dating, romantic rejection increased men's "hostile tendencies," measured as both aggressive tendencies toward the rejecting partner and hostile attitudes toward women more broadly.[11]

In other words, being "more of a bitch" is risky, since refusing to give men the attention, adoration, or service they desire makes some men very, very angry. More than 94% of far-right violent and nonviolent extremists in the United States between 1948 and 2021 were men.[12] Men commit 98% of mass shootings and at least 94% of sexual abuse.[13] Being "more of a bitch" is even riskier for nonwhite women, who are disproportionate victims of gun violence from intimate partners—data that are clear even with high rates of underreporting in marginalized communities.[14] The overall scale of the problem is staggering, with nearly twenty people per minute being physically abused in the United States by an intimate partner.[15] The outcomes are especially bad for trans women, who experience disproportionate incidents of violence compared to cisgender women, and for girls and women who are disabled, who are twice as likely to experience sexual violence in their lifetime.[16] LGBTQ+ people are often targeted with violence by men who are enraged at them simply for existing in ways that do not conform to their expected norms for gender expression or behavior. This is especially true for trans and gender-diverse people who are assaulted, as one violent attacker later described in trying to justify his violence, for "flaunting" their identity.[17] The very idea of "flaunting"—i.e., of being somehow excessively or abnormally public or flamboyant—illustrates what the philosopher Kate Manne has so thoughtfully argued: At its root, misogyny is about policing the behavior of anyone who does not adhere to patriarchal norms and expectations.[18]

But these ongoing, ubiquitous cases of interpersonal violence are almost always treated as wholly separate from the kinds of episodic mass shootings and attacks that fall under the national security mandate of the federal (or any given state) government.[19] This happens even though enraged partners do not only pose a tremendous risk to the safety of their lovers: Their anger clearly can spill over to anyone who gets in the way. In well over half of mass shootings, the perpetrator shot an intimate partner as part of the rampage.[20] Relatedly, as many as half of the people killed in intimate partner violence are not the partner themselves.[21] Violent misogyny, stalking, harassment, and abuse of women or the LGBTQ+ community is a constant detail in reports of mass shootings or terrorist attacks, although it is barely acknowledged and even more rarely analyzed. In 2019, the *New York Times* detailed dozens of cases of mass shooters from across the ideological spectrum who share a common thread: "a history of hating women, assaulting wives, girlfriends and female family members, or sharing misogynistic views online."[22] Of all mass murders in the United States in 2018, 83% of the offenders had a history of prior violence against women.[23] That year was no exception. In case after case, misogynistic rage against women, the LGBTQ+ community, or prior reports of intimate partner violence are a documented part of perpetrators' histories, even when their official motives lie elsewhere (or are unidentified).

This pattern holds across a wide variety of violent plots, attacks, and mass shootings. The attackers who killed dozens at a Virginia university, a Florida LGBTQ+ nightclub, a Parkland high school, and a Maryland newsroom all had prior reports of stalking, domestic violence, or harassment of women.[24] Before he killed nineteen students and two teachers at an elementary school in Uvalde, Texas in spring 2022, the alleged assailant regularly threatened teen girls online with kidnapping, rape, and murder—an online experience so normalized that many youth who observed his digital rage dismissed it as simply a product of, as one teenager put it, "what online is."[25] Later that same year, in November 2022, an attack on a New York synagogue was narrowly averted when two men were intercepted by police at Penn Station with multiple firearms, a ski mask, bulletproof vest, a military-style knife, and a swastika arm patch. The media was understandably focused on the antisemitic nature of the imminent attack. But a year earlier, one of the men had bragged online about violently attacking a transgender person and said he was most proud of being "good at raping women."[26]

Some men's violent rage is directed toward the abstract enemy of "feminism" itself or the idea that women's gains come at the direct expense of men and white civilization more broadly, especially because white women are purportedly not having enough white babies. This type of misogyny often intersects with antisemitism or the scapegoating of Jews or racial and ethnic minorities for the so-called great replacement of white civilization.[27] It also directly targets "feminists" who are perceived to be taking away men's rights. The son of a New Jersey judge was killed in a 2020 attack on her home by an anti-feminist Men's Rights Activist (MRA) who had previously filed repeated unsuccessful lawsuits challenging the constitutionality of nightclubs' "Ladies' Night" promotions. He left behind nearly two thousand pages of written text infused with racist and misogynistic ideas, including a reference to his victim as "a lazy and incompetent Latina judge."[28] In dozens of other incidents—at a Black historic church in Charleston, a California synagogue, a Buffalo grocery store, and more—attackers blamed feminism, falling white birth rates, frustration with women who didn't meet their sexual needs, or blamed minorities for "raping" white women as motivation for their attacks.[29]

Other men become enraged enough to murder people just because women exist in ways that bother them. The eight people killed in a series of massage spa shootings in Atlanta—six of whom were Asian spa workers—were targeted because the 21-year-old man who shot them believed he was entitled to a life without the sexual temptation he felt they created. The victims' ethnicity is also key here, especially considering hypersexualized tropes about Asian women and the timing of tremendous anti-Asian rhetoric and violence during the COVID-19 pandemic. In other cases, men don't even have to be rejected to get angry enough to explode in violent rage—it's apparently enough just not to be invited. While a motive was never released, an early report from the 2023 Monterey Park shooting at a dance hall that killed eleven suggested the gunman was upset that a woman had been invited to the dance hall without him.[30]

In a growing number of other instances, misogynist and male supremacist perpetrators act out their rage in violent mass attacks that specifically target groups of women. Many of these attacks are committed at the hands of men in the violent, misogynist incel (involuntary celibate) movement, who lash out violently at women in anger at their inability to establish romantic or sexual relationships. Dozens of people have been killed over the past decade in misogynist incel attacks targeting women at a California sorority, a Florida yoga studio, an Oregon community college, and a New Mexico high school—in addition to similar attacks in England and Canada.[31]

It is worth noting that boys and men are not only the predominant perpetrators of violence in a culture that valorizes and rewards dominance and aggression as hallmarks of masculinity.[32] They are also victims of that same violence, as childhood victims of domestic abuse, bullying, and street fighting.[33] Boys and men are struggling in a bevy of ways that have only recently gained mainstream attention, including the labor loss of traditional male jobs in a postindustrialized economy, the declining percentage of men relative to women who earn higher education degrees, and the fact that men account for three-quarters of "deaths of despair" (overdose, suicide, alcohol abuse) amid surging reports of male loneliness, depression, anxiety, and isolation.[34] Two-thirds of men aged 18–23 report that "no one really knows me," while 25% of men under age 30 (and 20% of unmarried men overall) say they have no close friends. Half of American men say their online lives are more rewarding than their offline lives.[35] Mens' and boys' loneliness is also shaped by the fact that people spend less and less time in the company of other human beings more generally. In the United States, 15–24-year-olds spend 70% less time in person today with friends than two decades ago.[36] That's particularly meaningful given that the strength of adolescent friendships predicts a whole host of wellbeing measures in adulthood, from healthy romantic relationships to lower anxiety, aggression, and improved adult mental health overall.[37]

There has been periodic acknowledgment of how these outcomes are a part of a "masculinity crisis," with boys and men facing relentless messaging about being the problem while also facing pressure to conform to what has been called the "man box" in a culture that insists men are stoic and hard rather than emotional and soft, are providers and protectors rather than caregivers and supporters, and are strong, sexually dominant, physically tough, and hypermasculine.[38] The prevailing message that many boys and men receive is that men are inherently dangerous, violent, and bad in ways that can make manhood itself seem somehow shameful. These messages are rooted in real stories and revelations of the atrocious behavior of some men, from the #MeToo movement to Catholic priests' abuses of children and the dozens of men recently convicted in France of raping an unconscious woman over a decade-long period after her husband drugged her. But a steady diet of outrage at very real bad behavior by men—alongside too few opportunities to see positive male role models or for boys and men to be able to express pride or engage with meaning and purpose as men—has further contributed to the crisis of masculinity. There has been far less open discussion, however, about how that masculinity crisis is evolving into a misogyny crisis.

There is no question that masculinity is both more fragile and more policed than femininity. Sanctions are stricter for men who violate gendered norms than they are for women—in part because Western culture valorizes masculinity and devalues femininity. And masculinity itself is often performed through that devaluing of femininity, regardless of who performs it—i.e., trans women, gay men, or heterosexual women.[39] While girls and women are now allowed broader flexibility in embracing traits and activities traditionally seen as "masculine," the same is not true for boys and men who adopt traditional "feminine" traits or roles— as evidenced in differences in how parents respond to "feminine boys" or "masculine girls" and in the social sanctions and bullying that each group faces among peers.[40] In a modern patriarchal system, girls and women have more freedom to breach gender roles and expectations, but are less valued; boys and men have less freedom to reject social expectations about manhood and masculinity, but receive more automatic status and power. The implications for violence are devastating. A culture that rewards and expects boys and men to be dominant, aggressive, and violent ultimately produces and reproduces that same violence in ways that harm all of us.[41] And yet we fail to acknowledge, address, or prevent that from happening in any meaningful way.

The consequences of our inattention to the gendered dimensions of mass violence are not limited to fringe terrorist movements or violent attacks: They also affect and shape our broader democratic crisis, especially related to growing support for political violence. People who hold hostile sexist views are substantially more likely to express support for political violence and violent extremism.[42] The relationship is robust, reported across a wide range of national and ideological contexts, showing that hostile sexist and misogynist attitudes are often a bigger predictor of support for violent extremism than any other factor—including, in some countries, religiosity, age, gender, level of education, and employment.[43] These factors also affect rising violence against women political leaders in ways that fundamentally undermine inclusive democracies.[44] Online violence and abuse against women in politics aims to silence or punish women leaders, especially those who speak out about issues of gender equality.[45] Women politicians have been subject to beatings and killings, blackmail, extortion, and smear campaigns globally.[46] They also face the constant and quotidian problem of gendered media coverage that objectifies and trivializes women politicians alongside an "adversarial style of politics that enables and foments sexual harassment in legislative chambers."[47]

Taken together, these varied categories of violent harm rooted in sexism and misogyny reveal a crisis all the more shocking for how it is largely ignored. The data are crystal clear. Women are perpetrators of violence in many ways, including through support for white supremacist and other violent extremist movements and as domestic violent actors. But the most common—and least discussed—feature of mass shooters and violent terrorists is their manhood. And despite all the evidence about how boys and men are encouraged to see violence as "alluring and satisfying," as bell hooks observes, when individual boys or men are violent, "pundits tend to behave as though it were a mystery."[48] In fact, what Rebecca Solnit describes as the "pandemic of violence" is always "explained as anything but gender, anything but what would seem to be the broadest explanatory pattern of all."[49] The oversight is strikingly evident across a wide variety of government and nonprofit reports on terrorism and mass shootings. In the FBI's list of twenty-two "concerning behaviors" exhibited before mass shootings, gender does not appear a single time. Instead, warning signs are listed in ways that ignore gender itself, with categories like "interpersonal," "threats or confrontations," or "violent media use," despite the fact that the targets of those problems are likely to involve women or intimate partners.[50] We fail to see gender-based violence as ideological, in other words, even when it is rooted in dehumanization and categorical, identity-based hate. This is a failure with many ripple effects. We rarely count online or offline misogyny and gender-based harassment as hate speech. We do not classify intimate partner or sexual violence as hate crimes. Nor do we typically see misogyny included as part of hate group tracking or extremist incident monitoring reports from nongovernmental organizations or government agencies.[51] The silences in the data and reporting are as shocking as they are deafening.

Even more tellingly, the US government doesn't include gender or sexual orientation as categories within our national threat assessment classification of domestic violent extremism. The threat assessment classification system breaks domestic violent extremism into three major categories, with subcategories for specific types of extremism, like sovereign citizens or anarchists. In a variety of formal and informal ways, these categories help shape national security priorities, such as staffing decisions in federal security and law enforcement agencies, as well as attention through congressional hearings and staff briefings. Attacks motivated by gender or sexual orientation are folded into a catchall category of "other."[52] Even animal rights extremists—who pose a risk to property damage at wildlife facilities and laboratories but are considered a "low threat in the United States"—get a category.[53] Not so for gender or sexuality. This oversight is part of why existing approaches have done little to eradicate the problem. Gendered violence, at least in the US government assessment, is "other."[54]

It's hard to see a problem for which there is no category. It's also hard to conceptualize the scope of the problem when expertise about it is spread across many different areas of work. Experts who work at the intersection of gender and violence do so from at least three major starting points, each of which has its own subfields, conferences, associations, and nonprofit organizations developing interventions—too often in isolation from the others. First is work on patriarchy, nationalism, and gender, including research on sexism, masculinities, misogyny, misogynoir, and transmisogyny, often through scholarship in the social sciences and humanities. The second starting point is research and intervention work on violence against women and the LGBTQ+ community, especially through intimate partner violence, sexual assault, and sex and human trafficking, which tends to exist in more applied academic fields and schools of social work and public health. That form of violence is addressed in the United States at the local, state, and federal levels through law enforcement agencies, local domestic violence and rape crises centers, and the US Department of Health and Human Services and Department of Justice. Finally, work on violent extremism that addresses the growing problem of mass shootings, targeted violence, and domestic terrorist violence directly targeting women and the LGBTQ+ community or otherwise rooted in gender-based bigotry tends to take place in schools or departments of security studies, criminology, and terrorism, and is handled at the US government level by the Department of Homeland Security and its state equivalents. Across these disparate agencies, organizations, and fields, there is too often a lack of cooperation, with competition and turf wars for funding and attention all too common.[55]

One aim of this book is to stitch these areas of work together to see the full scope of the problem more clearly. By connecting these three categories, I hope to demonstrate how ordinary and everyday forms of sexist, misogynist, and anti-LGBTQ+ harm normalize and help mainstream violence in ways that create fertile ground for extreme gender-based bigotry and antifeminist misogynist ideologies to take root. I also connect these escalating patterns of hate and violence to a common thread in the virulent defense of traditional patriarchies, showing how gendered social changes—from increasing women's political and corporate leadership to a disrupted gender binary—are framed by far-right actors as an existential threat to the nation's way of life in ways that mobilize violence. But while violence itself tends to emanate from the fringes, the problems are much bigger than "extremists" per se. Extremist violence, as I argue throughout this book, is underpinned by and mobilized through conservative mobilization, mainstream normalization, and liberal silencing of misogyny and gender-based bigotry.

It's not just the defense of patriarchies in general that is mobilizing surges in political and hate-fueled violence. It is the defense of white patriarchy—in ways that illustrate how different forms of supremacism and hate overlap and mutually reinforce each other. The gendered dimensions of violent extremism are, as an audience member at a Penn State lecture helpfully framed during my January 2024 lecture, perhaps best thought of as "racialized gender"—a concept that is echoed in Francesca Scrinzi's work on the racialization of sexism.[56] Sexist and misogynist online cultures frequently overlap with racist and xenophobic ones—through banal ways like meme sharing and in violent ways like the targeted harassment of women of color or the framing of migrants and Muslims as a sexualized threat to white women. These dynamics are embedded in long histories. Lynchings of Black men in the American South in the post-emancipation era were often linked to rumors of savage rape—or to any perceived sexual advance on a white woman. And those lynchings aimed to both terrorize and emasculate Black men, often through literal castrations.[57]

It's worth noting here that the interactions between racism, white supremacy, and misogyny are complicated and sometimes counterintuitive. In recent years there has been an increase in far-right engagement and even white supremacist terrorist acts by individuals who are nonwhite. In May 2023, a Latino man who was both a neo-Nazi and part of violent misogynistic communities online shot and killed eight people at a shopping mall.[58] The former chairman of the extremist group Proud Boys is Cuban American Enrique Tarrio. Nonwhite individuals also engage in white supremacist extremism and terrorism overseas. In Singapore, a teen of Chinese ethnicity was placed under security restrictions in 2024 after being radicalized to white supremacist extremism online and developing an "intense hatred" of African Americans, Arabs, and LGBTQ+ individuals.[59] There are complex reasons why people of color might support white supremacist ideas and movements, including colorism and racism within and across ethnic groups.[60] But misogyny also plays a key role as an ideological glue, as scholars have pointed out in describing increasing support from people of color for Trump and broader far-right and 'alt-right' movements. As Daniel HoSang and Joseph Lowndes argue, whether expressed as patriarchal traditionalism, "street-brawling bravado," or online misogyny, "masculinity bridges racial difference for populist, fascist, and even white nationalist politics."[61]

Toxic online subcultures that are misogynistic can easily introduce or strengthen exclusionary ideas about national purity, degradation, and degeneracy that are racist and dehumanizing. And political violence that is ostensibly motivated by ideology has often targeted women leaders and elected officials with particular vitriol, harassment, and harm.

This is why I argue that it is impossible to understand the rise of the modern far right without recognizing how it is fundamentally gendered. Throughout this book, I aim to show how misogyny and other tactics of patriarchal enforcement underpin broader expressions of far-right violence and extremism. These gendered dimensions of violent extremism, however, are inextricably racialized, rooted in and intertwined with other hierarchies of exclusion and belonging.

Before turning to the strategies of misogynistic enforcement that I argue are hardwired into far-right extremism and other forms of mass violence, it is necessary to unpack trends in that violence and in the surging online misogyny that I argue underpins it.

The Rise of (Online) Misogyny and the Violent Far Right

On virtually every measure we have available, political and hate-fueled violence, which I refer to as "far-right violence," continues to surge in the United States.[62] Terrorism has fallen in the West overall, with 55% fewer attacks in 2023. But 76% of those attacks took place in the United States—the majority of which were attributed to far-right sympathies. And other forms of hate-fueled and political violence, including hate crimes, death threats, and harassment directed toward elected officials, poll workers, and other local leaders, have surged, with several categories (such as antisemitism, Islamophobia, and anti-LGBTQ+ hate) breaking records.[63] As of mid-2024, threats of violence and harassment against local officials were 30% higher than the same point in 2023 and 87% higher than the same point in 2022, with 2024 on pace to surpass the total number of threats from the previous year.[64] The climate of antisemitism and Islamophobia amid global fallout from the October 7, 2023, terrorist attacks in Israel and subsequent war in Gaza, the fear of political violence in the wake of two attempted assassination attempts on (then) former President Trump, and the threat of violence surrounding the 2024 US presidential election—and other 2024 and 2025 elections around the globe—continue to raise concerns about the threat landscape and possible spikes in violence.[65] In short, the problem of mass violence and far-right extremism, including hate-fueled and political violence, is increasing.

These same trends hold true for the gendered dimensions of extremist violence, and for misogyny more broadly.[66] The past several years have seen a rise in male supremacist violence, including threats, plots, and attacks from misogynist incels.[67] These developments have emerged alongside what is now understood to be a pervasive and proliferating climate of online misogyny, along with an ever-expanding digital ecosystem that makes it faster and easier to express and share hateful content and harass individuals. While it is difficult to quantify the exact amount of misogyny online or offline, misogyny and hostile sexism are regularly described as a "routine" part of women's daily lives, an emerging "established norm" of digital spaces, and an "epidemic."[68] Scholars have tracked significant increases in online misogyny starting in 2011,[69] not long after the advent of social media platforms alongside ongoing economic repercussions from the 2007–09 global financial crisis and the impact of significant racism in the wake of the election of the first Black US President. While the misogynistic ideas being expressed online are not new, online spaces and places offer novel ways to communicate those ideas.[70] Those new spaces, meanwhile, have helped transform previous men's rights discussions that were focused on family law, child custody, and mental health issues into more extreme misogynistic, violent, sexually explicit, and homophobic ideas.[71]

Misogyny is ever-present in offline spaces as well, in public spaces like nightclubs and music festivals and in professional spaces like the military, where scholars have made a causal link between American women's reduced interest in serving in the armed forces and the "unchecked proliferation of misogyny" that characterizes their lives.[72] But it is the ubiquitous and unrelenting nature of online misogyny that appears to be shaping patterns of violence. In one study of tweets in four hundred areas across forty-seven US states, researchers found that misogynistic tweets positively predict domestic and family violence.[73] A range of studies, as I discuss in depth in chapter 1, show that misogyny and hostile sexist attitudes are correlated with increased support for political violence and willingness to engage in it.

Even when they are not met with physical violence, victims of online misogyny still suffer from vitriolic threats and are sometimes forced out of the public eye. When the *Ghostbusters* movie remake was released in 2016 with an all-female lead cast, the Black leading cast member, Leslie Jones, was forced off Twitter by an onslaught of racist, threatening, and pornographic trolling.[74] Jones isn't alone. There is solid evidence that US adults are experiencing increased online harassment, often due to gender. Graphic rape and death threats have been described as a "standard discursive move" for expressing disagreement or disapproval of women online, as some men communicate in ways that not only challenge ideas, but also aim to scare and silence women's voices.[75] Overall, the share of Americans who report having been harassed online because of gender jumped from 20% to 33% from 2017 to 2020, while those harassed for sexual orientation also doubled, from 8% to 16%.[76] These figures resonate with my own experience online. When I first started writing in mainstream media outlets, a friend urged me to "never read below the line," referring to the comment section, because he knew it would contain not only legitimate critique, support, and engagement, but also ugly, hateful, gendered comments. He wasn't wrong—it only took one curious perusal "below the line" on an op-ed for me to never do that again.

The comment section problem is just one illustration of how easy it has become to harass women (and anyone else, for that matter) online. Direct messaging on social media platforms, live in-game voice chats, and other communication features of online spaces have made the use of gendered slurs, rape and death threats, and other forms of gendered discrimination a ubiquitous part of online engagement. New forms of digital media and the ever-present ease of smartphones enable the effortless sharing of sexually explicit photos and videos, including AI-generated images or videos and revenge porn, alongside cyberstalking, doxing, harassment, sextortion, verbal abuse, and hacking.[77] Social media doesn't cause these behaviors, but the platforms amplify and increase exposure to harmful and hateful content and spread misogynistic attitudes contagiously—in part because the structure of social media incentivizes angry and salacious posts, which garner more attention and are more likely to go viral.[78] Influencers and entrepreneurs who make a living from subscribed content, in turn, capitalize on these algorithms by selling outrage, which then directs additional anger and hostility toward the targets of any given short-form video rant—and when those videos garner tens of millions of views, it's easy to see how hate and threats become supersized. Meanwhile, the anonymity and homogeneous nature of communities online polarize people and also create a disinhibition effect that reduces the barriers to engaging in hateful and harassing ways. Taken together, the digital ecosystem has led to "emboldened and elevated vitriolic forms of misogyny."[79]

Some of this misogyny occurs at the hands of organized or semi-organized communities that deliberately target women in troll storms or violent plots and attacks. These male supremacist and misogynist incel communities have recently begun to garner the attention of national security experts and agencies, as I detail in chapter 3. But aside from this new attention to organized male supremacist groups, the problem of misogyny—and of women's security concerns more broadly—has "been historically absent" from traditional security discussions.[80] This is despite evidence, as I discuss in chapter 1, that support for online misogyny makes violent attacks by terrorist and extremist groups more likely.[81]

The ubiquitous, rampant experience of online misogyny deserves more attention—especially because not all misogyny can be attributed to intentional attacks by avowed misogynists. Some of it is traceable to changes in attitudes toward feminism, a rise in resentment, loneliness, discontent, and isolation among boys and men, and increased scapegoating of women for supposedly disadvantaging men. These effects are exacerbated for younger boys and men. While the share of Gen Z women who identify as feminists (61%) is higher than for any other generation of women, fewer Gen Z men (43%) than millennial men (53%) identify as feminist.[82] This means that Gen Z has both a large gender divide on issues of women's rights and a declining level of support among younger men, compared to older men, for those rights.[83] It's hard to imagine that those divides and changes are not affecting—or fed by—sexist and misogynist expressions online.

Women's experiences with misogyny, sexism, and other kinds of gendered discrimination are also reflected in shifting views in women's experiences of their own equality. In the United States, not only is adults' reported satisfaction with the treatment of women in society split along gender lines, but women are much less satisfied than men and their satisfaction has declined over time, from 61% in 2001 to 44% in 2021.[84] Here too, generational differences point to concerning trends. Gen Z women are the most likely group of Americans to report being treated disrespectfully by the opposite sex.[85] These trends in online sexism, misogyny, and attitudes toward feminism, women's rights, and other kinds of gendered bias and violence are both a catalyst and an outcome of the developments I trace in the rest of this book.

In the end, you have to be more of a bitch, as my sister argues, but also not too much of one. That's the crux of it. This quotidian navigation is an inextricable and underacknowledged part of the roots of and pathway to violent extremism. In a context with so much mainstreaming and social media incubation of hostile sexism and misogyny, taking a closer look at where those beliefs come from and how ubiquitous they are can help shed light on how pathways to violence begin as well as on where we might best be able to interrupt them. Our failure to connect everyday misogynist encounters and the normalization of sexist experiences with rising mass violence targeting a wide range of groups has left a gaping hole in our awareness of how to prevent it.

Before I turn in the rest of this book to unpacking the dynamics that underpin and drive that violence, some clarification of terms will be helpful.

Defining Violent Extremism, Patriarchy, and Misogyny

The Far Right and Violent Extremism

As in my previous work, I use the term "far right" to refer to a spectrum of supremacist and antigovernment ideologies, including those that set up hierarchies of superiority and inferiority between groups of people where the "other" supposedly poses an existential threat that must be met with violence. This includes white supremacist extremism as well as male supremacism, Christian supremacism, Western supremacism, and other extremist ideologies that justify and naturalize inequalities between groups. It also includes unlawful militias and paramilitaries and some conspiracy theorists, where the term "unlawful" in conjunction with militia or paramilitary refers to a difference between illegal, private citizen militias and lawful, government-organized militias that are referenced in state law and the US Constitution.[86]

There is messiness and blurriness in the terminology that is necessary and rooted in the ways different terms are used in different legal and scholarly contexts. And, critically, some hateful and supremacist ideologies, like antisemitism and misogyny, exist across the political spectrum. However, "far right" is the term used in databases like the Global Terrorism Index to refer to a wide variety of hateful types of extremism that pose the biggest or fastest growing threat across Europe, North America, and Oceania, making it a useful term to situate my analyses in broader discussions. As a result, in my analysis of the ways that misogyny is hardwired into pathways to mass violence, I maintain that the "far right" remains the best bad term we have available to capture a mix of violent, exclusionary, and harmful ideologies. I also use the term "domestic violent extremism" along with "hate-fueled violence" and "political violence" when I aim to capture broader or more specific forms of violent extremism in the US context, reflecting the terminology used by the US federal administration and expert analysts to refer to specific components of terrorist and extremist violence. I use the term "mass violence" as a more expansive term that captures mass atrocity attacks that are not labeled or identified as extremist or terrorist, often due to a lack of manifesto or motivation, but sometimes due to an inability to see male supremacism as an extremist ideology. And I use the term "violent extremism" more broadly when I am referring to extremist violence that is not exclusively far right.

Finally, while most of the violence I discuss is what I call far right, I also argue that this violence is made possible by actions from everyone. This includes the impact of nonviolent mobilization from conservatives on issues related to women's and LGBTQ+ rights, the normalization and legitimation of misogyny within the mainstream, and liberal silence about all of it. This book therefore addresses nonviolent ways that misogyny and gender-based bigotry play a role in potentially mobilizing violence, including through legislative action and erasure through book-banning and the demonization of LGBTQ+ people as "groomers."

Patriarchy

Patriarchy is simultaneously one of the simplest and most complicated terms I've ever had to define. In its simplest form, it is a gendered system that gives some men the power and resources to dominate women and some other men.[87] What becomes more complicated, however, is describing *how* that system of domination works and what it relies on. First and foremost, patriarchy insists on a rigid male/female binary that is depicted as natural or biologically determined—meaning that people's intelligence, behavior, or talents are based on genetics rather than by their social environment—and which privileges human capacities that are seen as male over those that are seen as female. Decisions about who falls on which side of the male/female binary rest on sociopolitical ideas about sex (i.e., biological features like anatomy, hormones, and chromosomes) and gender (i.e., social constructions of what masculine and feminine traits should be).[88]

Power is the most important feature of patriarchy, which becomes clear when we understand that patriarchy is more than a set of cultural norms: It is a system of social, economic, and political relations. In patriarchal hierarchies, some men not only hold more power, but they also impose policies and practices that perpetuate that power and the superior status that accompanies it, while ensuring that others (such as women and the LGBTQ+ community) are subservient. The word "some" is important here, because not all men dominate all women; some men who benefit from patriarchal systems also dominate other men who do not embody expected masculine ideals.[89] Some women, in turn, benefit from, reinforce, and uphold patriarchal norms and expectations,[90] in their own lives, in their familial and caretaking roles as mothers, wives, or daughters, and in the policing of gendered rules more broadly.

Historically, patriarchal power has manifested in legal restrictions that dictated who had the rights of full citizens, such as voting or the right to move about freely, enroll in schooling, work, or maintain their own financial affairs. In the United States, for example, women were the legal property of their fathers, brothers, or husbands until 1920, when the Nineteenth Amendment was passed.[91] In this way, patriarchal systems function like other systems of domination and exploitation, such as colonialism, in relying on a logic of supremacy and a belief that some people are entitled to the labor and attention of others because they are superior and therefore both more worthy and more capable. Patriarchy is also deeply intertwined with capitalist processes that have relied on the sexual division of labor and the use of women's "free" labor to maintain households and raise children—often compensating for the lack of broader social safety nets.[92]

These systems of domination have not been seamlessly implemented or maintained, of course; male-dominated societies based on ideas about justifiable exploitation, dominance, and subjugation have been created, resisted, and dismantled over the centuries—and in the contemporary world today.[93] And patriarchy has never been the only way to organize social, political, and legal relations, as Angela Saini argues in her comprehensive work on the complex histories of matriarchal and patriarchal societies in history.[94] There was nothing inevitable about the fact that patriarchy became the prevailing form of gendered relations in modern society. On the contrary: The world's various civilizations and communities historically had much greater variation in how they understood and classified gender, sex, and sexuality. European, colonial ideas about sex and gender were forced on supposedly "uncivilized" indigenous communities in ways that all but eradicated approaches that were often more fluid and expansive.[95] This includes Native American "Two Spirit" people who were considered neither men nor women, beliefs about gender diversity that encompassed individuals holding multiple genders, and scores of matriarchal and matrilineal indigenous societies across Native American, First Nation, and aboriginal communities.[96]

Today, Western cultures and societies are structured with a strongly fixed male/female binary, whose rules and expectations must be taught and reinforced throughout the life course. Patriarchal norms and expectations socialize boys and men, for example, to prioritize emotions and traits deemed sufficiently masculine (like strength, courage, toughness, and anger) while denying themselves a fuller emotional life that includes vulnerability, gentleness, caretaking, and intimate friendship.[97] Girls and women, meanwhile, are socialized toward submissive traits like being pleasing, demure, deferential, nurturing, and embracing roles as caregivers and keepers of extended kin relationships, and are often depicted as in need of protection. As the writer Chimamanda Ngozi Adichie puts it, "We teach girls to shrink themselves, to make themselves smaller." Girls can have ambition, she says, "but not too much."[98] These expectations also vary according to race, however—Black women and girls, for example, are often portrayed not as in need of protection but rather as invincible or strong in ways that contribute to a wide range of unequal treatment, from overwork and inadequate medical care to the adultification of Black girls.[99]

Part of the power of patriarchy is that it socializes boys and girls to blindly accept these defined roles while camouflaging those expectations, and inequality more generally, as a natural or God-given way of organizing human life.[100] Patriarchy is not only limiting for girls and women, in other words—it also steers boys and men into narrow "boy culture" ideals that have led to a "crisis of connection" and a lack of intimate friendships, with likely implications for rising isolation, depression, loneliness, and suicide.[101] It uses shame, in particular, as a tactic to keep people in line—because shame relies on a belief that we haven't lived up to an expectation—including societal pressure about what makes a man or a woman sufficiently feminine or masculine.[102] And shame, in turn, is a powerful mobilizer of violence.

Recent years have ushered in some changes in these gender norms, including around how masculinity is perceived and performed. While boys and men are still largely confined to a limited "man box" that insists on "hard" traits like stoicism, strength, dominance, and aggression over "soft" traits like emotional intimacy or caregiving, there is evidence that this rigidity is softening in favor of what scholars call "hybrid masculinities." But these changes have not helped to disrupt gendered power relations in significant ways.[103] Social norms about fathers' roles in parenting, for example, have undergone tremendous change in just a generation, as men take a more active role in their children's lives. But women still bear the disproportionate share of all caregiving—childcare, elder care, and household management—especially in countries with inadequate social safety nets, like the United States.[104]

In sum, there is no single, categorical system of patriarchal oppression in which all men, and only men, dominate all (and only) women. As has been thoroughly argued about race, not all people hold racist attitudes or beliefs, but virtually everyone lives within a system that privileges whiteness. The same is true for sex and gender. Not all men are male supremacists; but all men in patriarchal systems benefit from a logic of male supremacy, even as they also suffer from it. These benefits accrue in part through everyday practices of male domination that defend and reinforce male power in both private and public domains.[105]

Nor is it possible to speak of a singular patriarchy that affects everyone the same way.[106] Patriarchies themselves can only be understood—as so many Black feminist authors, including Patricia Hill Collins, bell hooks, Kimberlé Crenshaw, and others, have argued for decades—in conjunction with other forms of domination that intersect with gender hierarchies, including race, sexuality, social class, and caste.[107] This intersectionality, as articulated so thoroughly by Crenshaw, means that patriarchies are complex power structures.[108] The intersections across forms of supremacy are clear both in the logic that defines them (superiority and inferiority, a desire to restore or preserve domination, a sense of existential threat from perceived enemies) and in the intertwining of those same enemy groups. Sexism and anger directed at women of color is often not only misogynist but also racist—such as in media and policy depictions of Black women as "welfare queens" or white supremacist extremists' accusations of white women being "feminist race traitors" who don't have enough white babies.[109] It is impossible to understand any form of domination without seeing how all forms of superiority mutually reinforce and draw on one another.

Some people argue that the United States and other Western societies are now "post-patriarchal," with women having historically unprecedented freedom and choices, and outcomes on many measures of wellbeing and education now better for women than for men. It's only been a decade since the journalist Hanna Rosin declared, in a *Slate* essay, that the patriarchy is dead—as evidenced by the revolutionary progress of women seated in the US Congress and other powerful positions.[110] It's hard to quibble with her, at least if you take the long view. My mother was pregnant with her third child in 1974 before she was able to open a credit card without a male co-signer. It would be years more before she earned the right to legally challenge sexual harassment in the workplace or be protected against being fired because of a pregnancy. I had nearly graduated from college myself before spousal rape was criminalized, in 1993. It took another twenty years for women to earn the right to fight in military combat.[111] The *Obergefell v. Hodges* case that legalized same-sex marriage happened two years after that, in 2015. The progress we have made in women's and LGBTQ+ rights is undeniable, and worthy of acknowledgment—even as there is still so much more work to be done. That same progress, however, has misleadingly left public culture in a state of denial about ongoing inequality rooted in misogyny and gender-based bigotry.

It is my stance in this book that descriptions of the United States and other Western countries as post-patriarchal are premature. There has been real change in women's and LGBTQ+ rights and some softening of what masculinity and manhood look like (even as masculinity remains incredibly restrictive for many men.) But we have not seen parallel change in societal norms and expectations about gender roles or in the idea of a fixed gender binary itself.[112] Research on how peers react to transgender transition illustrates this paradox well. One study found when trans men transition in the workplace, their coworkers adjust relatively smoothly to the individuals' new pronouns and identity, but also quickly engage them in heterosexual gender rituals and expectations that reinforce gender binaries. Women coworkers immediately asked trans men to carry heavy items, unload boxes, or hang things in the office, for example, in ways that were different from when they identified as women. Colleagues' gender transitions, in other words, did not make people rethink the "naturalness of the gender binary."[113] On the contrary: By treating their trans men colleagues as men, these women reaffirm the dichotomy itself and the "naturalness" of men performing certain kinds of tasks.

Patriarchies are built on two pillars: a set of attitudes, beliefs, and ideas that rationalize and justify hierarchies of superiority and inferiority (sexism), and a constellation of processes that enforce patriarchal norms and expectations (misogyny).

Sexism

Not long after smoke billowed into my living room a few years ago, I was standing on the hearth of our century-old fireplace as a chimney sweep scooched out of it on his back, holding an iPad full of images of the flue and the liner. He frowned, flicking through photos of creosote buildup. And then he looked at me matter-of-factly and said: "I wish your husband was here so I could explain this."

Every woman I know has a pocket full of stories like this: banal sexist encounters in everyday life in the form of little asides or direct comments from men that belittle, or dismiss, or sexualize. Sexism is the set of attitudes and beliefs that defines women as inherently, biologically inferior to men. These are beliefs that depict women as less qualified, intelligent, rational, and capable than men—as unable, in the chimney sweep's understanding, of assessing interior chimney damage and deciding on a repair. They position women as not only less intelligent but also less important helpmates to the men who run the world and who make decisions on behalf of their wives, mothers, and daughters. Sexism takes a lot of different forms, both hostile (i.e., the notion that women are inherently deceitful, manipulative, oversensitive, and above all less qualified than men) and benevolent (i.e., the idea that women are inherently fragile, in need of protection, hurt by external roles that interfere with their so-called natural roles as mothers and homemakers, and need to be shielded from harsh jobs and environments for which they lack physical strength or constitutions).[114] Not unlike scientific racism, sexist ideas have persisted in part because of the impact of long-debunked research purportedly demonstrating women's inferior brain size or supposedly natural behavior like sexual chasteness—which subsequent scientific studies have demonstrated to be false.[115]

Sexism reinforces women's subordinate roles even as its benevolent form is often cloaked with a protectionist veneer of safeguarding women from dangerous jobs (like the military) that could harm their reproductive health or would be otherwise too strenuous. Russia, for example, has historically banned women from hundreds of professions—reduced in the year 2000 from 456 to 100 professions—and still does not permit women to work as miners, steelworkers, firefighters, or divers, among other occupations.[116] Whether benevolent and protectionist or hostile and dehumanizing, sexist beliefs reinforce and support patriarchal hierarchies. Regardless of the specific form, in other words, sexism is rooted in patriarchal traditionalism—the belief that women belong in the home, as wives, mothers, and in traditional homemaking roles and that they are weaker, less competent, and less capable than men.

Historically—and in some contemporary cases—sexist beliefs restricted women's roles to domestic domains, either through legal and formal policies or through informal cultural and social norms and expectations. The distinction between public and private spheres is central here—with men assuming control of the public sphere and relegating women to the private sphere. Sexist policies enshrined in US law ensured the ongoing subordination of women by restricting their rights to vote, to determine their own medical care, by requiring men to co-sign on leases, bank accounts, credit cards, or by restricting access to certain educational, athletic, or occupational environments to men only. Structural forms of sexist control still exist in some legal ways, including those that came with the loss of reproductive rights post-Dobbs and legislative actions to restrict contraception, penalize women who travel for abortion care, or restrict or ban gender-affirming medical care.

Earlier waves of feminist and LGBTQ+ mobilizing made tremendous progress in broadening access for girls' sports (through Title IX in the United States, for example), creating more equality in employment and pay, and broadening pathways for reporting and prosecuting harassment and sexual assault. But despite these gains in equality and access, sexist policies and practices continue to result in women's disproportionate material resources through unequal pay or retirement savings, inadequate family leave and childcare support, or other informal and formal disparities that lead to power imbalances and differences in wealth or status between men and women. Sexism also persists in informal ways in patterns like documented higher sales prices on cars sold to women or disparities in pay raises and promotions. These disparities disproportionately affect poor and working-class women and women of color, who often face the layered effects of racism, xenophobia, classism, and sexism.

Importantly, sexism is not merely a mode of interaction; it uses the male/female binary to maintain and defend the unequal distribution of social, political, and economic power.[117] And this means that eradicating sexism isn't just about gaining access to spaces that have been dominated for men—i.e., breaking through the proverbial glass ceiling. Rather, eliminating sexism requires challenging and unraveling the entire patriarchal system and its intersections with other forms of domination that have helped ensure systemic, structural inequality.[118] This also explains why disruptions to the gender binary have been so threatening to so many in the conservative and extreme right. The gender binary itself is an essential part of securing and maintaining power and the inequalities that result.

From the relatively privileged perch of my generation and background, I mostly absorb men like the chimney sweep as a kind of annoying residue, a left-behind legacy in an era when we largely have it better and easier than our mothers did. "I don't want my wife to be barefoot and pregnant," a roommate in a college group house once joked. "I want her to wear shoes in case I need something from the store." It was funny because it was ludicrous, because we knew we were a generation who didn't face those expectations. We fully expected to live transformed lives compared with the sexist barriers our mothers faced. Indeed, there is no denying that we do. After all, my own mother had attended that same college, a generation before, and paid for it herself by waitressing, after her father told her he wouldn't pay for college for a girl.

That kind of sexism—the type enshrined in either law or overt social norms—was all but inconceivable for my generation. And indeed, overtly sexist interactions are, thankfully, increasingly rare, at least according to the research on sexist beliefs. More and more people around the world reject overtly sexist ideas that claim women are inherently, biologically inferior to men in ways that justify their unequal treatment or require a man to make their decisions.[119] This is a big shift from just a few decades ago, when sexist attitudes were both normalized and enshrined in legal and private sector policies in banking, medical care, education, and more.[120]

As those formally sexist laws, policies, and official restrictions have gradually been repealed in many parts of the world, other justifications for inequalities between the sexes have endured that are often a result of cultural norms and expectations rather than laws and policy restrictions. Thus, the well-documented era of "girlie-girl culture," as Peggy Orenstein calls it, helps perpetuate sexist beliefs about women's appearance and capacities.[121] Sexist beliefs persist in the kinds of attitudes that could lead a chimney sweep to think only my husband could understand the complicated nature of creosote buildup, but also in the kinds of beliefs that place blame for sexual assault on how a woman dresses, how much she drinks, or whether she was walking alone at night.

Many women of my generation squared our shoulders and pushed forward with the optimism of youth who thought we were immune to sexism, rolling our eyes at the occasional sexist aside and the daily acts of cautionary prevention we take for granted as we navigate our personal safety. The more I study acts of mass violence—both directed against women and against other targets—the more I am convinced that what often seems like an irritating daily reality is actually an enabling condition and environment that nurtures, cultivates, and ultimately explains and mobilizes much of the violence we see in the world today. The sexism that underpins attitudes and beliefs about women's inferiority is just one part of the story, however. Misogyny—understood here as the hostile enforcement of patriarchal norms and expectations—plays an even more critical role in mobilizing men to mass violence.

Misogyny

Early one morning some years ago, a senior colleague who had done a performance review of my teaching the previous evening showed up in my office doorway, before anyone else had arrived. "I was struck by what you were wearing to teach a lecture on gender," he offered, apropos of nothing. "That short skirt, tight sweater, and those stiletto boots. It wasn't quite a catsuit, but . . ." His voice trailed off as I stood there, blinking, wondering how my tweed, knee-length skirt and fuzzy mock turtleneck could possibly look like a catsuit, while simultaneously realizing the catsuit was a fantasy of his own making and that the lights weren't even on in the office yet. He slowly shook his head, smiling, and then just wandered away into his own office, not far from the conference room where he would be voting on my tenure case within a few months.

The policing of girls' and women's attire—in the workplace, during the questioning of rape victims, or in school dress codes—is one of the most ubiquitous forms of misogyny, which I define (following Kate Manne) as strategies to enforce patriarchal norms and expectations, including the boundaries of acceptable masculine and feminine behavior. This definition differs from how misogyny is usually understood in popular use: as hatred of women. By seeing misogyny not as an individual belief but rather as a form of social policing, the definition I adopt here illustrates how this kind of control defends and maintains patriarchy and the continued subordination of women and dominance of men.[122] Misogyny is a means of regulation, especially in the face of rapid social change. It is both a continuation of age-old patriarchal values and systems and a backlash against progress and visibility in women's and LGBTQ+ rights.

Misogyny is intertwined with sexism, especially in its hostile form— but it goes a step further than sexist beliefs to capture the strategies of enforcement directed toward people who step out of line or reject patriarchal expectations.[123] Misogyny is the "foot soldier" of patriarchy, working to police the boundaries of acceptable behavior, contain and control violations through hostile threats and action, and ultimately enforce sexist beliefs in order to uphold gendered systems of power and domination.[124] This doesn't mean that all violence against women or the LGBTQ+ community is intentionally misogynistic or designed to reassert and defend patriarchies. Some violence against women, for example, is rooted in simple patriarchal entitlement—to women's bodies, attention, adoration, time, and service.[125]

There are many misogynies, because there are a variety of ways that patriarchal norms are enforced in a vast and diverse ecosystem of online and offline spaces and places—in ways that inform and mutually constitute each other.[126] Attacks on the LGBTQ+ community, for example, are part of misogynistic tactics aimed at defending traditional patriarchies and policing the boundaries of acceptable expressions of femininity and masculinity.[127] I generally use the term "gender-based bigotry" to capture this more expansive set of tactics and strategies, especially as an acknowledgment that misogyny is most often used to refer exclusively to hostile acts directed toward women. For brevity's sake, I sometimes use the term "misogyny" on its own, although readers should understand the term to include a broader range of gender-based harms aimed at defending and maintaining traditional patriarchies.

Misogynoir is a term coined by Moya Bailey to capture Black women's experience of anti-Black racist misogyny, especially through US digital and visual media.[128] It describes the mutually reinforcing racism and misogyny conveyed in popular culture, caricatures, consumer product marketing, and iconography that shapes public and policy perceptions through negative stereotypes of Black women's domestic servitude, sexual availability, unwillingness to work, or ability to withstand physical pain, to name just a few examples.[129] These are, as Patricia Hill Collins describes, "controlling images" that "make racism, sexism, poverty and other forms of social injustice appear to be natural, normal, and inevitable parts of everyday life."[130] Misogynoir shapes both overt experiences of exclusion and violence and everyday microaggressions experienced by Black women,[131] as well as public perception, policies, and media attention, resulting in trends like the erasure of Black women and girls from Amber alerts or missing persons publicity due to "missing white woman syndrome," which refers to the attention that missing white women garner in the media compared to the silence that often occurs when girls or women of color disappear.[132] In a moment of rising far-right extremism, Black women and girls are subject to the multiple impacts of what Alexandra Onuoha and colleagues call "far right misogynoir," which are distinctly layered forms of hate and bias rooted in both antidemocratic, xenophobic, anti-LGBTQ+ and supremacist ideas as well as racist and sexist ones.[133]

The chapters to come also use the term "male supremacism" and occasionally refer to "toxic masculinity" and a category of violent extremists known as "misogynist incels." Male supremacism is a set of beliefs that men are naturally, biologically, and genetically superior in ways that justify and rationalize the logical domination of women and LGBTQ+ people through social, political, economic, or legal hierarchies.[134] Male supremacism espouses a narrow understanding of masculinity that is sometimes called toxic masculinity—a view of manhood that requires boys and men to be stoic, unemotional, dominant, and aggressive and is associated with sexual entitlement and hostility toward women.[135] Incel (involuntary celibate) is a label that individuals self-identify with as part of a community of others who are involuntarily not having sex— it includes both men and women. The term "misogynist incels" refers specifically to incels who embrace male supremacist ideas that dehumanize women while simultaneously positioning them as something to which men are entitled.[136]

Whose Progress? The Cost of (White) Women's Rights

The 2020 kidnapping plot against Michigan governor Gretchen Whitmer was what ultimately motivated me to write this book. As the news broke, I fielded media inquiries from the yard of a rental house outside the city, where I had briefly decamped during the COVID-19 pandemic. I paced back and forth across the grass, urging journalists to consider not only the antigovernment premise of the plot but also its deeply misogynistic undertones. Within weeks, the media frenzy surrounding the Michigan plot was eclipsed by the presidential election and all that followed—including the January 6 insurrection. But the idea of a book calling out the misogyny underpinning violent extremism began to bump around in my head more persistently.

As COVID rates surged that winter, I began meeting friends and family at a regional park in Virginia. There, we could hike on the park's network of trails, or sit and talk, watching the river pass us by. Over the course of several visits, a construction site next to the park's parking lot gradually turned into a memorial—the Turning Point Suffragist Memorial, housed at Occoquan regional park because that land was home to the workhouse that had been the site of the famed 1917 "night of terror"—a brutal night of torture and abuse enacted upon thirty-three suffragists who were held there.[137] That night of terror—and the public attention to it—is often credited with shifting the public mood toward support for the Nineteenth Amendment.

Watching the memorial come into being got me thinking about the century of women's progress it commemorated, and about the backlash we continue to see in the form of rising misogyny. I was also reminded of how the story of women's rights has been curated in ways that often obscure the racial costs of that progress. The night of terror brought public attention and helped move the needle of sympathy toward suffrage, but real political will to give women the right to vote only came about because of the efforts of women leaders who made a deliberate decision to sacrifice racial equity to achieve (white) women's progress.[138]

"White supremacy will be strengthened, not weakened, by woman's suffrage," Carrie Chapman Catt, who led the mainstream arm of the US suffragist movement, told white politicians as she worked to secure the success of the Nineteenth Amendment. White women outnumbered Black men and women "by nearly half a million," Catt reasoned.[139] So giving women the right to vote would chip away at the patriarchy, but in return would secure the continued oppression of Black people in the United States, because the same methods used to ensure the disenfranchisement of Black men (like poll taxes and literacy tests) would affect Black women.[140] This was a controversial bargain for the white suffragists, who had previously been aligned with the abolition movement. But it was one that enough were willing to strike to secure the right to vote for (white) women.[141]

The new Suffragist Memorial glosses over that history in its twenty panels of text and photos, celebrating the bravery of the women who fought for seventy years for the right to vote, but ignoring or whitewashing the racial tradeoffs with language like "African American women were not consulted in the parade planning" about the first national demonstration for suffrage in 1913, for example. As a result, memorial visitors likely leave with little understanding about the strategy that white suffragists pursued—aligning themselves with white men in the name of white supremacy to secure rights for themselves, but leaving African

American, Latina, Asian American, and Native American women without full voting rights.[142]

I had planned to include this brief historical diversion as a cautionary tale—a reminder of the exclusions that are so common in the story of women's progress, and of the importance of a fuller, intersectional story. But when I returned to the memorial with two students in fall 2024 to fact check my original description, we also visited the nearby Lucy Burns Museum, housed in the Occoquan workhouse where suffragists were held and force fed to break their hunger strike. To our surprise, we discovered that the museum exhibit tells the story of suffragists' racism and exclusions very differently than the outdoor memorial. In the museum, there is a dedicated panel about the "African American Fight for Suffrage," and other sections with explanations of how Black voters were kept from voting. The National American Woman Suffrage Association (NAWSA) is described as being "focused on suffrage solely for white women," with the explanation noting that the exclusion of women of color was strategic, rooted in fear of alienating "the segregated, Jim Crow South," and also racist, driven by "bigotry, notions of white supremacy and fear of African American voting power."[143]

These two radically different approaches to the history of the suffragist movement—in a museum and a memorial on the same historical site—illustrate clearly that the curation of the past requires a series of deliberate choices that produce thinner and thicker versions of history. The memorial's story of the (white) suffragists' efforts was not exactly incorrect, but it was wholly incomplete. The museum's account was a fuller and more complex rendering. Since the story of women's progress so often fails to note the exclusions—such as the alliance white women struck with white men at the expense of Black and brown rights—perhaps it should be no surprise that we so often fail to acknowledge or recognize multiple layers of supremacism today. We too often fail to acknowledge the dual impacts of racism and misogyny that Black women experience, or the layered exclusions experienced by trans women and LGBTQ+ communities. And we also tend to see the racism and xenophobia of hate-fueled and political violence, while ignoring the gendered and misogynistic dimensions.

The suffragists—and all that followed in the women's and LGBTQ+ rights movements of the late twentieth century—did chip away at the patriarchy. But as the systems that helped legally ensure patriarchy's endurance as a system of domination and control began to fall away, it is no surprise that we have seen rising backlash in the form of increasing misogyny and gender-based bigotry. The patriarchy's gendered expectations and norms are today enforced primarily (though not exclusively) by social, rather than legal, control. Control of gender—of women's bodies, of trans visibility, of nonbinary pronouns, and so much more— is right in the thick of it.

Aims and Overview of the Book

An attention to gender and its intersections with white supremacy and mass violence is not novel in and of itself. Plenty of scholars have written about misogyny, patriarchy, and their intersections with racism and white supremacy, as articulated in the work of Black feminist scholars like Audre Lorde, Kimberlé Crenshaw, bell hooks, and Moya Bailey and Trudy.[144] In the extremism field, few have been listening. There are key exceptions, of course, especially from a core group of scholars who have worked hard to effect change at the intersection of gender and extremism.[145] However, when it comes to broader works on extremism, radicalization, and terrorism or mainstream policy reporting, gender is largely marginalized or absent.[146]

My hope is that *Man Up* will help to fill this gap and challenge the persistent underemphasis on gender in discussions about violent extremism and the pathways that lead to it. To do so, I advance three arguments throughout the book, using five case studies of misogynistic strategies used to police modern patriarchies: *containment, punishment, exploitation, erasure,* and *enabling.* I show that misogyny and gender-based violence in intimate and everyday settings are among the most reliable and unequivocal predictors of support for and precursors to mass, public, and targeted violence. I argue that recent increases in violent extremism are partially explained as violent retrenchment and reassertion of traditional patriarchy. And finally, I contend that all forms of hate and hate-fueled violence—including racist, anti-immigrant, anti-semitic, and Islamophobic ideas and attacks—are linked by the connective tissue of misogyny and gender-based bigotry.

To ground these arguments, I structure the book into three parts. In this introduction and in chapter 1, I review the book's themes and key definitions and what we know about the intersection of gender, misogyny, and violent extremism and about the gendered lenses that affect radicalization and recruitment into extremism. In the second part of the book, I turn to the five case studies that illustrate how misogyny underpins the mobilization of violent extremism. In chapter 2 (Containment: "Lock Her Up"), I dive into the language of sexist slurs, harassment, hostile sexism, and the toxic masculinity that fuels it, looking at how strategies like belittling and dehumanizing work to reinforce patriarchal ideas as they aim to put women and others who don't conform to patriarchal norms back in their place. In chapter 3 (Punishment: "Grab the Bitch"), I analyze violent misogyny as articulated through misogynist incel, men's rights, and broader male supremacist movements, with a focus on mass violent attacks and plots that target women, including with language like "kill them all and make them suffer."[147] In chapter 4 (Exploitation: #SaveTheChildren), I examine two consequences of the normalization of patriarchal superiority, arguing that acts of terrorism and mass violence need to be understood in concert with gendered exploitation and everyday violence through sex and human trafficking, intimate partner violence and the exploitative control of women and children. Chapter 5 (Erasure: "Don't Say Gay") looks at anti-LGBTQ+ movements, including their mainstreaming and normalization through legislative action, community-led initiatives to silence conversations about sexuality in schools, libraries, and curricula through book banning, attacks on "grooming," and the broader assault on gender-affirming care and medical transition. Finally, in chapter 6 (Enabling: The White Baby Challenge), I illustrate how women—especially white women—actively participate in white supremacist movements, examining white women's role in policing, enforcing, and ultimately enabling the white patriarchy.

In the final part of the book, I turn to prevention, looking at potential strategies to disrupt misogyny and violence. In the conclusion, I take up the question that is at the heart of so much of my research and work: What can be done to prevent violent extremism and mass violence? What would it look like to more clearly center gender in the field, and how would the landscape of prevention and intervention look differently because of that centering? In the epilogue, I issue a call to action— to anyone and everyone who can do better at recognizing and acknowledging the patterns, at intervening when they observe it, at raising and mentoring children differently, and in committing to challenge and change the gendered systems that constrain us and contribute to so much violence and harm. A final resources section offers an adapted excerpt of the guide, "Not Just a Joke: Understanding and Preventing Gender- and Sexuality-Based Bigotry," produced by my research lab PERIL in collaboration with the Southern Poverty Law Center. It includes a list of strategies parents and relatives, teachers and educators, counselors and therapists, coaches and youth mentors, faith leaders and others can take to address misogyny and potential violence. And it offers a comprehensive, US-based resource list for additional help on issues like internet and social media safety, sexual assault and gender-based violence, sexual health, and how to talk to kids about online and offline harms.

1

Gendered Gaps in Extremism
and Violence

"PEOPLE SEE WHAT THEY WISH to see," Erin Morgenstern writes in her novel *The Night Circus*, "And, in most cases, what they are told that they see." Of all the words I could use to talk about the absence of attention to the gendered dimensions of violent extremism, I keep coming back to one phrase: blind spots.[1] A blind spot is different than a lacuna, or a gap, or a chasm or vacuum or any of the other words that come to mind when I think about the absence of attention to gender and mass violence. While these other concepts imply that something is missing, a blind spot refers to an area that actually does exist, but is simply unseen by a driver in a rearview mirror because of the physical nature of the car. It has been extended, metaphorically, to suggest a degree of ignorance or a lack of judgment about a subject that is rooted in an inability to see it, often due to bias—and carries an inherent sense of consequence, of risk or danger that comes from the failure to see a problem. Blind spots are a weak point, a failing that puts drivers at risk of a collision, or metaphorically lead to deficiencies in judgment. In the case of violent extremism, the narrowmindedness that comes from blind spots has created a dangerous tunnel vision, leading the field to ignore or dismiss some of the most compelling evidence about trends, predictors, and warning signs of violent extremism. There are "examples of expressed misogyny or domestic violence in the personal histories of nearly all the perpetrators of the worst terrorist incidents and mass killings in Western countries in recent years," two senior advisors for the United Nations recently wrote, "which is remarkable because neither misogynist acts or expressions nor violence against women are typically reported and exhaustively documented."[2] Gendered blind spots are, I contend, our field's weakest point and most obvious failing.

The problem is not that we don't know enough about the gendered dimensions of violent extremism. We do know enough—but we have relegated most of that knowledge to a blind spot, looking directly past the evidence as we formulate arguments and theories and interventions that largely ignore the facts that are right in front of us in nearly every single case of mass violence. The good news about blind spots, though, is they are fixable. Any driver will tell you that all you need to do to deal with a blind spot is change your line of sight. You have to look straight at it.

What We Know: Gender and Political Violence

A straight look at the literature on gender and mass public violence, including terrorism and violent extremism, shows that scholars have spent decades painfully, painstakingly articulating a variety of ways that gender shapes radicalization, mobilization, and engagement in violence. Three areas of robust scholarship have already established a canon of evidence and theory: on the nexus of gender and nationalism, including the rise of the populist radical right; on gender roles in extremist movements; and on the role of masculinities, including toxic masculinity and aggrieved masculinity, in the recruitment and radicalization of men to a wide variety of extremist scenes and movements, from unlawful militias to white supremacist gangs.[3]

This literature has thoughtfully articulated the ways that nationalist and extremist movements rely on—and exploit—traditional gender hierarchies and norms that see women as the reproducers of the nation and men as its defenders. It has shown that women's roles in extremist movements are complex, including in increasingly less backstage and more leadership positions, and are often but not always mobilized through their relationships with fathers, boyfriends, and husbands.[4] Scholars have comprehensively traced how ideals about femininity, motherhood, and conceptions of manhood alongside ascribed masculine qualities like bravery, courage, strength, determination, and a willingness to be violent, are clearly linked to fascist and other extremist movements.[5]

These insights are well documented in contemporary research on far-right movements as well as in historical research, where a wealth of case study research has traced the centrality of a mix of chauvinistic nationalism, racist patriotism, unlawful militia movements, and conceptions of manhood to Western colonialist and imperialist projects over the past two centuries.[6] An expansive literature on gender and far-right populism in more recent years, especially across European cases, has come to similar conclusions about the role of modern masculinity and the weaponization of women's and LGBTQ+ rights to frame immigrants and Muslims as a threat to "Western values."[7] Taken together, these strands of research have confirmed that ideas about femininity, masculinity, race, and nationalism are inextricably intertwined in the construction and maintenance of extremist, populist, and nationalist movements and violence.[8]

These prior areas of scholarship have been essential in shaping my own thinking about gender and extremism, both in previous research projects and in laying a foundation for the arguments I make throughout this book. I also rely on a more emergent body of scholarship that builds on this canon in focusing specifically on misogyny and its relationship to radicalization and mobilization. Here, I find three areas of evidence and theory especially central to a better understanding of the gendered mobilization of extremism in areas of research that have been relatively less well-connected or -cited in the scholarship on violent extremism. I focus on these three areas in this chapter.

The first area draws on substantial quantitative evidence from national and cross-national surveys demonstrating a connection between hostile sexism, misogyny, and support for political violence and violent extremism. The second integrates insights from scholars in religious and gender studies who have clearly linked the centrality of US evangelical and Christian nationalist ideas about patriarchal authority to the current backlash against gendered social change. Finally, I draw on an exhaustive set of global policy reports and academic research documenting how sexual and gender-based violence, including sexual assault, kidnapping, trafficking, and torture, is both foundational to the ideology of violent extremism and is used as an intentional tactic of terror. Each of these three areas is articulated in greater detail in the remainder of this chapter, to create a foundation for the arguments throughout the rest of this book.[9]

Hostile Sexism, Misogyny, and Violent Extremism

In several recent studies across a wide range of national contexts, hostile sexism and misogynist attitudes emerge as significant—and in some cases, the biggest—predictors of support for political violence and violent extremism.[10] The relationship is substantial: In nationally representative survey data across several countries, hostile sexist attitudes are more important than religiosity, age, gender, level of education, and employment in predicting support for violent extremism.[11] Evidence shows that people who hold hostile views toward women and toward gender equality are more likely to hold extremist views, be intolerant of out-groups, support violent groups, and to participate in political violence themselves.[12] Hostile sexism also plays a role in support for populist and far-right political movements—it is, for example, a more important predictor of favorable attitudes toward Trump than religiosity, sexual orientation, race/ethnicity, education, age, marital status, and income.[13] In the UK, recent national representative survey research shows that misogyny predicts men's violent extremist intentions, their willingness to engage in interpersonal violence, and their support for violence against women and girls.[14] Holding higher hostile sexist views also makes people more likely to believe feminist conspiracy theories, which in turn predicts the acceptance of rape myths (such as the idea that women who are drunk are responsible for their own assault).[15]

Beliefs in traditional—or what is sometimes called "toxic"—masculinity are also connected to higher rates of interpersonal and political violence. Men who believe masculinity is defined by strength, dominance, power, and toughness and who hold a hierarchical view where women are less valued than and submissive to men engage in sexual and intimate partner violence significantly more than those who do not hold those views. These beliefs also correlate with participation in larger-scale political violence.[16] And the likelihood of violence increases when men believe that women are threatening the "natural order" of hierarchical male dominance.[17]

The relationship also works in reverse: Research studies have shown that support for women's advancement or empowerment through gender equality reduces the likelihood of a wide variety of harmful and violent outcomes—including rape and rape threats, domestic and intimate partner violence, and political attacks targeting women.[18] Support for women's advancement is also one of the strongest predictors of an individual's resilience to extremist radicalization in the case of Islamist terrorism, although more research is needed to know how this relationship works within far-right and domestic violent extremism. In recent research overseas, respondents who support the freedom of women to work outside the home and hold political office, to name two examples, were among the least likely to support violence.[19] Supporting violence against women or experiencing childhood exposure to violence in the form of domestic or intimate partner violence and bullying, on the other hand, is correlated with reduced resilience to violent extremism.[20] Across ideological and geographic cases, in other words, beliefs that justify and defend the superiority of men and the unequal distribution of economic, social, or political power between men and women[21] are foundational and consequential for violent extremism and the pathways that lead to it. These beliefs and attitudes are also clearly demonstrated precursors to violence against women more broadly.[22]

It's not just sexist attitudes that matter. Previous violent and misogynistic action against women and girls is a consistent red flag among mass shooters and terrorist actors. The list of terrorist actors with prior personal histories of intimate partner and domestic abuse, documented harassment, stalking, or online abuse of women and girls as precursors to their public rage is exhaustive. Misogyny and personal violence against women and girls is a "common element" in "nearly all" mass killers' personal histories, write Pablo Castillo Díaz and Nahla Valji as they document case after case of misogyny and violent abuse of women in the personal histories, written manifestos, and livestream comments of violent terrorists, mass shooters, and other violent attackers. This is the case in known attacks targeting women, of course, but also in cases where there has been little public attention to those histories, such as the 2012 Sandy Hook elementary school shooting, the 2013 Boston marathon bombing, and the suicide bombing at pop singer Ariana Grande's Manchester concert in 2017.[23]

Both quantitative and qualitative evidence suggests, in other words, that gender—and its intersections with racism and other forms of hate—should be among the very first factors we consider in understanding extremist motivations. Misogynist and sexist attitudes are foundational to mass violence and violent extremism—as a gateway to later radicalization, as a red flag or warning sign for subsequent violence, as an integrated part of all far-right ideologies, and as an ideology that motivates mass violence on its own.

How Does Misogyny Work to Mobilize Violent Extremism?

Scholars have spent significant time tracing how and why sexism and misogyny are so important to mobilization to violence. Some argue that the subjugation of women is a society's "first political order" in ways that shape how people act toward one another across groups. Whether men view women as equals, dehumanize them, exploit them, or violently dominate them reflects "foundational choices of the human collective" that can "bleed over" into group behaviors and choices and attitudes, including the perpetration of terror.[24]

Others suggest that social changes that have dismantled traditional gender norms, expectations, and hierarchies have been met with misogynistic backlash.[25] Support for online misogyny makes violent attacks by terrorist and extremist groups more likely—a finding researchers attribute in part to a call to reassert "traditional" norms and a rejection of "modernization," including the increased visibility and role of women in sociopolitical life amid an intensification of resentment over lost power.[26] If feminist gains are perceived to come only at the expense of men, then the humiliation, the shame of losing, is a part of the backlash. That backlash, notably, can be both reactive and preemptive, meaning that people can push back on women's and LGBTQ+ rights even when progress has been limited.[27]

In cases where there have been true gains, backlash is often rooted in a reality in which men's collective privilege in society is being reduced.[28] There is no question that economic shifts away from industrialized, manual labor work through automation, offshore manufacturing, and self-driving technology have decimated traditionally male-dominated jobs like mining, long-haul trucking, and heavy manufacturing. We are less likely to see all-white-male leadership teams and boardrooms. It's not economic anxiety or precarity itself that causes sexist (or racist) backlash, though—rather, it is the loss of relative status vis-à-vis women or minorities, which can lead men to see themselves as less masculine and fear that others see them as less masculine too.[29] In short: Men who perceive social and economic changes as threats to their own sense of status or position—and therefore embrace a sense of injustice and victimhood while navigating feelings of shame at a perceived loss of manhood—more readily lash out with misogyny.

It's a quick leap from shame and humiliation to anger and violence.[30] There is good evidence that men who feel "resentment toward their perceived loss of dominance and masculinity" may seek violent revenge to "restore power and control."[31] Men who feel their dominance or gender identity are threatened are also more likely to sexually harass women.[32] Even when it isn't articulated outright, men who feel insulted or reduced from the status, honor, authority, or superiority they believe they are entitled to in a world where there are winners and losers may embrace more masculine bluster as a result—more grabbing and boasting and taking and putting down of others—amidst a yearning for a perceived glorified past when "real men" were in charge and women knew their place in the gender hierarchy. These same feelings can also lead to an outright rejection of whatever one doesn't like—i.e., a refusal to accept the results, a rejection of the authority of the new boss, an insistence on error, fraud, or scapegoating who must be to blame for the current state of things.[33] This latter point—about scapegoating—is especially important in light of evidence that men's anger toward women also spills over into a desire for revenge "against ethnic minorities" and "society as a whole" as men seek to reclaim the power, status, or positions they feel are rightfully theirs.[34]

This connection has been explored thoroughly in discussions of why some American voters rallied around Donald Trump even after he was caught on tape talking about grabbing women's private parts without their consent. Many American voters did not rally around Donald Trump *despite* his hypermasculine and heteronormative bluster, but rather *because of it*.[35] This was true for evangelicals, whose support for Trump has been linked to an "embrace of militant masculinity, an ideology that enshrines patriarchal authority and condones the callous display of power, at home and abroad."[36] It was true for voters outside of the evangelical community, too. Trump was elected in 2016—and again in 2024—in part, because he was the kind of "real man" whose "rugged masculinity" reminded (white) voters of a time in America when "all was right with the world."[37]

A defensive stance toward patriarchy doesn't just motivate voters. It also mobilizes violence as a "response to insult" when men feel threatened by women's power, status, or position and seek ways to exert male dominance, power, and control.[38] This has long been understood as a key dynamic in patterns of domestic and intimate partner violence, rape, and sexual assault. Researchers have increasingly come to see the same patterns hold true for mass public violence, including violent extremism. Various acts of violence committed by men are driven by a combination of "misogyny, violated entitlement beliefs, masculinity threats and a desire for revenge."[39] This works through a mediating factor, according to recent UK data on misogyny and support for violent extremism. When men experience status or group threats to their in-group, they may seek to restore a dominant form of manhood or masculinity through hypermasculine attitudes and expressions—thus "performing" masculinity with expressions of perceived strength but also hostile, hateful, and violent attacks.[40]

The kinds of hostile sexism that underpin radicalization and mobilization to violent extremism don't materialize out of thin air. They are a well-documented continuation of centuries-old discrimination. Hostile sexism and misogyny—especially in its most recent iterations and growth—is also a clear backlash against progress as women and the LGBTQ+ community have secured more rights, representation, and power in economic, social, and political spheres. The rise of misogynist violence has been paralleled by a growing, trenchant defense of patriarchy and "traditional" family values in the face of significant and specifically gendered social change. There is perhaps no better way to illustrate how that works than through the lens of defensive patriarchalism in the growing mainstream movement of Christian nationalism.

Backlash, Traditional Patriarchy, and Christian Nationalism

Patriarchy—sometimes referred to in this context as "biblical patriarchy"—is part and parcel of the rapidly growing ideology of Christian nationalism,[41] which contends the United States is and should remain a Christian nation and that Christianity should be prioritized by the state.[42] Defense of traditional patriarchy plays a big role in Christian nationalism, as a wide variety of social changes—including gendered ones—are positioned as driven by forces of evil that must be fought with a militant, rugged masculinity that promises restoration of power, status, and tradition. Christian nationalism has swiftly garnered significant mainstream attention and support, including among elected officials and political candidates who have criticized the constitutional principle ensuring the separation of church and state and argued that religious rights should "supersede government."[43] This isn't just the language of campaign speeches. A September 2022 poll by Politico found that 61% of Republicans and 17% of Democrats believe the United States should declare itself a Christian nation.[44]

Even when it is not stated, Christian nationalism implicitly calls for the United States to be a white, Christian nation led by men.[45] Crucially, Christian nationalists believe Americans are an exceptional, chosen people who will eventually face an apocalyptic end-times battle. Tradition and traditionalism itself are positioned as a sacred, pure part of the natural world (or God's will). By extension, believers see a need to defend—including with force—traditional, patriarchal gendered norms that depict men as entitled to power, status, and positions of leadership, and women as in need of a strong hand to guide them. In this worldview, humans exist within hierarchies of racial, ethnic, and gendered differences—and each group's purity ostensibly needs to be maintained if individuals are going to have a sense of belonging and purpose. This us-versus-them thinking positions the "other" as a dire threat that must be defeated out of a moral duty to defend Christian values and prevent the nation from falling into darkness. Women and gendered issues are right in the thick of it.

Christian nationalists espouse a militant defense of biblical, patriarchal authority,[46] situating husbands as the breadwinning head of the household and wives as submissive, supportive homemakers and mothers who will raise children in an environment promoting chastity, purity, heritage, tradition, and family values. These ideals are not limited to adherents of Christian nationalism per se—they are widely embraced across conservative, fundamental, and evangelical Christian groups as well and among many communities across the United States more broadly. White evangelicals believe "men are natural leaders," while women oversee home and family life and are responsible for the moral upbringing of children.[47] They call for and celebrate the idea of a moral return to traditional gender roles and values in which men remain the head of the household, responsible for protecting and providing for their family.

Warnings about a catastrophic loss of traditional manhood are echoed in rhetoric from conservative and right-wing pundits and influencers. Tucker Carlson's Fox News 2022 special "The End of Men" ran with the tagline "Testosterone levels in American men are collapsing. Fertility is in decline. Is this the end of men?"[48] *Rolling Stone* magazine's analysis of the documentary described Carlson's "cherry-picked, decontextualized data" that is used to position a restoration of physical male dominance as an antidote to impending societal collapse. "Society's ills," so argues Carlson in what *Rolling Stone* describes as a "vaguely authoritarian" position, "can be pinned on men just not being man enough to keep everyone else in check."[49]

These frames about moral threats and gendered roles place mothers at the helm of warding off a wide variety of cultural threats to their families, the future of their children, and the nation writ large, including threats of an apocalyptic end times populated by invaders and rapists who threaten the purity of white women. The source of these threats is wide-ranging, including leftists, multiculturalists, communism, abortion, "radical" Islam, "woke" professors, globalists, immigrants, the decline of religion, gendered pronouns, transgender "warriors," and LGBTQ+ people. In the face of so many perceived enemies, traditional family values are called on to shore up a nation under siege, which can only be defended as part of a virtuous restoration of moral order and a hoped-for return to a lost Golden Age. Deeply rooted in metaphors of "pollution and purification, invasion and resistance, apocalypse and salvation, corruption and renewal," the nation's virtuous restoration is above all else gendered, because decline and weakness were "brought about by docility and femininity," and a "return to greatness" requires a reassertion of dominance, masculinity, and manly bravado.[50] Unlawful militia organizations in the United States, for example, have openly urged men to relocate to rural communities in order to get away from cities' "feminizing effects" and the resultant "sissification of society."[51]

This framing has been long in the making among Christian nationalist and mainstream evangelical Christians. The mobilization of evangelical Christian women in the 2016 election, in many ways, was the culmination of a decades-long effort by the Christian right to encourage "housewives outraged by moral decline . . . to get involved in politics."[52] In so doing, the Christian right also ensured that the issue of moral threats to Christian families and to the nation more broadly remained a front-line issue for voters. Women, meanwhile, need to be saved by men, by patriots, and by the church itself from the unnatural path of feminism and all the dangers it supposedly leads to—communism, wokeism, and more. Feminism is not only bad for women, in this framing, but women need to be rescued from it—in ways that echo the positions of fascist and authoritarian leaders across the centuries. The Nazi intellectual Alfred Rosenberg, for example, in 1930 called for the "emancipation of women from the women's emancipation movement."[53]

Perceived threats from enemies and evildoers have come fast and furious for the religious right, especially with regard to gender and a wide range of cultural changes over the past decade-plus, including the legalization of same-sex marriage, changes in the rights of transgender people, and the growing awareness and acceptance of gender as a spectrum. Generations play a significant role in these transformations, as we can see in rapidly changing norms that are breaking down a long-standing gender binary in ways that directly shape how people identify and express their own gender. Less than half of 1% of American adults over age 50 identify as trans or nonbinary, for example—but that percentage jumps to 5% of adults who are younger than 30 (and 1.6% of those aged 30–49).[54] This statistic illustrates how understandings of gender have shifted rapidly, in large part driven by a younger generation that has embraced a wider range of gender expressions and identities in their own lives and communities.

These kinds of changes to gender norms come only a decade after Germany became the first country to introduce a third gender option on its passports, in 2013, followed by Canada and more than a dozen other countries globally. The US State Department introduced a nonbinary gender category on US passports in April 2022, reflecting a change in federal government recognition that also appeared in registration forms for White House visitors—until the second Trump administration.[55] The US Census has proposed adding new questions about gender that would include gender assigned at birth as well as current gender identity, including transgender and nonbinary options.[56] These changes are happening across the globe. When I landed in the Kathmandu airport in June 2023 to attend a UN meeting, I logged into the airport visa kiosk and discovered that Nepal includes a third gender option for visa applications. On a coffee table at the hotel later that day, I picked up the latest version of the Nepalese *Smart Family* magazine, whose cover featured makeup artist and LGBTQIA+ community advocate Anish Tamang, sporting colorful, gender-fluid makeup and nails behind a banner title "Celebrating Inclusivity in Nepal."[57]

Years before these developments, legal and policy changes around gender issues were already galvanizing Christian evangelicals to political action to fight a perceived culture war. This included the Pentagon allowing women into combat in 2013 and the American Civil Liberties Union's lawsuit against a bakery owner for refusing to make a cake for a same-sex wedding. When the US Supreme Court ruled in favor of same-sex marriage in 2015, followed by an Obama administration challenge to North Carolina's restrictions on transgender bathroom usage, evangelicals stoked "a sense of embattlement" among followers.[58] For white evangelicals and Christian nationalists, changes in women's and LGBTQ+ rights were "insults to American manhood" that challenge "the position of straight white men who saw themselves as rightfully superior."[59]

It is hard to overstate just how important these trends have been for political developments, especially during the years leading up to Trump's 2016 and 2024 presidential wins. Rapid social changes have been met with significant backlash—articulated in part by the rising use of gendered slurs, epithets, and attacks I analyze in chapter 2, through rising political and hate-fueled violence, and through the vast and growing number of state legislative actions to prohibit gender-affirming care, as I discuss in chapter 5. This backlash can be understood as a rejection of challenges to social expectations about gender and what it means to be a woman or a man. It is also rooted in the insecurity of some men who fear displacement or losing power that they believe is rightfully theirs and which they believe violates the natural or God-given order of things.[60] That fear of displacement is linked to what has been called a "crisis of masculinity"—in which men who are falling behind on many economic, educational, mental health, and social measures seek new ways to reassert their power, sexual prowess, domination, or aggression.[61]

In this way, white evangelicals and Christian nationalists helped fuel a sense of urgency about social changes that purportedly pose a threat to moral, Christian values in ways that would inevitably lead to national decay unless thwarted by the righteous. These frames were highly gendered. Evangelical support for Trump was driven in part by a core desire for "real manhood"—his promises to make America great again "played on people's fears of being laughed at. A heroic leader whose aggressive, militant masculinity was not "restrained by political correctness or feminine virtues," for many evangelicals, was just the ticket.[62] As Du Mez explains: "With the forces of evil allied against them, evangelicals were looking for a man who would fight for them, a man whose testosterone might lead to recklessness and excess here or there, but that was all part of the deal . . . Trump embodied 'American strength,'" and would project that globally as well.[63] In so doing, Trump would make America great again and restore white American men to their rightful and unquestioned superiority.[64] The very framing of the 2016 Trump campaign around national decline and promised restoration was gendered, straight from an authoritarian playbook that aims to "reverse shifts in social norms that threaten patriarchy."[65]

The same dynamics held true nearly a decade later, as Trump campaigned for the 2024 presidential election. White evangelicals continued to be both a strong source of support for Trump amid a steady stream of reports that their congregants are vulnerable to conspiracy theories, propaganda, and disinformation. In repeated surveys, white evangelicals report high agreement with a range of conspiracy theories, including 31% who believe that "Donald Trump has been secretly fighting a group of child sex traffickers that include prominent Democrats and Hollywood elites."[66]

In sum, rapid growth in evangelical Christianity and a resurgence of Christian nationalism were partially rooted in a sense of urgency and backlash against gender-specific concerns and social change. These developments helped fuel a mainstreaming of antifeminist ideas. When that backlash to gendered social change evolves toward violence— including support for violent extremism—it can expand into a full-blown embrace of the use of sexual and gender-based violence as a strategic and ideological aim.

Gender-Based Violence as Extremist Ideology and Tactic of Terror

Most of the academic literature—and global policy guidance—on the issue of sexual and gender-based violence and extremism is quite recent and draws heavily on cases of broader conflict and war. One major review dates the first English-language published article on sexual violence and war to 2001, describing the growth in the field since then as "explosive," with over one hundred articles across disciplines now garnering well over two thousand citations.[67] During that same period, the United Nations and the International Criminal Court have published dozens of guidelines on the issues of sexual and gender-based violence in conflict settings, including those affected by terrorism. These reports, guidelines, and academic analyses have clearly established that sexual and gender-based violence against women, men, girls, and boys—including rape, sexual assault, and genital or sexual mutilation, sexual trafficking, sexual slavery, forced prostitution, forced marriage, forced reproduction, and other forms of gender-based and sexual violence—is a tactic of terror. These and other strategies are used by terrorist groups across the ideological spectrum to subjugate and terrorize communities, maintain territorial control, recruit and reward fighters, promote particular aspects of extremist ideology, finance terrorist operations or create revenue and income streams, and create a supply of future fighters.[68]

The vast majority of attention has focused on these issues within the context of Islamist extremism, where there are ample cases of sexual and gender-based violence that have helped increase global awareness.[69] This includes the kidnapping and sexual enslavement by the Islamic State in Iraq and the Levant (ISIL) of Yazidi women, Boko Haram's kidnapping and forced marriage of Nigerian schoolgirls and their use of them as suicide bombers, ISIS's publicized beheading, stoning, and other killings of LGBTQ+ people, Al-Shabaab's use of abduction, rape, and forced marriage as a strategy of territorial control, and the systematic and widespread rape, sexual mutilation, and sexual torture of women and girls during the October 7, 2023, terrorist attack in Israel by Hamas.[70] These are cases of deliberate, organized, and large-scale sexual and gender-based violence designed to "increase the pain and humiliation" of victims and witnesses, including family members.[71] They are a part of core operational and financing strategies among a wide range of Islamist terrorist groups.

There is ample evidence, however, that white supremacist and neo-Nazi groups also regularly use sexual and gender-based violence as a tactic of terror, despite a much thinner public and academic discourse about it. The willingness to see the problem among Islamist terrorists, of course, is partly founded in the greater ease with which Westerners observe and analyze sexual and gender-based violence when it's "over there," at the hands of Black and brown terrorists. Documented, repeated cases of neo-Nazis charged with running sexual trafficking and prostitution rings, both in the United States and across Europe and Russia, receive much less attention. In just one recent example, a neo-Nazi was arrested in 2022 while plotting the mass rape of white women as part of a group called Rapekrieg.[72] More broadly, the ubiquitous trolling and harassment of women in online and offline contexts by far-right influencers and their followers often calls for or incites actual violence, including through rape and death threats targeting feminists or women who promote views that challenge conservative and right-wing positions.[73]

Ideologically, white supremacist extremism is fundamentally gendered, with a central obsession centered on white birth rates, demographic change, and white women's reproductive capacity. Far-right narratives and rhetoric—and popular conspiracy theories like the so-called Great Replacement—emphasize the nation's or white civilization's survival in the face of demographic change in ways that are inherently related to the subjugation of women and their roles as reproducers of the nation, mothers, and housewives.[74] This is what Kathleen Blee refers to as the gendered rhetoric of white supremacist movements, which position themselves as the bulwark against a host of threats and promise to "protect vulnerable and endangered majority-group women (white, citizens, heterosexual, dominant religion) whose childbearing and childrearing is essential to the future of the majority race, nation, or religion."[75]

Violence against women purportedly enacted by racial minorities also plays a prominent role in the propaganda, recruiting tactics, and justifications for terror in extremist actors' manifestos and statements. Specifically, the idea that white women's bodies must be protected from a threat of sexual violence from racial and ethnic minorities and immigrants has been key to white supremacist violence against Black and brown men and communities. White women's wombs are battlegrounds for white supremacists, who see "the birth of each white child as an act of war," in Kathleen Belew's words.[76] Women are expected to protect, preserve, and deploy their own bodies to produce future warriors—including by guarding their sexuality against miscegenation and impure cultural or religious influences. In this way, white women's sexuality is both guarded and regulated by extremist groups.[77]

Gender-based violence is also directed toward men and boys by far-right groups—especially those who identify as LGBTQ+ or who otherwise are accused of violating expected norms of masculine behavior. And while much gender-based violence is sexual in nature, not all of it is. Domestic and intimate partner violence, femicide and mass shootings targeting women or the LGBTQ+ community, forced labor, or other acts of coercion and harm are also common.[78] This points to a constant refrain in far-right groups, in which the protection of white women is a key part of public propaganda, but those same women are often abused in private settings.[79] These groups also profit from the exploitation and abuse of women and girls. As chapter 4 details, there are ample cases of white supremacist groups running prostitution rings or otherwise profiting from the sale of women's bodies, including through sold footage of rape and assault on the dark web.

Sexual and gender-based violence is not just a side effect of terrorist and extremist activity for the far right, in other words. It is an integrated, core part of the ideology, radicalization process, and financing of white, western, male, and Christian supremacist groups and movements. It is a deliberate, targeted tactic of terror designed to exert control over women and their reproductive functions in the name of racial, ethnic, or civilizational growth.

Conclusion

In the novel *Pet*, Akwaeke Emezi writes that things don't have to be seen to be true. It may be "easier not to look," she contends, but "a thing that is happening happens whether you look at it or not."[80]

Both an established canon of scholarship on gender, nationalism, masculinities, and extremism and an emerging cluster of evidence in less attended to but nonetheless essential areas of research have clearly demonstrated that gender is a foundational component of racist, xenophobic, nationalist, and supremacist ideologies, movements, and terrorist tactics. This includes Christian nationalist backlash to the fragmentation of a fixed gender binary as well as Islamist and far-right extremist sexual exploitation of women and children. It also includes a bevy of new evidence revealing that hostile sexism and misogyny are the most reliable predictors of support for political violence and violent extremism.

This brief review of the established scholarship and data on gender and mass violence makes clear that our failure to understand the gendered dimensions of rising far-right violence is consequential in many ways. We understate the extent of the harm by failing to classify intimate partner and sexual violence as hate crimes. We underestimate the potential for early patterns of gendered harassment, stalking, assault, and violence to be warning signs, red flags, and boot camps for later mass violence. We fail, again and again, to see that misogyny is hardwired into extremist ideologies and is a core mobilizer of violence.

Across the following five chapters, I analyze how misogynistic ideas and tactics incubate hate and open pathways to violent extremism, looking at five strategies that enable gendered harm and mobilize extremism. I call these Containment, Punishment, Exploitation, Erasure, and Enabling.

PART II

Strategies of Enforcement

2

Containment

IN THE FALL OF 2022, I had just finished an appearance on CNN to talk about the October attack on Nancy Pelosi's husband, Paul Pelosi, when a voicemail pinged into my work phone from a Texas phone number. "Hey, watching ya on CNN this morning," drawled the caller, who then shared a leading conspiracy theory about the Pelosi attack. He then quickly turned tack: "And why is it that you transsexual people are always front and center on the news . . . god help you man, if you can't look at yourself in the mirror dressed as a woman and say I'm ugly as fuck, I'm a man, then you have no sense of anything. Shit, bitch."

Ten minutes later, a second voicemail pinged in, after the caller had apparently done some research and decided to correct his trans-hate with some regular old misogyny. "Hey," said the same caller, with a more menacing tone: "Looks like I mighta made a mistake. It looks like you might have a pussy after all. You're just fucking ugly as shit is your problem. You look like an ugly fucking man. Look at that ugly fucking nose, those beady eyes." And then, after a bit more ranting, he added: "P.S. I don't think that bitch, that's the governor of Michigan, was in any kind of problem as far as being kidnapped. . . . You fucking cunt."[1]

I get a lot of hate mail, and it will come as no surprise when I tell you it's almost all from men.[2] The few women who reach out to me in anger often express conspiracy theories (such as "January 6 was a hoax," as one woman claimed in a recent voicemail) or else attack me for my presumed political views, occasionally with colorful language, like another woman's creative accusation that I am a "rat demon fascist." Overall, women stick to a standard playbook of complaints, focused on the ideas I express and their disagreement with them. It's men who go the extra mile, peppering their critiques of my ideas with slurs like *bitch, cunt, whore*, with attacks on my appearance, or with insults directed toward identities they falsely think I hold, like the antisemitic tropes (*ugly fucking nose, beady eyes*) and anti-trans hate in the Texas caller's voicemail.

Men's rage-fueled calls and emails reveal more than they likely know about the roots of their anger. They are often most upset that I am not controllable, or containable—I am a woman, in Kate Manne's wording, *in a man's world*.[3] I am not in the place they think I belong—and so they want me gone, and quickly. I should "jump off a building and stop wasting our precious oxygen," as someone named "Nazi Boy" recently wrote, or "get a heart attack," in the words of another email. One man sent his profanity-laced message from a fake email account with the phrase "stay in the shadows." Like so many other men, he urgently wants me to get out of public view—as another caller illustrated as he raged across my voicemail following my May 2023 congressional testimony: "Why don't you *go back to the shithole* you came out from under, you fuckin' piece of shit, you communist fucking whore." These men are incredibly straightforward in these requests, even when they are not especially hostile. "I am asking you to GET OUT," one man wrote rather politely in a recent email, using all caps, without specifying where I should leave from or where he would like me to go. In fact, none of them seem to care very much where I end up, as long as it is not here, as another man made clear in an antisemitic email: "Go rub your hands together elsewhere." These men want me silent, invisible, out of sight, and most importantly, far from power of any kind. They even say this in incredibly direct language, as an email from a guy named Zack made clear: "You will never have control."

These men are ostensibly angry about the words and ideas I expressed on television or before Congress. In the end, though, what I said seems to matter less than the fact that I said anything at all. They want me to *go back*, to *go elsewhere*, to stop being *always front and center*. When they can't come up with sufficient substantive complaints about the content of my public remarks, they pivot to gendered attacks. Even in their complaints about my actual ideas—like dismissing the kidnapping threat against a sitting governor—their rejection of my words includes a gendered attack—*you fucking cunt, you dumb broad*—in an effort to diminish my expertise by labeling me stupid or saying I am no more than a sexual body part.

In the end, these callers are unoriginal. Their words aim to patrol gender boundaries with insults and violent threats in order to "ensure that women and girls are either kept out of, or play subservient roles in, male-dominated areas."[4] The attacks focus on my intelligence and competence, physical or sexual attractiveness, aim to undermine my sense of safety as a woman (such as through rape threats), or dehumanize me with the use of animal terms or sexual body parts. They undoubtedly aim to belittle and disparage—but they are also attempts to control and contain. The Texas man's chief complaint—that I was *front and center*—is the most telling part of his entire rant. As has often been said, if you've always been in a world where public figures or leaders look like you, apparently the inclusion of others can feel like oppression.

The desire to control and contain, to keep women in their place, explains why so many sexist and misogynist metaphors involve motion. Send Her Back, Lock Her Up, Hold Her Down, Ditch the Witch, Joe and the Ho Got to Go. Women who are publicly visible are a particular target—stated in graphic slurs, brutal rape threats, explicit imagery, and more that they should stay down (down girl), or that they will have to break out of their place (the home, the kitchen).[5] The goal of these misogynistic attacks is to police the rules of women's engagement in public space—to limit that engagement to pleasure (pornography), service (domestic help), or support ("eye candy" on the arm of a powerful man), and to punish women for resisting those roles. The widespread online use of the phrases "go back to the kitchen" and "your body, my choice" in the wake of the 2024 US presidential election, as some men sought to reclaim power over women and their bodies, is just one example.[6] Women who are "visible and audible" attract the highest levels of violent abuse.[7] This kind of territorial gender policing is true for the

LGBTQ+ community too, who for so long and in so many places today are still forced to be *in the closet*—to be invisible, out of the public eye, not front and center, not "flaunting" their identity, in the words of one violent attacker. Like so much of my own hate mail, LGBTQ+ people are told to move away, to #BEGONE, in the words of hate speech targeting a Montana LGBTQ+ friendly church in July 2023.[8]

For generations, gendered expectations in patriarchal societies have divided the worlds of men and women into two spheres: the public sphere of politics and economics, and the private sphere of the home—or of what ancient Greeks referred to as *polis* (city-state) and *oikos* (household and family). As Angela Saini argues, in ancient Athens, "the boundary between these two spheres would come to define a woman's place."[9] And when women cross that boundary, or when LGBTQ+ people successfully claim equal civil rights to marriage or the use of the pronouns they identify with—they are met with efforts to put them back in their place.

Thus, women are jokingly described as being *kept barefoot and pregnant*—a phrase that evokes, as Katherine Jamieson writes, "a vivid threat of entrapment: the one-two punch of immobilization in the domestic sphere by dint of both biology and culture." Keeping women dependent on their men by ensuring they were perpetually "in a state of pregnant servitude" is the ultimate form of control—one that has been managed and policed by women as well as by men, all in the name of preserving traditional family order, family values, and ideals of domestic motherhood and housewifery.[10] The popular "make me a sandwich" meme, directed by men at women online in meme or text form ("Stop talking politics, bitch, and go make me a sandwich") in order to discredit or insult women, is one frequent example.[11] But keeping women in the kitchen is also key for white supremacists obsessed with white birth rates and the patriarchal order, for whom control of women is part and parcel of the supposed restoration of white civilization. After all, Hitler used the notion of "Kinder, Küche, Kirche" (Children, Kitchen, Church) to define what the Aryan woman's world should look like: dedication to children, husband, the home, and the Christian church.[12] Her world should not, by any stretch of the imagination, include being *front and center.* Women who violate the unspoken rules about where they belong are met with swift reminders to stay in their place.

One of the clearest recent examples is the massive online vitriol and outrage the pop star Taylor Swift faced when she began regularly appearing in the stands at football games during the 2023–24 season to cheer on her boyfriend, Travis Kelce. Swift commanded only a handful of seconds of the possible airtime in each game—calculated at 0.46% of the airtime across multiple games, and just 0.36% of the Super Bowl—and yet this miniscule amount of attention generated massive misogynistic vitriol from outraged and angry men online. As Jeanna Kelley wrote for SB Nation, "We probably saw more of Taylor Swift on her VISA commercials that aired during those games than actual shots of Taylor Swift at the games."[13] Men's online complaints about the attention Swift garnered quickly morphed into more aggressive backlash. Widely circulated, AI-generated, deepfake pornographic images of Swift set in football stadiums were viewed tens of millions of times—leading a bipartisan group of US senators to introduce legislation to criminalize the creation of nonconsensual, deepfake sexualized images.[14] The feminist campaigner Laura Bates describes this backlash as "just the new way of controlling women. You take somebody like Swift, who is extraordinarily successful and powerful, and it's a way of putting her back in her box. It's a way of saying to any woman: it doesn't matter who you are, how powerful you are—we can reduce you to a sex object and there's nothing you can do about it."[15]

There are a wide range of tactics used to keep women and LGBTQ+ people in their place, each of which merits an entire book of their own. Their tools include violence in the form of rape, harassment, stalking, assault, bullying, online abuse, intimate partner violence, revenge porn, trolling, and mass attacks, as well as more ordinary tactics like belittling, demeaning, shaming, derogatory speech, and school dress codes that police girls' clothing choices. These tools are containment strategies. Women who say no—or ignore, or reject, or simply exist on a spectrum that doesn't match what some men believe they are entitled to (service, labor, sex, power, attention, a life without temptation)—are transgressive. They break the rules, and therefore must be punished.

Some of these tools have already been analyzed in great depth, like the "mansplaining" Rebecca Solnit details in *Men Explain Things to Me*, which help to "warp everyday life and allocate more credibility, audibility and consequence to some people than others."[16] The assumptions about competence (and incompetence) that medical professionals and others make about Black women whose experiences of pain are systematically ignored or denied, as Tressie McMillan Cottom has so painstakingly analyzed, are another example.[17] Other tools are analyzed elsewhere in this book, such as the legislative erasure of the LGBTQ+ community. I offer two of these ubiquitous forms of casual sexism and misogyny as examples here: the use of gendered verbal attacks using slurs, epithets, or hateful words, and the policing of (white) femininity.

The Misogynist Toolbox:
Slurs as a Form of Containment

You don't have to be more of a bitch, as my sister advised all those years ago, to be called one. "I'm going to have to kill a bitch," the hitman hired to bludgeon a New York mom to death in 2015 told his getaway driver, as if the task were an irritating errand.[18] "Snatch and grab, man," a militia member said to an FBI informant in summer 2020 as he plotted the kidnapping and execution of Gretchen Whitmer for supposed "tyranny." "Grab the fuckin' governor. Just grab the bitch."

"Bitch" is one of a host of terms that I have come to think of as terms of containment. Everyday forms of containment are misogynistic tactics aimed at policing women's or LGBTQ+ people's behavior by using sexist and homophobic slurs, threats, harassment, ridicule, silencing, and belittling. These might be contrasted with structural forms of containment I discuss in chapter 5, which refers to legal and legislative strategies to put women, sexual minorities, and gender-diverse people back in their place through restrictions on reproductive rights, banning of books, the framing of trans or gay people as a threat to children as "groomers," or attacks on gender-affirming medical care.

I regard epithets as part of this toolbox of misogynist tactics. As a category of speech, slurs are derogatory terms that are usually used to disparage or belittle others. They are motivated by the speakers' emotions and attitudes and have the effect of insulting and threatening targets.[19] They express contempt, derision, and hostility while attempting to degrade or erode the confidence, authority, power, or joy of the target. They convey disregard and disdain. Thus, when Donald Trump said to former *Access Hollywood* host Billy Bush that he "moved on her like a bitch," he was both bragging about his own prowess and depicting the woman he described as pitiful. Later in the same conversation, he gloated about his ability to grab women "by the pussy" without waiting for their consent, noting that "when you're a star, they let you do it. You can do anything."[20] The term "bitch" polices the boundaries of supposedly acceptable feminine behavior. So when a porn producer recently argued that he doesn't hate all women, "just stuck up bitches," he was asserting what kinds of women are acceptable to hate—those who do not give him the deference, attention, or admiration he feels entitled to.[21]

In this way, gendered slurs are not only disparaging—they also have an enforcement function as they work to police people's actions and censure them for not behaving the way they are supposed to (in the speaker's view).[22] This means that slurs and epithets like "bitch" and "cunt" are not just insults—they are also misogynistic strategies of containment. Gendered slurs often focus on behavior that is seen as needing to be disciplined for not adhering to patriarchal norms and expectations. They attack women's autonomy, independence, dignity, and intelligence; they discredit, dehumanize, stifle, and silence.[23] Sexist and misogynistic name-calling suggests that women are too power-hungry (*bossy, nasty*), or that men aren't masculine enough (*wimp, pansy, sissy*). They are words that accuse people of doing their gender badly.[24]

Bitch is a good example. It is a popular slur directed at powerful or ambitious women whose behavior is cast as uppity, difficult, or aggressive. As the actress Bette Davis famously said, "When a man gives his opinion, he's a man. When a woman gives her opinion, she's a bitch."[25] *Bitch* positions women as not only assertive or powerful, but inappropriately so—or else insufficiently feminine, deferential, gentle, helpful, or pleasing.[26] Such behavior is deemed so aggressively unnatural that it can only be unhuman, best described with a word that refers to a dog.[27]

However, the epithet is lobbed not only because women have supposedly abandoned their natural roles, but also because they have simultaneously stolen men's entitlement to positions of leadership. Powerful
women are therefore not just unnatural, they are emasculating, robbing
men of their roles, their power, and ultimately their manhood—as in
the case of a "*castrating bitch*."[28] The slur communicates that women's
choices—in their rejection of gendered social expectations about their
proper place or role—threaten the patriarchal order.[29] The aim of such
epithets is both to belittle targets in ways that make them less powerful,
less of an authority, and ultimately to contain them by eliminating or
reducing the space for women to take on public roles.[30] Popular though
it is, *bitch* is just the tip of the iceberg in the world of gendered slurs,
directed both toward women in the public sphere and ordinary women
experiencing everyday online harassment.[31] A wide range of insults attack women's intelligence (*bimbo, stupid, idiot, dumb broad*), sanity, rationality, or stability (*crazy, hysterical, psycho*), perceived attractiveness
(*ugly, fat, old*), actual or imagined sexual behavior (*slut, skank, ho, floo-
zie*), position women as no more than a sexual body part (*cunt*), or reduce them to domestic service tasks (*dishwasher, babymaker*).[32] Animal
slurs are used both derogatorily, to dehumanize or depict as ugly (in
addition to *bitch*, common examples are *heifer, fat pig, landwhale, dog,
cow, porker, horseface*), to sexualize and reduce women to sexual roles
(*cougar, kitten, wildcat, fox, bunny*), or to otherwise diminish them
(*chick*). In particularly vile online subcultures, women are dehumanized
with words like *foids* (female humanoid) or *roasties* (a vulgar term for
labia) or are referred to by categories of purportedly more attractive and
unattainable women (*Stacys*) and average (*Beckys*) women. Derogatory
slang exists for entire subcategories of women, like those deemed attractive except for their face (*butterface*) or seen as overbearing or too aggressive (*battle axe*).[33] Racist terms (e.g., *noodlewhore*, for Asian women)
also abound. Notably, the use of body-based slurs like these allows men
to forcibly make gender visible in virtual or online contexts where it
would otherwise be invisible and where there is no physical presence
to attack or disparage.[34] In otherwise nongendered virtual interactions,
in other words, gendered slurs, homophobic language and imagery, and

misogynistic attacks act as performative "virtual manhood acts" to enable men to reclaim power and reassert the status hierarchy, keeping women, men, and trans or nonbinary people "in line" with patriarchal norms and expectations.[35]

These strategies of containment also affect boys and men who are deemed not masculine enough, who are policed with pejorative insults that clarify the hierarchy in which heterosexual, cisgender men who conform to traditional expectations for strength, machismo, and stoicism are higher status than women, gay, or nonbinary people who express more femininity. Slurs typically disparage men by calling them women's body parts (*pussy*), imply they are too feminine (*sissy*), disparage their masculine courage, prowess, or physique (*fat-ass, coward, weakling*), suggest they are homosexual (*fag*), label them as weak and overly submissive to women (*cuck*), imply they are only good for roles as providers (*wallet*), troll them for being too kind or sympathetic toward women (*simp*), or describe them as uncoordinated (*throws like a girl*).[36] Boys might also be told to man up, toughen up, or don't cry. Such slurs police the boundaries of what is considered acceptable masculine behavior—thus the word "sissy" does not just imply a man or a boy is sensitive or timid but that he is more sensitive or more timid than men should be.[37] Other slurs are used to demonize the entire LGBTQ+ community and create a moral panic (*groomers*).[38]

Gendered slurs and epithets like these can only be understood in a world with strict rules about what it means to be a man and a woman—which are enforced by what scholars often call "gender policing." These rules—the boundaries of acceptable gendered expression—vary across national, cultural, and historical contexts, and are subject to rapid change as competing ideas about gender roles and norms challenge and shift societal expectations.[39] Even when gendered expectations are contested, there are some expressions that become culturally ideal at any historical moment, creating widely accepted norms about what a "real man" is, for example, and how he behaves.[40] Boys learn early that there are clear rules associated with manhood—including that they should not cry, should be physically strong, should eschew intimate friendships as they enter adolescence, and must be the primary household earner as adults.[41] Violations of those rules that venture into perceived feminine ways of being are then met with social shame, ridicule, bullying, or violence, as boys or men who refuse to adhere are branded a "pussy or a faggot," as weak and inferior and not masculine. For some men who experience or anticipate these social sanctions, violence becomes a "means of asserting dominance and thus proving superiority" in ways that offer the possibility of undoing shame and restoring honor.[42]

Gay men and boys are more frequent targets of gender policing than heterosexual boys and men, but research suggests that as same-sex relationships have become more socially accepted, this kind of policing is less about homophobia than it is about "proper" notions of masculinity. The kinds of homophobic bullying that gay boys face in school, for example, is more accurately understood as gender policing—whereby youth use social sanctions to defend, enforce, and reproduce the gender binary and essentialist ideas about being a man or a woman.[43] This helps explain why researchers have found that being gay (engaging in same-sex intimacy) is increasingly accepted among American youth, but being a "fag" (nonconforming, embodied expressions of sexuality seen as "flaunting" gay identity) is met with harassment—because the latter is the bigger transgression of gender norms.[44] This is one way that social norms about gender and sexuality are simultaneously challenged and reproduced— with progress in one area (greater support for same-sex relationships or marriage) advancing at a different pace than in other domains (strict ideas about expressions of masculinity and being a man).[45]

In some cases, these cultural ideals and expectations evolve into what is called "toxic masculinity," creating unhealthy and extremely narrow restrictions on "manly" qualities and limiting men's emotional and physical expressions to characteristics like anger, strength, aggression, and dominance.[46] This is what Mark Greene of The Good Men Project calls the "man box" of American masculinity—in which "real men" are tall, strong, stoic, heterosexual athletes and sports fans. These men embody the idea of the "man's man," which remains the primary caricature of a leading man in Hollywood or a dominant force in politics, finance, or sports. Such expectations are reinforced by both men and women and are remarkably durable over time, even as each generation challenges some parts of the man box. Donald Trump is just one recent example—his supporters have barely blinked at his repeated misogynistic and disparaging descriptions of women or assertions that men with power can touch women against their will.[47]

Not everyone adheres to prevailing ideas about masculinity—and even those who do can end up feeling like "prisoners" of an unattainable set of expectations.[48] And it is worth noting that the prevailing kind of masculinity in the United States—with its insistence on toughness and its valorization of violence and anger—is especially dangerous given the ease with which guns can be purchased and carried in many states. Research has shown that young men's views about the attractiveness of guns and even fantasies they might have about mass attacks are closely tied to issues of a desire for power and perceived threats to masculinity and status.[49] And youth who hold stronger male supremacist views also hold stronger beliefs about their safety being tied to owning guns or having others around them be armed.[50] These findings bear out in horrific episodes of mass violence, too. Prior to his rampage, the attacker at a California sorority wrote that buying his first handgun gave him a "new sense of power."[51]

This context helps explain the ubiquity of gendered slurs, especially online. In one study of the use of slurs in a one-week period on one social media platform,[52] researchers found more than 2.5 million tweets with the word "bitch," and an additional 400,000 with the words "cunt," "slut," or "whore."[53] During Hillary Clinton's presidential campaign, the use of the word "bitch" on Twitter spiked from a daily average of 400,000 to more than 900,000 on election day, with the words "Clinton" and "bitch" often appearing together.[54] Merchandise sold during the 2016 election included t-shirts with the phrase "Life's a Bitch, Don't Vote for One."[55]

The decades-long harassment of Hillary Clinton is one of the most textbook cases of misogynistic policing.[56] Even as a campaigning spouse to future President Bill Clinton, Hillary was pillorized by critics who saw her as a power-hungry, unnaturally aggressive, ambitious, and domineering bitch. This supposed domination was also sexualized; *Spy* magazine's 1993 cover depicted Hillary Clinton as a riding crop-wielding dominatrix in black leather and fishnet stockings.[57] She was nicknamed "Shrillary," called a *nasty woman*, and fielded relentless calls to "Lock Her Up," including among protesters who chanted it outside her home in late 2020.[58] This latter phrase reflects what Kate Manne describes as a "desire for her containment." Calling for Clinton to be locked up was, quite literally, an attempt to put Hillary Clinton back in her place—to punish her for violating patriarchal expectations and seizing power out of the hands of men.[59]

Clinton is hardly alone. Around the world, women in politics have reported marked jumps in threats and misogynistic hate over the past several years, as women journalists, elected officials, and other public figures have received bomb threats, death threats, and other harassment and online abuse.[60] This is nothing new, of course—as phrases like "Ditch the Bitch" and "Wicked Bitch of the West" directed decades ago at Pat Schroeder, US Representative from Colorado, make clear.[61] But online spaces and new modes of communication—like memes, short-form video, and deepfake video—have fueled exponential growth in the circulation and sharing of misogynist attacks against prominent women. Hate memes directed at Nancy Pelosi were ubiquitous at national rallies prior to the January 6 attack on the US Capitol—often with her image adorned with devil's horns or a swastika in ways that aim to link her to evil, to fascism, demons, or authoritarianism. Her attackers often "addressed" her by her first name only, including the singsong "Where are you, Nancy?" that insurrectionists called out as they attacked the Capitol, and the "Where's Nancy?" uttered by an attacker at the Pelosi home in fall 2022.[62]

This kind of harassment and violence against women in politics, Mona Lena Krook argues, specifically aims to exclude women from the political sphere, rooted in beliefs that women should not have the right to participate in society outside the home with the same rights as men.[63] This can be both a backlash against women's political participation specifically and against feminism more broadly, especially as antifeminism itself has gained strength globally as part of a broader far-right attack on "gender ideology" and women's and LGBTQ+ rights.[64] The tactics of such attacks are broad and varied, but Krook highlights two in particular that are especially relevant for online spaces, both rooted in semiotics and the use of images, language, and symbols to render women either invisible (annihilating their public presence) or incompetent (arguing women's roles are incongruent with public leadership). A wide range of strategies are deployed to these ends, including silencing, ridiculing, objectifying, slut shaming, mansplaining, and ultimately removing women from their public roles.[65]

It's not just women in power or leadership who grapple with misogynistic insults, sexism, or violence. Tens of thousands of ordinary women have posted stories anonymously just to the online Everyday Sexism Project in recent years. There are terrible, extreme accounts of violent rapes, sexual abuse by parents and friends, of physical groping and catcalling in public spaces. But there are also stories of casual sexism and misogyny experienced in ordinary, everyday ways: girls who are constantly told to smile, to lighten up, to learn to take a joke, to accept that "boys will be boys." "You're not cute enough to be raped," a male friend told one young woman when she asked for a ride home from a pub. (The report echoed Donald Trump's claim that he could not have raped accuser Jean Carroll because "she's not my type.")[66] Misogynistic and sexist comments like these are often couched as jokes, which can make it harder to challenge them.[67] Those who do report—at work, at school, to friends, to parents—are often silenced, shamed, dismissed, and blamed. People don't "want to acknowledge it, or talk about it," Laura Bates describes, in ways that effectively normalize and excuse everyday forms of sexism.[68]

Marginalized women are targets of multiple forms of hate and harassment. This includes girls and women with disabilities, who are disproportionately affected by sexual violence.[69] And it includes what Trudy and Bailey have coined misogynoir to refer to the twin enforcement mechanisms of white patriarchy experienced by Black women, who face layered forms of racism and misogyny.[70] This is part of what Crenshaw calls intersectionality: the multiple and simultaneous experiences of oppression faced by individuals who hold identities in more than one marginalized group. For example, women of color may experience their engagements in professional life in ways that have been described as "space invaders" or "bodies out of place," as repeated examples of women politicians of color being denied entry to office spaces, rejected from "members only" elevators, or asked to fetch coffee illustrate all too clearly.[71] In the summer of 2019, then President Trump attacked several congresswomen of color in a series of racist tweets, suggesting they "go back" to "the crime-infested places from which they came."[72] Although he didn't name them, he was widely understood to be referring to Representatives Alexandria Ocasio-Cortez, Ilhan Omar, Rashida Tlaib, and Ayanna Pressley[73]—four congresswomen of diverse ethnic and racial backgrounds.[74] Trump wasn't the only one attacking these political leaders. The four women were repeatedly taunted with chants to "send them back"—words that insist they go back to their place, to anyplace— whatever it takes for them to stop being *front and center*. Those same calls were echoed or copied in the propaganda of white supremacist and neo-Nazi groups. The National Alliance, for example, called for immigrant deportations with a flyer saying "Send Them Back. They can't make White babies."[75]

Policing (White) Femininity

Slurs aren't the only containment tactic in the misogynist's toolbox. Policing physical expressions of femininity and appearance is an equally common strategy of enforcement. Women's physical appearance— especially in the public realm—has long been dictated by strict norms that are rarely breached and that center on signaling good motherhood and respectable, moral citizenship without treading too far into men's spaces. As women began entering traditionally male occupations in greater numbers over the past several decades, women's physical appearance first aimed to imitate men's attire (through business suits with giant shoulder pads, for example) or restrict appearance in ways that maintained a pleasing, hostess-like engagement (such as through weight requirements that mandated slimness for flight attendants).

These standards for beauty and appearance are often embedded in ideas about "respectability" ingrained in white, elite ideals, morals, and values that intersect with gender, race, and social class.[76] In the end, as

Tressie McMillan Cottom thoughtfully argues in *Thick*, these expectations are less about standards of beauty or appearance than they are about the "preferences that reproduce the social order." These are normative expectations that dictate what is the proper way to look—in ways that have often reinforced or upheld white, male desires.[77] These expectations range from popular ideals around slenderness to implicit or explicit standards for "professional" makeup, jewelry, and hairstyles that promote racist and racialized ideals around beauty, respectability, and discipline.[78]

Rigid standards for expressions of femininity are regularly contested, of course, including by second-wave feminists who rejected these expectations entirely on the logic that wearing makeup or spending too much time on cosmetic grooming was a betrayal of feminist ideas in favor of conventional, mainstream expectations of femininity.[79] But even as second-wave feminists rejected traditional norms about women's physical appearance, women in power or leadership roles were often still held to restricted (if unstated) expectations about hair length and color, feminine (but not too bold) makeup, and clothing choices that largely reflect social norms and expectations about white femininity. Neutral colors, small jewelry, modest nails and makeup, nothing flashy or bold: These were markers of respectability that women acquiesced to in order to break through the glass ceiling.

Norms began to change radically when a younger, more diverse group of women elected officials and public leaders entered professional careers—and in turn, those women of color were faced with tremendous onslaughts of misogyny and racism regarding "rules" of proper feminine behavior that policed both parts of their identities. These intersecting forms of racist and sexist experiences are common for women of color, especially in public-facing roles.[80] Black and Latina women must grapple with the effects of constant stereotypes in Hollywood characters, caricatures, product marketing, and popular culture, while simultaneously being sanctioned for a perceived failure to conform to standards of white respectability and femininity.[81]

Sonia Sotomayor, for example, was advised by President Obama's staff to change her signature red nail polish to a neutral color during the confirmation hearings for the Supreme Court. As *Latina* magazine later reported, she did so for the hearings, but at the subsequent White House celebration, Sotomayor held up her fire-engine red nails for the President to see, and pulled back her hair to show black and red semi-hoop earrings. Nearly a decade later, when Alexandria Ocasio-Cortez wore red lipstick and hoop earrings as she was sworn in to the US Congress in 2018, she tweeted that her inspiration was Sotomayor, and told followers "Next time someone tells Bronx girls to take off their hoops, they can just say they're dressing like a Congresswoman."[82]

Sotomayor and Ocasio-Cortez showed that refusing to conform to white patriarchal expectations about feminine respectability is a radical, transgressive act, a kind of breaking of the rules that dictate appearance.[83] They also eschewed white second-wave feminist arguments that dictated a wholesale rejection of cosmetic grooming. In so doing, Sotomayor and Ocasio-Cortez are part of a wave of women of color who advance a different pathway for feminine appearance. This is a third wave of feminism that argues it is possible to embrace high heels and makeup and "girly" things without compromising one's identity as a feminist or a powerful woman. Thus, the feminist writer Chimamanda Ngozi Adichie can sign on as a brand ambassador for a makeup company, for example, and argue that feminists can also care about how they look—echoing, in some ways, the frustrated words of indie singer Ani DiFranco from a quarter-century ago, as she lamented that "people talk about my image like I come in two dimensions. Like lipstick is a sign of my declining mind."[84]

The policing of white femininity is just one example of how containment works for women of color, who experience multiple oppressions as they are faced with misogyny alongside racism, Islamophobia, or anti-immigrant beliefs. Part of the reason why people are so quick to police perceived transgressions of femininity or masculinity has to do with cultural norms that dictate expected behavior—and those norms are racialized, gendered, classed, ableist, and more. Women who break unspoken rules about femininity and moral public presence find their transgressions are swiftly met with misogynistic enforcement strategies.

Those strategies intend to contain or make women conform to the box they are deemed to belong in—with containment strategies like belittling, rejecting, or simply asserting they should "go back" to some other place (regardless of where they were born, live, or belong).

Policing the behavior or appearance of women in online and offline contexts are clear strategies of containment. How do those commonplace tactics open pathways to more violent misogynist and male supremacist ideologies and actions? In the next chapter, I interrogate the violent online and offline groups and spaces that make up a vast and ever-expanding ecosystem of male supremacist beliefs and violence. Before we turn to those worlds, it is necessary to articulate how pathways from ordinary and everyday expressions of misogynist and gendered norms—like the slurs and containment strategies described in this chapter—can open pathways to more virulent and violent worldviews.

Gateways and Rabbit Holes: How Everyday Sexism Incubates and Mobilizes Violent Misogyny

If the patriarchy is dead, as Hanna Rosin claimed in that 2013 *Slate* essay, we'd better tell the internet. Online spaces are rife with every imaginable form of sexism and misogyny, from vile harassment of women in online gaming and chat rooms to women influencers touting the benefits of "Trad Wife" (traditional wife) lives.[85] There are many different everyday entry points to the kind of violent male supremacist radicalization that has led to mass attacks against women, the LGBTQ+ community, and other targets, but the trajectory is remarkably common across different pathways. I describe three here: the online worlds of gaming, memes and short-form video, and self-help influencers. All three of these areas of online engagement are often fun, engaging, therapeutic, and productive spaces that provide meaningful ways of spending time with friends or learning new skills. They are also spaces that can introduce or cement toxic masculinity and misogynistic ideas about women and gendered relationships.

Online Gaming

It's no secret that extremists exploit gaming sites. Various reports have shown that online gaming chat rooms and in-game chats—or related sites and servers on platforms heavily populated by gamers, like Discord and Twitch—have been used by extremists to share extremist content, network and plan violent action, recruit other players to supremacist movements, and livestream attacks.[86] Some 3.3 billion people play video games—representing a third of the global population—and the majority of online gamers report they have been exposed to extremist content while gaming.[87] That content—and the grand mythologizing in the broader fantasy worlds the games convey—is often highly gendered. Boys and men still comprise the majority of online gamers and developers, and are overrepresented in characters within games, although there have been significant efforts to introduce more gender and racial diversity to the industry. But even as the percentage of women gamers has grown, 75% of women report being harassed while gaming and nearly two-thirds admit to hiding their gender (through the use of male avatars or names, for example).[88]

The attention to possible radicalization in online gaming has mostly focused on the risks that live chat or text communication features create for grooming and recruitment. Such vulnerabilities have been well-documented in games oriented toward younger children, where there are reports of extremist actors trying to plant seeds among children to help undermine the legitimacy of parents or the authority of other adults as a starting point for grooming them to accept supremacist ideological views.[89] And they have also been thoroughly analyzed for older teen and young adult recruits, where extremists in online chats focus on encouraging young men to embrace an angry stance toward the mainstream that they feel has rejected or let them down. Such recruitment in online gaming chats often happens through a subtle conditioning of young men toward a reactionary political outlook that is hostile to progressivism, less tolerant of diversity, and inclined to reject ideas about structural or systemic and historical discrimination.[90]

This kind of engagement happens with regularity. Megan Condis notes that within the game *League of Legends*, once every six or seven games, "you'll see someone whose username is something racially or gendered or sexually inappropriate or whatever, or someone who spams in chat and is like, 'Hitler was right,' or whatever. And the question is how often is that a person who is just hoping that someone's going to respond so that they can jump into private chat and be like, 'Come check out my neo-Nazi forum,' and then how many of them are just people who are being edgy and memeing or whatever, right?"[91]

In-game chats can be deeply problematic even when they are not populated by extremists seeking to intentionally recruit new members to formal groups. Gaming chats are also deeply misogynistic, according to a 2024 analysis of in-game chats by the Extremism and Gaming Research Network (EGRN) and gamer reports in a 2022 survey from the United Nations Office of Counterterrorism (UNOCT).[92] They are peppered with a constant stream of toxic, racist, homophobic, and misogynistic content that desensitizes, dehumanizes, and ultimately can radicalize individuals through a broader normalization of hate.[93] Eighty-five percent of the UNOCT survey respondents reported witnessing problematic or toxic behavior in gaming spaces, mostly through verbal abuse within in-game chats or using voice-based communication. A third reported seeing significant amounts of misogyny, racism, xenophobia, or homophobia. This included hate directed toward every imaginable targeted group, including the casual use of slurs and comments like "ur gay" or "you play like a girl."[94] In this way, even when the games' content is benign or when there is no extremist recruitment taking place in deliberate ways, the games themselves can anchor ultracompetitive, hypermasculine communities of players who foster and incubate extreme ideas. Gaming thus becomes a kind of "proving ground" for boys and young men as they negotiate masculine status by using sexualized language and slurs that police the appropriate boundaries of sex and gender.[95] And because this takes place during an affective, enjoyable experience of gaming together, boys and young men engage in these behaviors while creating social bonds, a sense of belonging, and group membership in ways that weave racist, misogynist, and homophobic ideas into an experience that fosters emotional and social connections with others.[96] Similar patterns have been shown with fraternal bonding in sports locker rooms—but the virtual arena opens up this type of participation for a broader range of boys and young men, including those who are not athletically inclined.[97]

Similar kinds of misogynistic, racist, and homophobic harassment and trolling take place in online gaming communities outside the actual games, in Discord servers and Reddit forums and other spaces where disaffected gamers express and catalyze discontent about changes games have made to introduce more diverse characters. In the spring of 2024, a harassment campaign with aspirations to become "Gamergate 2" targeted the gaming advisory company Sweet Baby Inc with false, conspiratorial accusations of secret interference in gaming companies' narrative designs.[98] The original Gamergate saga was a 2014 series of vile misogynistic threats, doxing, and abuse lobbed at women in the gaming industry that had long-lasting effects on male supremacist mobilization online. In the 2024 version, an angry mob of online trolls—including a Brazilian-based man who set up an entire Steam curation group and Discord server dedicated to unmasking the supposed conspiracy—accused Sweet Baby Inc of forcing gaming companies to conform to "woke ideology" and add more racially and gender-diverse characters. The company's employees, along with others who have spoken up in defense of Sweet Baby, have been threatened, abused, harassed, and doxed online.[99]

The narrative framing within games can also help normalize and legitimize misogynistic views. Games offer an immersion into a variety of worlds laden with masculine bravado—from military simulation games to mythical worlds laden with violent or apocalyptic ideas rooted in an all-or-nothing, good versus evil binary that valorizes hypermasculinity and promotes ideals about men as violent heroes and martyrs. These are often fantastical settings that lean heavily into masculine stereotypes or misogynistic ideas, couched in survivalist and dystopian ancient worlds, wars between mortal beings and magical realms, and wilderness quests. And through features like "mods"—tools that allow gamers to create and publish their own content—games include hypersexualized or naked female characters or embed other antifeminist content.[100]

There is no evidence that game storylines—or even the violence within games—contributes directly to offline violence or radicalization.[101] There is evidence, however, that gaming spaces are laden with gendered toxicity,[102] and that extremists leverage narratives within games to help position "violent extremists as protagonists who battle ideologically opposed forces."[103] Some of the fantastical and violent ideas common in digital gaming narratives have been exploited in far-right propaganda, including Viking-themed and doomsday prepper tropes or in far-right extremist ideologies that celebrate and valorize violence, call for system collapse, support conspiracism, and dehumanize enemies.[104] Violent video games and the communities they anchor reflect and foster fantastical, mythical moral worldviews that are fundamentally gendered in often grandiose ways—where violent actors are brothers and honorable men of this age, whose women play a submissive but key role in replicating the nation and ensuring its racial purity. Other games directly promote far-right ideological content that embeds misogynistic ideas right into the game's structure, such as the game *Lock Her Up: The Trump Supremacy*, which describes itself as a "fast-paced survival shooter" pitting players "against the endless ambitions of Madame Hillary and the Globalists." The promotional text asks whether the protagonists will "survive each onslaught and finally be able to Lock Her Up?"[105]

Narrative frames and concepts like this are undoubtedly channels for sexist and misogynist ideas. And there are other aspects of gaming that are linked to terrorism and mass violence, such as "gamification," which refers to the ways that the design elements of games are being used outside of games—like in the creation of online "kill count" scoreboards to compare the "success" of terrorist attacks and aim for a higher "score," or the use of GoPro camera helmets to livestream attacks.[106] It is the online gaming community itself, though, that helps to introduce, strengthen, and normalize sexist, racist, and misogynist slurs, comments, and attacks as part of the ordinary act of playing. In some ways, these chats reflect existing social dynamics in the offline world and its ongoing challenges of racism, sexism, and homophobia—but in digital gaming chats, dehumanizing content is often unchallenged and spreads easily.[107] And harmful content is often introduced as part of communities that young men seek out to help them improve their game—in ways that can lower resilience to the community's toxicity because of existing trust and relationships within the group. In this way, gaming communities can introduce, reinforce, and strengthen ideas that can ultimately radicalize individuals toward violence. This includes community language that introduces and reinforces ideas like violent accelerationism, which promotes societal collapse as desirable and inevitable, or nihilism and the meaninglessness of life, or the mass shooter fandom and idealizing of mass killers—all while embracing a gendered view of a dichotomous world driven by good and evil, sin and salvation, darkness and light, in which real men fight back against an ever-growing set of existential threats and can be cleansed and redeemed by sacrificing themselves in the name of a just cause.

In anonymous online forums and in post-arrest interrogation videos, in written manifestos, interviews with "former" extremists, and in post-deradicalization memoirs, men who embrace violent extremism repeatedly describe themselves—or violent actors they admire—as heroic martyrs who are challenging an unfair world—often while simultaneously expressing tremendous misogyny, sexism, and complaints about white women's reproductive role and declining white birth rates. Demographic change is perceived as posing an existential threat to racial purity and ultimately to white civilization—as reflected in the popularity of the Great Replacement conspiracy theory on gaming forums and sites—and white women are to blame for not reproducing enough. Many violent far-right actors believe they are sacrificing themselves through their own discipline and commitment, making an offering that brings glory to them personally and racial restoration or rebirth of their people or civilization more broadly. Those ideas can be strengthened and mirrored in online gaming communities, especially those with abusive, racist, misogynistic, or hypermasculine norms and environments.

These ideas don't come from video games, any more than they originate in social media or online platforms more broadly. They can be quickly reinforced through the world of online gaming, however, and the grand myths and fantasies expressed there. It bears emphasizing that games do not turn anyone into violent attackers. Young men who are already isolated and angry or who are encountering racist, misogynist, or other hateful ideas elsewhere, in online communities or in their off-line lives, may find those arguments echoed in the immersive world of violent video games—and the like-minded communities of gamers in them.[108] In short, the often hypermasculine and misogynistic communities that emerge within and across apocalyptic and fantastical digital games can reinforce gendered and racialized ideas about heroic defense of purity, sacred civilizations, and threats of contamination while valorizing violence. And they do this while offering live chat features that open literal pathways to violent extremist scenes and groups through relationships, invitations, or engagement with others who already hold extreme and violent ideas.

Video games are played by millions and millions of young people—the vast majority of whom never become radicalized. The kind of time and expense game creation takes—with sophisticated production, coding, and design costs and needs—means that individuals are unlikely to create games for the purpose of intentionally sharing misogynistic ideas—rather, in the gaming world, those ideas are more of a byproduct of community norms and behaviors. A faster, more organic, and more intentional visual sharing of toxic masculine ideals and messages is literally at everyone's fingertips—in the meme-crafting and short-form video-making worlds of their smartphones.

Memes, Misogyny, and Masculinity

A digitally savvy younger generation has honed their visual media skills on image-sharing sites like Instagram and Snapchat, video platforms like YouTube and TikTok, and a variety of other online sites for sharing memes and vlogs, podcasts and images. This means that teens and young adults are no longer only the consumers of hateful and extremist propaganda that is produced by formal, organized groups. They are its active producers—especially in witty, irony-laden memes, curated photographs, and short-form videos. Sexist, misogynist, and gender-policing memes are in the thick of it—not only as a supporting role in other kinds of hate or harm but as online incubators of dehumanizing content that are so ubiquitous online that they easily draw ordinary users in.

Memes situated in obscure internet subcultures have fueled violent extremist and terrorist action in surprising ways. A meme referencing a coming "second civil war" mobilized terrorist actions affiliated with the Boogaloo scene across several states during the COVID-19 pandemic, including among alleged members of Boogaloo scenes who were later charged with plotting to kidnap the governor of Michigan. A few years earlier, a cartoon character named Pepe the Frog, originally created by Matt Furie for the comic "Boy's Life," suddenly became co-opted by the "alt-right"[109] in part through a series of memes depicting Pepe with racist and antisemitic iconography.[110] Within a year, the connection between Pepe the Frog and the US far right was so strong that Hillary Clinton denounced Pepe publicly, and the Anti-Defamation League added the cartoon character to its hate symbols database.[111] Through a series of moves only explicable through the lens of online subcultures, the Pepe meme evolved into a flag for a mythical land called Kekistan ruled by a frog-headed man-god Kek—which then moved outside the realm of online caricatures and started showing up in physical settings.[112] The flag appears prominently in photos from the 2017 white supremacist Unite the Right rally in Charlottesville, Virginia. It also waves on a flagpole and was strewn across the shoulders of a combat fatigue–dressed insurrectionist wearing a red Make America Great Again hat at the US Capitol on January 6, 2021.

Before they can even potentially fuel violence, racist and misogynistic memes begin their lives in ordinary online spaces where youth spend time. They are shared widely in group chats, which help young people follow rabbit holes of hyperlinks into increasingly offensive sites and subcultures. For an isolated-but-highly-networked online generation of youth, trading memes, messages, and embedded short-form videos from TikTok, Instagram Reels, or YouTube Shorts is a way of connecting that can quickly desensitize and normalize hate. Racist, misogynistic, and dehumanizing ideas are introduced in ways that are framed as "just a joke," with all the plausible deniability that phrase carries. Thus there are memes that make light of the Holocaust by comparing extermination gas chambers to a pizza oven, or that compare Black people to various animals—all motivated by an online youth culture that provokes with salacious, mocking, offensive humor aimed at getting *"lulz,"* online shorthand for laughing out loud. By framing hateful content as ironic, Raúl Pérez argues, the modern far right made racist humor into something enjoyable.[113] This is what I have called the weaponization of youth culture that helped fuel the far right prior to and following the Charlottesville Unite the Right rally. Irony, satire, humor, and sarcasm were tools that the far right used to position itself as an edgy youth counterculture resisting and provoking a boring, triggered, adult mainstream.[114]

Many of the memes and videos circulating among youth are organic, crafted and modified and circulated by teens themselves. Others are deliberate propaganda that takes advantage of the changing visual landscape of our communication worlds to embed violent, hateful, and extremist content in accessible forms. Social media and video platform algorithms clearly struggle to weed out racist, antisemitic, and transphobic content, even recommending banned content to young users.[115] Young boys in particular report seeing a steady feed of hateful content in their feeds—with few places in their lives where they can openly discuss what they are seeing, what it means, and its broader impact.[116] In one recent study, sock puppet accounts for a 16-year-old boy that searched for gender-normative content (like sports, video games, gyms) on TikTok and YouTube Shorts were fed antifeminist, manosphere-related content within minutes. And if the account showed interest by watching that content, within 2–3 hours, the vast majority of recommended content was antifeminist and manosphere-related content. Boys receive this content even when they don't search for it, in other words.[117] Algorithms that privilege misogynistic or salacious posts help desensitize and normalize hateful, conspiratorial, and violent content. Eventually, shocking content becomes less shocking.

Antifeminism and memes focused on issues of purity, morality and immorality, sexual promiscuity, and Christianity are especially popular. Online spaces are rife with jokes and memes related to issues of consent and virginity, along with male supremacy memes (e.g., comments or jokes about differences in brain size between men and women) and memes conveying anti-abortion and antifeminist content. One common set of memes depict a slender "trad girl" dressed in demure clothing with long, blond hair and light makeup and compare her, invariably, to a "lefty woman" (unkempt, unhinged), a "slut" (provocatively dressed, heavily made up), or a "liberated feminist" (tattooed, dyed hair, tight clothing). In one well-known meme comparing a "liberated feminist" to a "Tradwife" (traditional wife), margin text describes the tattooed, heavily made-up feminist with phrases like "sleeps around to improve her self esteem but it only makes her feel worse," while the Tradwife is described as having a "slim figure from her healthy homemade meals and active lifestyle." White supremacist and nationalist text often accompanies the images by describing the liberated feminist as "only attracted to black men" or having "aborted her black baby last year" while the Tradwife "loves her family, race, and country in that order."[118]

The policing of women's sexuality—in memes and other forms—raises an intriguing contradiction within white supremacist movements. On the one hand, women are celebrated as nurturers whose men would defend them against all manner of threats to their purity—and thereby help secure the future of white civilization and traditional patriarchy. The Proud Boys, for example, use a slogan "Venerate the Housewife." It is only housewives—women positioned in subordinate roles—who are put on a pedestal, however, and only under specific conditions. Within white supremacist and other far-right movements, women are held to strict standards about sexual purity and chastised for behavior that violates those standards. And in those scenes, women are often the victims of domestic and intimate partner violence and abuse—a phenomenon whose intersections with violent extremism are only beginning to be seriously explored.

Part of why memes policing women's sexuality find a foothold at all is because of the ubiquitous presence of gendered ideas and rules about issues of purity, promiscuity, and shame as well as weakness, strength, defense, and protection as it relates to masculinity, the bonds of brotherhood, a call to be honorable men, and traditional family values. These concepts can underpin violent mobilization, but they also help recruit and radicalize people who are already receptive to the idea of fixed gender norms and rules for behavior.

These memes don't exist in isolation. Memes and short videos policing women's sexuality are just part of the widespread exposure that many teens have to violent content about women, including violent pornography that deliberately violates and dehumanizes women of color. The pop star Taylor Swift faced backlash in spring 2023 when she began dating singer Matty Healy, who had admitted to masturbating to hardcore pornography that degrades Black women on a website called "Ghetto Gaggers." He made the admission on a podcast hosted by two comedians known for their use of "ironic bigotry," with frequent use of racist slurs and accents.[119]

Healy's admission was shocking but not terribly surprising in light of data showing that a majority of youth have seen pornography as teens, starting at an average age of 12—in ways that suggest they are learning about sex, sexuality, and relationships through their consumption of content that is often violent, aggressive, and racist. Over half of teens who have viewed pornography report having seen pornographic content that was violent or depicted rape, choking, or someone in pain.[120] Online pornography is rife with video content that dehumanizes, abuses, and degrades women with name-calling and physical acts of violence.[121] Pornographic images that viewers may regard as innocent pleasure also include digitally altered, graphic images of real women, including politicians.[122] Researchers already know this both normalizes and fuels sexual violence.[123] It can skew teens' beliefs about whether people like to be hit, spanked, slapped, gagged, or choked during sex.[124] Two-thirds of US women college students report that a partner had choked them during sex, often without their consent—a phenomenon that researchers tie to repeat exposure to sexual strangulation in violent pornography.[125]

Frequent exposure to pornography also increases endorsement of rape myths, which are false beliefs that place the blame for rapes on survivors rather than perpetrators.[126] And it is also correlated with boys' thinking that forcing someone to have sex is ok.[127] In light of research showing that men who perceive threats to their gender identity view more pornography that is degrading or demeaning to women and evidence suggesting impacts of pornography on sexually aggressive attitudes and behaviors,[128] it's hard not to imagine that exposure to violent porn isn't also affecting the growth of violent misogynist incels and the broader male supremacist manosphere—as discussed more in the next chapter.

Memes and video shorts that police women's sexuality, appearance, intelligence, competence, and ambition have many layers of consequences. They directly disparage, humiliate, and degrade women and girls. They also become a gateway to scientific racism, antisemitic conspiracy theories, and calls for violence against an existential threat. This doesn't mean those kinds of jokes or memes are only important because they play a supporting role in some other kind of hate or harm. Rather, I use the notion of "gateway" content to refer to hateful ideas that are so ubiquitous online that they draw ordinary users in. Once young men are part of servers, group chats, or discussion boards that share misogynistic content, inevitably, antisemitic, racist, or conspiratorial content is not far behind.

Taken together, the combination of misogynist, racist, and hateful ideas in online games and memes contributes to a kind of digital "redpilled" awakening for legions of young men who believe they are seeing the pieces fit together in ways that reveal the true nature of the world. The red pill is a pop cultural reference used widely in far-right youth subcultures. It comes from a scene in the 1999 film *The Matrix*, in which the protagonist Neo was given the choice to take a "red pill" (and be introduced to the hidden reality of the manipulated world) or a "blue pill" (return to a happy state of ignorance).[129] The idea of a hidden but true nature of the world we live in has been a compelling frame to help rationalize the disaffection many youth feel, and has been especially appealing to young men who seek help with depression, isolation, or anxiety—and ultimately find it in a rigid gendered worldview that promises them dominance, status, and power over all others.

Self-Help Forums

Online self-help searches may seem like an unconventional starting point for pathways to mass violence. Young men seeking guideposts in the transition to adulthood, though, often discover a world of online spaces rife with influencers who offer a set of "success" strategies (often at the price of a monthly subscription) to get their lives together. These influencers contribute to a broader online culture in youth spaces that is obsessively focused on men's bodies, physical fitness and body image, self-improvement, and discipline, sometimes alongside what is described as "looksmaxxing," which are online communities focused on enhancing men's faces, including through plastic surgery to build stronger-looking jawlines or chins.[130] These fixations on appearance, which are a flip side of the beauty standards that can lead young women to develop eating disorders, body dysmorphia, or obsessive use of plastic surgery, can also lead to disordered eating or obsessive fitness regimes and steroids use in boys and men.

Boys aren't the only ones who encounter gendered influencers online. Girls and young women may encounter Trad Wife (traditional wife) influencers who encourage women to embrace roles as submissive homemakers and mothers, decked out in 1950s housewife heels and dresses—or they may follow false self-help or spiritual influencers who promise wellness or success in business or relationships but instead lure women into human and sexual trafficking.[131] But male-oriented self-improvement spaces can open pathways to radicalization in ways that increase the risk of violence as traits like discipline, strength, and masculine prowess are linked to defense of a nation or Western civilization writ large. In these spaces, men are often urged to renounce porn and masturbation, commit to working out, getting buff, and embrace sexual morality and purity in ways that often evoke college fraternity boy rituals. The Proud Boys' initiation rituals and rules, for example, include restricting the frequency of masturbation and agreeing to be beaten up by other Proud Boys members until they can name five kinds of breakfast cereal.[132]

Guidance for self-improvement in these online spaces is strict, predictable, and often very effective at initiating real changes that do help youth feel better—from making their beds each morning to drinking more water. A recent thread on the anonymous 4chan political discussion imageboard /pol/, for example, emphasizes a three-month transformation plan with no processed food, no fast food, and a commitment to maintain discipline and eat only healthy food. Some of these kinds of plans come from self-help influencers who are legitimate fitness experts offering concrete strategies for change that have meaningfully helped legions of users build healthier habits. But in other cases, popular influencers and creators promise tangible "success" (wealth, sex, power) in plans that are accompanied by tremendous amounts of misogyny, racism, or other harmful content. There is perhaps no better example than Andrew Tate and his outsized influence on teenage boys across the globe.

In January 2023, I began fielding calls from journalists who had heard from parents and teachers that teenage boys were expressing a surprising number of misogynistic ideas in class or at home. This was no surprise to me or my team in my research lab, the Polarization and Extremism Research and Innovation Lab (PERIL): Two years earlier, we had all listened as a middle school mom in a webinar complained that during the highly online period of pandemic learning, her son had adopted new misogynistic beliefs so severe that he no longer would listen to her as an expert on anything, because she is a woman. And throughout 2022 and early 2023, a variety of news reports began to warn parents and teachers about an uptick in violent misogyny being expressed by teenage boys.[133] Teachers in the UK, Canada, United States, and elsewhere have reported impacts like a "huge increase in rape jokes" among boys, as well as comments that casually praise men as better than women and refusals to do assignments handed out by a woman because "women should only be housewives."[134] One teacher reported hearing a young student in the playground introduce his girlfriend to a group, and "as soon as she was out of earshot he was asked by several friends if they could 'have a go' with her."[135]

Some teachers and education experts blame this disturbing increase in part on creators like self-described misogynist and online influencer Andrew Tate, who was arrested in December 2022 in Romania on charges of organized crime, human trafficking, and rape.[136] Tate amassed millions of followers on social media—mostly teenage boys and young men—before being banned from Facebook, YouTube, TikTok, and Instagram. Among other repugnant statements on social media, Tate has compared women to property, argued that women bear some of the responsibility when they are raped, and bragged about seeking sexual conquests with 18-year-old women because younger women are easier to "make an imprint" on.[137] While teaching dating academy tactics to degrade and manipulate women, he compares women to dogs, advocates for their physical abuse as a mechanism of control, and says he believes that they shouldn't drive or work outside the home. If a woman accused him of cheating, he told his followers, "it's bang out the machete, boom in her face and grip her by the neck. Shut up, bitch." It is hard to overstate Tate's popularity with boys and young men. In February 2024, a new UK report revealed that one in five men between age 16 and 29 view Tate favorably.[138] Data from the United States reveal similar trends: In 2023, 18–23-year-old men were more likely to say they trust Andrew Tate (20%) than then-President Joe Biden (15%).[139]

Tate doesn't only peddle misogyny and abuse of women. He also embeds it within an ecosystem of self-help and self-improvement guidance, urging young men to get up off the couch and embrace a gym-bro-culture that rejects therapy and believes depression isn't real. Tate covers hateful content in an affable, joke-filled delivery style, offered in monthly subscription content promising self-help strategies alongside money-making and self-improvement tips. And he does so while appearing to be a maverick who bucks mainstream norms, which has a particular appeal to boys and young men.[140] Tens of thousands of boys and men— some claiming to be as young as 13—paid anywhere from $49.95 to $147 per month for access to Tate's content.[141] Performative, chest-thumping masculinity is part of the package: Tate flaunts wealth, flashy cars, yachts, and mansions as symbols of status and success. The performative aspect has even become a shield for Tate: In a statement to NBC News denying allegations of misogyny, he called himself a "success coach" who plays an "online character."[142]

Tate's content wouldn't be so effective if it wasn't reaching boys at a moment when they are in a well-documented crisis of loneliness, isolation, and inhibition about how to engage in a world that often presents them as "inherently dangerous."[143] Researchers liken Tate's approach to the kinds of psychological manipulation common in cults and multilevel marketing tactics, including the use of coercive control and promises of financial success from a charismatic authority who bonds followers and fosters a sense of community that is inherently exploitative. Tate's "The Real World" community, which evolved out of a previous subscription service Tate called "Hustlers University," had over 100,000 members as of August 2024, each of whom enters a chess-like hierarchy on the platform in which they can advance through the ranks from pawn to bishop, knight, and king—under the guidance of professors and captains—by increasing active participation on the platform.[144]

By situating self-help and self-improvement within an anti-feminist, anti-liberal "wokeness" stance, Tate and other misogynist influencers scapegoat women's progress and the broader progressive mindset as damaging to men and to the God-given natural order of things, including traditional gender roles. Conspiracy theories that evoke antisemitism as part of antifeminism are a part of the deal: Tate and his followers, for example, blame the "matrix" (the international liberal order) for suppressing the Truth—which alludes to the manosphere's broader commitment to "red-pilling." Men are being duped, according to Tate, and if they would just wake up, they too can become wealthy, desirable, and ultimately seduce endless numbers of beautiful and subordinated women who will serve their needs.[145]

Tate doesn't only appeal to teenage boys; he amassed a following among some conservative Muslim men, especially following his conversion to Islam and his praise of the "traditional" family structure of Muslim countries, "where a woman obeys their man."[146] Tate's statements validate these followers' patriarchal belief system, in which men remain heads of households and women are subservient actors who support them. As Rasha al Aqeedi explains, Tate's embrace of Islam is based on "the very Islamophobic stereotypes that many Muslims have fought against" and which are now "attracting the toxic masculinity types to Islam." After he converted, for example, Tate claimed he was collecting bricks so he could stone his partner if she cheated on him—an allusion to the Shariah punishment for adultery that is not practiced in the vast majority of Muslim-majority states.[147]

Tate is far from being the only driver of rising misogyny, including within the burgeoning online self-help space. Online extremism expert

Milo Comerford points out that there are "thousands of Andrew Tates out there" offering up antifeminist content. There are plenty of other relationship "coaches" online, teaching seduction and manipulation techniques, or railing against women's progress as having come at the expense of men and as a threat to the God-given natural order of things.[148] And these ideas spread rapidly into the mainstream. In 2019, an all-male, mock student government in Kansas proposed repealing the Nineteenth Amendment giving women the right to vote, leading to an apology from the sponsoring organization. Women's rights campaigner Laura Bates reports that over the past few years, her visits to schools now have a "new normal": boys in the audience trying to challenge her with false statistics about rape. A 2020 UK survey found that half of young men believe feminism has gone too far.[149]

Tate and other online fitness coaches and self-help influencers' emphasis on the "natural order" is key to radicalization pathways. It doesn't take long in online spaces frequented by young men to encounter a belief in women's and men's traditional roles as part of the "natural order of things"—a concept that also lends itself to anti-LGBTQ/anti-trans beliefs and scientific racism. Women in these scenarios are sometimes described as not at fault—they don't understand, aren't wired the right way, and need a man to take control. This idea of human difference being hardwired makes it a short leap to race science and its belief in racial differences in IQ and intelligence. And that—like nearly every final destination in hateful online spaces—leads directly to antisemitism and conspiracy theories about Jewish orchestration in the name of power.

Conclusion

These three examples show how ordinary and everyday spaces and places can act as incubators of hate or pathways to violent beliefs. The ubiquity of sexist and misogynist ideas in online gaming, memes and short-form videos, and among some popular self-help influencers, is a troubling trend that has consequences for boys' and men's relationships, propensity to violence, and ideas about consent, pleasure, and romantic partnerships. These ideas shape what boys and men think being a "real man" is, especially vis-à-vis women, and increase the pressure they may feel to act that way. The misogyny they embrace, in turn, assists in establishing ways of thinking that help to amplify and reinforce exclusionary ideas about national purity, degradation, contamination, and degeneracy, which can create fertile ground for scientific racism. Meanwhile, a steady flow of depictions of minorities (such as Muslim, Black, or Latino men) as a threat to white women's sexual purity and safety bolster xenophobic, nationalist, and anti-immigrant claims. The concepts of misogyny and white supremacy are ultimately inextricable.

As we have seen all too often recently, the toolkit misogynists use is not limited to verbal attacks or memes. In fact, if you can't contain women with words, the strategies of misogynists are bound to expand toward violence. The next chapter explores the burgeoning world of violent male supremacy.

3

Punishment

"GRAB THE BITCH"

ON A FRIDAY EVENING in November 2018, a 40-year-old man opened fire in a second-story yoga studio in Tallahassee, Florida, killing two women and injuring four others, along with a fifth man, before his weapon malfunctioned. It's hard to imagine a case with more red flags from ongoing and escalating violence toward women. The shooter had a decades-long history of harassing, stalking, and assaulting women. He wrote songs, stories, and screenplays with fantasies of torture, rape, and murder of women, with titles like "Stalker" and "Locked in my Basement." In dozens of separate incidents over the course of years, he was kicked out of apartments, jobs, family birthday parties, teaching positions, and the military after repeated incidents of unwanted touching, harassment, stalking, and battery against girls and women or for using school district devices to search for pornography involving yoga and cheerleaders. He was arrested several times and completed court-mandated counseling with a sex addiction therapist. His parents were so afraid of him that they slept with their door locked when he was in the house.[1]

That Florida yoga studio attack—along with other mass shootings targeting women at a California sorority and a series of Atlanta massage spas, a Toronto vehicle-ramming attack, and an attack at a New Jersey judge's home, which in total killed over two dozen people and injured dozens more, have thrust violent misogyny and misogynist incel (involuntary celibate) extremism into the public eye. The US Department of Homeland Security funded a project on violent incels as part of its 2022 grant program on terrorism and targeted violence prevention, for example.[2] And when the Colorado-based Counterterrorism Education Learning Lab (CELL) revamped and overhauled its Denver visitors' center in 2023, they added an entire new display section on male supremacism and misogynist incels, which has equal footing alongside educational displays on Islamist terrorism and other forms of domestic violent extremism.[3]

Yet even as the problem garners more attention, male supremacist violence is still often relegated to a category of "other" threats[4] or dismissed as the personality problems of challenged individuals rather than an ideological belief system on its own. The misogynistic and gendered dimensions of extremist movements are often ignored or brushed aside in media reports, policy analyses, or during prosecution. Defense attorneys for the Michigan militia members charged with plotting the kidnapping of the state's governor dismissed the alleged extremists' language—in which they repeatedly referred to Governor Gretchen Whitmer as a bitch or a "tyrant bitch" while plotting her kidnapping and execution—as just "big talk" and "blowing off steam."[5] After a man killed eight people in Atlanta spas in 2021, the police chief initially explained the shooter's actions as rooted in his being "fed up" and "having a really bad day."[6] That explanation came only a few years after a Texas police chief described the actions of a white man who sent mail bombs to Black community members as an "outcry of a very challenged young man talking about challenges in his life that led him to this point."[7] It's not just legal authorities who have helped minimize violence and misogyny. Ordinary people also normalize online hate as part of the cost of engaging. After the Uvalde, Texas, gunman's attack on an elementary school, his extreme misogyny and violent threats against teen girls online came to light. Teenagers who had observed his digital rage said they didn't report it because it's just "how online is."

Yet misogynist, anti-women, and antifeminist rhetoric is nearly always present in accounts of terrorist radicalization or motivation. The white supremacist terrorist who killed seventy-seven individuals, mostly children, in Norway in 2011 wrote that feminists were waging a "war against boys" and should be blamed for low white birth rates. The 2019 terrorist attacker in Hanau, Germany peppered his manifesto with incel references, while another attacker that same year in Halle, Germany listened to vile, misogynist lyrics on the day of his attack in a song that has been dubbed the "incel anthem."[8] The Buffalo terrorist shooter who murdered Black people at a grocery store referenced birth rates more than forty times, repeatedly noting that "white birth rates must change."[9] The neo-Nazi who murdered eight people in an Allen, Texas shopping mall in May 2023 left behind extensive writings detailing violent fantasies rooted in an expansive belief system about "real" manhood, violence, and the defense of nation and race, which included a "fixation with sex, pornography, and punishing women by violently raping them."[10]

The problem goes well beyond terrorist attacks, of course. In February 2024, a new report revealed that K-12 schools overseen by the US Department of Defense had experienced a 400% increase in reports of unwanted sexual behavior since 2019, from ninety-nine incidents in the 2019–20 school year to more than five-hundred three years later.[11] And men and boys have rapidly embraced tech-enabled innovations in gendered harassment, including revenge deepfake porn and AI-generated nude deepfake image and "undressing" apps—the latter having made disturbing inroads into middle and high schools across the United States.[12]

As security and counterterrorism specialists have belatedly begun to recognize the problem, male supremacy has gradually become more systematically integrated into understandings of violent extremism,[13] although attention is largely limited to misogynist incels.[14] This focus on male supremacist violence and violent incels is both welcome and overdue—but it is also important to ensure that new energy and attention toward violent incels does not obscure the presence of a much broader male supremacist spectrum. That broader spectrum includes not only violent incels but also a growing and toxic mix of men's rights activists (MRAs), antifeminist ideologues, and other misogynists. It is impossible to understand the full impact of misogyny on violent extremism and terrorism if we narrow the focus to one specific group.

The previous chapter argued that slurs, epithets, and hostile sexism are strategies for containing and controlling women and LGBTQ+ people in ways that can pave the way for targeted gender-based attacks. Mass atrocity attacks emerge from and are inexplicable without these more ordinary forms of misogyny and gender-based violence.[15] I turn here to the fringes where such violence is often incubated, encouraged, and celebrated, looking specifically at both online and offline manifestations of violence targeting women and the LGBTQ+ community. This type of mass targeted violence is part of a broader set of misogynist tactics to enforce rules and norms about gender and sexuality—and punish violators of those norms.

As a reminder, sexist attitudes—based in beliefs about natural differences between the sexes and the preference for or privileging of men's traits and abilities—can lead to differential treatment across sex and gender categories. Misogyny takes those beliefs a step further by acting as an enforcement strategy that seeks to punish or restore violations of patriarchal norms. As Kate Manne argues, the goal of misogyny is containment: to put those who breach or reject patriarchal expectations back in their place. For men enraged by a wide variety of these perceived violations, violence becomes an acceptable tactic to reassert their power and suppress it among anyone who does not adhere to the rules. Those perceived violations of norms rest on a core set of assumptions and beliefs known as male supremacy.

Understanding Male Supremacy

The school year was barely underway in fall 2023 when my research lab, PERIL, was contacted by a school after a group of middle school boys circulated AI-generated nude photos of their female classmates. It was not the first such inquiry we had—nor the last—as school leadership teams across the country grapple with the impact of toxic online spaces on their school communities. The specific use of generative AI to create deepfake nudes had already swept the nation in a wave of similar incidents at middle and high schools, enabled by increasingly realistic technology that puts a victim's face onto an existing nude body or "undresses" a clothed image. These nonconsensual, AI-enabled images and videos are easy to produce through free apps and have been used for harassment, sextortion, and bullying. Schools, parents, and communities are scrambling to catch up. Fewer than a dozen states currently have legislation that imposes civil or criminal penalties for creating deepfake pornography, although Congress did take up the issue in January 2024 after deepfake nude images of Taylor Swift in football stadiums were viewed tens of millions of times. The vast majority of deepfake images are both sexually explicit and created without the victim's consent.[16] In the case of middle and high school perpetrators, their victims are most often other minors, steering the use of deepfake nude and undressing app technology into the realm of child pornography.

The nonconsensual generation of images with the support of artificial intelligence is a new and troubling phenomenon. But it is also just the latest iteration—and rests on the shoulders—of age-old dynamics in which men and boys often feel entitled to sexual gratification, attention, and service from women, with or without their consensual participation. There is significant research showing that boys gain social currency and bolster their heterosexual and masculinity "creds" by sharing nonconsensual images of girls.[17] Tech- and AI-enabled image sharing, sexual harassment, and abuse is a clear, if novel, example of male supremacy, which is a toxic expression of patriarchal systems and the sexism and misogyny that underpin them. In this chapter, I analyze the ideology and violent expression of male supremacy through a focus on three cross-cutting themes apparent across all its forms: an obsessive desire for purity, anger at a perceived loss of power and status, and deep-rooted fears about worth and respect. These themes crystallize in anti-feminist ideas and conspiracy theories and mobilize violence organized around control and punishment.

Male Supremacism: Purity, Power, Worth, and Control

While eighth grade boys were busy figuring out how to "undress" the girls in their grade with free apps online, intelligence experts and extremism scholars were tracking the troubling online growth of a wide range of groups and subcultures across the male supremacist spectrum. Eventually dubbed the "manosphere," these groups and spaces are linked by and help to reinforce several sets of emotions and mental states: an obsessive desire for purity, anger at a perceived loss of power and status, and fear about a lack of worth or respect. A bevy of online spaces offer conduits for these emotive states, directing them into anger toward feminism, a sense of entitlement to women's service and attention, and a desire to control and punish women who don't conform to their expectations. These online spaces and the dialogue within them have helped to fundamentally reshape how young men see and understand issues related to gender, sexual consent, perceived injustice, and who is to blame for their personal problems and grievances. While many of these issues existed in prior men's rights movements, the online nature of the manosphere has helped shift these earlier discussions into more misogynistic, sexually explicit, homophobic, violent, and racist forms.[18]

Male supremacism is the belief that men are naturally, biologically, and genetically superior in ways that justify and rationalize the logical domination of women through social, political, economic, or legal hierarchies. These ideas do not only target women—the kinds of biological essentialism male supremacists rely on also reject anyone who does not fit within a naturalized and fixed gender binary, including trans men and women and the broader LGBTQ+ community. Nor are these ideas only believed or enforced by men—some women also help to uphold male supremacist beliefs. Male supremacy also establishes hierarchies of superiority and inferiority within men, positioning a certain kind of man—referred to in some male supremacist circles as alpha males, or chads—as superior to everyone else.[19] Anyone who doesn't fit the ideal, macho mold is seen as posing a threat to men and to the "real man" masculinity they embody.[20]

There's nothing new about the concept, of course—male supremacy was enshrined in law and social norms in most places for generations. But the core ideas of male supremacy—including their most violent manifestations—have surged in popularity as part of a decades-long retrenchment of traditional patriarchy and antifeminism and an explosion of broader misogyny and antifeminism in the social media era.[21] These developments are partially due to the increases in online misogyny that I detailed in the introduction. But they are also related to broader antidemocratic and authoritarian trends in the United States and globally, which have focused heavily on gender, control of women's reproductive capacity and abortion rights, LGBTQ+ rights, and the policing of gender binaries, trans communities, and broader expressions of autonomy and freedom.[22]

As an ideology, male supremacy intersects with other forms of supremacist beliefs, including white supremacy, Christian supremacy, and Western supremacy. Research shows that it is also linked to a wide range of other problematic traits and beliefs. People who report agreement with male supremacist statements are more likely to be socially isolated, express greater mental distress (loneliness, anxiety, depression, and posttraumatic stress), more support for racist and antigovernment ideas, and report more viewing of gun-related media.[23] Male supremacists score high on beliefs in authority and social dominance and are fixated on hierarchies and rankings. They also tend to espouse conspiratorial thinking, irrational suspicion, narcissism, and expressions of entitlement, while embracing a victimization-grievance narrative that situates their personal problems within a broader conspiracy of male harm orchestrated by feminists and women.[24] Male supremacist ideas exist across the ideological spectrum, from Islamist to white supremacist and antigovernment militia movements. But male supremacy is not just a supportive player in other extremist belief systems—it also exists within a category of its own, in part because of its rootedness in specific forms of anger and backlash against feminism and women's progress, which male supremacists generally believe has disadvantaged men.[25] At its core, this anger reflects fears about a loss of status, worth, respect, value, and power—manifesting in attempts to control, punish, and reassert dominance.[26]

Feminism as the Enemy: Men's Worth, Power, and Status

"Some men," Chimamanda Ngozi Adichie argues, "are threatened by the idea of feminism . . . their sense of self-worth is diminished if *they* are not 'naturally' in charge as men."[27] Indeed, if one thing is abundantly clear across male supremacist spaces and ideas, it is their shared sense of anger at feminism, either in openly hostile ways or through complaints that feminism has gone too far. Feminism is blamed for softening or "sissifying" men, making them weak, too reliant on modern conveniences, lacking authority over their households, and unable to protect or provide for their families.[28] In these spaces, the movement for equal rights and representation is viewed as part of a broader "war against men" as workplace competition displaces men from their natural roles as providers and simultaneously prevents women from assuming their God-given roles as mothers.[29] Men's crises are framed as intentional suffering at the hands of feminist "extremists" or "feminazis," such that problems ranging from divorce, child custody, child support, or men's high rates of suicide or domestic violence cases with male victims are blamed entirely on feminism.[30] Women's gains, in other words, are seen by some men as a direct challenge to their own sense of worth and value, which is itself rooted in traditional ideas about gendered roles.

After years of research on far-right propaganda and messaging, members of my research team in the Polarization and Extremism Research and Innovation Lab (PERIL) have come to think of both antifeminism and antisemitism as either the starting point or the final destination for virtually all propaganda and conspiracy theories online.[31] Our experience isn't an isolated one. A recent report from two UK-based NGOs describes misogyny as "widespread" within antisemitic spaces on the messaging app Telegram, with "pro-rape comments" and discussions of sexual violence especially common.[32] It doesn't really matter which rabbit hole you start down, though. Whether you begin perusing climate change discussions, immigration forums, or chat rooms dedicated to gun safety, you don't have to go very deep into most comment sections before the scapegoating begins. And feminists (along with Jews) are most often enemy number one.[33]

Anger at feminism—and feminists—takes a variety of forms. Some men deploy a lens of victimhood, arguing that men are discriminated against and women should be punished "just like men are" as they justify hostile action and violence.[34] Relatedly, some men's anger and irritation is a hostile reaction to a sense that girls and women are being

promoted and prioritized over men—in part through the visible popu-
larization (and commercialization) of "Girl Power" feminism and the
multitude of school and extracurricular programs meant to boost girls'
and women's engagement in everything from boardrooms to science
labs. This can create a feedback loop between popular feminism and
popular misogyny, driven in part by a narrative that suggests feminism
itself is a threat: to men's roles as dominant leaders and heads of
household, to their self-confidence, manliness, and self-worth, to traditional femininity and masculinity, or to broader work culture, tradition,
social norms, and family values.[35]

But antifeminism isn't limited to men's anger about "Ladies' Night"
promotions or "take your daughter to work day." Antifeminist arguments are imbued with claims that women are intrinsically manipulative, deceitful, irrational, untrustworthy, undermining, and that they are
controllable only with a firm physical hand. Feminism is blamed for
luring women away from their "natural" roles as mothers and homemakers and therefore is to blame for low white birth rates and—in the most
conspiratorial form of this claim—white genocide. Still other arguments suggest that capitalism itself is to blame for pushing women into
the workforce in ways that have made them unhappy, as they have abandoned true desires for marriage and children,[36] or that feminism is incompatible with traditional, natural, and moral values.[37] These ideas are
often echoed right in the mainstream. US Vice President J. D. Vance
once said that professional women "choose a path to misery" when they
prioritize careers over having children, for example.[38] In other cases,
antifeminists call for a reduction in women's rights based on the supposedly natural state of their subservience to men and their purported
intellectual and physical inferiority.[39]

Anger toward feminism itself easily bleeds into gendered conspiracy
theories that argue feminists and others are deliberately and secretly
working to undermine traditional values, dismantle families, and enact
sinister plots against men in order to secure more power for women.[40]
This is especially consequential because exposure to gendered conspiracy theories is known to shape harmful views toward violence against
women (such as endorsement of rape myths—beliefs that women are

to blame for their own rapes or that men are victims of false accusa-tions).[41] Conspiracy beliefs are associated with a variety of indicators that are constantly evoked in male supremacist spaces—powerlessness, anomie, low self-esteem and interpersonal trust, uncertainty, a lack of personal significance, resentment, and hostility. Belief in conspiracy theories fuels animosity toward scapegoats—including feminists—who are positioned as malevolent, dishonest enemies orchestrating politics and society to secure power for themselves. These beliefs are also linked to support for violent political actions, how morally accept-able people believe violence is for achieving goals, and readiness or intention to engage in violent extremism.[42]

Antifeminist conspiracy theories are easily intertwined with misog-yny and ideas about male victimization, including claims that women falsify accusations of rape or domestic abuse or are unfairly privileged in divorce and child custody cases.[43] Some antifeminist conspiracies bleed into anticorporate and antigovernment ideas, like the conspiratorial claim that plant-based food or soy burgers are being deliberately pro-moted to reduce testosterone or increase estrogen levels and turn men into "soy boys" to help the United Nations achieve its goal of making every man "a collared dog of an empowered female office worker."[44] Other antifeminist conspiracy theories are intertwined with antisemitic conspiracism, such as arguments about an orchestrated "Great Replace-ment" of white civilizations with multicultural ones that supposedly relies on abortion access and reproductive rights to reduce white births. Conspiracies about a hypothetically Jewish-led "Cultural Marxism" that aims to achieve the intended goals of the failed Marxist revolution by moving the battle to one of ideas and policies rather than a labor revolt are another good example. "Cultural Marxism" is blamed for a wide range of progressive policies, including gender-neutral bathrooms and pronoun usage and other gendered developments that the far right per-ceives as dismantling Western civilization.[45] The far-right terrorist who murdered seventy-seven people—mostly children—in Norway in 2011 wrote a 1,500-page manifesto blaming feminism, Nordic approaches to gender equality, and the demise of patriarchal male roles as part of a cultural Marxist project of multiculturalism. In his worldview, feminists and cultural Marxists alike must be eradicated—leading to his primary target of a summer camp for the Norwegian Labour Party.[46]

Antifeminism is a clear recruitment narrative, ideological justification, and direct mobilizer to violence for a wide variety of antigovernment and supremacist groups and violent actions. The man who killed fourteen women as part of a 1989 attack on women engineering students at Montreal's Ecole Polytechnique, for example, said he was "fighting feminism."[47] An antifeminist lawyer who claimed that women are the "real oppressors" attacked a New Jersey judge's home in 2020 and murdered her son.[48] Millions of men are members of online groups dedicated to men's rights and antifeminist issues, including the 600,000 subscribers in the subreddit r/pussypassdenied who are dedicated to dismantling "female privilege" and the more than 419,000 who subscribed to r/TheRedPill, focused on discussion of "sexual strategy" and conquest and laden with degrading discussions about the sexual subjugation of women, before Reddit shut it down for content that violated its policies on bullying and harassment.[49]

The same ideas that mobilize these kinds of violent actors have gradually become more and more mainstream, as growing numbers of men report believing that feminism has caused harm to modern society. A recent national survey in the UK found that more Gen Z men than boomers believe feminism has done more harm than good (16% of Gen Z versus 13% of over-60s men).[50] In the United States, 2022 polling data show that 37% of Americans overall—with higher numbers among men (62% of Republican men and 46% of Democratic men under 50)—believe that feminism has done more harm than good.[51] In 2023, 16% of American youth aged 14–30 report believing a number of male supremacist statements, including that women can't help but be attracted to those who are higher status than they are, that women use feminism to gain an unfair advantage over men, that modern society prioritizes women over men, and that men with high testosterone levels are the most attractive to women.[52]

Millions and millions of people, in other words, are at the very least skeptical of feminism. Devoted antifeminists take that skepticism several steps further by positioning feminism as a betrayal of natural, God-given, or biological differences between the sexes. Antifeminists argue that "real" differences between men and women are not only hormonal or biological (i.e., related to testosterone or average upper body strength), but also are evidenced in concrete differences in emotions and dispositions. These rigid dichotomies also help explain how antifeminism so easily bleeds into anti-trans hate. And those purported differences between men and women are used to justify the maintenance and defense of a hierarchy of superiority and inferiority that is both gendered and racialized. White men are deemed superior and are therefore entitled to more power, esteem, and the service of women and minorities. This sense of men's God-given, naturally justified entitlement is deeply engrained in far-right ideology, and feminism is an automatic enemy of it. Even some male supremacists who self-identify as excluded from the alpha male hierarchy (such as incels) see feminism as the source of all men's problems.[53]

With antifeminist ideas already prevalent in the mainstream, it is not surprising to see that male supremacist ideas are increasingly normalized among teenage boys and young men—in ways that also affect their behaviors and actions. Egregious, violent ideas that incubate in the manosphere—including calls for rape and mass attacks against women—spread easily across both fringe and mainstream online fora, chat rooms, and comment sections. There are many ways this happens, including through the pervasive reach of US gun culture. Despite many changes to social norms about gender, marriage, and fatherhood, men still encounter—and reinforce—a constant set of messages about the importance of being both providers and protectors to their success as men. In the United States, for example, this includes the idea that men should own and be willing to use a firearm to defend their families with violence as part of "real" manhood[54]—making the potential use of a gun into an occasionally necessary and honorable social duty that men perform on behalf of women and children.[55] Evangelical influencer James Dobson, for example, advises parents that "boys are biologically driven to like guns" and that denying them is tantamount to giving in to radical feminists' efforts to "feminize boys" and make them gay.[56] The linking of manhood with guns and the willingness to use them is especially important in light of declining economic opportunities for men, which researchers argue has made the "provider" role more precarious for men in ways that enhance the appeal of the protector role.[57] And it is a reminder of how strongly manhood is linked, especially in American culture, with a willingness to be violent. "Masses of boys and men," as bell hooks argues, "have been programmed from birth on to believe that at some point they must be violent, whether psychologically or physically, to prove they are men."[58]

Feminists aren't male supremacists' only "enemy." The aggrieved entitlement that the manosphere cultivates—in which men are entitled to women's bodies, emotional support, and subservience to men[59]—is often highly racialized. Thus we see memes widely circulating about "white sharia," a fascist-patriarchal fantasy state that would force white women into subservient roles, restrict their freedoms and rights, and ensure they have sufficient white babies to stem the "Great Replacement" or "white genocide." Scholars of gender and nationalism have extensively documented the foundational ways that gender and race intersect in supremacist ideologies.[60] This bears out in empirical data showing that the targets of online misogynist and male supremacist communities' rage include not only women but also a wide range of perceived enemies of men. A 2022 analysis of over 20,000 online posts across a variety of male supremacist, misogynist incel, and other chauvinist or men's rights online spaces by a team of researchers at the International Centre for Counter-Terrorism found that women (and terms that relate, like girl, chick, female, feminism, wife, and whore) were by far the most frequently identified adversaries, but other targets included certain kinds of men (chads, dudes, bros), the LGBTQ+ community, Muslims, Jews, and the left/liberals.[61] The same pattern is found in broader white supremacist extremist movements, which direct social hatred and rage not only toward racial minorities but also toward a broad range of groups they see as "antagonists of the white race," including women, the LGBTQ+ community, and the federal government. This latter point illuminates how important it is to understand systems of domination and beliefs about the relative superiority or inferiority of groups in an intersectional way, as the scholar Kimberlé Crenshaw has argued.[62]

Entitlement and Control as Foundational Premise

Male supremacists don't generally want to eradicate women, even though they sometimes violently punish them. On the contrary: Their worldview requires women's participation as subservient support players. Because male supremacist ideology is based in the premise that straight, masculine men are superior to women and LGBTQ+ people, men and women are logically divided into categories in which some people (men) hold power and dominate all others. Male supremacists view all women as fundamentally, absolutely, and always inferior to men, and see men as therefore entitled to women's servitude (sexually, domestically, and in the care of children and household).[63] These ideas are shared widely in accessible, humorous, and "just a joke" formats, like memes that refer to women as dishwashers and sandwich-makers.

In male supremacist belief systems, women as well as men are expected to adhere to strict expectations about masculinity and femininity in ways that both control the range of possible gendered expressions and establish clear rules on what is deemed appropriate feminine (and masculine) expression and who gets to perform it in what contexts.[64] Male supremacists don't expect that everyone will adhere to their belief system—especially since they generally view women as innately selfish, sneaky, and manipulative. Rather, male supremacists view women as subhuman or inferior beings who are "undermining patriarchal social orders" when they reject their "rightful" roles—and therefore women can and should be violently harassed or harmed into subservience.[65] Anyone who refuses to adhere to these norms and to the broader patriarchal social order is subject to punishment.[66] Sanctions can be even more severe for Black women and other women of color, who have to grapple with both racism and sexism.[67]

These ideas have translated to violent action all too frequently, in no small part because violence against women is not only tolerated in male supremacist spaces online but is openly and ubiquitously valorized and glorified. The goal of male supremacist terrorism is to secure women's compliance with patriarchy—or punish them for refusing to comply—both by hurting individual women and forcing all women to "live with

the threat of being hurt."[68] Those who take violent action are celebrated as heroes. Terrorist actors like the Santa Barbara shooter (who
attacked a college sorority) are lauded as "saints"—among others, the
white supremacist extremist Andrew Anglin once described himself as
the "self-appointed spiritual successor" to the California shooter.[69] That
shooter's initials (ER) have become a verb in calls for violence (i.e.,
encouraging others to "go ER" in a gender studies class or in other places
where feminists can be targeted).[70] Such violence is also fueled by the
constant dehumanization of women online, along with the casual celebration of violence and harassment directed toward them. One of the
neo-Nazi men arrested for plotting an antisemitic attack in New York
City in 2022 had previously shared online that he had violently attacked
a transgender person and described himself as "most proud of being
'good at raping women,'" according to an assistant district attorney on
the case.[71]

In other cases, women are not just targeted with rage as a means of
punishment; they are attacked violently as a strategy of elimination.
The six Asian women and two others gunned down in a rampage at
three Atlanta massage parlors in the spring of 2021 were killed because the
21-year-old gunman believed he deserved to live in a world without the
sexual temptation he believed they created for him. It's hard to think of
a clearer example of how mass violence can be generated from a sense
of entitlement and male supremacist reasoning. Violent attacks against
women in cases like these—as well as in domestic and intimate partner
violence and misogynist incel attacks—are not only or even primarily
about sex. Rather, they are rooted in what Kate Manne describes as
"some men's toxic sense of entitlement to have people look up to them
steadfastly, with a loving gaze, admiringly—and to target and even destroy those who fail, or refuse, to do so."[72] Raised in a religious household
and addicted to sex, the Atlanta shooter had already been kicked out of
his house by his parents and belittled by a friend for watching porn. But
rather than own up to his own addiction or take responsibility for it, he
blamed the women he felt were responsible for his failings. The attack
was not only a male supremacist one—it was also deeply connected
with racist stereotypes and hypersexualized tropes of Asian women.

Asian and Asian American women had already borne the brunt of the COVID-19 pandemic spikes in hate against the AAPI community, with three-quarters of Asian American and Pacific Islander women, in spring 2022, reporting racism or discrimination during the previous year. Notably, like so many other mass attacks against women, it was difficult for authorities to recognize the attack as anything other than the personality problems of an individual man.

Ultimately, although male supremacy is sometimes understood as hatred of women, it is even more fundamentally about control of women, their bodies and choices, and the kinds of gendered expressions deemed appropriate for both men and women. Many of the well-documented emotions that underpin forms of supremacist extremism—such as fear, resentment, anger, rage, hatred, or indignation about threats and status—are manifested in male supremacism through "expressions of hypermasculine thuggery" that normalize violence as an acceptable or desired reaction to perceived threats.[73] Control is central to this process.

In the worst cases, male supremacy fuels the violent defense of a system in which certain kinds of men dominate and hold power. And because these online and subcultural manosphere developments are growing within a broader social and political context in which control of gender and sexuality are at the center of community and parent protests and moral panics, it's not surprising to see the growth of male supremacist ideas in both fringe and mainstream spaces. The past few years have seen growing citizen protests and violence at drag performances and story hours, hundreds of legislative actions across dozens of states to restrict trans and gender-diverse people's rights to medical care, and widespread banning of books from libraries and school curricula for mentioning anything related to sexuality or gender identity—issues taken up in more depth in chapter 5. These debates and protests have provided fertile ground for extremist ideas about control of women's bodies, sexuality, and reproductive rights to fester and grow.

Mainstream legislative actions and fringe violent actors alike are just the tip of the iceberg when it comes to the misogynistic underpinnings of violence. Over the past decade-plus, a broad and fluid set of male supremacist places and spaces online has helped foster and incubate the mainstreaming and normalization of antifeminist hate and gender-based bigotry.

Punishment: Violent Misogyny in the Online Manosphere and Offline Worlds

"Look, I hate women. I think they deserve to be beaten, raped and locked in cages." So spoke the founder of the white supremacist blog *The Daily Stormer* in 2018.[74] On /pol/, a user posted the comment and asked whether "this kind of talk" might be going too far, noting that "I'm not a cuck. Liberal women should be punished by shame, beatings, and executions depending on their crimes against their people, just like men are, but Anglin is going too far with this shit. It just turns off guys who simply want to remove women's voting rights, not treat them worse than animals."

It's hard to overstate the impact of the internet and its frequently hostile communication style as a fundamental driver of rising male supremacist beliefs. Communication is widely documented to be more hateful, toxic, or mean when expressed under the cloak of internet anonymity, which can also contribute to a lack of inhibition or shame for behavior that would otherwise make most people cringe.[75] Harassment, trolling, and cruel comments laced with sexist, misogynist, and racist slurs are a constant reality in online spaces. Unmoderated forums—which both reflect toxic content and actively produce and reproduce that toxicity—are especially problematic. In those spaces, users become gradually desensitized as they encounter and share ever-more salacious content that seeks to shock and imbue a sense of power through offensive provocation. One study showed that rape is mentioned every twenty-nine minutes on incel forums, and in those discussion threads, 89% of users expressing a stance did so in support of rape. An additional 5% of posters expressed a belief that rape was wrong, but for non-moral reasons, such as one comment arguing rape was "unimaginative" and it would be better to "reduce a woman to nothing."[76] Extreme desensitization and dehumanization is a clear consequence for users steeped in toxic forums like these.

Hateful and violent misogynistic forums are just one part of a loosely networked set of formal and informal online male supremacist communities and men's rights activists' groups known as the "manosphere," which valorize and engage in toxic online harassment and targeted violence directed toward women.[77] Although the ideas (and some of the groups) that are central to the manosphere have deep and long histories, the online ecosystem itself is rooted in the 2014 Gamergate saga and the reactionary torrent of misogynistic hate, trolling, doxing, online threats, and abuse that was directed against women in the gaming industry during that period.[78] Over the years that followed, on message boards and channels across a variety of online spaces—notably 4chan's /r9k/ channel—vile misogyny and praise for violent incel shooters helped fuel a subculture with a broad set of concepts establishing violence as a laudable tactic to punish women for depriving supposedly "beta" men of sex while giving it freely to "alpha" men.[79] Scores of alienated young men found a validating culture in online spaces which laid blame for their problems at the feet of women, feminism, and the LGBTQ+ community.

It didn't take long for this burgeoning and increasingly misogynistic online culture to intersect with other forms of hate across the internet. Gamergate and the subcultures it spawned were readily incorporated into the "alt-right" and broader attacks on politically correct culture, feminism, social justice warriors, and the liberal left's supposed efforts to indoctrinate youth.[80] This carried over into the offline world, too. After far-right provocateur Milo Yiannopoulous championed Gamergate and its fight against the "social justice warriors" and "snowflakes" of the overreaching liberal left, he became a journalist at Breitbart, the far-right news network once headed by former Trump advisor Steve Bannon. As I have argued previously, the contemporary far right in the United States, including the emergence of the alt-right and the online ecosystem that supported it, is unimaginable without these gendered developments.[81] Recent research has clearly documented correlations between male supremacy beliefs and a range of other far-right and harmful ideologies and beliefs, including authoritarianism, antisemitism, racist and anti-immigrant beliefs, and conspiratorial thinking.[82]

Toxic misogynist online spaces didn't just help spawn the contemporary far right. They also helped amplify and expand men's rights groups that had existed offline for decades. Men's rights movements were rooted in reactionary challenges to second-wave feminism in the 1970s and complaints about women's preferential treatment, with a particular focus on fathers' rights in divorce, child custody and child support cases, and claims that domestic violence services unfairly prioritize women and ignore male victims.[83] Over time, men's rights activists gradually shifted their focus from fathers' rights and family law to include more messaging around sexual politics and rape, including on college campuses, with claims ranging from feminist cover-ups of male victimization to a supposedly rampant state of false allegations in the context of a feminist-led "moral panic" on rape culture.[84]

Today, there are a variety of overlapping forms of antifeminist, misogynistic white supremacist extremism, and other factions of the manosphere and broader male supremacist cultures online. They have a range of aims, but they all share a commitment to antifeminism and a belief in the notion of a red-pill awakening to the harms supposedly visited upon men. The forums themselves, meanwhile, foster what psychologists call "cognitive distortions"—ways of thinking that can be self-defeating and harmful, such as all-or-nothing thinking, catastrophizing, and overgeneralization. On male supremacist forums, these kinds of cognitive distortions help reshape the way young men see their own problems as part of a broader set of perceived injustices blamed on women writ large.[85]

Performances of toxic masculinity abound, both across the online manosphere and in offline groups that espouse antifeminist and anti-LGBTQ+ beliefs. The Proud Boys, for example, a self-described "Western chauvinist" group labeled a terrorist entity by Canada and New Zealand, emerged as a men's-only street fighting club with initiation rites that include submitting to a beating from other members and agreeing to forgo masturbation.[86] Several members of the Proud Boys' leadership were sentenced to decades-long prison sentences in late 2023 after convictions on the rare charge of seditious conspiracy for their roles in the January 6 insurrection at the US Capitol. Nationalist expressions are also common across male supremacist spaces, as men bemoan overly liberated women in countries like the United States and espouse the benefits of supposedly more subservient women from regions like East-ern Europe and Asia.[87]

Like the broader range of extremist ideologies circulating online, most of the male supremacist movement exists outside of organized groups or scenes. But there are plenty of organized and semi-organized groups and communities driving violence too. Each group or community is orga-nized around a particular set of grievances or strategies to exploit, seduce, or control women. The manosphere links together a variety of men's rights groups, including the Men's Liberation Movement (MLM) and the Men's Rights Movement (MRM), alongside the online male suprem-acist community Men Going Their Own Way (MGTOW), who advo-cate opting out from feminist-run society and refusing all relationships with women until the utopian ideal of full male power over women (in-cluding removal of women's rights) is achieved.[88] Some groups in the manosphere openly espouse forced servitude, spousal rape, or rollbacks on no-fault divorce laws. There are fringe Nazi occult groups like the Order of Nine Angles (O9A) that promote Satanism, advocate for rape, pedophilia, and sexual violence to help accelerate the collapse of social norms, and use child sexual abuse material (CSAM) as part of initiation practices.[89] In 2023, a former US army soldier was sentenced to forty-five years in prison on charges of providing national defense information to the O9A and attempting to murder US military members.[90] Other subcultures online coalesce around "coaches" who teach manipulative dating techniques and men's "self-help" tactics—which have racked up millions of followers with a level of popularity that is hard to overstate: The misogynist influencer Andrew Tate, for example, was one of Google's most searched for people of 2022.

One of the early groups in the manosphere were PUA (Pick Up Art-ist) communities, which describe a "sexual marketplace" and rate women based on their Sexual Market Value (SMV), a subjective value of sexual attractiveness assigned by men based on factors like physical appearance and age, but which also decreases if women have too many sexual partners, among other factors.[91] SMV is also racialized for both men and women, with white men purportedly getting an "instant SMV boost" based on white privilege and the supposed greater desirability of white men,[92] while the misogynistic terms that target women of color are also often racist.[93] PUA communities eventually created a kind of "seduction industry" of influencers who advise men on strategies for manipulation; devoted followers seek guidance on ways not only to seduce women but also to overcome things like the euphemistic "last-minute resistance" (LMR) in order to ensure they can have sex.[94] PUA communities and the broader MRM inspired a popular online forum created in 2012 called r/TheRedPill, named for the 1999 *The Matrix* movie reference to an awakening (in this case, about supposed feminist control, women's manipulative power, and men's victimization). Discussions in r/TheRedPill, whose anonymous founder was later revealed to be an elected Republican lawmaker in the New Hampshire state legislature, focused heavily on sexual strategy and conquest through personal transformation from "beta" to "alpha" masculinity. But posts were also laden with anger and public degrading of women, whose sexual subjugation is one part of a broader project of putting women back in their place and reasserting patriarchal manhood.[95]

The PUA world ultimately evolved directly into the violent misogynist incel world, most notably when one of the PUA community's followers, a 22-year-old man, killed six people in Santa Barbara in 2014 in a targeted attack on a university sorority. That attack was followed by targeted attacks by misogynist incels across North America and in the UK over the years to come that were often inspired by the Santa Barbara shooter, making misogynist incels the best-known movement or community to come out of the manosphere—and the one that has gotten the lion's share of belated media and law enforcement attention to male supremacist extremism.

Incel (involuntary celibate) is a label with which individuals self-identify as part of a community of others who are involuntarily not having sex. Incel forums and communities online have "grown exponentially" in both popularity and toxicity in recent years in ways that have played a clear role in normalizing harmful speech and misogyny targeting women online.[96] While there are women who identify as incels (known as femcels), online incel communities are primarily made up of men who are angry at their inability to get the sex they want and feel they deserve. Incels are highly focused on physical appearance and the idea of "lookism," which places attractive and unattractive people on a desirability hierarchy that leaves unattractive individuals without sexual or romantic partners.[97] There are subgroups within and across incel communities online, including "Black Pilled" incels—a play on the notion of the "Red Pill"—who are nihilistic and see no chance for anything other than an isolated, lonely life without sex or the adoration of a woman.[98]

The term "misogynist incels" refers specifically to incels who embrace male supremacist ideas that dehumanize women while simultaneously positioning them as something to which men are entitled.[99] They are filled with rage directed toward women they perceive as attractive and hypersexual but undateable (called "Stacys"), who deprive "beta" men of sex that is disproportionately taken by muscular, hot "alpha" men (called "Chads"). Chads supposedly hoard women and sex in ways that leave lesser men without. This latter point is crucial, because misogynist incels are not only angry at women; they also direct their rage at men who are viewed as more sexually successful than they are.[100] Misogynist incels have been responsible for some fifty deaths in the United States and Canada since 2017.[101] Notably, incels are not only misogynistic— they also interlace their misogyny with racism when targeting women of color. In a recent analysis of nearly four million comments on a popular incel discussion board, researchers found that racist misogynistic posts are present in nearly 9% of discussion threads, while 30% of participants have used a racist misogynistic term at least once.[102]

Not all incels call for violence. But violent talk and rhetoric is a big part of the incel community's online spaces, which are flooded with "deliberately provocative" shitposting, satire, and ironic humor in ways that are also intended as a "strike back at feminism and women's increased rights."[103] Those discussions have become more extreme and violent over time, reflecting broader trends within the manosphere in which newer communities are "more toxic and misogynistic" than older ones.[104] The incel community has its own belief system, comprised of a variety of false claims, myths, and pseudoscientific beliefs, including the belief that women only mate with higher-status males (hypergamy), prefer white men (Just Be White, or JBW), and the rule of 80/20 (that the supposed top 20% of genetically superior men have access to the top 80% of women, leaving the bottom 80% of supposedly inferior men to compete for the remaining 20% of women).[105] Misogynist incels commonly refer to women as "femoids" or "foids"—an abbreviation of "female humanoid"—or through derogatory sexual terms like "holes" or "roasties" (a vulgar word for labia) in ways that help dehumanize women and sanitize calls for violence against them.[106] Women are described as having a declining "sexual market value" that leads to an inevitable "hitting the wall" as they age and are no longer attractive or reproductively useful. In one recent incel forum discussion about the podcast "Fresh & Fit," which often portrays misogynistic views, a commenter describes the women on the podcast, who are purportedly around 21–24 years old, as looking "completely used up and old," and "appear to be 27ish due to them being in the process of hitting the wall."[107]

What we know about the manosphere is shaped by the dominance of studies of English language and Anglo-American contexts—in part because even in non-native English settings, violent misogynists sometimes still use English to communicate (through manifestos or videos) with global audiences.[108] The 2019 terrorist attacker in Hanau, Germany, for example, expressed signs of deep misogyny and resentment toward women in his manifesto, which he wrote in English, suggesting that the audience for his violence was global rather than only national.[109] There is some research, however, showing that the manosphere is thriving outside of Anglo-American contexts, including in a comprehensive set of groups with hundreds of thousands of followers in the Spanish-speaking manosphere and a specific set of online groups and communities in the Indian manosphere, where Western ideologies are blended with local, historical, and religious references that are specific to Indian culture.[110]

Part of the delay in the broader recognition of the threat from misogynist incels (and other male supremacists) is tied to a controversial discussion about the role of mental health as it relates to incels. There is a documented high prevalence of depression, loneliness, suicidal ideation, and autism within the incel community, which can bias observers toward a view of incels as only mentally ill or simply struggling with social relationships rather than being ideologically motivated toward violence in ways that are both predictable and preventable.[111] Misogynist incels score high on measures of victimhood—rooted itself in male sexual entitlement and misogyny—and tend to ruminate over past instances of victimization and perceived discrimination in ways that gravitate toward revenge thoughts against those who they believe have wronged them.[112] Thus, what originally may have been legitimate personal grievances about their own isolation and exclusion can be easily converted and channeled, especially through toxic online forums, into more generalized scapegoating, blame for personal problems, and extreme rage directed toward feminists, women, and alpha men.[113]

There is evidence of higher rates of neurodiversity among incels, and there are frequent discussions of autism within incel discussion forums.[114] One survey shows that nearly a quarter of incels self-report autism symptoms, while more than half of the perpetrators in seven incel-related cases of violence had characteristics of autism—figures that must be interpreted with care due to their self-reported or retrospective nature following homicide-suicides.[115] It is also important to note that misogynist incels also sometimes use autism and their autism diagnoses as a way of justifying their misogyny and violence, either because they claim to lack empathy or because of grievances about how "normie" women will reject autistic men.[116]

The intelligence and law enforcement communities—and the broader fields of terrorism and violent extremism—have gradually come to recognize the significant threat misogynist incels present, with dozens of research articles published about these communities over the past few years alone.[117] In February 2024, a 24-year-old self-identified incel was sentenced to six years in prison—thereby becoming the first incel to be prosecuted on US federal hate crime charges—for plotting to "slaughter women" out of "hatred, jealousy, and revenge" in a mass attack on an Ohio university, where he hoped to get a "kill count" of at least three thousand victims. Investigators uncovered disturbing search histories and memes on his phone, including one depicting a woman being raped at gunpoint.[118]

With so many ways to embrace and express misogyny, antifeminist ideas, and rage against women online, it's not surprising to see an impact of growing male supremacist and other extremist ideas on rights in the offline world. The glee with which white supremacists reacted to the loss of the constitutional right to abortion in the United States is one of the clearest examples in recent times.

Entitlement and Control: The Case of Reproductive Rights and Anti-Abortion Mobilizing

On the afternoon of June 24, 2022, my phone pinged with the news of the US Supreme Court's decision in the landmark *Dobbs v. Jackson Women's Health Organization* case, which was a challenge to a Mississippi law banning abortion after fifteen weeks of pregnancy. The case had reached the Supreme Court after a lower court struck down the state ban as unconstitutional. The state of Mississippi asked the high court to both uphold its abortion ban and to rule that there is no constitutional right to an abortion in the United States.[119] In agreeing to hear the case, the Court considered the constitutionality of abortion for the first time in nearly fifty years. Its June 24 ruling overturned *Roe v. Wade*, the 1973 Supreme Court decision that had established Americans' constitutional right to an abortion without government interference. The *Dobbs* decision thus took away the constitutional right to abortion, marking the "first time in history that the Supreme Court has taken away a fundamental right."[120]

That decision took on a horrifying set of implications just a few weeks later, when a former Marine who led a neo-Nazi group called Rapekrieg was arrested after plotting in New York to organize a mass murder of minorities and mass rape of "white women to increase production of white children."[121] The Rapekrieg plot was one more reminder of the insidious ways that white supremacy, male supremacy, and violent extremism go hand in hand: Minorities and white women are targets of an ideology that seeks both to reduce nonwhite populations and to increase white ones. For this and other white supremacist extremist groups, the mass murder of minorities and the mass rape of white women are twin goals oriented toward maintaining a white majority nation.

Control of women's reproductive capacity is a key feature of white supremacist extremists' goals as they seek to counter long-standing demographic trends and preserve white majority societies in the face of what they believe is an orchestrated plot to end the white race and replace it with multicultural societies. White supremacists' conspiratorial beliefs about demographic change have existed for decades, in the form of an antisemitic conspiracy theory called "white genocide" and an Islamophobic conspiracy theory called "Eurabia."[122] But they have gotten new life as the global "Great Replacement" conspiracy has grown and been mainstreamed.

Fears related to a supposedly orchestrated replacement of white majority societies are a major driver of white supremacists' compulsion to control women and their reproductive rights. On the one hand, abortion is seen as part of the so-called white genocide plot and as one factor leading toward the extinction of the white race. This isn't only happening on the fringe, but is also echoed very clearly in the mainstream. As *Time* magazine reported, several weeks before the *Dobbs* decision was handed down, Matt Schlapp, leader of the Conservative Political Action Conference, told reporters that overturning *Roe* would be a positive step toward fixing the US immigration problem. "If you're worried about this quote-unquote replacement, why don't we start there?" he asked. "Start with allowing our own people to live."[123] The loss of *Roe v. Wade*, in this scenario, directly serves some white supremacist extremist goals—as long as it is white babies who cannot be aborted.[124] As NPR has reported, "prominent white supremacists have at times called for abortion to be banned only for white women but for it to be accessible and even free for women of color."[125]

The same contradictions hold true for rape. The rape of white women by nonwhite men is used to generate outrage and treated as a "rallying call to unite and fight back"[126] in ways that are deeply historical and contemporary all at once. Hitler promoted a conspiracy theory that Jews were orchestrating the rape of white Aryan women by Black soldiers to destroy the white race by "bastardization"—similar to a 1920s Ku Klux Klan antisemitic conspiracy about a Jewish plot to orchestrate mass rape of white women by Black men.[127] The Ku Klux Klan and

other racist vigilantes repeatedly lynched Black men who had been accused of raping white women—or even those who had been (falsely)
accused of merely looking at a white woman the wrong way, as was the
case with the brutal beating and murder of 14-year-old Emmett Till. At
the root of all of this racist violence, conspiracy theorizing and outrage
is the idea that the purity of white women (and thereby the white nation) must be protected from degradation or sullying at all costs—
especially through impregnation by men who are not white.

But rape is considered by some on the far-right spectrum as acceptable, even desirable—if it produces white babies. Voluntary reproduction matters too. In far-right forums online, users have discussed the
"pro-white" approach of having large families of white children, thus
promoting their goals and ideology "through procreative means."[128] It
is worth noting that these mainstream and fringe debates about the production of white babies, the replacement needs of white civilizations,
and the "need" to reduce births among women of color, immigrants, and
others deemed "undesirable" for the white nation have echoed across
history in other racist policies related to fertility and the control of
women's bodies, including mobilization against abortion rights, and
forced sterilizations of women of color. Women of color and low-income
women are also much more likely to bear the brunt of the consequences
of the *Dobbs* decision and the broader domino effect of diminishing
access to reproductive and material healthcare.[129]

This is where the state of reproductive rights in the United States
post-*Roe* becomes especially chilling. Supreme Court Justice Samuel
Alito's opinion reversing *Roe v. Wade* referred to data from the Centers
for Disease Control and Prevention describing an insufficient "domestic
supply of infants" to meet the demand for infant adoption in the United
States.[130] He also cited Justice Amy Coney Barrett's December reflection during oral arguments that forced pregnancy is not a "meaningful
hardship" because unwanted babies can be surrendered through
"safe haven" laws. These kinds of justifications for dismantling reproductive rights reduce women to vessels charged with producing babies
for the good of the collective. Control of women's bodies—and entitlement to them—is essential in these scenarios.

It's important to note that most mainstream anti-abortion activists denounce explicitly racist and white supremacist groups. Racist justifications for abortion restrictions are clearly on the fringes. But it's not a stretch to see how mainstream arguments about the need for more babies to counter "replacement" or produce a sufficient "supply of infants" benefit white supremacist extremists, their obsession with demographic change, and their desire to increase white birth rates. These arguments have been around for nearly two centuries. As early as the mid-1900s, physicians argued against abortion rights because of low white birth rates and the fear that "undesirable" groups were gaining traction.[131] The solution was to "force middle- and upper-class white women—who had the most access to detect and terminate unwanted pregnancies—to bear more white children."[132]

White supremacist extremists' anti-abortion activism has a long history in the United States. In the 1980s, the Ku Klux Klan created wanted posters listing abortion providers' personal information. The subject of the first wanted poster, created by Randall Terry, who founded the anti-choice group Operation Rescue, was murdered in 1993 in Florida. His successor, also targeted by a wanted poster, was killed the following year. Tom Metzger, founder of an Aryan white supremacist group, noted that the killing was acceptable if it "protected Aryan women and children." Throughout the 1990s, racist skinhead groups, KKK chapters, and other white supremacists regularly joined anti-choice protests at abortion clinics, seen as part of the "Holy War for the pure Aryan race," in the words of one white supremacist group. Much of the white supremacist anti-abortion rhetoric is also deeply antisemitic, linking abortion to the antisemitic conspiracy theory about white genocide, arguing that Jews profit from abortions, or that they control Planned Parenthood.[133]

These same claims bolster white supremacist extremists' anti-abortion rhetoric today. As Seyward Darby told *Time* recently, white supremacists ultimately want "a series of policies, including making white women have more babies, by force if necessary."[134] And it is this landscape in which the group Rapekrieg, which has overlapping membership with other neo-Nazi extremist and terrorist groups, like Rapewaffen and Atomwaffen, operates. In this white supremacist extremist worldview, the mass rape of white women is seen as desirable because it can lead to more white babies. The former marine arrested after the *Dobbs* decision had allegedly written a group plan to conduct both mass killing of minorities and mass rape of white women in order to create a white ethno-state, describing rape as "an extremely effective tool against our many foes."[135] He allegedly planned an attack on a synagogue, got a New York City police officer to purchase his weapons, and used his military training to train other neo-Nazi group members. The layers of danger here cannot be overestimated.

Groups like Rapekrieg are fringe extremists whose violent plots clearly constitute terrorist action. But in a post-*Roe* world, a plot to force women to become pregnant, however fringe it might be, takes on a whole new meaning. White women aren't only victims of this worldview. They play an active role across the far-right spectrum, including some who actively promote women's roles in restoring white birth rates.[136] Challenges to reproductive rights must be understood within the broader context of entitlement and desire to control women's bodies and—for at least the white supremacist fringe—protect the purity of the nation and the white race.

Conclusion: From Punishment to Exploitation

There is no question that the online and offline worlds of male supremacist extremism have done tremendous harm—both in terms of physical violence and in the creation and circulation of dangerous rhetoric, propaganda, and misogynistic ideas. These worlds have helped convert what are often legitimate grievances experienced by boys and men—and the emotions those grievances can fuel, including anger, shame, and humiliation—into scapegoating and vile misogynistic violence as an ideology of hatred. But abuse and exploitation of women doesn't require a commitment to a formal male supremacist ideology. It's also taking place right in our homes, our neighborhoods, our towns, and in online and offline spaces targeting children and women for exploitation. These are the issues I turn to in chapter 4.

4

Exploitation

#SAVETHECHILDREN

ON A SUNDAY AFTERNOON in December 2016, a man armed with a loaded AR-15 assault rifle and revolver walked into Comet Ping Pong, a neighborhood pizza restaurant in leafy northwest Washington, DC, that is popular with local families. He had driven up the east coast from North Carolina believing he was going to rescue child sexual slaves from tunnels in the restaurant's basement, based on disinformation he gleaned from the viral far-right PizzaGate conspiracy that falsely claimed a group of Democrat elites were running a child sex abuse ring in restaurants, including Comet Ping Pong.[1] After he fired several shots inside the restaurant and subsequently realized there were no child sex slaves present, the attacker surrendered to authorities.

The Comet Pizza attack was one of the earliest signs that the far right's previous obsession with pedophiles and child trafficking had become both supercharged and oddly mainstreamed. False claims about pedophilia and the LGBTQ+ community had animated white supremacist and Nazi ideology and violence for decades. But #PizzaGate and the sprawling network of QAnon conspiracies it helped fuel made abundantly clear that the issue of child trafficking didn't just mobilize an extremist fringe. When combined with massively circulating disinformation and conspiracy theories, fears about the exploitation of children have driven the recruitment and radicalization of millions of mainstream Americans to antidemocratic beliefs and egregious acts of interpersonal and extremist violence—including in ways that terrorist groups have used to their direct advantage.

Conspiracies about human trafficking are just one of many ways that the issue of exploitation helps mobilize mass violence, including terrorism. The breadth and depth of the tactics and strategies of sexual and gender-based violence and harm show that exploitation is not just a side effect of terrorist and extremist violence, nor a wholly separate issue. On the contrary: Terrorist and extremist groups and movements rely on and systematically enact sexual and gender-based violence—or promote disinformation about it—for strategic and operational aims.

This is not a new claim in the literature on terrorism, but the discussion about gender-based violence has been almost exclusively rooted in Islamist forms of terrorism, where there are dozens of United Nations reports and academic analyses of the exploitation of women and children by Boko Haram, Al-Shabaab, ISIS, and Hamas. There is much less attention directed toward the systematic or spontaneous use of gender-based violence in far-right, neo-Nazi, or antigovernment movements and scenes.[2] I explore here what I call five overlooked pathways through which gender-based violence in intimate and interpersonal spheres predicts, enables, or otherwise should serve as a red flag or warning sign for radicalization and subsequent mass violence and domestic violent extremism. This includes the mobilization to violence based on disinformation and conspiracy theories about sexual trafficking described above, alongside four additional categories: perpetrator histories of domestic and intimate partner violence, including stalking, harassment, rape, and revenge porn; exploitation through commercial sex trafficking and organized prostitution; engagement in child exploitation and child pornography; and the use of gender-based and sexual violence for ideological goals, including through propaganda about the subjugation of women and the LGBTQ+ community and about white birth rates in the face of demographic change. These brutal, dehumanizing, and exploitative behaviors are sometimes individually acknowledged as part of antidemocratic and far-right extremist pathways, but they are rarely understood as systemic and operational tactics that can further strategic extremist goals. This blind spot, like so many others related to gendered issues in extremism, must be remedied.

How False Child Trafficking Information Fuels Violence

Throughout the twentieth century, fringe neo-Nazi and white supremacist groups regularly called for crackdowns on pedophilia, both as a way of garnering support from ordinary citizens and as a cloak for false claims and attacks on the LGBTQ+ community.[3] But over the course of the past decade, social media and other online spaces fueled the spread of a wide range of conspiracy theories that transformed the far right's false claims linking child molestation with gay men into a full-blown moral panic about protecting children from the risks posed by "gender ideology" and its corrosive effects on traditional families.[4]

That obsession evolved into a sprawling web of conspiracies about an orchestrated child-pedophile, Satan-worshipping ring run by a cabal of Hollywood and political global elites—loosely organized under the umbrella of QAnon, whose supporters believed they were following a trail of breadcrumbs that would reveal the Truth about the deep state. QAnon believers who thought they were using clever decoding and puzzle-solving detective work falsely accused a raft of celebrities, politicians, and ordinary people of being perpetrators or victims of child trafficking, leading to tainted reputations as well as death threats, harassment, kidnappings, and murders.[5] There were conspiracy-fueled violent attacks on a wide variety of physical sites believed to be locations where child sex abuse or trafficking was taking place, including the Hoover Dam, a US Navy hospital ship, the home of the Canadian Prime Minister, and the US National Butterfly Center, which was forced to shut down in the wake of threats after it became falsely identified as a migrant trafficking site.[6]

QAnon wasn't only focused on child sexual exploitation; its conspiracies were wide ranging, including the belief that John F. Kennedy is still alive and that COVID-19 was an orchestrated scam aimed at delegitimizing Trump and removing him from office.[7] But it was QAnon's sweeping false claims about child trafficking that did the most harm, inspiring violent action, luring millions of people from across the political spectrum into a spiraling network of disinformation and conspiracy theories, and preventing actual victims from getting help. When a QAnon influencer falsely linked the online shopping website Wayfair to child trafficking in 2020 by suggesting that highly priced home décor products with girls' names on them were a channel for the sale of human children, millions of people shared the claims online and flooded national trafficking hotlines before the claims were debunked by Wayfair and the US Department of Homeland Security.[8] One anti-trafficking organization estimated that the time it took to investigate false Wayfair claims prevented them from responding to forty-two actual trafficking cases.

The Comet Ping Pong Pizza attack may have rung the first alarm bells about conspiracy-fueled violence—but the Wayfair conspiracy showed that disinformation wasn't just a problem of the violent fringe, raising red flags about just how big the pace and scale of the problem was and how rapidly things could get worse. The Wayfair conspiracy drew millions of new believers to the world of child trafficking conspiracies—including a woman who was trampled to death at the US Capitol on January 6 after Wayfair conspiracies drew her into QAnon and its #hashtagged links to election disinformation.[9] By the fall of 2020, an astonishing 41% of US adults reported believing that "elites, politicians and/or celebrities are involved in global pedophilia rings and we need to #SaveOurChildren." That same year, one in five Americans self-identified as QAnon believers,[10] and by 2023, more than 30% of evangelical Christians believed at least some part of QAnon.[11] The conspiracy also spread quickly on a global scale, inspiring terrorist and extremist violence in countries like Germany, where a 2022 plot to assassinate the Federal Chancellor and overthrow the government at the hands of a rapidly growing group of antigovernment conspiracy theorists who promote QAnon was narrowly averted. Among those arrested for the plot were over two dozen current or former soldiers or military reservists, a judge, three police officers, and a pilot.[12]

It's hard to overstate the damage that QAnon conspiracies have done to democracy itself, including by undermining the public's ability to distinguish fact from fiction, mobilizing threats and acts of violence, and acting as hashtag channels to broaden the reach of a wider range of conspiracy theories, health and election disinformation, and anti-immigrant propaganda.[13] Belief in QAnon conspiracies has divided and destroyed countless families in well-documented, heartbreaking ways.[14] But those beliefs also have done tremendous damage beyond interpersonal relationships. QAnon channeled hateful content, mobilizing targeted violence and harassment as a surge of propaganda and false claims linked LGBTQ+ communities to pedophilia, including through accusations of threats that children were being "groomed" by gay teachers, coaches, or online predators.[15] The far right's obsession with child sexual abuse, supersized through QAnon, became a clear cloak for anti-trans and anti-LGBTQ+ scapegoating and fearmongering.[16]

QAnon's integration into the pro-Trump MAGA world helped mainstream conspiracy beliefs further, including through the retweeting of QAnon claims by President Trump and QAnon supporter and US House of Representatives member Marjorie Taylor Greene. In the 2020 US general election, ninety-seven candidates with ties to QAnon were running for office, including one in seven of women Republican congressional candidates.[17] Before the election, QAnon supporters were already swept up in pro-Trump fixations that Satan-worshipping pedophiles are running the country and that true patriots can and should use violence to eradicate them. But after Trump's 2020 defeat, the cross-pollination of conspiracy theories got even worse, as massive amounts of online disinformation connected through hashtags brought #SaveTheChildren and #StopHumanTrafficking closer together with the #StopTheSteal and #MAGA worlds. A broader pool of Trump supporters, Christian nationalists and evangelicals who already believe apocalyptic end-times prophecies helped indoctrinate millions of Americans with claims about a coming biblical storm that would sweep away evil leaders and bring about a righteous restoration to power of President Trump. In this way, conspiracies that were originally based in false claims about a child trafficking network of Democrat elites drove thousands of people to the US Capitol on January 6, 2021, to try and subvert US democracy.[18] Today, millions of US adults continue to believe disinformation about the 2020 election and conspiracies about the January 6 attacks on the US Capitol. Fully one-quarter of Americans—and one in three Republicans—believe the FBI instigated the January 6 attacks.[19]

Extremist groups were quick to jump on the QAnon bandwagon. White supremacist and far-right extremist groups online have issued instructions for how to co-opt and recruit QAnon followers, especially by using disinformation about child sex trafficking. In January 2021, a white supremacist channel on Telegram with several thousand followers posted, "The bottom has just fallen out from underneath their world-view, they are extremely open to radical ideas when framed simply and reasonably . . . the elites are baby eating pedophiles." The Proud Boys—who are designated a terrorist entity by US allies like Canada and New Zealand—posted content online lambasting Hollywood for being a "den of parasites feasting on the blood of children"—a direct reference to antisemitic blood libel conspiracies that are at the core of QAnon beliefs.[20]

PizzaGate and the sprawling web of QAnon conspiracies showed how disinformation and conspiracy theories about child trafficking had the power to recruit and radicalize millions of people to extremist violence. Absurd conspiracies and false claims about the need to rescue children in danger led to real harm through kidnappings, murders, violent attacks, and ultimately an insurrection. These conspiracies didn't just emerge out of whole cloth, of course. QAnon believers were primed to believe child trafficking claims after years of horrific revelations of actual pedophilia, sex trafficking, and other sexual abuse convictions of men who were either among the most familiar and trusted figures in families' lives (Catholic priests, Boy Scout troop leaders) or prominent elites in the political, financial, sports, and media worlds. Media coverage of accusations or criminal charges of rapes, assaults, and sexual coercion by Hollywood's Harvey Weinstein, financier Jeffrey Epstein, the *Today Show*'s Matt Lauer, Penn State assistant football coach Jerry Sandusky, and Stanford University swimmer Brock Turner—along with the ongoing revelations of the entire #MeToo movement—undoubtedly made it easier to believe claims of orchestrated pedophilia and child trafficking. (It is worth noting that these public cases often generated significant public sympathy for the perpetrators of rape and harassment, alongside comments like "it's impossible to flirt anymore"—i.e., that one cannot flirt without being accused of sexual harassment.)

Media revelations of very real and abhorrent sexual abuse scandals make the moral panic around sex exploitation and child sexual abuse a little more understandable. But the sad and ironic truth is that as QAnon believers were recruiting millions of people through an obsession with invented, false cases of child exploitation, the biggest spikes in harms to real children and vulnerable women weren't coming at the hands of prominent public figures or an imagined cabal of global elites. Violence was coming from those much closer to home.

Domestic and Intimate Partner Violence:
Red Flags and Boot Camps

Around the same time millions of Americans became obsessed with the Wayfair conspiracy, the United States began to see serious increases in nearly every imaginable category of sexual and gender-based harm. Already-high rates of domestic and intimate partner violence jumped at least 8% in the country during the pandemic, while resources and services available to victims declined or were diverted to COVID-19 medical needs.[21] The same period saw an upsurge in child abuse and maltreatment despite plummeting reports to authorities as mandatory reporters like teachers and school counselors no longer saw most students in person.[22] Rates of rape have increased in the United States nearly every year since 2013, when the FBI revised the definition—while well over half of rapes go unreported to begin with.[23] And murders of trans and gender non-conforming people in the United States have sharply increased in recent years. At least 288 trans and gender non-conforming people were killed in the United States between 2017 and mid-2024.[24]

There is significant evidence showing that prior violent acts in the domestic and intimate partner sphere—sometimes called "intimate terrorism"—are a warning sign for public, targeted, and extremist violence.[25] A history of gender-based violence against lovers, sisters,

mothers, and wives—along with expressed grievances against women—
is a clear risk factor for later public and mass violent engagement, including in both Islamist and white supremacist extremism.[26] The vast
majority of perpetrators of mass murder in the United States had a prior
history of violence against women.[27] This is true for terrorist actors
more broadly, who often have previous histories of violent behavior
against women through intimate partner violence, stalking, harassment,
rape threats, sexual assault, honor killings of girls and women in their
families, and more.

Domestic and intimate partner violence is far more common than
terrorism, of course. Over 40% of women and over a quarter of men in
the United States report having experienced sexual violence, physical
violence, and/or stalking by an intimate partner.[28] Over half of women
will experience physical sexual violence in their lifetime.[29] In the United
States, two dozen people per minute are victims of rape, physical violence, or stalking—the vast majority of whom are women.[30] And violence against women affects women of color disproportionately in the
United States—with well over half of Black, multiracial, and American
Indian/Alaska Native women experiencing sexual violence, physical
violence, and stalking during their lifetime.[31] Globally, the statistics are
even worse. Some fifty thousand women die at the hands of their partners or family members annually. As the United Nations puts it in a
recent global study on homicide, the most dangerous place for women
is their home.[32]

Not all men who are violent at home go on to become violent extremists or perpetrators of mass harm (not that the lack of that trajectory makes their domestic and interpersonal violent crimes any less
horrific). But there is clear evidence that histories of domestic and intimate partner abuse and violence should be recognized as a highly relevant red flag or warning sign for potential radicalization.

There are several explanations for why intimate and domestic partner
violence might create pathways to later mass violence or radicalization.
Some scholars suggest that enacting violence at home shapes how men
think about the utility of violence itself as a tool to achieve a goal. In this
way, domestic and intimate partner violence becomes a *"boot camp* for

terrorism" by both lowering men's inhibitions to violence and shaping their beliefs about its efficacy.[33] Men who engage in "the very personal and intimate disempowerment of women at the household level" would thus be more likely to see terrorism as a tactic to achieve their goals.[34] This bears out in global data showing that the level of women's subordination and disempowerment at home is significantly related to rates of terrorism at the national level.[35] This explanation is also upheld by consistent evidence showing that support for violence against women is the biggest predictor of support for violent extremism.[36]

Another set of explanations looks at the relationship between radicalization and childhood trauma related to the experience of domestic violence and physical abuse in the childhood home. In life history interviews, white supremacist extremists in the United States report adverse childhood traumas at much higher rates than the general population, including nearly half who report having been the victims of childhood physical abuse (in comparison with 28.3% of American adults overall).[37] The domestic violence literature has clearly established an evidence base for an intergenerational cycle of violence, in which boys who grew up in a household with a physically abusive father are more likely to perpetrate domestic violence in their own households as adults.[38] Men who enact violence against domestic and intimate partners may also be grappling with their own childhood traumas from witnessing or being victims to violence from their fathers or other men in the home. That trauma, in turn, may have an impact on radicalization pathways, including through mental health struggles that can create vulnerabilities to conspiracy theories or propaganda. It is worth noting, however, that white men who commit mass shootings and extremist attacks are more likely to be described as mentally ill compared with other terrorists, whose extremism is typically seen as purely ideologically motivated. Far too often, the implication is that mental illness is the reason for their radicalization and violence, which I have argued is a critical mistake. Mental illness is just one of many vulnerabilities that can drive people to extremist actions—not its cause.[39]

These are plausible explanations. Private violence may well become a training ground for subsequent public violence. And men who are violent at home or in their personal lives may well be acting on childhood traumas that also impact the likelihood of their subsequent public rage. But ultimately, these contentions still fit within what I suggest is the more compelling explanatory frame: Domestic and intimate partner violence is, at its foundation, an attempt to control and contain, to assert power and authority. Domestic and intimate partner violence is not only about the control of a single woman, but rather is about control of all women.[40] Men who are violent against lovers, sisters, mothers, and wives do so to assert, maintain, or defend their own dominance and demand deference to their entitlement to status, power, and service from others. Both types of male violence—private, intimate, and public, terroristic—are rooted in misogynistic attitudes, an impulse for power and control, and the violent defense of the patriarchal order and the clarity of roles and purpose it provides for many men.[41] Men who enact violence against women in their personal lives often do so in anger based in aggrieved entitlement and rage directed toward women because of a perceived loss of status and identity in the patriarchal hierarchy.[42] This type of aggrieved entitlement is also a risk factor for the perpetration of mass violence.[43]

Violence against women and children in intimate and familial domains is ultimately related to questions of power, domination, and control in ways that we ought to understand as similar and predictive of violence on a larger scale, especially through political or mass attacks. Analyzing histories of—and a sense of entitlement to—behaviors like coercion and threats, intimidation, emotional abuse, and other forms of isolation, economic abuse, control, and manipulation of intimate partners, spouses, children, or others—is critical to understanding the behaviors of violent men more broadly.[44] This is true for neo-Nazis and formal members of white supremacist or Islamist terrorist groups. But it is also true for mass shooters whose ideological motivations are muddied. The mass shooter who attacked a Uvalde, Texas, elementary school in May 2022, for example, had repeatedly engaged in misogynistic threats against teen girls online, threatening them with rape, kidnapping, and other physical harm.

Violence directed toward intimate and domestic partners is a clear and well-documented part of the pathway toward mass, public, and terroristic violence. But men who aim to exert power, control, and dominance over women don't just lash out against them in violence; they also seek to exploit them for their own pleasure, for financial gain, and for other strategic aims. Commercialized sex exploitation is one such strategy.

Sexual Trafficking and Extremist Violence

Several dozen members of a violent white supremacist gang were indicted in 2018 for methamphetamine distribution amid a series of crackdowns on drug trafficking among Aryan white supremacist gangs nationwide. Buried deep in a plea agreement, a brief aside casually revealed another kind of trafficking taking place alongside the drug running, as the alleged perpetrator was "known for having young women stay at the property in exchange for labor, drugs, and sex."[45] This is just one of several cases of systematic sexual exploitation and trafficking linked to organized white supremacist extremism, including the sale of women and their forced servitude for men's sexual and labor needs.

In his research on commercial sex exploitation and white supremacist groups, the investigative journalist Jordan Green uncovered details of heinous crimes.[46] One woman described being drugged and raped by several men who filmed her and sold the footage on the dark web. Another woman said she was kept in a drug house and raped before she was purchased by another man who kept her in servitude. Notably, these cases—like many others—were not pursued by law enforcement and are therefore undocumented in the data both on human trafficking and on white supremacist extremist group crimes.

The omissions of any charges for sexual assault or trafficking in the cases Green was investigating are especially problematic in light of two well-documented ties: between illegal drug operations and white supremacist gangs and between drug trafficking and sex trafficking—crimes the US Drug Enforcement Administration (DEA) describes as "inextricably linked."[47] Federal and state authorities have broken up at least a dozen neo-Nazi and white supremacist gangs with charges of drug trafficking in recent years, sending scores of individuals and networked groups to prison after mass arrests in West Virginia, California, North Carolina, Texas, Arizona, Utah, and more.[48] But when white supremacist extremists are charged with drug trafficking and other crimes, the details of those arrests, including media coverage, rarely refer to sex trafficking and sexual assault, even when witnesses report it. The well-documented connection between the two kinds of crimes makes it a safe bet that at least some of the white supremacist extremist groups trafficking in drugs are also engaged in some form of commercial sex exploitation. But since overloaded investigators and prosecutors likely find it more efficient to pursue cut-and-dried cases related to weapons and drug charges, counterfeiting, money laundering, or other racketeering activities than having to rely on traumatized witnesses in sexual assault, rape, or sex trafficking cases, especially if the end result is the same in terms of sentencing, we lack the data to know how big the problem really is. This is also amplified by the ways that the law enforcement and legal communities often minimize or look past violence against women—as in the examples of police spokespeople describing mass shooters or extremist actors as having had a "bad day" or acting "fed up." The end result is that victims of commercial sex exploitation are left with little justice, support, or recourse, since the crimes against them are left undocumented.

It's not that we can't see the connection between extremist and terrorist actors and sex trafficking. The far right is clearly obsessed with fears about sex trafficking in patently false and conspiratorial ways, related to QAnon claims or false allegations of "grooming." And there's plenty of analysis of sexual and gender-based violence and exploitation in Islamist terrorist and extremist groups. But analysts and experts have either willfully or ignorantly looked away from the problem in the case of domestic extremism, even though there is a long history of white supremacist and far-right groups engaging in organized sex trafficking. There is ample historical evidence that groups like the Ku Klux Klan used the systematic rape of Black women during "nightriding," riots, and mob action as a method of intimidation.[49] Neo-Nazi and white supremacist groups like the Sonnenkrieg Division and the neo-Nazi groups Rapekrieg and Rapewaffen regularly make public statements advocating for sexual violence against women or have been documented as systematic abusers of women through violent assault, abuse, and rape, including by calling for mass rape of white women to produce more white babies.[50]

Perhaps the most systematic and widespread case of white supremacist sex trafficking and abuse was under the Nazis, whose routine rape and torture of Jewish girls and women, often in front of their parents or during mob rapes in riots like those of the infamous *Krystallnacht,* was part of their campaign of terror.[51] The Nazis established over five hundred brothels across Europe where tens of thousands of women were raped and forced into sexual slavery in servitude to military officers, soldiers, and police. Brothels were also established in Nazi concentration camps, where women were raped as part of compulsory conversion therapy for gay "pink triangle" prisoners and as incentives and rewards to prison leaders and forced laborers. The brothels were highly and viciously regulated, like so many other Nazi policies; men had to secure a special "SS brothel permit" and were only allowed to rape women of the same racial group (i.e., "German" or "Slavic"), while women experienced forced abortion and sterilization.[52]

The extreme right's sexual exploitation of women for strategic and financial gain is much more widespread than the historical Nazi case. In Greece, regional control after World War II was often at the mercy of anticommunist paramilitary organizations, which ran prostitution rings and other criminal enterprises with the tacit permission of the state, who needed the paramilitaries to help police and maintain order.[53] Much more recently, intelligence reports revealed that both senior leaders and rank and file members of Greece's neo-Nazi Golden Dawn party, which won 7% of the national vote in 2012 and secured eighteen seats in Parliament, were involved in human trafficking and prostitution.[54] Other cases occasionally make international news, such as when Germany declassified its files in 2016 on a torture colony in Chile run by a Nazi pedophile, where victims were abused as sex slaves over three decades.[55]

In the United States the largest white supremacist prison gang, the Aryan Brotherhood, which boasts 20,000 members nationwide, runs several criminal enterprises, including a male prostitution ring.[56] There are also reports of Aryan Nation and other white supremacist spin-off groups being involved in commercial sex exploitation and trafficking.[57] Such exploitation is a persistent problem in Europe, too. Fourteen members of a neo-Nazi group were recently arrested in Spain for a raft of criminal activity, including coercive prostitution. The prostitution ring, among other illegal enterprises, helped finance the group's activities, which the local police described as "mainly related to attending music and sporting events to disseminate hatred, hostility and violence towards vulnerable or rival groups."[58] In 2013, seven members of an Austrian neo-Nazi group were caught running an illegal prostitution network, alongside other criminal activities including weapons and drug trafficking and arson attacks.[59]

Prostitution and sex workers are a common target of attacks by the far right as well, including with horrific violence and propaganda that links prostitution, moral depravity, and a permissive, decadent left. Even though the Nazi regime ran a state-sponsored network of brothels, Nazi ideology also framed prostitution as a moral degeneracy and a vice brought about by the Weimar regime—one that must be eradicated for the purity of the nation.[60] After pornography and prostitution became legal in eastern Germany post-German unification, neo-Nazi gangs began attacking sex shops, gay bars, bordellos, and red light districts, framing those activities as dirty, corrupt, and Western.[61] A Russian neo-Nazi was recently arrested for forcing twelve prostitutes to march naked in the streets of St. Petersburg, having previously declared a "war on prostitutes."[62]

The problem of sex trafficking and the sexual exploitation of women is much bigger than the activities of organized extremist groups, of course. Andrew Tate's online community "The War Room," which is packaged as a next-step learning opportunity for paid subscribers, teaches men how to groom women for intentional financial sexual exploitation online. For an entry fee of $8,000 and additional charges ranging from $12,000 to $18,000, men subscribe to programs like the PhD course ("Pimping Hoes Degree") to learn how to seduce women, make them fall in love and believe they are in a genuine relationship, and then manipulate them to sell themselves in the webcam porn industry or on OnlyFans. Tate's strategies have been likened to multilevel marketing initiatives, as the invitation to "The War Room" is framed as an exclusive, members' only inner circle opportunity—but with a financial commitment that can lead subscribers into significant debt while they learn how to sell and exploit women for profit.[63]

In the end, the lack of data on organized human and sex trafficking by white supremacist and neo-Nazi gangs and groups makes it impossible to know the true scope of the problem, how systematic it is, or how often the much more frequent charges of racketeering, drug trafficking, weapons charges, or other charges obscure additional crimes related to the commercial sexual exploitation of women. This is a problem in the field of human trafficking more broadly, where research is scant on the connection between gangs and sex trafficking, even though significant amounts of commercial sex exploitation have been documented to be at the hands of organized gangs and networks.[64]

What we do know is that white supremacist and other domestic extremist groups exploit women for much the same reason that any other human trafficker does—because it brings them pleasure or profit, because it gives them control and power, and because they can. The cases that have been documented of contemporary and historical neo-Nazi and white supremacist groups running prostitution rings and other criminal trafficking enterprises make it clear that commercial sex exploitation is operationally useful to some far-right extremist groups, for financial gain and for ideological and strategic aims.

Even if it is limited to fringe extremist and terrorist groups, organized prostitution and sex trafficking—and violent attacks against it—clearly have the potential to further far-right operational and financial strategies and tactics in ways that deserve greater attention, better reporting and data transparency, support for victims and survivors, and strategies and resources for prevention and intervention. We need more research situating the already expansive policy work on the use of rape and sexual violence as a weapon of war and an instrument of terror within our broader understandings of masculinity, patriarchy, and gendered power relations.[65] We also need to understand how commercial sex trafficking and the sexual exploitation of women and children is a part of what feminist scholars call rape culture, which describes a broader environment in which rape, rape threats, and sexual violence are normative in people's lives.[66]

Part of what makes sexual violence so normalized is that people are too often exposed to it at very young ages, including as victims and survivors. In this light, it is critical to acknowledge that trafficking and commercial sex exploitation is only one type of horrific perpetrator harm. Another category that is repeatedly linked to neo-Nazi and other far right extremists is the possession and circulation of child sexual abuse material.[67]

Child Pornography, Child Exploitation, and White Supremacist Extremism

"Why do neo-Nazis keep getting arrested for child sexual abuse material?" a VICE journalist wrote in July 2023, detailing repeated cases of white supremacist extremists charged with possessing indecent images and videos of children and toddlers, sending or requesting nude photos in exchanges with minors, or attempting to groom or have sex with minors.[68] In just one such example, the alleged former leader of Atomwaffen, a white supremacist terrorist organization, was accused by prosecutors in 2020 of "trading child pornography," having reportedly kept a folder of child sexual abuse material on his computer.[69] In 2019, a member of a white supremacist group that promotes incest as a strategy for maintaining the purity of their bloodlines was arrested on embezzlement charges; other members of the group had previously been convicted on incest and felony child abuse charges.[70] In case after case over the past several years, men who come under suspicion of plotting far-right terrorist attacks or are investigated in the wake of targeted threats are found during investigations to have child sexual abuse material (CSAM) on their computers, tablets, and phones.

Some of this relates back to a persistent and pervasive culture in the online manosphere in which underage women and minors are sexualized in the context of broader misogynistic ideas about physical appearance, beauty, age, and the fertility needed to reproduce babies. The concept of "hitting the wall," in which women are deemed too old to be dateable and thus have a declining or expired "sexual market value" that culminates in a "sexpiration date," captures this clearly. A 2024 analysis of social media channels that promote "hitting the wall" narratives by the group Diverting Hate found that manosphere channels that promoted this narrative in specific videos experienced increases in subscribers of up to 25%. The higher "sexual market value" placed on younger women and girls, who are seen as more pure, naïve, and controllable, is closely linked to what researchers describe as a "pedophilic-type mindset" prevalent on incel sites, where preteen girls are depicted as objects of desire. The misogynist influencer Andrew Tate also argues that women are more attractive at age 18 or 19 than at 25, describing the teens as more appealing because they are less sexually experienced.[71]

But child abuse is also part of a larger story of power and domination in ways that matter in the analysis of extremist child exploitation. Age is not often considered within analyses of exploitation and inequality—an oversight made worse in the case of Black girls, for example, who are often adultified (perceived as older and less innocent than white girls) and whose rapes by white men historically were often not counted within child sexual assault classifications. Age is a factor that should receive much more attention in analyses of exploitation. Children and adolescents are structurally vulnerable to control and domination by adults in ways that enable the ongoing prevalence of child sexual abuse—including by extremist groups and their members.[72] And even in horrific cases of child rape, media coverage often centers on the perpetrators and the impact on their lives, as Roxane Gay points out about the gang rape by eighteen men of an 11-year-old girl in Texas—the New York Times coverage of which was titled "Vicious Assault Shakes Texas Town." The article focused on how the men's lives were changed and the town "ripped apart" by one awful incident—rather than focusing on the 11-year-old girl "whose body was ripped apart." These stories are shaped, again and again, through the lens of power and subservience, of whose lives are deemed most fundamentally altered by even as egregious a case as the gang rape of a child.[73]

Child exploitation is yet another issue where abuses perpetrated by Islamist and international terrorists have been well documented, especially related to the kidnapping and forced marriages of schoolgirls, re-cruitment and radicalization of minors, and the use of child soldiers.[74] Experts have had much less to say about domestic or far-right extrem-ists' engagement in the same kinds of horrific abuse, even though public revelations over the past few years about both casual and organized use of child exploitation by domestic extremist groups has made that over-sight glaringly obvious.

In the fall of 2023, the FBI issued a warning about a cluster of new violent extremist groups originally operating under the name "764" (sub-sequently renamed and reorganized into more than a dozen offshoots and subgroups) which bear disturbing similarities to the militant extrem-ist group Order of Nine Angles (O9A).[75] O9A is an occult accelerationist group—whereby acceleration refers to groups and movements that aim to catalyze the collapse of social, economic, and political systems. O9A promotes neo-Nazi, antisemitic, and fascist beliefs and calls for an over-throw of Western civilization by subverting democratic and civil values and norms through criminal sexual violence and obscene acts of cruelty against children, animals, and others.[76] Obscure, fringe, and dangerous, O9A came to the broader public's attention in 2020 when Ethan Melzer, an active duty US soldier, was charged with a variety of offenses, includ-ing planning to murder fellow servicemen and providing sensitive opera-tional details about his unit to members of O9A. In spring 2023, Melzer was sentenced to forty-five years in prison.[77]

The FBI warning about a new network of similar groups came later that same year. Although the 764 network of groups is not predomi-nantly white supremacist in its ideology, their members have often been arrested in possession of Nazi material or have otherwise been engaged in networks and sites promoting violent extremism, mass shootings, or racially and ethnically motivated ideologies.[78] In August 2024, the Royal Canadian Mounted Police issued its own warning about the groups, noting their ties to ideologically motivated violent extremists and their use of youth-oriented social media and gaming platforms and apps.[79] The groups' strategies focus primarily on online child sextortion and child sexual material production and distribution produced in part by convincing minors to livestream, photograph, or record intimate images, acts of self-harm, or abuse of other children that are then used to sextort and dox them.[80] The groups engage in several horrific forms of abuse—and encourage new members to engage as well—including creating videos of animal abuse, acts of torture, incest, rape, abuse of other children, self-harm and self-mutilation, and bestiality.

All of these groups work to groom victims online, including through the in-game chats of multiplayer video games for children, like Roblox and Minecraft. They have an active presence as of January 2024 on nearly every mainstream gaming and social media platform, including TikTok, Instagram, YouTube, Roblox, X (previously Twitter), Snapchat, Discord, Twitch, Steam, Mega, and Telegram and also meet minors over Omegle, a random-connection app that arranges conversations between strangers online. Victims often later become abusers and recruiters for the group.[81] Both O9A and 764 and its offshoots see child sexual abuse and harm as a strategy and a "necessary prerequisite" for members to eventually enact acts of terrorism and larger public violence.[82] Their goal, as the 2024 Canadian law enforcement warning explained, is to "manipulate and control victims to produce more harmful and violent content as part of their ideological objectives and radicalization pathway."[83] These strategies are consistent with well-documented similarities in grooming techniques used to exploit children sexually and to recruit and radicalize them toward extremist and terrorist ideologies.[84]

While there are clear patterns of child sexual abuse, pedophilia, and sexual violence against minors among neo-Nazis and white supremacist extremists, it is also the case that the far right is obsessed with fighting "groomers" and supposed child exploitation by queer people. Propaganda and conspiracy theories across the far-right spectrum are often tied to an obsessive focus on child trafficking and pedophile rings, as illustrated by QAnon and described earlier in this chapter. Immigrants and refugees are also positioned as sexualized threats from whom white women must be protected—as in hateful language like "rapefugees." We also see it in conspiratorial language about the Democratic or elite cabal, racist descriptions of immigrant rapists, and the concept of "rape jihad" within extremist propaganda.[85] Sexual violence enacted against women and children is thus foundational to far-right extremism and is simultaneously used to rally support for the far-right through mobilizing calls to men to protect women and children from that same type of violence.

The exploitation by some men of women and children for sexual, labor, or other service roles—and the ubiquitous use of violence in the intimate sphere—is enabled and maintained by belief systems that assume and violently enforce the subjugation of women and the LGBTQ+ community as part of extremist ideology. The ideological use of sexual and gender-based violence is a foundational tactic of terrorism.

Ideological Use of Sexual and Gender-Based Violence and Control

White supremacists' gendered and natalist beliefs are an essential part of their racist and nationalist fantasies. Women's reproductive capacity is a relied-upon feature of the maintenance and defense of the white nation, and therefore white women's supposed purity must be controlled, maintained, and defended by men. These concerns are rooted in white supremacist fears that white reproduction rates are not as high as the population growth among nonwhites—which is why the issue of declining white birth rates and increasing immigration is a constant obsession with the far right and white supremacists.[86] The far right's hostility toward women's reproductive autonomy, in turn, is a natural outgrowth of an ideology that requires a steady supply of white babies to reverse demographic trajectories and maintain or restore a white majority nation.[87] The slogan of the white supremacist group Women for Aryan Unity, for example, is "Securing our future one child at a time."[88]

Women are charged not only with birthing and reproducing the (white) nation but also with cultivating and nurturing it through traditional roles associated with food and cooking, educating children with homeschooling curriculum, and providing generalized "feminine softness" in the family domain.[89] To this end, white supremacists make ample use of propaganda, narratives, or ideological rhetoric that insist women reproduce in order to repopulate a race or civilization and that women remain in domestic roles as mothers and housewives. These roles are then framed as natural, God-given roles whose sanctity can't be violated. White supremacist mobilization against abortion must be understood in this context.

Of course, not all women are held up as pure, Aryan breeders. Some women—like those who are sold, trafficked, and exploited for operational and financial goals—are seen as disposable. Others—especially white women who date or marry nonwhite men or raise nonwhite children, are labeled "race traitors" or "anti-white bigots" who deserve punishment.[90] White supremacist beliefs include a fear of forced race mixing, which is seen as part of a genocidal plot against white civilization.[91] The former leader of the white supremacist National Vanguard described "racemixing" as a "crime worse than murder," whose perpetrators are killing "the infinite generations of our future."[92] Terms like "polluting wombs," "race treason," or "bedroom genocide," used to refer to interracial relationships or the children they produce, capture white supremacists' extreme paranoia and anxiety surrounding demographic change.[93] The much-used white supremacist phrase "Day of the Rope" (DOTR), taken from the white supremacist novel and revolutionary playbook *The Turner Diaries*, refers to a coming day when opponents, including white women who have relationships with nonwhite men, will be publicly executed by hanging, their corpses left in the streets with signs labeling their supposed offenses, including phrases like "I betrayed my race" or "I defiled my race."[94] The phrase "Day of the Rope" regularly appears on white supremacist propaganda.[95]

Ideological arguments that rest on the subjugation of women and the LGBTQ+ community are a key radicalization tactic for white supremacist groups. In the United Nations' November 2023 report on sexual and gender-based violence related to terrorism, this dimension of sexual and gender-based violence is described as prevalent among extremist movements that are based on "xenophobia, racism, and other forms of intolerance." These ideologies require the control of women's "bodies and reproductive health to breed a generation of future group members or promote the survival of one ethnic or racial group over another." Extremist groups motivated by white supremacy, the report argues, view women as both subordinate to men and simultaneously essential to the survival of the nation.[96] Arguments about white birth rates and white women's reproductive obligations have proven especially powerful for extremist groups in light of the popularity of the so-called Great Replacement conspiracy, which claims white civilizations are being deliberately replaced by a cabal of Jewish or Muslim elites who promote multicultural societies in order to secure and consolidate their own power. Claims of an orchestrated "depopulation agenda" being pushed by elites and "enemies of whiteness" are peppered with rants against contraception, abortion, and feminists who prioritize careers rather than motherhood.[97] The Great Replacement (or localized versions of it, like Eurabia, a conspiracy that says Muslims are orchestrating the replacement of Christian Europe) have motivated terrorist attacks in Norway, New Zealand, and across the United States. Those terrorist actors have left behind manifestos, letters, or written posts that obsessively ruminate on "white birth rates" as part of their ideological rants.

What's Next? AI- and VR-Generated Misogyny and Violence

On a boring afternoon in the middle of COVID-19 lockdowns, I found myself in my basement, trying on a pair of virtual reality (VR) goggles for the first time after a friend recommended a boxing workout. I didn't realize I should change the settings from the previous (much taller) user, and suddenly a very tall man with hyperinflated biceps and broad shoulders came at me with fists flying. I felt an immediate physical sense of panic— sweaty palms, high-alert, tingly nervous system, and rapid breathing, as I threw my fists into a rapid flurry. It took me about thirty seconds too long to remember that I could simply remove the glasses and be back in my brightly lit basement among my hilariously laughing family.

Funny though it was, that basement boxing moment was also a sobering one, as I realized that virtual reality experiences have the potential to induce the same kind of visceral, physiological reactions in a victim of an attack as a physical assault might, even though there was no physical touching or harm being done. Shortly after the boxing incident, Meta opened up its virtual reality social media platform, Horizon Worlds, for beta testing, and a woman was immediately virtually groped.

She described another player's "floating hand" virtually rubbing her chest, ignoring her entreaties to stop, and then chasing her around, "making grabbing and pinching motions" near her chest and then shoving his hand toward her virtual crotch and making a rubbing motion. "There I was," she later described, "being virtually groped in a snowy fortress with my brother-in-law and husband watching."[98]

If there's one thing we have learned in the early days of artificial intelligence and virtual reality advances, it's that their capacity to generate hateful and harmful content stretches the imagination of what humans could have previously conceived. We now know that the three-dimensional aspect of virtual reality can trigger the same kinds of nervous system and physiological reactions as the fear generated in a physical attack. And artificial intelligence–generated imagery and videos now create fakes so realistic that users are hard-pressed to identify them as fake. The use of AI-generated nude photo "undressing" apps by middle school boys and the use of AI images to create and circulate child sexual abuse material have already caught school principals and law enforcement officials alike off guard.[99] Other problems related to tech-enabled exploitation are also rapidly escalating, including the financial sextortion of teens, which jumped 20% in just the six months between October 2022 and March 2023.[100] It is clear that strategies to prevent exploitation—and to support victims and survivors—have to evolve much more quickly if we have any hope of addressing the harms of new technologies, which I take up in greater detail in this book's conclusion.

Conclusion: Recognizing Sexual and Gender-Based Exploitation as Core to Far-Right Movements

The five overlooked pathways examined in this chapter—showing how exploitation and gender-based violence are both a spontaneous and a systematic, sustained, and operational part of far-right movements— should raise major red flags about what we have been missing in current analyses of white supremacist and other antidemocratic and domestic extremist movements. These are dehumanizing tactics that exploit and systematically harm women and children in the name of furthering and financing strategic goals and aims of antidemocratic, conspiratorial, and white supremacist movements and ideologies. But these issues have long been overlooked or ignored by local, state, and federal authorities as well as by the counterterrorism divisions of organizations like the United Nations, whose near-exclusive focus on Islamist movements and demonstrated aversion to intervening in far-right and far-left extremist movements is rooted in a sense that the latter is the domestic problem of member states rather than an international or global issue. I have previously argued that this framing is a mistake because of the globally interconnected nature of white supremacist and antigovernment movements and ideas. But the presence of so much gendered exploitation as a core part of far-right movements—as detailed above—should also raise the possibility of more serious and sustained intervention from global organizations like the UN, which could lean into existing mandates to engage within member states to prevent sexual and gender-based violence.

Margaret Atwood once wrote that men feel threatened by women because they are "afraid women will laugh at them," while women feel threatened by men because "they're afraid of being killed."[101] Looking straight at some of the most egregious and nauseating aspects of gendered exploitation, as I have tried to do in this chapter, is a critical part of recognizing and responding to the foundationally gendered nature of far-right extremist movements. But while the kinds of exploitation I discussed in this chapter have been happening right under our noses, another tactic of gender-based harm has accelerated rapidly—namely, the erasure of LGBTQ+ communities and a wide variety of gendered civil and reproductive rights.

5

Erasure

"DON'T SAY GAY"

The past was erased, the erasure was forgotten, the lie became the truth.

—GEORGE ORWELL, *1984*

IN JANUARY 2023, a group of fifteen people stood outside the entrance to Disney World in Orlando, Florida, waving Nazi flags and signs that read "Destroy all Pedophiles," "White Pride Worldwide," and "DeSantis 2024 Make America Florida."[1] An anti-pedophilia Nazi protest at Disney World might have seemed like the peak moment in what has been several years of American moral panic around LGBTQ+ issues, exemplified by Florida's 2022 "Parental Rights in Education" bill (also known as "Don't Say Gay"), which prohibits discussion of sexual orientation or gender identity prior to fourth grade, and requires that such discussions be "age appropriate" thereafter. The Walt Disney company became a target of far-right rage after it condemned the legislation and vowed to help repeal it.[2] But the Nazi Disney World protest wasn't the peak. On the contrary: It wasn't even the last Nazi Disney protest that would take place that year.[3] And the conflict spread well beyond Florida, as 2023 became the fourth consecutive record-breaking year for anti-LGBTQ+ legislative action, with six hundred legislative bills introduced in forty-nine states to challenge trans people's rights, nonbinary pronoun use, gender affirming medical care, trans athletes' sports team participation and bathroom usage, and more.[4] The pace continues to accelerate: In 2024 alone, the American Civil Liberties Union tracked 533 anti-LGBTQ+ bills in the United States.[5] And on the day of his inauguration in January 2025, President Trump signed an executive order titled "Defending Women from Gender Ideology Extremism and Restoring Biological Truth to the Federal Government," which establishes an official US policy of recognizing only two sexes (male and female), revokes protections for transgender military personnel and prisoners, bans the use of federal funds for gender-affirming medical care, and establishes restrictions on trans women's access to rape shelters, among other requirements. The executive order rescinds more than a dozen existing federal documents on transgender equality, including guidance from the Department of Education, the White House, and more.[6]

It's hard to imagine a more rapid series of perceived cultural threats to ardent defenders of patriarchy than recent social changes in how we experience and express gender and sexuality. The past decade has seen a radical shift away from the idea of a fixed gender binary, the normalization of gender-fluid pronouns, increased visibility of the trans community, and a growing number of young Americans who report preferring non-monogamous or polyamorous relationships and do not plan to get married.[7] It's no surprise to see backlash against these changes both increasing and developing new layers of strategies. If violators of the patriarchal order can't be contained in their box, can't be punished into compliance, and can't be exploited in ways that serve traditional patriarchies, the next step is to try to remove or eradicate those violators altogether. This is what I call erasure.

Erasure as a concept has been thoughtfully articulated by authors writing about Native American and indigenous communities, the experience of disability, how rape victims are treated in the legal system, and the LGBTQ+ community's experiences with medical care.[8] It can refer to the silencing or deliberate omission of credit for ideas, as Moya Bailey and Trudy explain about their names so often being absent from discussions of misogynoir, a term they coined.[9] Erasure can mean rendering entire communities invisible, such as through the bans of books and curricula with any content related to sexual orientation or gender identity, leaving behind deleted reading lists and open spaces on library shelves. This is the erasure the author Toni Morrison speaks of in *Burn This Book*, referring to the "erasure of other voices" as novels go unwritten, plays unstaged, films cancelled, languages outlawed, and writers' questions challenging authority are never posed, resulting in a whole universe "being described in invisible ink."[10] Erasure can also mean physical removal from spaces like bathrooms or sports teams, such as through legislation prohibiting transgender students and athletes from existing in spaces that correspond with their identities. It can refer to efforts to reduce or eliminate a population from existing at all, as in the case of laws prohibiting medical professionals from providing gender-affirming care to minors or through the discriminatory treatment of trans people by medical professionals.[11] Erasure doesn't only mean rendering invisible—it can refer not only to a removal but also a shrinking of rights as a means of restriction and control, as with reproductive rights and the loss of the constitutional right to an abortion in the United States.

In this chapter, I build on these prior articulations to elaborate on two major types of gendered erasure that should be understood as strategies of misogynistic containment and enforcement that normalize, legitimize, and mobilize violence, including on the extremist and terrorist fringe. As a reminder, misogyny is an enforcement mechanism, or set of tactics, intended to help maintain or defend patriarchal norms and expectations. The tactics of erasure I focus on here are legislative bans of reproductive and gender-affirming healthcare, and knowledge erasure through book and curricular bans and attacks on gender and women's studies in universities. These types of conservative mobilization of misogyny, I argue, critically underpin violent extremism and other forms of interpersonal and mass violence. Legislative and curricular erasure is a key example of what I call ordinary and everyday ways that misogyny is normalized, legitimized, and mainstreamed—which ultimately creates the conditions in which more extreme forms of misogyny and gender-based violence can flourish, including from the fringes. I conclude with an explanation of how these tactics of erasure have helped motivate extreme acts of harassment, threats, and violence against LGBTQ+ communities and their allies.

Legislative Erasure

Florida's Don't Say Gay policies didn't come out of thin air. The state has a decades-long history of organized opposition to homosexuality, including through legislative action in the 1950s, '60s, and '70s that resulted in the first ban in the nation on gay adoption and legalized housing discrimination based on sexuality.[12] The national context matters too—Florida's legislation came after years of nationwide homophobic fearmongering, false claims about the LGBTQ+ community "grooming" children for sexual abuse or trying to make them gay, and conspiracies about liberals and democrats as complicit supporters of pedophilia. Just before Florida passed the "Don't Say Gay" Bill, the governor's press secretary, Christina Pushaw, referred to it as the "Anti-Grooming Bill" and tweeted that anyone who is against it is "probably a groomer" or at least doesn't "denounce the grooming of 4–6-year-old children."[13]

These descriptions are rooted in false, age-old claims that homosexuality is pathological or sexually deviant and that gay people are psychopaths, perverts, or pedophiles—claims that over the years have led to mob vigilantism, medical intervention, conversion therapy, and vice purges.[14] In the post–World War II era, fears about child molestation and "stranger danger" were linked to ideas about healthy masculinity and deviant effeminacy, with pamphlets warning that the traditional, patriarchal family and home was a safety buttress against an outside world filled with potential predators.[15] These fears of the "other" relied on homophobia to craft a moral panic that could help whip up nationalist sentiments and reassert a strong, masculine nation in the wake of war.[16] No matter, of course, that these claims ignored the well-documented fact that most child sexual abuse is not perpetrated by strangers, but rather by relatives or individuals known to the child. The facts notwithstanding, these moral panics have created a false but persistent linking of homosexuality, molestation, and child predation.

Homophobic moral panics must be understood in light of conservative and far-right attacks on gender and diversity more broadly, in which feminism, LGBTQ+ rights, and multiculturalism are deemed a collective threat to traditional families and values as well as to the nation and

Western civilization. These frames are often deeply antisemitic and white supremacist, in part through conspiracy theories like the Great Replacement, that falsely claim Jews are deliberately orchestrating social change to secure more power and eradicate white Christian majority populations. The Florida legislation, for example, had the full weight of Christian nationalism behind it—at a moment when Christian nationalism and its antidemocratic, white supremacist, and patriarchal ideology was surging.[17] Just a few months before the Nazi Disney World protest, Florida Governor Ron DeSantis quoted the New Testament Book of Ephesians as he called on a crowd to "put on that full armor of God" and stand firm against "the left's schemes." "You'll be met with flaming arrows," he warned, "but the shield of faith will stop them."[18] This was classic Christian nationalist rhetoric, twisting biblical scriptures to mobilize Americans to a righteous, good-and-evil fight against the so-called degradation and degeneracy coming from a morally bereft or perverse left.[19] Issues related to gender and sexuality are right in the thick of it.

In the end, the Florida "Don't Say Gay" legislation was just the tip of the iceberg amidst a national legislative scramble to erase decades of gains in women's and LGBTQ+ rights.[20] These gains included the 2015 *Obergefell v. Hodge* decision that legalized same-sex marriage and the Obama administration repeal of the transgender ban in the military. The Obama administration had also issued new federal guidance confirming that transgender students are protected by Title IX—the US federal civil rights law that prohibits sex discrimination in educational settings.[21] In response, a slate of new organizations mobilized to counter momentum in gay and trans rights, often by framing these changes as part of a nefarious "gender ideology" or agenda that aims to indoctrinate children against their parents' wishes.[22] They stood up websites, associations, and campaigns to share anti-LGBTQ+ pseudoscience research and try to reverse federal guidance that secured rights for transgender students. Within a decade, their efforts had managed to introduce hundreds of bills across the country that rolled back protections for transgender people and prohibited gender-affirming care for minors—often based on false arguments about harm that fly in the face of what the medical field knows, for example, about the importance of trans people's health and well-being.[23] Similar efforts worked to roll back reproductive rights through banning and restricting abortions, challenging health insurance contraception coverage, and redefining the concept of "children" to include frozen embryos. By mid-2023, legislative efforts to erase LGBTQ+ and women's rights had accelerated so quickly that the Human Rights Campaign (HRC), the largest LGBTQ+ civil rights organization in the United States, declared a state of emergency for LGBTQ+ people in the country for the first time in its 40+ year history, and issued a companion guidebook to help travelers and residents in hostile states stay safe.[24]

Erasing and Controlling Bodies

White supremacists have long promoted homophobic arguments rooted in the supposedly unnatural character of sexual activity that doesn't lead to reproduction of the white race, positioning same-sex relationships as "cheating the race" with treasonous crimes against nature.[25] The broader fight to erase and control bodies is rooted in similar claims about nature. Those claims animate the far right's fight against "gender ideology" in wide-ranging ways, targeting many of the choices people might want to make about their own bodies—including the right to abortion and contraception, sex education in schools, nontraditional families, their sexual orientation or gender identity, or whether they can choose to engage in sex work.[26]

Much of the mobilization about gender in recent years has centered on trans people's identity and gender-affirming care for minors. Anti-trans activists have made fearmongering claims that demonize trans women as predators who pose a threat to "real" women and girls in bathrooms, locker rooms, or prison wards. They spread disinformation and make pseudoscientific claims that contend gender-affirming care amounts to experimental, state-sponsored sterilization which disfigures children, that trans youth are in the throes of some sort of psychic panic, or falsely claim all gender-affirming care involves surgery, which the American Academy of Pediatrics (AAP) does not recommend for minors.

There are undoubtedly reasonable questions to ask about gender-affirming care and how it should be provided to both adults and minors.[27] However, there is a consistent medical consensus in the United States about the standard of medical care for minors diagnosed with gender dysphoria—a disconnect between the sex they were assigned at birth and their gender identity. That consensus includes a broad swath of mainstream medical associations, including the American Academy of Pediatrics and the American Medical Association, who have clearly established standards for gender-affirming care as including mental health care, puberty blockers, and hormone treatments.[28] Anti-trans mobilization ignores this medical consensus and the established standard of care in the field.

Florida's efforts to restrict transgender youth and adults' rights became "an incubator for anti-trans legislation."[29] Anti-trans efforts have met with sweeping success around the world and across the United States, including at the federal level, in part through a consistent framing about gender ideology and the threats it supposedly poses to traditional families and the nation itself. Political leaders in Hungary, Spain, Turkey, Russia, and elsewhere have referred to "feminazis," "gender jihadism," "cultural terrorists," "gender dictatorship," and described gender ideology as "totalitarian"— reflecting a view of gender fluidity, LGBTQ+ relationships, and other transformations in gender and sexuality as unnatural, existentially threatening to traditional families, and destructive to the nation.[30] These arguments are also intertwined with anti-immigrant rhetoric in ways that link "natural" reproduction of the nation to racial and ethnic purity.[31]

These same strategies have now surged in the United States. In 2017, the Trump administration repealed the Obama administration's Title IX guidance, removing Title IX protections for transgender students. In 2020, the state of Idaho passed the first transgender athlete ban, and the following year, Arkansas passed the first ban on gender affirming care— both bills that were drafted by outside groups (Alliance Defending Freedom and the Family Research Council). In 2021, a legislation plan written by three conservative groups—the Alliance Defending Freedom, the Heritage Foundation, and the Family Policy Alliance—laid out a plan for states to restrict LGBTQ+ rights based on religious freedom and parents' rights. The following year, Florida passed the "Parental Rights in Education Bill," also known as "Don't Say Gay," banning discussion of sexual orientation or identity in schools and allowing parents to sue schools if students are introduced to content deemed not age appropriate. States across the country jumped on the bandwagon.

In the year 2023 alone, 185 bills were passed to ban gender-affirming healthcare across the country. Two new bills in Arizona target gender fluidity, with one encouraging parents to report books that "promote gender fluidity or gender pronouns" and a second requiring both a guardian and a teacher to approve students' pronouns.[32] The medical community has pushed back, arguing that attempts to ban gender-affirming care are extraordinary acts of interference by politicians that have "the sole purpose of threatening the health and well-being of transgender youth."[33] But the pace and scope of the bills has only increased, including in a broad swath of areas related to reproductive health, where dozens of bans or new restrictions on abortion have been introduced across the country.[34] In 2024, Alabama became the first state to legally define frozen embryos as children, meaning they cannot be discarded. Within a few days of the ruling, several fertility clinics paused or closed their IVF treatment facilities.[35]

The impacts of this rapid legislative erasure have been far-reaching, including through a series of witch hunts targeting athletes and students who are seen as not conforming to their expected gender identity, even when they are not trans or nonbinary. Starting in 2022, Utah passed a series of laws banning gender-affirming care for minors, requiring public school and government buildings' locker room and bathroom usage to align with the sex of individuals as assigned at birth, and banning transgender athletes from participating on girls' sports teams.[36] After the athletic ban, a state school association warned lawmakers it had received complaints about students who didn't "look feminine enough," and investigated a state champion after questions were raised about the athlete's biological sex—including by secretly examining school records back to kindergarten before reporting "she'd always be a female."[37] In February 2024, a member of the Utah State Board of Education posted a photograph on Facebook of a Salt Lake City high school girls' basketball team, falsely claiming one of the players was transgender. The post unleashed a troll storm of threats and abuse against the child, who was provided with security by the school district.

There is nothing uniquely American about anti-LGBTQ+ mobilization, of course. The LGBTQ+ community continues to be persecuted by state and nonstate actors in dozens of countries around the world, where same-sex relationships are criminalized, punishable in some cases with the death penalty.[38] But there is something new about the accelerating pace of recent legislative bans and actions in the United States and the framing of those bans under the umbrella of "parents' rights." It's also worth noting that there is substantial resistance across the United States to these bans, including through several counterchallenges that are underway. LGBTQ+ rights advocates continue to press for legal rights, filing lawsuits to challenge state employee healthcare plans' lack of coverage for gender-affirming care and in 2020, securing protection for the LGBTQ+ community through federal sex discrimination laws. Nevertheless, it's clear that legislative erasure is affecting the LGBTQ+ community's quality of life, sense of safety, and willingness to be "out" publicly.

Bans are not the only problem, of course. LGBTQ+ people experience disproportionate amounts of hate-based harassment, bullying, and violence—with nearly two-thirds of LGBTQ+ respondents in one recent survey reporting harassment, compared to just over one-third of non-LGBTQ+ respondents.[39] Experiencing hate-based harassment directly—as reported by 65% of marginalized group members in the United States—impacts a wide variety of indicators of health and well-being. LGBTQ+ people are about twice as likely, for example, to have difficulty concentrating, sleeping, or to experience anxiety and fears about future harassment.[40] Even when it isn't directly experienced, violence against members of one's own identity group produces fear and heightened vulnerability through what is called "vicarious victimization." These feelings of vulnerability and fear shape how people live their daily lives as they make choices to reduce the risk of violence against them—in ways that can make daily life feel "unlivable," marked by fear, suspicion, and self-imposed restrictions on activities.[41]

Living with hypervigilance against violence and harassment in this way adds to the impact of legislative erasure on marginalized groups' well-being. LGBTQ+ youth are already at high suicide risk compared to other adolescents; 2021 Center for Disease Control (CDC) data reports that 26% of lesbian, gay, and bisexual youth had seriously considered a suicide attempt in the past year, compared to 5% of heterosexual youth. Public health scholars warn that hostile laws that limit clinical care and education will exacerbate the kinds of stigma, mental and emotional stress, and identity-based victimization LGBTQ+ youth will experience. Adults are also affected in negative ways. LGBTQ+ teachers in Florida have described the legislation's chilling effect and pressure to self-censor discussions of their families, partner, or identity.[42] Parents and families of LGBTQ+ youth are also experiencing stress. One recent survey found that the "Don't Say Gay" bill led 56% of LGBTQ+ parents in the state to consider moving out of Florida, while 21% described themselves as "less out" within their communities.[43] Another survey of LGBTQ+ parent families found that 14% were actively in the process of relocating from Florida.[44] The tactic of erasure—including through silencing, removal, or eradication—is working. And alongside LGBTQ+ targets, a wide range of collateral erasures are also taking place, as teachers, librarians, and school board members resign in droves.

Erasing Knowledge:
Bans, Burnings, and Attacks on Gender Studies

After just nine months on the job, a town librarian in Idaho resigned in 2022, describing a "political atmosphere of extremism, militant Christian fundamentalism, intimidation tactics and threatening behavior" from a group of angry parents who wanted the library to preemptively ban a list of four hundred books that the library did not actually own.[45] That same year, a Texas librarian resigned, citing her fear of book banning intimidation tactics: "Who wants to be called a pornographer? Who wants to be accused of being a pedophile or reported to the police for putting a book in a kid's hand?"[46] Across the country in New Jersey, a high school librarian described feeling sick as she watched a public school board meeting where a parent accused her by name of "grooming" her 16-year-old son for letting him check out a library book with LGBTQ+ characters and descriptions of sexual activity.[47]

Some of the nation's most beloved public servants—librarians and schoolteachers—are suddenly on the front lines of the gender wars, navigating new mandates to review book content while being falsely accused of grooming and pedophilia. Hundreds of community members showed up at a 2023 Florida board meeting in protest after a fifth grade teacher showed her class a Disney movie that portrayed a gay character. That teacher resigned; another teacher in the same district who also resigned spoke at the board meeting, imploring parents to understand that "No one is teaching your kids to be gay! Sometimes they just are gay. I have math to teach. I literally don't have time to teach your kids to be gay."[48]

Those two teachers are now data points in the surging shortage of thousands of teachers in Florida—a shortage that has more than quadrupled since 2010. The gap won't be filled anytime soon with new teachers, either. While 8,000 students earned education degrees in Florida's higher education sector in 2010, that number has dwindled to somewhere between 2,000–3,000 students.[49] And Florida isn't the only place struggling. Teachers leave their jobs for a variety of reasons, of course, but the political climate affecting educators' lives is one of them. A third of K-12 teachers surveyed in 2022 said they will leave the profession within the next two years, many of whom cited new restrictions on LGBTQ+ content as part of their decision.[50] The erasure of allies from the classroom marches along.

The story of the gendered dimensions of extremist mobilization, as this recent history illustrates, is also a story about knowledge and expertise. For the American far right, education is the predominant scapegoat for the supposed decline of Western, Christian civilization and far-right ideological values. There is a long history of conservative mobilization around sex education in schools, of course, with periodic controversies erupting about whether and how schools should teach about contraception, homosexuality, abortion, or premarital abstinence as a standard.[51] Other issues like school dress codes, sexual assault policies, support for

LGBTQ+ clubs, and transgender rights related to bathroom or sports team participation are a constant source of controversy, protest, and parent engagement as well. The current moral panic about school curriculum related to race, gender, and sexuality—as exemplified by a wave of book bans in schools and libraries since 2021—is just the latest battleground issue, this time framed around parents' rights to determine what kind of content their kids read in schools or public libraries.

The parents' rights movement latched onto LGBTQ+ themed books and curricula sometime in the early pandemic period, right around the time millions of Americans were going down QAnon rabbit holes as they tried to #SavetheChildren from purported networks of Democratic elite child sex traffickers. Claiming they were asserting their rights to protect their own children from exposure to sexual content and the "leftist agenda,"[52] parents began filing complaints about school curricula and books, based on content related to sexual orientation, gender identity, as well as race and the teaching of slavery, the Holocaust, or other atrocities. Nearly six thousand books were temporarily or permanently banned across forty-one US states between July 2021 and June 2023, mostly because of content related to sexuality or racism. As a result, children in those schools are no longer allowed to read stories about kids who have two mommies, or about puberty and the changes their bodies might go through. The acclaimed graphic novel, *Maus*, about the Holocaust, has been banned, along with Nobel Literature Prize winner Toni Morrison's *Beloved* and *The Bluest Eye*.[53]

The pace and scope of the bans has rapidly accelerated, with book banning jumping 33% from the 2021–22 to the 2022–23 school year,[54] often in "copycat ban" fashion or initiated by the same group of "serial filers" of objections.[55] The increase is more significant for books that have been permanently removed from schools, where four times as many books (1,263) were permanently banned in 2022–23 compared to the year before (333).[56] Emerging reports from the 2023–24 school year are even more striking. One Florida school district closed libraries, covered bookshelves with black paper to protect students from "objectionable or illegal" content, and ultimately pulled more than 1,600 books from its shelves for special review in 2023—including dictionaries, encyclopedias, and world almanacs—because they mentioned "sexual conduct."[57]

It's not just book bans that are sweeping the nation. The past few years have seen a series of surreal book burnings staged by elected officials, candidates, and religious leaders, whose viral videos evoke the Nazi book burnings of 1933. In February 2024, a Missouri candidate for secretary of state released a video of her burning what she called "grooming books," which had LGBTQ+ inclusive content. Her campaign issued a statement calling for an end to library books about "sexualization, indoctrination and grooming of children," warning of the "ideologies that the radical left loves to push on children" and affirming the candidate's position as against "all drag shows around children, pride flags in classrooms, teachers with pronouns, people wanting to 'change' genders, and people that can't even define what a woman is."[58]

Libraries and schools are not the only target for attacks on knowledge. The extreme and conservative right also have set their sights on colleges and universities, which they see as hotbeds of liberal bias that indoctrinate students with a "woke," leftist agenda. Gender is a key target for such claims, drawing on recent changes in campus practices related to gender-neutral bathrooms and the growing use of alternative pronouns. Campuses are said to be sites of "subversive leftist activity," inundated with radical "feminazis" who will emasculate or usurp men of their rightful power and place and brainwash impressionable young students into submission to political correctness.[59]

Gender is only one part of conservative and far-right attacks on higher education. The Trump administration issued a controversial executive order against diversity and inclusion practices in 2019, and although that guidance was later overturned, the ideas were quickly picked up at the state level. In June 2023, Texas governor Abbott signed a law into effect banning all DEI offices from public universities in the state—becoming the second state to do so, after Florida.[60] Over the course of that year, twenty states either considered or implemented bans of diversity, equity, and inclusion (DEI) programming at public universities, part of an organized anti-DEI campaign that is rapidly spreading from higher education to the corporate world as well.[61] In

January 2024, the Florida Board of Education voted to remove a required sociology course from the curriculum of all twelve public universities in the state, replacing it with a new American history course.[62]

But gender studies remains at the heart of much of the conflict, called out by far-right and conservative pundits and activists who believe feminism and a disrupted gender binary along with gay rights and multiculturalism more broadly are collectively undermining the West, the nation, capitalism, and traditional Christian values.[63] According to this logic, universities pose a serious danger to Western civilization, Western values, and the Christian religion in ways that amount to what one right-wing writer warns is "cultural treason."[64] Far-right favorite Jordan Peterson describes universities as having been "hopelessly corrupted by their adoption of 'women's studies.'"[65] Far-right provocateur Milo Yiannopoulos created a post–secondary education "Privilege Grant," for which white men were exclusively eligible, so that they could be "on equal footing with their female, queer and ethnic minority classmates."[66]

The most extreme case hails again from Florida, where Governor Ron DeSantis staged a takeover of the public honors college New College of Florida and vowed to remake it into a bastion of conservativism. He replaced the trustees with a new group in 2023 who immediately set about erasing as much as they could. They eliminated gender studies, which a trustee described as an "ideological movement" rather than an academic discipline, closed the DEI office, fired the campus librarian, who is a member of the LGBTQ+ community, and eradicated gender-neutral bathrooms.[67] Thirty-eight of the college's ninety faculty members resigned, and a "large number" of students left to attend college elsewhere.[68] In 2022, DeSantis also introduced a bill known as Stop W.O.K.E. (Stop Wrongs to Our Kids and Employees), to restrict teaching or workplace training related to race and gender, with a particular focus on critical race theory and the idea that groups of people may hold privilege or be oppressed based on race or gender, but its implementation was blocked by a Tallahassee judge, who called it "positively dystopian."[69]

Florida offers some of the most extreme examples, but they are not isolated ones. Across the United States and Europe, gender studies is regularly attacked and discredited as a supposed instrument of "gender ideology" that decries supposedly "real" scientific evidence from fields like biology and evolutionary psychology[70] while corroding and destroying traditional gender roles, undermining family values, and promoting a nefarious elimination of "natural" differences between the sexes.[71] These US developments are part of a broader global assault on knowledge and expertise undermining public confidence in factual information—creating vulnerabilities to propaganda and extreme ideologies and making people less willing to believe real information or images.[72]

Far-right attacks on knowledge and expertise, including gender studies, exist in the context of what Tom Nichols calls a "campaign against established knowledge."[73] This includes attacks on the credibility of facts and arguments, specialized experts, and the free press. The mainstream right's declining trust in higher education, combined with a growing populist climate of anti-intellectualism and broader attacks on expertise, creates fertile ground for more-extreme attacks on higher education, including gender studies, from the far right. The challenge to traditional gendered roles—by feminists, "woke" university professors, gender studies departments, and more—is seen as not only threatening but also positioned as intentionally manipulative, part of orchestrated efforts by corrupt elites and social justice advocates to undermine the nation's traditions and purity. The overall effect nationally has been a weakening of the legitimacy of sources of knowledge and trust in the kinds of expertise that historically help build shared ways of understanding and explaining our worlds,[74] while reassuring voters that a stronger state (and authoritarian strongman) is needed to protect the pure people from the threat.[75] Anti-gender attacks—including those rooted in homophobia, transphobia, and misogyny—are also tactical strategies that splinter coalitions and divide political allies with moral panics and dystopian threats about the catastrophic demise of "natural" or traditional ways of life—in ways that destabilize democracy itself.[76] In this sense, attacks on gender studies, "gender ideology," and the broader LGBTQ+ community have helped legitimize, normalize, and mobilize antidemocratic movements, including extremist violence.

How Erasure Normalizes
and Mobilizes Violent Harassment and Threats

Thirty-one members of the white supremacist Patriot Front group were arrested in June 2022 on charges of conspiracy to riot at an Idaho Pride event. The men had traveled to Idaho from ten states, equipped with riot gear, shin guards, shields, and at least one smoke grenade. Other men at the parade walked through the crowd carrying long guns and pistols and unfurled a banner with a false anti-LGBTQ+ narrative about harming children.[77] Elsewhere, white supremacists, neo-Nazis, and the self-described "Western chauvinist" Proud Boys have recently harassed attendees at Toledo's Love Fest celebration, protested at charity events, children's story hours, and outside of the entrance to Disney World.[78] Members of the Proud Boys showed up at a school board meeting in Illinois because of book ban discussions, disrupted a drag queen story hour for families in California, and protested at a North Carolina LGBTQ+ themed story hour.[79] In Bozeman, Montana, in May 2023, masked neo-Nazis gathered outside a local bookshop to disrupt a Drag Story Hour, holding signs that said "Pedophiles Not Welcome" and "Queers Hurt White Kids."[80] At a Florida charity event that featured drag performers alongside other musicians and singers, including an eight-year-old dancer, Nazi protesters held signs that read "Drag queens are pedophiles with AIDS," and projected "Child grooming in progress" and "Pedophilia must be punished by death" on a wall.[81]

Calls to curtail women's or LGBTQ+ rights are known "early warning signs for extremist violence"[82]—and as we have seen those rights be erased across the United States, we are seeing violence follow in short order. The same anti-LGBTQ+ rhetoric and propaganda ushering in legislative bans catalyzes hostile action from opportunistic neo-Nazis, white supremacists, and other domestic extremist groups whose false claims about grooming and pedophilia—and promises to eradicate it—are increasingly being normalized and legitimized by ever-more mainstream statements from elected officials, school board members, parents, and other community groups. Both Islamist and white supremacist extremists have long and well-documented histories of homophobia and of harassing, abusing, and attacking members of the LGBTQ+ community. The 2016 Islamist terrorist attack at the Florida Pulse nightclub, which killed forty-nine people, was the deadliest act of violence against the LGBTQ+ community in US history.[83] But now, legal banning has emboldened extremists who "believe they have the force of the law behind them."[84] The result has been year upon year of record-breaking hate crimes, harassment, murders, and attacks on the LGBTQ+ community.

The data are painfully clear across every available source. In the United States, between 2022 and 2023, anti-LGBTQ+ propaganda distributed by white supremacists jumped 141%, moving from sixty-eight reported incidents in 2022 to 164 in 2023.[85] The previous year, according to a joint report from GLAAD and the ADL, there were 356 extremist incidents targeting LGBTQ+ people from June 2022 to April 2023, followed by additional 145 extremist anti-LGBTQ+ incidents during Pride month in June 2023.[86] The incidents took place in forty-six of fifty US states and in the District of Columbia, and about half were perpetrated by individuals with ties to extremist groups. Drag events were a particular target, with 161 attacks in the United States from January 2022 through March 2023, including violent protests, vandalization, bomb threats, and a firebombing.[87] And FBI hate crime data—which are historically underreported to begin with—show that hate crimes targeting gender identity increased 33% in 2022, while hate crimes focused on sexual orientation and anti-LGBTQ+ sentiment each jumped 14%.[88]

Each of these data points represents a story that has left victims and survivors reeling. In August 2023, a 66-year-old woman (who did not identify as LGBTQ+ but considered herself an ally) was shot and killed by a man who yelled homophobic slurs at her after she confronted him for tearing down the Pride flag from the front of her California clothing shop. Two soldiers were arrested in Virginia in February 2024 for tearing down a Pride flag from the home of a gay couple five times over several months.[89] Neo-Nazis and other white supremacist extremists along with other anti-LGBTQ+ activists have repeatedly slashed, burned, removed, or defecated on Pride flags at private homes, government buildings, and businesses, or have harassed attendees at Pride parades as well as local restaurant owners.[90] The list goes on, and on, and on.

The trans community is especially vulnerable, including through high rates of online transphobic comments (including calls for trans genocide), the use of incorrect or insulting pronouns (like "it"), which aim to deny and erase trans identity, and far-right attacks on trans people as mentally ill, unnatural, dangerous, and an existential threat.[91] In the United States, at least forty-one transgender people were killed in 2022, marking a decline from the record-breaking fifty-nine transgender people who were killed the year before, which made 2021 the most violent year on record for the trans community.[92] Over the past seven years, at least 288 trans and gender non-conforming people were killed in the United States.[93] While many of those murders are understood by the public and in the media as motivated by interpersonal or intimate partner violence, the disproportionate amount and degree of violence enacted on trans men and women must also be understood within the context of pervasive transphobia within and across far-right movements—and increasingly within the conservative mainstream as well.[94]

Transgender youth are disproportionately affected, including through high rates of bullying, attempted suicide, and less access to mental healthcare.[95] Trans women are particular targets, with the overwhelming majority of online transphobia being directed at trans women—a trend researchers attribute to the fact that the social value placed on men and masculinity is so high that it is "unthinkable" that trans women would "trade down" in their gendered identity.[96] Black transgender women, furthermore, bear the brunt of transmisogyny and are the disproportionate victims of fatal violence against trans people.[97] This is likely due both to high rates of violence motivated by anti-transgender bias and its intersections with racism, and because victims' transgender or gender-expansive identities can create pathways of exclusion that put them at risk through a lack of housing or employment, or through participation in survival sex work, which affects Black women disproportionately.[98]

That same intersectionality also extends to the intersection of racist and antisemitic tropes with anti-LGBTQ+ incidents and propaganda. In the 2022 data, over a third of the 356 anti-LGBTQ+ incidents also cited antisemitic tropes, and thirty incidents also cited racist tropes.[99] In just one recent example, a 28-year-old dancer was killed in Brooklyn after a group confronted him with racist and homophobic slurs while he was dancing and vogueing with a group of friends.[100]

The problem is not limited to the United States; anti-LGBTQ+ hate crimes have increased in Europe and Canada, and in 2022, violence against the LGBTQ+ community in Europe and Central Asia reached its highest point in a decade. In 2023, Uganda passed anti-LGBTQ+ legislation that includes the death penalty in some cases, which has since inspired a "domino effect" of anti-LGBTQ+ laws across Africa, in part through the influence of American evangelicals.[101] But the United States bears an outsized proportion of anti-drag activism, including the highest number of violent incidents. It is also the only country across the West to have both a substantial number of mainstream elected officials involved in anti-drag activism or promoting "save the children" conspiracies. The rest of the world is listening—the United States is a major exporter of anti-LGBTQ+ propaganda, including anti-drag rhetoric and the "groomer" slur.[102] The United States is also the origin of the QAnon conspiracy theory, which relies heavily on a narrative about protecting children from predatory sex traffickers and groomers and which has subsequently spread to countries around the globe.

The targets of violence and rage about gendered social changes are not only wide-ranging, but encompass places not previously thought to be vulnerable. Bookstores, public libraries, Disney World, and school board meetings have all faced surging threats, harassment, and violent protest. Medical providers, clinics, and hospitals have also been targeted for offering gender-affirming care and treatments. In 2022, after false claims about its gender-affirming care circulated on Twitter, Children's National Hospital in Washington was threatened with violence.[103] Those threats followed bomb threats against Boston Children's Hospital and other violent threats against hospitals in Phoenix, Pittsburgh, Seattle, Akron, Ohio, and Nashville, Tennessee, all targeted because of their gender care programs.[104]

Like all forms of domestic extremist mobilization, the erasure of LGBTQ+ people and rising violence against them would not work if it were only perpetrated by men. Women, including some who identify as feminists, have played a significant role in spreading disinformation and pseudoscientific claims about the LGBTQ+ community, especially through groups like Moms for Liberty, which has successfully led many of the school curricular bans nationwide, and by groups of radical feminists who oppose the inclusion of trans women (sometimes referred to as Trans-Exclusionary Radical Feminists, or TERFs, a term credited to online blogger named Viv Smythe).[105] Radical feminist opposition to trans-inclusion has a long history, rooted in the same kinds of gatekeeping that led white American suffragists to exclude Black women or British women to denounce hijras in the 1870s. Anti-trans feminists rest their arguments on two core beliefs: that transgender women are not legitimate as women and therefore not worthy of inclusion in the fight for women's rights, and that women's liberation can only take place through men's absence or removal.[106] They also position transgender women as a physical threat, depicting trans women as disguised male predators who pose a threat in bathrooms and locker rooms.[107] Proponents often cloak anti-trans views with softer language, using terms like "gender critical" feminism. Anti-trans feminism became well known to the public through the controversy surrounding *Harry Potter* author J. K. Rowling, who has regularly made transphobic statements while insisting they are about protecting children from harmful hormone treatment, protecting "real" women in bathrooms from the predatory threat to safety that trans women supposedly represent, or claiming that trans activists are "erasing" the concept of biological sex. Rowling personally funded a new domestic violence support center in Scotland which explicitly excludes trans women, arguing that the center offers "woman-centered and woman-delivered care." Meanwhile, trans women and especially trans women of color are at a much greater risk of intimate partner violence and sexual assault compared to cisgender women.[108] Transgender women experience violent victimization at a rate of 86.1 incidents per 1,000 people, compared to cisgender women's 23.7 for every 1,000 people.[109]

Conclusion: The Refusal to See

"Erasure is a form of oppression, the refusal to see," Chanel Miller writes in her memoir, *Know My Name*, about her rape by Stanford swimmer Brock Turner and her treatment by the legal system afterward. The notion of blind spots, as in a driver's rearview mirror, implies that the viewer is not at fault, that people's inability to see a problem is a feature of their lived environment. This isn't entirely inaccurate—patriarchal norms and expectations are so ingrained in our society that it is understandable that so many people either look straight past them, or else tacitly or explicitly enable and support them. But some blind spots are deliberately, aggressively constructed and defended, as Chanel Miller persuasively argues. Sometimes we refuse to see them, or we deliberately create them through removal, erasure, containment, and any number of other strategies designed to keep certain kinds of people in their box, in their place, unseen and therefore nonthreatening to the patriarchal order.

In this light, it should be abundantly clear that the gendered lenses through which we need to understand far-right recruitment and mobilization go far beyond attacks on women. Gender-diverse and nonbinary people, the trans community, and LGBTQ+ people more broadly are heavily targeted in ways that make clear that the misogyny driving far-right violence encompasses a sweeping range of targets. The erasure of LGBTQ+ rights, the erasure of allies who resign from their jobs as teachers and librarians, the impact on LGBTQ+ people who feel they have to be less public, to be back in the closet, to be more invisible—is a horrifically powerful tactic of misogyny. That tactic, like all strategies of misogyny, aims to reassert the dominance of traditional patriarchal norms, expectations, laws, and rules. And it's working.

As this chapter has already demonstrated, none of these tactics—including erasure—would work if they were only enacted and supported by men. The example of TERFs shows clearly how women—including some feminists—are actively engaged in policing the boundaries of gender and sexuality. In the next chapter, I look at the role that white women play in enabling, supporting, and mobilizing violence in white supremacist and other antidemocratic extremist movements.

6

Enabling

THE WHITE BABY CHALLENGE

THE MARTYRING OF VICKI WEAVER began shortly after she was shot by a federal agent's stray bullet while holding her infant daughter. She had been standing behind the door of her family's off-the-grid Ruby Ridge, Idaho cabin amid a multi-day standoff in August 1992, as US Marshals tried to arrest her white supremacist, antigovernment husband. Their 14-year-old son, Sammy, had already been shot and killed. After Vicki died, Randy and their surviving children laid siege with her body for four more days. At a roadblock protest down the hill, white supremacists and antigovernment activists held signs with warnings like "Your Family Could Be Next." The Weaver family was later awarded a $3.1 million settlement from the US government for the wrongful deaths of Vicki and Sammy.[1]

A homeschooling mother who died unnecessarily and tragically at the hands of the government was an easy choice for far-right martyrdom. Vicki Weaver—whose oft-circulated image in hate group spaces depicted her barefoot, standing outside in a white dress, looking pure, demure, docile, and in need of protection in ways that fit neatly into the outlines of white supremacists' ideas about who women are and what they should be for the movement.[2] She was ideologically committed, as evidenced by repeated threatening letters she sent to local government officials describing her refusal to bow to the "evil commandments" of "your Lawless government,"[3] but also spent most of her time raising children and selling huckleberries and wood to help feed the family. She was unarmed inside the cabin when she was shot. Her death was used by antigovernment and white supremacist forces to warn of the danger the state poses to white families and their women. As Aryan Nations pastor Carl Franklin later explained, "When the Feds blew the head off Vicki Weaver, I think symbolically that was their war against the American woman, the American mother, the American white wife . . . This is the opening shot of a second American revolution."[4] In her death, Vicki Weaver linked the fight for white families—and the protection of white women—with the fight against the government.

White women are no less a mobilizing force for the far right today—as articulated by the white supremacist activist Lana Lokteff, who recently declared that "when women get involved, a movement becomes a serious threat."[5] But during the post–Ruby Ridge decades, women's visible roles shifted from passive, protected mothers and backstage organizers to frontstage leaders, active recruiters, and participants in violent action. There is no question that it is men who continue to dominate the extreme right globally—and that they are responsible for most of its violence, much of it against women.[6] And it is also true that traditional domestic roles, especially motherhood, continue to be a mobilizing force for women. But women are no longer relegated to domestic tasks alone, and their increasing roles have broadened the reach of the far right in critical ways.

Nearly thirty years after Ruby Ridge, another far-right woman was shot through a door—this time by a Capitol police officer during the January 6 insurrection—and immediately martyred. But while Vicki Weaver was killed while passively holding her baby behind a door, Ashli Babbitt, a US Air Force veteran and QAnon supporter, was shot trying to break one down. After she died, the far right valorized her as a patriot and a resistor who died fighting tyranny.[7] Her face now adorns flags, fliers, memes, and other images depicting her as the Statue of Liberty and a symbol of white resistance, with slogans noting she should "rest in white power."[8]

The story of how Vicki Weaver became Ashli Babbitt is the story of how within far-right political movements women moved from being mothers and reproducers of the nation to being violent defenders of it. In less than three decades, women shifted from backstage supporter and protector roles to political leaders and violent actors. This happened in three overlapping stages. Women first were activated to political engagement through their roles as mothers working on behalf of their families' needs. Soon after, as QAnon beliefs swept across the country, millions of women moved beyond a sense of duty to protect their own families as they were called on to defend all children, who were supposedly at risk from a Satan-worshipping network of child traffickers. In the hashtagged and hyperlinked world of social media, it was then a short leap from QAnon's #SavetheChildren hashtag to the insurrection's #StormtheCapitol one. In this third phase, a broader, national defense narrative called on citizens to defend the country from tyranny and usher former President Trump back into power. Thousands of women answered the call on January 6. By the time we get to Ashli Babbitt, the motherhood that defined Vicki Weaver's martyrdom isn't a necessary frame for political activism at all. The women of January 6 were violent actors all on their own.

Lady Liberty in Action

Like other women at the US Capitol, Ashli Babbitt mobilized first and foremost as a defender of her nation, not her family. She was part of a generation of women who had already broken through barriers in all-male domains like the military, firefighting, and the corporate world, and her political engagement reflected that. She traveled to Washington believing she was part of a righteous and violent storm of ordinary people who were called upon to reinstate Trump and turn darkness into light—beliefs she acquired through QAnon, which has radicalized millions of women to believe in a network of conspiracy theories.[9] And she did so with considerable prior combat skills. Her fourteen-year military service included four years of active duty during two wars, when she deployed to Afghanistan and Iraq. Afterward, as part of the Air National Guard, Babbitt was part of a security division that regularly trained with riot shields and clubs as part of civil disturbance preparedness. She was shot alongside a group of rioters trying to break through the locked, barricaded doors to the House of Representatives Chamber, where dozens of elected officials and their staff were holed up.[10]

Among those rioters were women who left ordinary lives and jobs as health professionals, a florist, a realtor, a school therapist, and an elementary school teacher, all mobilized over a relatively short period of time through mass disinformation about the US presidential election. Many of those women used language that referenced their role vis-à-vis the men they were traveling with, describing "all my boys behind me" or calling on supporters to join the physical attack because "we need strong, angry patriots to help our boys." But they were violent actors in their own right. At the Capitol that day, women smashed pipes through windows and posted videos from inside the building saying they were searching for House Speaker Nancy Pelosi "to shoot her in the friggin' brain."[11]

The engagement of so many women in a violent attack at the US Capitol—representing 14% of the federal arrests to date[12]—is a deviation from decades of relatively low formal engagement in the far right by women. Just 6% of violent and nonviolent far-right extremists between 1948 and 2018 were women, with a burst of violent engagement by women bumping that percentage to 11% by 2022.[13] This isn't to say that women like Vicki Weaver were irrelevant to far-right movements. Across history, white women like her enabled the violent vigilantism of the men in their lives, even as they eschewed formal roles or membership in groups. They handled a range of essential domestic tasks, from the sewing of the KKK's white supremacist robes to childrearing, cooking tasks, and the organization of logistics for large gatherings.[14] Women published newsletters with homeschooling tips and recipes intended to help raise pure, white families to secure the future of white civilization. And they were at the helm of significant nonviolent organizing and grassroots opposition to school segregation and racial integration, making fliers, organizing pickets, running consumer boycotts, and launching neighborhood petitions[15]—mobilizing activities permissible within the broader far right because they could be folded into women's primary roles and identities as mothers, wives, daughters, and homemakers. At kitchen tables and living room meetings, women leaned into these roles to justify their engagement and to recruit and mobilize others.[16]

Those roles began to shift from backstage to frontstage roles in the early twenty-first century. The path to Ashli Babbitt still includes a lot of mobilization of mothers. But it has also moved well beyond the family protection narrative to embrace a broader and more violent defense of the nation. It's a pathway that begins just over a decade after Vicki Weaver died, when a conservative woman political leader sought to mobilize other women to political leadership by convincing them that political activism was an act of good motherhood. Sarah Palin and her "Mama Grizzlies" galvanized the support of millions of women in the United States—and made them the dominant force of Tea Party local leadership.[17]

Mama Grizzlies: Mothers as Defenders

Following her 2008 vice presidential run, Alaska Governor Sarah Palin coined the term "mama grizzlies" as she called on moms to band together and rise up against big government policies that would "attack their cubs" and weren't "right for our kids and for our grandkids."[18] Conservative women across the country rallied. Palin—and in turn, the Tea Party— were core to what became a conservative reframing of women's issues around motherhood and family protectionism that asserted women's autonomy from government dependence. Government regulation, according to this logic, was not only patronizing to women but also threatened their own liberties and their children's futures. Fighting back against the fiscal threat posed to their families by big government was framed as a maternal obligation—part of a mother's charge to protect their families and their children's future standard of living. Good motherhood thus became a political act for conservative women. Rejecting big government was seen as moral engagement by good mothers who were expressing care for their families and their children's future wellbeing.[19]

Palin and the Tea Party recruited women at the local level by linking good motherhood to specific, conservative political positions. But this approach also reframed and reclaimed the mantle of feminism itself.

Modern liberal feminism, Tea Party activists argued, promotes a patronizing approach that fosters dependence on the government and incorrectly prioritizes reproductive rights over all else. In contrast, conservative feminists argued they were resurrecting the true purpose of the women's movement by promoting autonomy from government dependence and replacing it with self-reliance and personal responsibility.[20] This framing helped mobilize legions of conservative women who had previously taken a back seat in political movements and activism. That empowerment hinged on adopting an antigovernment position that framed skepticism of government as good motherhood.

Conservative women's engagement in the Tea Party didn't come entirely out of thin air. It built on earlier mobilization by antifeminists like conservative activist Phyllis Schlafly, whose anti–Equal Rights Amendment activism helped derail the ERA's ratification in the early 1970s. Schlafly's mobilization was based in arguments that equality would hurt women and create a moral decline. Women's correct place, according to Schlafly, was "in the home as a wife and mother."[21] But even though it wasn't entirely new, gendered Tea Party mobilization did launch an entirely new type of visibility for a larger number of women in conservative and far right political leadership roles. Within a decade, we would see the same empowerment drive the rise of women nationalist and far-right political leaders in Europe, like France's Marine Le Pen (National Assembly of France party), Italy's Giorgia Meloni (Brothers of Italy party), and Germany's Alice Weidel (Alternative for Deutschland party). Many of those women, in turn, rose to power by blending feminist arguments with far-right stances on family values, immigration, and defense of the nation. Both traditional family values and women's rights, so the argument goes, are threatened by Islam, Muslims, and immigrants writ large. This is what Sara Farris calls "femonationalism"—the exploitation of feminist, gender equality concepts to promote xenophobic, nationalist, anti-Islam, and anti-immigrant policies.[22] This deployment of feminist themes for exclusionary goals has helped to position immigrants, Muslims, and trans or queer people as "threats to the sexual order" of the nation.[23] In this way, racist and anti-gender arguments both mutually constitute one another and help to buttress nationalist and xenophobic rhetoric.

The Tea Party was extinguished by Trumpism and faded quickly from the public's memory. But it demonstrated that gender-related mobilization was a powerful force—as we would see again just a few years later, when the majority of white women voted for Trump in 2016, 2020, and 2024. The Tea Party also left an enduring legacy in the valorization of women's political engagement *through* their roles as mothers and homemakers, which laid the groundwork for a right-wing social media world that warned of the dangers of feminism, the appeal of a simpler, purer time, and urged women to embrace their "natural" roles as wives, mothers, and homemakers while railing against immigrants, feminists, Islam, and anyone deemed a threat.

Like so many aspects of our social and political lives, narratives about traditional families and the special role of women in safeguarding them became supercharged by the online world—led in large part by a digitally savvy generation of women social media influencers who exploited it with livestreamed video blogs, Instagram posts, and other ways of connecting directly with millions of followers to share their message and spread the word. There is simply no way to understand the path to Ashli Babbitt—and the hundreds of women who stormed the US Capitol on January 6—without taking a closer look at how those social media platforms were used to recruit and radicalize white women.[24]

Insta-Conspiracy:
Social Media and the Radicalization of White Women

Propaganda relies on images, and the far right is no exception. From dehumanizing cartoons under the Nazis to white supremacist photos of nursing women with headlines like "Fight for White Rights!"[25] aesthetics have always been central to the far right's message. As the mainstream social media world shifted to visual and video-based content, the far right was ready to exploit it—often at the hands of women. No longer relegated to domestic tasks, today women use social media channels and other online platforms as leaders, working to recruit and radicalize other women—and men—into white supremacist extremism, conspiracy beliefs, and more.[26]

Across the online ecosystem, far-right content designed by and for women has proliferated. There are Instagram accounts with beautifully curated images—typically of a blond woman with small children, standing in a field of wheat or next to a little deer in a dappled-light wood—with labeled warnings about purity, the need to defend whiteness, "European heritage," or white territory. In one recent social media post, a woman with an elaborate blond braid and a flowy white dress faces away from the camera, moving across a field toward a wild tangle of grasses and lavender-hued blossoms. She is reaching behind her to grasp a larger, presumably male white hand, creating a sense of the viewer being drawn after her. It looks like any other carefully curated advertisement, until you notice the block text overlaid on the image: "When You're White, There's No Upgrade, Don't Mix."[27]

On imageboard and short-form video-based platforms, women share far-right propaganda, spread election disinformation and conspiracy theories, and promote women's roles in reproducing white, Western civilization—all packaged within relatable content that is livestreamed right from their homes in ways that allow them to publicly maintain their own roles as homemakers, mothers, and wives.[28] Far-right women influencers online embed xenophobic and exclusionary ideas within reactionary nostalgia for a simpler time—with distinctive gendered roles—while calling on other white women to help counteract demographic change by having more white babies.[29] They intersperse personal stories of their own "red pill" awakenings to the dangers of feminism with relatable content about the joys of embracing their "natural" roles as mothers and wives.[30] The seeming contradictions in these frames—as women become "front-stage" promoters of antifeminist content urging other women to celebrate traditional roles as behind-the-scenes homemakers—go unacknowledged.

These influencers gain bigger audiences through alignment with conservative mainstream online subcultures, like the Tradwife movement—which calls on women to embrace traditional gender roles by eschewing paid work outside the home, dedicating their lives to domestic fulfillment through the care of household, submission to husbands, and rearing of children.[31] In Tradwife and adjacent spaces, women are encouraged to reject feminism, embrace "sovereign midwifery," and reject hospital birth in favor of having babies "outside the system" in ways that are often linked to ideas about a purer, traditional, back-to-nature lifestyle that is free from government influence, sometimes with antisemitic dog whistles about global cabals. These ideas sometimes bleed into conspiracies like QAnon as well as support for authoritarian discipline and the exclusion of women from voting rights in favor of a sole, male head-of-household vote.[32]

Tradwives intentionally adopt submissive roles while valorizing white men's roles and "sense of great importance" as the forgers and center of Western civilization—while framing gendered roles as biblical, biological, and natural.[33] This valorization of tradition, heritage, and a romanticized past against a seemingly chaotic and unnatural present made it especially ripe for co-optation by the far right,[34] who have promoted these choices as empowering for women who find modern feminism and the constraints of balancing work and motherhood impossible and who should return to a simpler, more fulfilling life.[35] Shared affinities between the far-right and Tradwife communities for images of a happy, nostalgic embrace of tradition, motherhood, increased birth rates, and concerns about social decline help make the boundaries between extreme and traditional or conservative ideas more porous,[36] as do the shared explicitly heterosexual frame and exclusion of gender-diverse, trans, and same-sex marriages in favor of promotion of "traditional" family values.[37] In this way, the hyperlinked and hashtagged world of social media and online spaces facilitates women's rising engagement in hateful and antidemocratic movements as extremist content spreads easily between mainstream and fringe platforms and channels.

It's no mistake that motherhood features so prominently across these women-led online spaces. Motherhood has always been a powerful way to attract and mobilize women's engagement in activism. It helps "depoliticize" their actions by positioning them as acting on behalf of their children and families.[38] But it is also used to defend women's engagement in violent movements or to mitigate culpability in criminal activities.[39] In several women's January 6 legal defenses, motherhood was used to make women appear more sympathetic by emphasizing their caretaking roles and status as "good" mothers and grandmothers who nurture and are devoted to their husbands and families.[40] Motherhood is also a useful symbolic tool for the far right, evoking tradition and family values and encouraging a rejection of modernity in favor of a utopian past that can be great again. The symbolic value of motherhood even extends to the nation itself. After the September 11 attacks, one of the "most popular pieces of amateur propaganda," as WIRED described it in 2001, depicted "Mommy Liberty," a gun-toting Statue of Liberty holding a child swathed in an American flag.[41]

Motherhood is also explicitly weaponized in racialized ways, especially related to declining white birth rates and fears of a so-called great replacement. A YouTube channel called Motherland, described as a pronatalist, pro-family, and pro-nation place for the far right, offers a forum to discuss conception, pregnancy, childbirth education, and "everything related to trying to become a mom."[42] It's only a few clicks from there to a broad online world that blends pro-natalist, empowered motherhood rhetoric with anti-multiculturalism, white ethnonationalism, and hate frameworks, often providing a "softer face" for extreme ideas.[43] One of the best known examples is a blog run by Ayla Stewart, also known as "Wife With a Purpose." Stewart's original interest in feminist, pagan, raw foodist-vegan spaces evolved into a militant belief in women's obligations as homemakers and mothers, and finally into a "virulent strain of white nationalism."[44] She eventually issued a "white baby challenge" to encourage white women to have at least as many white babies as she had had—six—in order to compensate for the threat to white civilizations supposedly posed by falling birth rates and demographic shifts.[45]

These ideas have always been a part of far-right and white supremacist movements, even in the offline world. A 2017 article in the white supremacist magazine *American Renaissance* described women as providers who tended gardens, helped with the harvest, preserved food, and cultivated "raw talents" in schoolrooms, holding "the home front when our men were called to defend us from invaders."[46] But in the online era, women found entire new audiences for gendered propaganda in ways that broadened the reach of fringe propaganda to millions.

It doesn't help that some of the same messages are shared by mainstream leaders. The white baby challenge, for example, came on the heels of a tweet from then-Iowa Representative Steve King in which he warned: "We can't restore our civilization with somebody else's babies."[47] It's a call with strong echoes of the eugenicist pro-natalist push in the 1920s and 1930s, which called for a "four-norm" birth rate among white, native-born, middle-class Americans.[48] Similar policy proposals are supported today by far-right political parties in Europe, who are working to advance public policies that would lead to increases in white birth rates. France's Marine Le Pen, for example, advocates policies that would encourage "French" women to have more than two children—including by increasing family allowances for families who have "at least one French parent."[49]

In ways even the Tea Party did not anticipate, Sarah Palin's "mama grizzlies" thus became racialized in the years that followed, with good motherhood and traditional gender roles linked to protection both of children and of white civilizations more broadly. These new women far-right online influencers leaned into the same persuasive strategies that were so successful for the Tea Party, urging women to embrace their role as nurturers and homemakers but in explicitly political ways. And they called on men to defend white women against all manner of threats to their purity—and thereby secure the future of white civilization.

It didn't take long for these same strategies to be deployed by a broader range of conspiracy and antigovernment movements, especially when the COVID-19 pandemic pivoted so much of our lives online, where social media and online channels became superhighways to conspiracy content and antigovernment mobilization. There is no better example of this than QAnon—and Ashli Babbitt and millions of women like her were right in the thick of it.

QAnon Moms

Before the pandemic, it's unlikely that anyone would have pegged a woman like Ashli Babbitt—a veteran and small business owner—as a conspiracy theorist. She lacked the stereotypical qualities Americans had come to associate with conspirational thinking: typically a slightly unhinged, wild-haired, usually white male character who spent his time in a basement apartment mapping ridiculous connections on his wall. There are still plenty of tin-foil hat hoax defenders out there. But the pool of conspiracy theorists has grown dramatically, driven in part by suburban yoga moms and the supercharged disinformation sharing of the social media era.

The QAnon conspiracy began when an anonymous 4-chan poster named Q Clearance Patriot, or Q, began leaving cryptic messages for a core group of dedicated decoders who created a kind of scavenger-hunt, puzzle-solving culture aimed at uncovering the "Truth." Its core mythology was a single absurd idea about an orchestrated pedophilic, Satan-worshipping ring run by a cabal of Hollywood and political global elites who practiced human child sacrifice in order to harvest adrenochrome from abused children.[50] That core belief echoed centuries-old antisemitic ideas about blood libel—a false conspiracy about a secret cabal of world-controlling Jews who traffic in children for their blood.

Not everyone who came to believe in QAnon was fully down the rabbit hole of Satan-worshipping child-sex ring conspiracies. QAnon soon broadened to include a "sprawling spiderweb of right-wing internet conspiracy theories" that had both antisemitic and anti-LGBTQ+ components. It developed an entire pro-Trump set of conspiracies through claims that Democrats like Hillary Rodham Clinton were part of the cabal of pedophile elites, who it was said were also plotting against President Trump.[51] QAnon thus became an integrated component of the pro-Trump MAGA world, including through QAnon claims retweeted by President Trump and QAnon supporter and US House of Representatives member Marjorie Taylor Greene. Today, fully 15% of Americans are QAnon believers who think a cabal of Satan-worshipping pedophiles are running the country. The same percentage believes that "patriots may have to resort to violence" to get rid of those pedophiles and set the nation on the right path again. Even more (20%) believe a biblical-style storm is coming that will result in a clean sweep of the evil leaders and a righteous restoration of those who deserve to be in power—namely, President Trump.[52]

Beliefs in a coming "storm" drove thousands to the Capitol on January 6. But it was the child trafficking claims that first mobilized an unusual number of women to violence. QAnon supporters, many of them women, threatened or attacked multiple sites believed to be child trafficking locations (including a Tucson cement plant, the Hoover Dam, and the National Butterfly Center). The violence included several murders, as well as abductions or kidnapping plots of children, often by mothers who believed their children had been taken away by Satan worshippers or pedophiles. QAnon women were violent in other ways, too, including one woman who livestreamed her attempt to "take out" Joe Biden while trying to enter a US Navy hospital ship she believed was being used as a child trafficking site. Some of this violence was specifically fueled by a subgroup of QAnon known as "QAnon moms," who believed they were rescuing children from pedophilia rings, torture, rape, murder, or Satan-worshipping groups at the hands of global elites.[53] Hashtags like #SaveTheChildren helped connect broader groups of parents to these claims and broaden the pool of conspiracy believers.[54]

Hashtags helped share and spread conspiracies that manipulate mothers' fears about their own children and mobilize them to violent action or political engagement. But one reason why the conspiracies made so many inroads to women is because they became amplified through an unexpected connection from the wellness community to QAnon.[55] Alternative health blogs and yoga communities had long been sites where skepticism of traditional medicine and a propensity for alternative models of health and wellness thrived. During the pandemic, that baked-in suspicion of medical expertise created inadvertent gateways to entire rabbit holes of conspiracy theories and disinformation, much of which calls on women to protect children from exploitation or harm. This got worse during the pandemic, when anti-vax communities helped introduce false claims about COVID-19 and vaccines to the wellness and holistic health world. Alongside posts about the power of turmeric to boost immunity against COVID, yoga and alternative health communities quickly found their online worlds inundated with broader disinformation that called on them to "question established truths." In some cases, this turned into what some researchers have dubbed "conspirituality," in which practices like yoga, spirituality, and holistic health intersect with conspiracy theories.[56] Conspirituality and the broader wellness community's culture of themes like enlightenment, self-interrogation, skepticism, and an openness to new awakenings proved to be fertile ground for QAnon in especially gendered ways.

Certain kinds of women's spaces, especially online, thus became a connector to QAnon in ways that fueled and broadened women's receptivity to conspiracy theories and anti-vax propaganda that later bled into antigovernment protest and extremism, especially through intersections with QAnon. Mom lifestyle influencers who embraced the QAnon conspiracy integrated posts about child trafficking into their regular content feeds with home decorating, cooking and childrearing tips, creating a challenge for parenting website editors, who have reported an uptick in conspiracy theory posts.[57] In this way, the QAnon world converted the protective motherhood frame that was ubiquitous in the Vicki Weaver era to a broader narrative calling for the defense of all children. This more public-facing rescue and heroism role was carried through hashtags and hyperlinks to an ever-broader community of women who came to believe they were called upon to defend the nation and its freedoms, and to fight against tyranny, traitors, and anyone who threatens a way of life deemed worth saving. When their President called on them to come to Washington to defend the nation from a stolen election, they were primed to act.

It's easy to understand why calling on women to protect children from unimaginable harm is effective. But during the early days of the COVID-19 pandemic, women mobilized against the government for much more banal reasons. They wanted haircuts.

Waking the "Sleeping Giants"

By early 2020, women were starting to move onto the front lines of right-wing movements. In the early weeks of the COVID-19 pandemic, women were front and center at state capitol protests, expressing anger and frustration with shutdown orders and holding signs with words like "tyranny" and "open up." Social media users quickly berated some of the protesters for their signs. "If you get infected with Coronavirus & you die," one person tweeted alongside a photograph of a Wisconsin woman holding a sign that read "I want a haircut," "I doubt you or anyone else will care what your hair looks like." Another commented: "What are a few million deaths when Karen needs a haircut?"[58] But women were not deterred. In one image circulated by the news media, a North Carolina woman stands with her arms held high, brandishing a neon-colored sign that reads: "You woke a sleeping giant."[59]

The sleeping giants might have awoken, but in the early months of antigovernment, coronavirus protests, women still took a back seat to the heavily armed men who stole the show. Men with long guns swarmed the Michigan Capitol in April 2020 in a protest that later looked like a trial run for the January 6 assault on the US Capitol, and notably was in a state with a woman governor who was later targeted with an antigovernment, misogynistic plot. Men wearing full camouflage militia garb with semiautomatic weapons slung across their chests showed up at other protests, carrying the whiff of violence.[60] Hundreds appeared in the all-black tactical gear of the Boogaloo bois, signaling a call to civil war. The women were there, waving their signs. But it was the armed men who signaled the potential for violence—at least until January 6, 2021, when that dynamic abruptly changed. Women engaged in the Capitol insurrection as highly violent actors, leaders, and organizers of the violence.

More than one hundred women have been arrested in connection with the insurrection so far. Some of the women faced misdemeanors, but others faced felony charges—and around 10% of them are accused of having either engaged in or conspired in violence.[61] Their alleged behavior on January 6 is consistent with what experts have argued for years—namely, that women play a more significant role in far-right extremist movements than is often acknowledged.[62] At the Capitol that day, women were not taking place in violent action as mothers. They were defending, or so they thought, the nation, their party, their President, and their constitution.

The weaponization of motherhood itself never went away—it marches on, alongside a new narrative about the fight against tyranny and the protection of freedom. And motherhood continues to rear its head in a different domain, especially as conspiracy theories about a "great replacement" of white, Western civilization began to ramp up. The reproductive role of white, childbearing women is essential to the production and reproduction of the desired white nation. The surprising implications of this connection became horrifyingly clear in the wake of the loss of women's reproductive rights with the overturning of *Roe v. Wade*, as I discussed in chapter 3.

Conclusion: From Victims to Violent Actors

As the extremist fringe moves more and more into the mainstream, we shouldn't be surprised to see women stepping up and leading the charge. Men have always been urged to mobilize men and join white supremacist movements for the sake of women, often through language about defending and protecting women against "invaders" or "rapists."[63] But white women have never only been passive players in racist and extremist movements.[64] They were at the helm of the fight against school integration in the United States and have long played key roles in the creation and maintenance of various forms of institutional racism.[65]

On the extremist fringe, women still represent a significant minority of violent and nonviolent engagement. And to be clear, women also are often victims of misogyny, harassment, or worse at the hands of men within those movements. Kathleen Blee's research on women in white supremacist movements has described racist skinhead men who refer to women in their group as "oi toys" (a reference to women in the skinhead scene who serve men sexually) and who are proud to dominate their wives or girlfriends.[66] Far-right women influencers and propagandists receive regular threats of rape and violence by extremist group members as well as critics.[67] For the far right, women are almost always viewed through, and valued for, their relationships with others—as daughters, as wives or lovers, and above all as mothers. But as the story of how Vicki Weaver became Ashli Babbitt illustrates, women are useful to the far right in ways that go far beyond their roles as mothers—even as motherhood continues to be a primary mobilizing force. Women are held up as a justification for violence against the government or others deemed a

threat. They help to soften or rebrand the face of violent actions or supremacist ideas. And they have long mobilized others to the movements
by weaponizing good motherhood, the obligation to reproduce white
civilization, and the purported need to protect—and control—white
women's bodies. We underestimate the power of women at our own
peril. They are not merely enablers of far-right extremism but rather are
core to its creation and maintenance in powerful ways.

PART III

Centering Gender

Conclusion

CENTERING GENDER: WHAT CAN WE DO?

Let it be known: I did not fall from grace.

I leapt
to freedom.

—ANSEL ELKINS, "AUTOBIOGRAPHY OF EVE"

From Othering to Centering Gender

"Misogyny doesn't mobilize violent extremism," a funder interjected confidently across the screen of a spring 2024 Zoom call, after I'd raised the issue. "I mean, it's not as if these guys want to wipe women off the face of the earth." Even after so many years of seeing gendered issues get sidelined in discussions of extremist violence, I was caught off guard by his certainty that gender wasn't a factor in the very issues he was seeking to combat. It's not that he is wrong about white supremacist men needing white women—after all, the fantasy of a white ethnostate and the restoration of white, Western civilization that features so heavily in white supremacist propaganda depends on white women's complicit or forced participation in birthing and rearing white children. There could be no ethnostate if women were wiped "off the face of the earth." And yet it's hard for me to wrap my head around the idea that the desire for elimination should be the main criterion by which we gauge gender's relevance for violent extremism.

The erasure of gender as a factor in so many expert assessments about rising political and hate-fueled violence and domestic terrorism is both telling and dangerous.[1] Ignoring gender—whether in our national security framework or in our public awareness—muffles the scope of the problem we face. It leads us to ignore early warning signs of mass violence that often present in intimate partner violence, stalking, rape threats, sexual assault, and attacks on the LGBTQ+ community. It makes it impossible for us to see the ways in which ordinary and everyday forms of sexism and misogyny create fertile ground for more violent beliefs and actions to thrive. And it limits the scope of what we see as vulnerabilities, gateways, or pathways to radicalization and the enactment of violence. Our inability to acknowledge and address this simple connection has led to catastrophic mistakes in how we understand and respond to violent extremism and contributes to what is an utter failure to stem targeted violence—creating missed opportunities to prevent escalations that have ultimately cost thousands of lives.[2]

Centering gender would require us to acknowledge that gendered issues are both a foundational part of radicalization and a primary catalyst in mobilizing to violence. This would force us to consider how other variables often linked to the prevalence of terrorism might actually also be gendered—for example, a sense of economic precariousness "puts masculinity in crisis" in ways that can lead men to see violence as a way of restoring manhood.[3] Similarly, the lack of belonging and desire for a sense of meaning and purpose so often discussed as vulnerabilities for radicalization and recruitment to violent extremism are also highly gendered in a social era in which increasingly isolated boys and young men are experiencing a demonstrated "crisis of connection."[4]

In my efforts to center gender in analyses of violent extremism, I advance three core arguments across the course of this book. First, I show that misogyny, hostile sexism, and prior acts of gender-based violence are demonstrated precursors to, predictors of, and catalysts for support for public, political, and hate-fueled violence. Second, I argue that the surges we are seeing in violent extremism and the parallel growth in online and offline violent misogyny, antifeminism, and hostile sexism ought both to be understood as part of a retrenched defense of traditional patriarchy. And finally, I argue that misogyny and gender-based bigotry in both online and offline forms act as a connective tissue that amplifies and reinforces many kinds of hate. Antifeminism, anti-LGBTQ+ hate, and other forms of gender-based harm fuel and underpin antisemitism, Islamophobia, anti-immigrant conspiracies, and anti-Black racism. In the following sections, I summarize key points for each of these three arguments before turning to the main purpose of this concluding chapter: What, if anything, can we do to reverse these trends? What might work to counter misogyny and gender-based bigotry and reduce the threat of violent extremism?

Misogyny as Predictor and Catalyst

Misogyny is both a predictor of violent extremism and a catalyst that mobilizes it. Prior acts of violence toward women are a known precursor to later acts of mass violence. But misogyny also acts as an incubator that reinforces ideas about entitlement, superiority, and the expected subordination and servitude of others. This deeper normalization of misogyny and hostile sexism is also a predictor of support for public acts of mass violence and terrorism in ways that we have too often failed to acknowledge.

One of my students recently related how her mother had advised her as a preteen to be rude to men who catcalled or bothered her, since they would take advantage of her being polite or kind. But when she later followed that advice, a man pressing her for personal information in a coffeeshop got frustrated and accused her of "stonewalling him." He had to be escorted out of the business when the harassment didn't stop. There has been much public discussion about the heartbreaking "talk" that Black parents have with their children about racism and especially about how their sons should act if they encounter the police.[5] There is less public attention to the parallel conversation parents must have with their daughters: how to stay physically safe from men. And girls and women today must navigate street harassment in real life while dealing with a constant flow of misogyny online. After I gave a talk on this book's chapter "Containment" at Penn State University in early 2024, the first person to approach the podium afterward was an undergraduate who lamented how desensitized she had become to the misogyny and violence against women that crossed her social media feeds all day. Her daily experiences with misogyny and sexism had become so normalized—and so mainstreamed—that she literally had stopped noticing them. That normalization and mainstreaming is a big part of what prevents us from recognizing the breadth and depth of gendered dimensions of violent extremism.

This book connects the ordinary sexism and misogyny so casually embedded in many experiences of daily life with endemic and rising hate crimes, targeted violence and mass shootings, political violence, and domestic terror attacks. The throughlines are infinite: from the sexist chimney sweep to the misogynist mass shooter, from the online harassers of Gamergate to Trump rally chants like "send her back" and "lock her up," from the demonic memes of Nancy Pelosi to the violent attack on her husband Paul in their home. A host of gendered issues work to recruit and radicalize people to violent far-right extremism in ways that are all too rarely discussed as part of the core issues in extremist violence.

Even in cases where misogyny is acknowledged—such as in violent incel attacks—it is rare to see those acts of violence described as "interconnected within an existing continuum of sexual violence and gender equality that are prevalent in society," as a UN report on the sexual violence Hamas perpetrated in Israel on October 7, 2023, notes.[6] Much of what we miss about gender and mass violence in the United States and globally boils down to our inability to see that everyday forms of gendered discrimination and hostile forms of violence exist on the same spectrum. Violence against women—in mass or everyday forms—can't be understood as wholly separate from women's ordinary experiences with catcalling, the insistence that they "smile," and their constant negotiations about safety in big and banal ways: where to sit on public transportation, where to park in parking garages, whether to take the stairwell or the elevator, if it's safe to take the shortcut through the park.

The one area where there is now significant acknowledgment about the gendered dimensions of extremism is the misogynist incel and the male supremacist manosphere, which are the subject of chapter 3. The growing willingness of the United States and global policy community to recognize the problem of misogynist incels is laudable. But the same community still tends to dismiss misogyny and gender-based bigotry, even in its most violent forms, as an individual psychological problem of a single bad actor, rather than an issue rooted in the normalization of misogyny in the mainstream. In the end, it appears that it is easier to acknowledge the most extreme cases of male supremacist violence in its mass shooter and violent incel forms than it is to do the challenging and banal work of understanding and confronting how everyday forms of sexism and misogyny exist on a continuum that enables the mass violence of radicalized actors.

This is not unlike what so many scholars of race have formidably argued about white supremacy—namely, ordinary and everyday racism underpins structural and systemic forms of exclusion, discrimination, and terror, by helping perpetuate ongoing racial discrimination, normalizing white dominance, and mainstreaming racist ideas and their legacy in the treatment of Black people and other racial and ethnic minorities. Ordinary and everyday forms of white supremacy leave an ongoing legacy of disparities in healthcare, policing, school quality and educational attainment, inherited wealth mortgage and loan rates, home appraisal values, life expectancy, and more.[7] White supremacist extremism cannot be meaningfully confronted without also addressing these everyday racist beliefs and practices, as scholars like Ibram X. Kendi have so persuasively argued.[8] My hope is that this book has demonstrated that the same thing is true for ordinary misogyny and sexism.

Violent Extremism and the Entrenched Defense of Patriarchy

The containment, punishment, exploitation, erasure, and enabling that I analyze in this book's empirical cases are not new tactics—they have existed for centuries as part of the silencing and control that is essential to the maintenance of patriarchy. But the scope and pace of these tactics has accelerated dramatically in recent years, revealing a contradiction that might explain part of the blind spots we have on issues related to gender and mass violence. On the one hand, most overt and legal forms of hostile sexism have decreased, opening the doors to more powerful positions for women in economic, political, and social domains and more rights and recognition for LGBTQ+ people. On the other hand, misogyny—understood as the enforcement mechanism used to defend patriarchal norms and expectations—has surged, especially online. This makes understanding sexism and misogyny as two different but related parts of patriarchal systems of domination even more essential.[9] And it also shows that progress in formal rights and recognition does not automatically mean that changes in norms and expectations will follow.

The logic of patriarchy requires a commitment to a fixed gender binary, to heteronormativity, and to the establishment of hierarchies in which men are deemed superior to all subordinated others.[10] Violent misogyny—and its intersectional forms on targeted sexual, ethnic, racial, and religious minorities—are reactions to transgressions of patriarchal expectations, norms, and the erasure of formal laws that support men's domination. As Kate Manne argues, misogyny targets those who "trespass on men's historical turf and threaten to *take something from him.*"[11] Misogyny is a punishment, an enforcement mechanism, and a way of policing, condemning, and subordinating women and LGBTQ+ people.

That policing happens in part because patriarchal norms are so entrenched in mainstream society that rapid changes unsettle the foundational assumptions that help us process and understand what we see and experience every day. Patriarchy is one of many kinds of mental and cultural scaffolding—what cognitive scientists call "schemata"—that we all rely on to make sense of the world.[12] These scaffolds are preexisting mental structures that rely on assumptions, rules, and norms that people gradually acquire starting in childhood and continue to refine across the life course. Navigating our daily lives would be impossible without them, because they allow us to take conscious and unconscious shortcuts as we rapidly receive, process, and interpret bits of often-incomplete information throughout our days and across our lives. Many of the foundational parts of patriarchy—the unquestioned power and status given to men, the rigid gender binary, the fixed idea of marriage as only between one man and one woman—are a part of our mental and cultural scaffolds.

But those foundational parts of patriarchy, and the norms and values associated with it, are changing rapidly. The past decade in the United States has brought legalized same-sex marriage, the introduction of a nonbinary gender category on passports and government surveys, and the steady march of trans visibility. We have seen significant leaps in representation, access, and equity for women and the LGBTQ+ community in key areas of political, corporate, and academic leadership, including the opening of entire domains like military combat, and the normalization of everyday practices like accessibility to gender-neutral bathrooms.[13]

All of this means that the cultural scaffolding of traditional patriarchies is changing in ways that require our entire society to reorient some of its entrenched ways of thinking. And as that starts to happen, we are also seeing virulent backlash from conservatives and far-right actors who insist on a fixed gender binary and seek to maintain other traditional patriarchal norms and expectations. That backlash—delivered through violent harassment and attacks as well as through legislative erasure—should be understood as a response to the disruption to the scaffolding of traditional patriarchy and the perceived transgression of its norms, rules, and hierarchies. As bell hooks argues, patriarchal norms and expectations about manhood create a sense of entitlement to power, attention, and support from others that make some men "feel that their very existence is threatened if these privileges are taken away."[14] The resulting domino effect has borne out in patterns of violence over the past few decades, as hooks maintains. When men's identity, status, and power as financial providers and protectors became less central as women gained equality in the workforce, and as they lost power and supervisory control in the workplace, incidences of private violence in the domestic sphere increased.[15]

There are many different flavors of backlash, depending on the type of entitlement that underpins them. There is the kind of backlash against men's perceived loss of power and status that drove a men's rights activist to target a New Jersey judge's family. There is the backlash against women who don't pay men enough attention, as illuminated by misogynist incels and male supremacist attacks on women who ignore, reject, or refuse men's sexual advances, as we have seen in mass shootings in California and Florida. There is backlash against women who don't put men's needs first, even when those needs are defined as a life without the sexual temptation that women supposedly create, as we saw in the Atlanta spa shootings. There is rage that targets other groups after first incubating in toxic online subcultures that are deeply misogynist, as illustrated by the Uvalde, Texas, elementary school shooter's online rape and kidnapping threats against teen girls. And there is rage that erupts against the closest vulnerable people—men's wives and children—in repeated instances of domestic and intimate partner violence that are precursors to more than half of mass shootings in the United States—as witnessed in repeated attacks, including the Pulse nightclub shooting.

The manosphere—and online spaces more broadly—have radically shaped the ability of this backlash to be embraced by the mainstream, especially as conservative rejection and demonization of gendered social changes became folded into broader hostile anger at progressive movements, "woke" campuses, diversity, equity, and inclusion (DEI) curricula, and more. A vast online ecosystem of misogynistic hate has been growing for over a decade, as I trace in greater depth in chapters 2 and 3, helping to normalize online misogyny and hate through tactics like casual shaming and the use of slurs to coordinated harassment campaigns, rape threats, and death threats.[16] As fringe extreme ideas moved out of subcultural spaces online and into alt-media ecosystems, they were able to build broader, more influential support in mainstream publics. This in turn has helped shift public attitudes away from progressive social changes, resulting in what Julia Ebner describes as the "mass adoption of extreme ideas" which is "characterized by violent escalations of liberal versus illiberal visions of the future." Those escalations are evident in culture wars about library books, in the political violence of January 6, and in extremist violence targeting anyone deemed a threat to the white patriarchal order.[17] This explains what I mean when I argue that far-right extremist and many other forms of mass violence can only be understood within the context of conservative mobilization, mainstream normalization, and liberal silencing of the misogyny and gender-based bigotry that underpins and enables that violence.

The point about white patriarchy and backlash illuminates the third major argument of this book: Misogyny and gender-based bigotry act as a connective tissue that amplifies and reinforces many kinds of hate.

Intersectional Hate: Misogyny as Firestarter and Connective Tissue

Centering gender in our efforts to counter rising hate-fueled and political violence will only succeed if we acknowledge and address the many ways the foundational nature of gender and misogyny intersect with and mutually reinforce white supremacy, Christian supremacy, and Western supremacy, along with some kinds of conspiratorial thinking and antigovernment extremism. Gender and misogyny are part and parcel of radicalization and the mobilization to violence, even when the target of extremists' rage lies elsewhere.

One way this happens is through frames around the need to protect white, Christian women's bodies and purity from the threat of contamination from immigrants, racial and religious minorities, and other purported threats to white women's safety. This is often done through the suggested or implied threat of rape by immigrants or ethnic minorities, in ways that have been widely acknowledged as key to the justification of white supremacist and anti-immigration policies, from segregation laws to border restrictions. The protection of white women has long been a rallying cry for men on the extremist fringe.

White women themselves play a key role in these kinds of mobilization. Even as white women are exploited and abused by men in extremist movements, many of them also work assiduously to support those same men in acts of violence and the spread of hateful ideology, as a robust scholarship from Black feminists and others has consistently demonstrated. This is illustrated by calls from white women for other white women to produce white babies for the future of the white nation. White women are instrumental in mobilizing men to join white supremacist movements (to defend them against "invaders" or "rapists"), but also as individuals who "support, participate in, and promote white supremacy, hate, and racialized violence" themselves.[18]

Another way gendered and racialized exclusions overlap is through conspiracies with multiple scapegoats. Different forms of hate and exclusion are interconnected and mutually reinforcing—and one way that happens is when virulent misogyny links a wide range of offline and online hate. Feminism gets blamed for purportedly stripping away men's opportunities, for example, which easily bleeds into other conspiracies that explain how the deck is stacked against white men. Or a single umbrella conspiracy with multiple protagonists—like the Great Replacement—blames Jews, Muslims, and feminists all at once for supposedly orchestrating a replacement of white civilization through immigration, abortion, the disruption of the gender binary, and abandonment of white women's "natural" roles as mothers and reproducers of the nation. Conspiracies about white genocide and misogyny are not only "kindred spirits," as Chris Wilson argues, but amplify each other through a kind of enhanced victimhood that does "more to radicalize white males than they would separately."[19]

White supremacist goals of establishing ethnostates—and accompanying fantasies of restoration and a phoenix-like rebirth of white civilization—are premised on white women's reproductive capacity and their complicit participation in birthing and rearing white babies. The obsessive focus on white birth rates, demographic change, and conspiracies of "replacement" are most often framed as anti-immigrant, Islamophobic, and antisemitic, but their misogynist and gendered dimensions are just as central. Antifeminism, antisemitism, anti-trans ideas, anti-immigrant conspiracies, and anti-Black racism are mutually reinforcing.

The fact that so many domestic violent extremist attacks have both gendered and racialized dimensions demonstrates that racism and misogyny are inseparable in the minds of many perpetrators, whether through rants about white birth rates in mass shootings targeting Black communities or through hypersexualized tropes about supposed threats from racial, ethnic, and religious minorities. In deep and abiding ways, the scaffolding of patriarchy, misogyny, and male entitlement (to power, to authority, to domestic labor, to women's bodies) underpins the resurgence of white supremacy and other forms of far-right extremism. Different forms of hate rely on similar hierarchies of superiority and inferiority that are co-constituted and inextricable from each other.

This matters for prevention, too. Reducing one set of hierarchies will help with other forms, but it is never enough to address one form of superiority without acknowledging its intersection with other forms of hate. We are lucky to live in an era, as my colleagues and I remind ourselves every day in my research lab, where there is an emerging body of evidence about what works to prevent people from being persuaded by supremacist propaganda and to be more confident about the integrity of the information they encounter.[20] Building resilience to conspiracy theories, propaganda, hoaxes, rumors, gossip, and online scams is a critical part of lifelong digital and media literacy needs. And part of that resilience requires addressing the intersectional, racialized, and gendered dimensions of the hateful and harmful content we encounter in our ordinary lives.

Reclaiming, Resisting, Persisting: Countering Misogyny

How can we counter this "tidal wave of misogyny," in the words of one elementary school teacher?[21] And how can we prevent it from fueling violent extremism? Strategies to counter and prevent rising misogyny and male supremacist violence must be holistic, multilayered, and lifelong. One of the simplest ideas comes from clear evidence that increasing support for women's advancement and for gender equality reduces the likelihood of a range of violent outcomes—including rape and rape threats, intimate and domestic partner violence, and politically motivated attacks targeting women.[22] Support for women's advancement is also one of the strongest predictors of an individual's resilience to extremist radicalization in Islamist terrorism. Survey research in Bosnia and Herzegovina, for example, found that respondents who support the freedom of women to work outside the home and hold political office, among other factors, were among the least likely to support violence.[23]

More research on this relative to far-right and domestic violent extremism is sorely needed to determine whether improving support for women's equality and advancement would also reduce violent extremism outcomes in the domestic arena.

Increasing support for gender equality is intrinsically valuable, of course—not only because it reduces violence. And it is the kind of outcome that will result from many layers of intervention and preventative work, including in collaboration among partners who are already working to combat these issues. This includes programs that work to prevent domestic and intimate partner violence and interrupt patterns of intergenerational violence, anger management programs, and sex therapy programs, especially if they focus on how a desire for sex (as articulated by incels for example) may act as a placeholder for a desire for attention, admiration, and adoration from a partner and a wish for intimate connections and relationships. It also includes a host of programming from men's work communities that help men heal and embrace more holistic identities that reduce disconnection, loneliness, and isolation and allow for greater vulnerability and engagement with caregiving, empathy, nurturing, and connection with others.[24]

Digital and media literacy programming that helps people build skepticism of propaganda and conspiracy theories, critical thinking skills, and a better ability to reject harmful content is essential. Evidence from pre-bunking approaches that equip people with better tools to avoid manipulation is especially promising.[25] So too are civic education and civic participation programs that foster a sense of belonging, community, purpose, and meaning. Programs that model and encourage healthy relationships with people across all genders and backgrounds are critical. And there are plenty of existing interventions in adjacent fields that could be modified—drawing on cult deprogramming, gang dropout work, and salafi-jihadist deradicalization. There is no need to completely reinvent the wheel.

There is no way to interrupt patterns of rising misogyny and gender-based violence, though, if we don't acknowledge their roots in our everyday norms and expectations. Recruitment, radicalization, and mobilization to mass violence in the name of misogynistic or male supremacist ideas starts with ordinary cultural norms and quotidian expressions of patriarchal masculinity and the insistence that it be the sole organizing framework for social relations. Seeing gender beyond a fixed binary and helping understand gender expression as a spectrum is one way to disrupt the foundational gendered nature that underpins so much of the far-right backlash we currently observe. Similarly, rhetoric that scapegoats feminists, calls for a return to traditional patriarchal norms and values, demonizes LGBTQ+ people, or otherwise positions the defense of patriarchy as part of an epic, good-and-evil battle for the moral core of the nation should be called out as dangerous. Misogynistic actions and sexist beliefs act as incubators that increase men's vulnerability to and exposure to violent extremism.[26]

There is plentiful guidance on some aspects of these tasks, such as how to handle ordinary and everyday forms of misogyny and toxic masculinity, including gendered slurs, harassment, catcalling, and other attacks. Women are often advised to ignore it; others argue that women should reclaim slurs like "bitch," the way many in the LGBTQ+ community have embraced the slur "queer" and reclaimed it as a prideful expression.[27] Reclamation, or appropriation, are well-documented phenomena in which in-group members embrace slurs that are used against them as an expression of pride or belonging to the group.[28] When Donald Trump used the phrase *nasty woman* during a 2016 presidential debate with Hillary Clinton, it was immediately reclaimed by supporters who turned it into a badge of honor, complete with merch and fundraising for Planned Parenthood.[29] Women have been encouraged to reclaim the slur "bitch" for decades, at least since Jo Freeman's classic *The Bitch Manifesto* argued that "A woman should be proud to declare she is a Bitch, because Bitch is Beautiful."[30]

Others turn misogyny into political mobilization. In the wake of misogynistic attacks against presidential candidate Hillary Clinton, supporters used the backlash—and the rollback of reproductive rights—to mobilize voters and to recruit a generation of new women candidates to run for office. When the midterm 2022 elections included a hashtag calling on voters to #Repealthe19th, or advocating for "household voting," in which the male "head of household" would presumably dominate, Hillary Clinton tweeted, "It turns out women enjoy having human rights, and we vote."[31] Indeed, young women drove those election results, including the rejection of six states' attempts to ban abortion in law and the approval of three states codifying the right to abortion in law (California, Michigan, Vermont). There was still significant backlash to women asserting themselves in the election, of course—Fox news host Jesse Watters reacted to the strong Democratic preference among single women in the 2022 election by lamenting on air that these "ladies" need to get married and "just settle down," admonishing men to "go put a ring on it," presumably so that their wives would vote Republican.[32] And the backlash against women following the 2024 presidential election in online and offline spaces illustrates just how powerful a force misogyny still is. After I appeared on PBS News Hour in December 2024 to talk about the surge of post-election online misogyny, I received several messages relating what women and girls were experiencing in person, from unwanted grabbing of a woman college student in public with the words "we can do that now," to a middle school girl being told by a boy in the hallway to go put on her handmaid's dress.[33]

In the end, one of the clearest implications of the rise of misogyny, male supremacy, and other forms of gender-based bigotry is that proposed solutions will never work if they fail to address why so many boys and men find sexist and misogynist ideas appealing—despite the counterintuitive fact that men also suffer from the effects of patriarchy. Men have ended up with more power, status, and resources because of sexist beliefs, laws, and policies. But the norms and expectations imposed on boys and men by traditional patriarchies have also left them more isolated, with fewer intimate friendships, than girls and women. And in other ways, men are experiencing real declines. Their college attendance is lower, as is their life expectancy, compared to women. In the end, male supremacy has not been very good for men either. As the political commentator Natalie Wynn puts it, "Maybe the average man is also oppressed by the system that feminists call patriarchy."[34]

What Boys Need: Modeling Healthy Masculinity

"I wish adults would stop being so sanctimonious," a high school student told me in the spring of 2023, when I asked his class what they thought adults could be doing better to help them navigate the misogyny they see online. In a different conversation nearly a year later, a younger group of boys advised one of my college students against any interventions that are "preachy," and lamented that there was no place for boys to discuss the awfulness they see online—including what they described as a relentless stream of racist, misogynistic memes and You-Tube Shorts—with a trusted adult.

What these boys already know is that shaming, judging, or embarrassing youth can drive them further online, where their shame is easily converted to anger directed toward "triggered snowflakes" who haven't yet woken up to the reality of the worldview they've adopted.[35] Countering with facts also doesn't work, because those facts are sometimes seen as part of a supposedly broader shadowy conspiracy against men.[36] Worst of all are approaches teens deem "cringey," which can fuel further backlash and ridicule.[37] One school administrator in the UK warned that there are "lots of videos on TikTok" of kids "making fun of" school assemblies about Andrew Tate. Teachers who "talk down to students," take patronizing positions as adults who know better, or refuse to acknowledge there is anything good about an online influencer can lead students to shut down.[38]

With these cautions in mind, there are important steps parents, teachers, and other adults can take to address rising misogyny among the boys and young men in their lives. The most important step adults can take is to be involved in children's lives and stay aware of how kids spend time online, what they see and experience there, and how the risks of those engagements are evolving. Schools should keep parents and students informed of new threats—like the 764 groups and other sextortion or grooming tactics—as part of their safeguarding role and media literacy coursework.[39] Schools can and should also work to educate parents and students, including through updated health and consent-focused, gender-inclusive sex and relationship curricula, about the impact of ubiquitous violent pornography on teens' and young adults' understandings of sexual consent and pleasure. The impact of violent-porn-as-sex-education is seen in research on high numbers of young people now reporting being choked during sex,[40] but also in the repeated lack of understanding that some men have about what consent and healthy sexual relationships look like. One man on trial for rape, for example, said he thought the victim was crying because his penis was too big, while a 14-year-old accused of rape told a teacher who asked why he didn't stop when the girl was crying that he thought it was normal for girls to cry during sex.[41]

Too few children or teens have places where they can openly share and discuss with trusted, nonjudgmental adults what they see online and how it might be shaping their beliefs, attitudes, behaviors, and relationships. Experts say the best approach combines curiosity, nonjudgment, and messages from mentors who matter to youth.[42] Discussions should include an acknowledgment that online communities have benefits as well as harms, opening the door to discussions about young people's values and whether or not online influencers reflect those values. Youth mentors beyond teachers are especially important. For example, athletic coaches can integrate discussions about healthy masculinity, treating women with respect, and rejecting violence into coaching, as programs like Coaching Boys into Men have shown.[43] Ongoing digital literacy training is also key, such as approaches that work to teach youth about how bad actors may seek to manipulate or groom them for their own profit.[44] Boys and young men need consistent, positive messaging and opportunities to engage with supportive communities that do not include toxic ideologies or scapegoating.[45]

Effective prevention must take seriously the ways we raise boys into men and the messages they receive about masculinity and femininity in that process. We have spent decades celebrating and promoting girls' ability to be anything they want to be, from coders to scientists and astronauts—in ways that challenged and helped break barriers established by traditional sexist ideas about women's roles and capabilities. But we have spent comparatively less time teaching boys how to be feminists themselves or challenging how traditional patriarchal norms have limited boys' abilities to form deep and intimate connections as they grow up.[46] This tradeoff between promoting girls' and women's empowerment and leaving boys out of the conversation—or ill-equipped to challenge the boxes they have found themselves in—isn't an inevitable one, as Shirley Chisholm reminds us, noting that even as women work toward more rights and freedom, men too can "work toward their freedom from the traps of their own stereotypes."[47]

Boys need guidance and support to navigate what they see online, such as abusive and degrading behavior in violent pornography, and learning what it means to be an ally and what a broader range of healthy masculinity looks like as they grow into adults in a culture that promotes and privileges violence, stoicism, dominance, and hardness while rejecting and devaluing softness, vulnerability, sensitivity, and emotions.[48] Boys and men also need positive messaging about manhood itself, especially during a moment when much of the discourse posits men as inherently dangerous, toxic, harmful, and violent. Helping boys navigate the transition to adulthood in ways that offer a sense of meaning, purpose, social wellbeing, and belonging—in contrast to the current trends of isolation and loneliness—is essential. All of this requires acknowledging that violence at the hands of men—whether against intimate partners or terrorist targets—can't be explained with models of individual deviance, mental health, or personality problems alone. The violence I talk about in this book can only be understood in the context of a broader structure of power relations between men and women and a culture that has valorized violence more generally, and especially as a hallmark of "real" manhood.[49]

In the face of rising online misogyny, all young people—especially teenage boys—need early, consistent, and positive engagement with men who embrace connection with others, who engage with empathy and love in caregiving roles, and who are role models for respectful treatment of women. Insisting on rigid, stereotypical ideas about masculinity that link manhood to toughness and the willingness to use violence confines and boxes men into limited roles and ways of relating to others—in ways that contribute to men's lack of intimate friendships, isolation, and mental health challenges. At the same time, outreach to boys and men who are already exposed to rigid ideas about manhood must be done with care and empathy. One suggestion from practitioners is to leverage men's wellness organizations to engage people who spend time in the manosphere in ways that validate and foster connection, while offering alternative ways of manhood and helping divert people toward positive influencers and channels that offer healthier discussions on male friendships and men's health.[50] As bell hooks advocates, instead of insisting that "real men must prove their manhood by idealizing aloneness and disconnection," we need to reshape manhood around connection and connectedness.[51] Recognizing and celebrating more flexible ways of defining manhood—as not only embracing measures like protecting and providing but also connecting with, caring for, and supporting loved ones, including through platonic friendships— would reduce the fertile ground in which extremist ideas can take root and thrive.[52]

The best offense is a good defense that helps youth recognize and reject harmful and hateful online content whenever they encounter it. It's far easier to prevent teens from going down the rabbit hole than it is to pull them back out. But to do so effectively, teachers, parents, and other adults need all the help they can get. When my research lab followed 1,500 parents for a year after they read our parents' and caregivers' guide to online radicalization, we found that three months after our intervention, over 150 of them reported they had created or joined a group of other parents to talk about the harms their children were experiencing online.[53] Even when parents and other adults want to help, they may not know how—and they need help and support as they figure it out.

Parents, teachers, and coaches aren't the only people on the front lines. Community groups, small business owners, mayors' offices and county governments, mental health counselors and adolescent crisis centers can all work to incorporate messages about healthy masculinity, digital citizenship, and online safety into their work with young people. They can also demonstrate allyship and support in the face of skyrocketing anti-LGBTQ+ mobilization. After members of the Proud Boys mooned protesters at a pro-Trump rally in December 2020 while wearing yellow and black kilts made by an LGBTQ+ owned company, the owner publicly denounced the group and declared he would "turn hate into love" by using the proceeds to fund anti-racist work. He donated $1,000 to the NAACP.[54]

What Policymakers Can Do

Parents, teachers, and practitioners shouldn't be left on their own to work out solutions. There is a lot that local, state, national, and international policymakers can do. First and most importantly, policymakers at all levels should center the needs of victims and survivors of gender-based violence, with a commitment to attend to marginalized groups who are too often invisible in these conversations—especially Black, Latina, Native American, and Asian American women. In the wake of violent incidents, the tendency to focus on perpetrators of harm—along with promises of investigations, accountability, and carceral solutions—almost always leaves victims on the margins. Survivors need spaces for healing and restorative commitments to repair physical damage after graffiti or other attacks on homes and storefronts, economic support to address wage losses and medical bills, and an invitation to participate in conversations about prevention and justice.[55]

Local, state, and national leaders—as well as policymakers on the global stage—can amplify the evidence about the role that misogyny and gender-based bigotry plays in mobilizing terrorism and mass violence. This would require acknowledging that the problems of male supremacy and gender-based bigotry are more than just a fringe personality issue among an isolated group of dysfunctional men. Nor is the problem limited to bounded and definable extremist groups. On the contrary: Most men who express misogynistic hate online are unlikely to be part of a formal extremist scene or group.

Third, terrorism and extremism threat assessment protocols should be revised to explicitly include prior acts of gender and sexual violence as a risk factor for radicalization to terrorist action. Other countries have already made tremendous strides on this front. In August 2024, the UK opted to treat extreme misogyny as a form of extremism.[56] A few months earlier, New Zealand's Classification Office released a report confirming that misogyny is a "common thread" in the propaganda of extremists who committed mass murder.[57] In 2023, Canada issued an explicit strategy to better integrate prevention of extremist violence with work on gender-based violence and online misogyny as part of a six-year (2023–29) action plan on Women, Peace and Security.[58]

These governments are responding to the clear evidence from nearly every individual terrorist actor over the past three decades that a range of hostile actions, including sexual harassment, abuse, assault, and exploitation targeting women, children, or LGBTQ+ people, are known precursors of radicalization to extremist violence. More than half of mass shooters previously abused a partner in documented domestic and intimate partner violence. Men with histories of gendered violence "are more prone to endorse and internalize misogynistic and hypermasculine attitudes," which can affect both their exposure to extremist narratives and how susceptible they are to them.[59] At a minimum, centering gender requires considering individuals' histories of perpetrating or supporting violence against women and girls as red flags, risk factors, or warning signs for subsequent targeted violence on a larger scale.[60]

Policymakers can also systematically include gender-based violence and gender training as a foundational aspect in the training and preparation of all government agencies responsible for targeted violence and terrorism, and simultaneously integrate training on male supremacist extremism and the nexus between misogyny and violent extremism into agency work on intimate partner violence, sex trafficking, and other forms of gendered interpersonal violence. Part of this work will require a hard look at internal sexism and patriarchal structures within institutions and workplaces that can impede recognition of the problems and the willingness to address them.[61] Training needs include explicit education for prevention partners as well as law enforcement, prosecutors, and courts on the relationship between online misogyny and violent extremism, and on the potentials for harm from technology-related and AI-generated sexual and gender-based violence and misogyny.[62] Relatedly, attorney generals can work to create enhancements for sex trafficking and related offenses to add a penalty to existing criminal charges. Such enhancements might incentivize law enforcement to consider offenses related to sexual-based violence and the exploitation of women and children alongside racketeering, drug and weapons trafficking, and related cases. However, it is important to note that sex offender laws in the United States have been disproportionately applied against Black men, who are already often positioned as hypersexualized and dangerous.[63] Care must be taken to ensure that enhancements aimed at making sexual exploitation visible within white supremacist scenes do not add to this existing bias.

Authorities at all levels of government—including supranational organizations—should incorporate training and guidance for practitioners on the link between trafficking, violence against women, and terrorism. Terrorism risk assessments should be revised to include human trafficking as a potential risk of terrorism financing. Financial intelligence units should receive specific guidance on this. Law enforcement investigators, prosecutors, and courts should acknowledge and pursue charges related to sexual and gender-based violence and sex trafficking when it occurs alongside drug trafficking, weapons offenses, and other racketeering charges, even if the latter charges are easier to pursue. And victims of trafficking at the hands of extremist and terrorist groups must be acknowledged as victims of terrorism who are entitled to the relevant support, compensation, and therapeutic resources.[64] Finally, the United Nations should continue to work across all relevant terrorism and educational offices toward more significant prevention and countering of gender-based violence within and across terrorist and extremist movements.

Public health policymakers can advocate for support for affirming care environments for LGBTQ+ communities in hospitals and medical facilities and for expanding training and support for practitioners and clinicians to reduce stigma and create a culture of care for gender-diverse patients and for victims of gender- and sexual-based violence. Medical providers who work in sexual health clinics, mental health facilities, primary care clinics, and emergency or urgent care facilities need opportunities and incentives for ongoing training on these issues, including through professional associations.[65]

Social media and technology companies should prioritize misogyny and gender-based bigotry in all its forms as a key issue for trust and safety divisions. TikTok is currently the only social media platform that explicitly names misogyny as a form of hatred, although other platforms, like Reddit, recently updated their hate speech or safety policies to include prohibition of hateful content related to gender, sex, or sexual identity.[66] Some companies have pivoted in the other direction, though. In January 2025, Meta CEO Mark Zuckerberg announced the company was ending its fact-checking program and introduced changes to content moderation that now allow users to say that women are property or LGBTQ+ people are mentally ill.[67] Overall, it is clear that social media companies can do significantly more to address misogyny directly and to reduce harmful content couched in dog whistles, humor, or irony. This requires ongoing training to recognize and remove hateful content that violates policies, but also regularly updating and revising those policies to incorporate new kinds of derogatory language, coded speech, and hateful images that incite violence or otherwise cause harm. It is important to pursue these changes with an eye toward the protection of free speech, however, in order to guard against censorship while still removing content that is illegal, incites violence, or violates company policies. Companies also need to provide clear and easily accessible reporting mechanisms (and appeal processes) to keep users safe.[68]

Finally, policymakers can fund, evaluate, and help distribute evidence-based programs that aim to interrupt and challenge broad and pervasive social norms that support the use of violence against women and children, link it to masculinity, or present violence as an acceptable (or valorized) solution to problems. Reducing and addressing violence against women is a desirable social goal on its own—and it can help prevent and combat violent extremism.[69] Partnerships with schools, sports clubs and teams, faith communities, youth organizations like Campfire programs or Boy and Girl Scouts, neighborhood clubs and other local community groups and organizations are essential to helping implement and expand programs across a wide range of social domains.

Key Takeaways:
How the Mainstream Mobilizes Extremism

Throughout this book, I have argued that part of our failure to address rising domestic violent extremism is embedded in our inability to acknowledge its gendered roots. With few exceptions, discussions of gender are absent, marginalized, or treated as a historical case study in both intelligence analyses and prevention efforts related to terrorism and extremist violence. Aside from occasional references to toxic masculinity or to the growing engagement of women in the far right, there has been little serious attention in the mainstream media or policy worlds attributed to the gendered aspects of extremist mobilization or radicalization. This blind spot has held firm even in the face of the visible rise of groups like the Proud Boys—a men-only, self-defined "Western chauvinist" group that openly espouses misogynist views and engages in street-brawl violence and anti-LGBTQ+ protests.

The most obvious, and least discussed, common trait of violent extremists is their manhood.[70] This doesn't mean that only men are responsible for increasing misogyny or its consequences. On the contrary: Systems of patriarchy are upheld by women as well as men, and the misogyny that acts as the enforcement arm of patriarchies—alongside the supremacist and antigovernment extremisms that are reinforced by it—requires the active engagement and participation of women.

If there was ever any doubt about the scope of the problem, the data from the past few years should make abundantly clear that sexual and gender-based violence is an enormous problem in the United States— including through the exploitation and trafficking of women, girls, and boys. And as repeated cases of real trafficking, violence, and exploitation have shown, some of these abuses are systematically and tactically a part of domestic extremist groups' ideology, financing, and strategies for recruitment, radicalization, and mobilization to violence—in ways that are far too often ignored.

Our inability to see how ordinary and everyday expressions of sexism, gender-based bigotry, and misogyny are intimately intertwined with violent extremism is consequential. This is true for our failure to take seriously mass violence that targets women and the LGBTQ+ community, which has often been dismissed as rooted in the mental health or personality problems of individual violent actors. But it is also true for our understandings of mass violence mobilized by white supremacy, Christian supremacy, and Western supremacy, and in mass shootings of undefined ideology—almost all of which are committed by men with personal histories of violence or violent fantasies against women.

While there has been much discussion about the ways the extreme has gone mainstream (including in the title of one of my previous books), throughout this book I approach the question of rising far right extremism from the opposite perspective, examining how trends in the mainstream create a kind of mental scaffolding that enables greater receptivity to widely circulating propaganda, disinformation, and racist and misogynistic ideas that originate on the fringes. What happens if we approach sex and gender as a primary organizing framework that mobilizes extreme violence? Other scholars have made formidable efforts to do this in ways that I build upon here. I aim to remedy key oversights in current analyses of domestic violent extremism, while elevating existing academic scholarship on rising misogyny and gender-based bigotry for a broader public audience.

The oversights to be corrected are many and varied. They include the way that gendered aspects are nearly always an afterthought in media coverage and scholarly analyses of extremism. There is the near-total omission of gender in any substantial way in the US classification and warning sign systems for domestic violent extremism and mass shootings. And there is the fact that gender is so often relegated to the expertise of a specialized few or, rarely, as a single, add-on chapter or section of a chapter in more general books on extremism. In this regard, my own scholarship is no different. Although issues of gender and misogyny have been central to my work, they haven't been centered in it. This book aims to change that. As Thomas Wolfe wrote in *You Can't Go Home Again*, "I have to see a thing a thousand times before I see it once."[71] The strategies used to enforce, reassert, maintain, and defend patriarchies, as I have detailed throughout this book, are expansive. They include violent attacks and threats aimed at containment and punishment, such as rape, assault, harassment, stalking, trolling, and doxxing. They include exploiting and abusing women and children for financial and strategic ends. And they also include a bevy of everyday tactics like silencing, mansplaining, belittling, demeaning, shaming, sexualizing, gaslighting, and condescending. What these tactics all have in common is their use as punitive strategies meant to enforce patriarchal norms and police anyone who rejects or violates those expectations. They aim to put women and LGBTQ+ people back in their place, or punish them for taking men's place.[72]

These tactics would never succeed if they were only used by men. Nor would they work without so much support from within the mainstream. In this book, I trace five major strategies used by both conservative and extreme right actors that are aimed at reasserting the nation's patriarchal scaffolding: through containment, punishment, exploitation, erasure, and the enabling support of white women. This includes the mainstream embrace of punitive backlash tactics as a protective defense against contamination from gendered social changes, which are framed as a threat to the nation's (and the family's) purity. But it also includes male entitlement to women's bodies, a belief in hierarchies of superiority and inferiority based on sex, the valorization of women's roles as mothers, wives, and caregivers, and sexist beliefs about power and leadership. These gendered understandings—and the patriarchy they seek to maintain—create a kind of mental scaffolding that enables greater receptivity to widely circulating propaganda, disinformation, conspiracy theories, and racist and misogynist ideas that originate on the fringes. Ultimately, I argue that combating the rise in violence we face today requires a much deeper look at the gendered lenses that shape our everyday lives—and an understanding of how those gendered understandings establish cognitive footholds for more violent forms of misogyny and extremism to take root and grow.

In the end, the simplest and most important takeaway from this book is this: The mobilization of violence on the extreme far right is enabled by rising misogyny and hostile sexism in the mainstream. This means that combating the rise in violence we face today is an impossible task if we don't also work to combat the gendered harms in our everyday lives—while simultaneously exposing their intersections with all forms of hate, wherever and whenever we encounter them.

Epilogue

MY "OH! SORRY, MA'AM" ERA

I WAS JOGGING in my DC neighborhood recently when a man cat-called me from behind. As I threw a glance over my shoulder—revealing to him that I am presumably around the age of his mother—he stood up straight and took a step back, raising his hands up with palms facing me, and said with a chagrined face, "Oh! Sorry, ma'am."

Of all the gendered anecdotes I carry around in my pocket, my "oh sorry ma'am" story is met with the most hilarity. It's such an absurd set of contradictions: Should I be annoyed that I was catcalled? Glad to receive an apology and some measure of apparently age-based respect? Or, as one friend noted, ought I to be pleased that from some angles, I meet an objectification standard that attaches sexiness to youth?

This story doesn't just prompt laughter among my friends. It also tends to generate reflection, especially among women in their forties and fifties, of their own experiences noticing that the "quality of the gaze," in one colleague's words, has tangibly shifted. As women age, men's gazes do not linger quite as long, or as appraisingly. The looks feel less threatening. This may be what women mean when they describe the invisibility that comes with age—an easing of attention. Some women describe missing these interactions. But when a male friend asked me what it felt like, the first word that popped into my mind was this: liberating.

The liberation from men's shifting gaze is connected to the answer I always give in response to the common icebreaker question about the best superpower. No question: I would choose invisibility. The power and freedom, the autonomy and liberation that would come from an unthinking run in the dark, a hike in the woods without hypervigilance, a walk through the parking garage without keys threaded through my hand, is unimaginable. It isn't only women who feel this fear, I know. Men are also afraid of other men and their potential violence. But women, as a 2024 viral "man versus bear" phenomenon illustrates (in which women weighed in on whether they would feel safer running into a bear or a strange man in the woods), live with a bigger and more relentless set of fears, founded in their tangible experience.[1] A large number of women in various online videos about the comparison insist that they would pick the bear—for a variety of reasons, including that they know what to expect from a bear and how to survive the encounter, and they know that people would believe them about being attacked by a bear.[2] Those answers are driven by hard life experience. About a third of us, as I recently explained while describing why I would choose the bear, have already been held down or hit by a man.[3] That prior experience guides our hypervigilance, our decision making, and our choice of the bear, who we presume would at the very least not enjoy the pain inflicted, nor blame us for it.

The question of who, exactly, women are afraid of merits both reflection and acknowledgment. I have tried to make it clear—in this book and throughout my life—that there is no place for demonizing men as a group. Change can only come with the full engagement of allies, including the majority of men who abhor and fight just as hard as I do for a world without the interpersonal and mass violence caused by a small minority of their peers. I believe that most men reject and abhor violence against women and others—but I also know that it is impossible to know which kind of man any particular man is, which is why women have little choice but to act as if every man they meet is a potential predator or violent actor. This, I know from conversations with male friends, is a frustrating and unfair predicament to be in as a man.

Of course—of course—it is not all men. But even that acknowledgment is complicated by the fact that the specific phrase #NotAllMen is used in various online discussions to disparage or undermine discussions about violence against women.[4] I would ask men who feel defensive about these issues to pay attention to any number of periodic news stories that regularly illustrate why women sometimes feel like it might be all men—because these episodic revelations show that the number of men who have willingly engaged in horrific abuse of women when given the opportunity is almost unfathomable. As I write, for example, I am reeling from the news of fifty-one men on trial in France after a man drugged his wife and let dozens of men rape her repeatedly, over several years. Police identified at least seventy-two separate men in video footage, and fifty are on trial alongside the husband. The men have offered various defenses, including that they thought it was ok because her husband had given permission.[5] Reading about that trial reminded me of how my high school boyfriend, who was a couple of years older than me, warned me before I left for college that I should never go upstairs at a fraternity party, not even to use the bathroom. Having already lived on a college campus, his advice was specific and sobering: Do not trust anyone at a party, always have a buddy, and always keep my drink with me—guidance I remember passing on to other women across dining hall tables and on the dormitory floor. It's easy to understand, in this context and considering news stories like the French trial, why some women feel the claim "not all men" rings hollow.

There is no obvious end point to the relevance of these questions— especially because sexualized violence and harassment—in catcalling or other forms—is just one part of the story of misogyny and gender-based bigotry. As I write, I am assailed with headline after headline of ongoing attacks on women, especially those in power. Female Secret Service agents were harassed and attacked relentlessly after the assassination attempt on Donald Trump, facing claims that women's biology—height, strength, or other factors—should rule them out from protective detail. President Biden's announcement that he would not seek reelection and would instead support Kamala Harris unleashed massive amounts of misogynistic and racist vitriol, including attacks on Harris's supposed "childless" status (she is a stepparent of two children) and broader claims by Republican vice presidential candidate J. D. Vance that the Democrats are run by childless cat ladies who are weakening family values.[6] The attacks on Harris remained relentless throughout the election season, and after the election morphed into a broader range of misogynistic attacks referring to women as "bitches and babymakers" or "property" who had been put back in their place and taught their lesson for trying to vote based on their bodily autonomy.

The tension between recognizing real progress and responding to genuine backlash is also generational in important ways. While I was writing this book, my women friends often reflected on how their experiences differed from their mothers' or their daughters' lives in ways that were often complicated emotionally. They explained that they had sometimes experienced a brushing aside of sexism and misogyny from older generations of women—who may have seen overt, explicit, and hostile forms of sexism and misogyny as the price of entering the workforce or of banal life activities like walking down the street. In my own experience, older women have sometimes expressed that the challenges younger women face today are less significant than those struggles—or have occasionally dismissed and justified ongoing discrimination and harassment, arguing that everyone had to go through it or that it is a rite of passage. On the other hand, I have also heard plenty of concern from older women about how younger generations of women and LGBTQ+ people have sometimes overlooked or dismissed the experiences of older generations as irrelevant in the modern, digital landscape of communication where they spend time. These tensions are natural and noteworthy but are also not inevitable, and ultimately distract us, I would argue, from a shared project of change.

As I now start to apparently age out of the kinds of everyday sexualized experiences that had, for so long, been such a normalized part of my ordinary life, my own laughter at the "oh sorry ma'am" moment is matched by a sense of frustration and sadness. Is it any better for a younger generation than it was for me? I'm left with a strong feeling that it is not. That man on the street apologized because of my age. But he was not apologizing because he sees something fundamentally wrong with catcalling at all.

I relate this story as part of a call to action for women like me, who feel the quality of the gaze shifting. That invisibility is its own kind of superpower—and brings its own set of obligations. Silence, as so many scholars have previously articulated, is its own form of violence, and is a part of the domination of others.[7] Women enable, support, justify, and defend patriarchal power and violence in many ways. We justify our own inequalities and burdens because we have sometimes signed up for it, whether on a literal committee or classroom parent list or in a marriage. We bargain with the tradeoffs, and sometimes forget that there might be a different way forward—one that must start with speaking and stepping up for ourselves and for others. We also fail, again and again, to invite men into this conversation and ask for their partnership in these efforts.

I have also failed to do this, in varied ways throughout my life and career—and perhaps most notably in this very epilogue, whose first draft didn't include a single word about what men could do. A reviewer rightfully called me to task on this, pointing out that this book would never make a difference if it were only a call to women. She was right. It must also be a call to men to recognize and acknowledge the patterns and the problems, to step up and speak up, to raise their children differently, and to commit to change. There are so many ways that men can catalyze that change, in both ordinary and extraordinary ways, from engaging with fuller awareness about unequal service burdens in their workplaces and homes, to speaking up when other men engage in misogynistic behaviors or gender policing. Men can pay attention to the advantages that have benefited them and try to rebalance. One of my colleagues, for example, regularly shares social media posts with lists of women scholars that journalists should contact instead of going to the same few (male) sources. But most importantly, men can model, teach, and mentor boys and other men—on their sports teams, in their youth groups, in their classrooms, and in their households—toward a way of being a man that embraces a fuller set of emotional options and ways of caring for others. Men can model how to engage with girls, women, and the LGBTQ+ community differently, to commit to being an ally, and to know how harmful online content can shape their expectations about relationships, consent, and pleasure.

There are endless other examples of what each one of us can do to challenge and change the gendered systems that constrain us. My hope is that this book, unflinching and difficult though it may be to read, will generate conversations, brainstorming, and new ways of addressing the contradictions and the possibilities for change. Writing it took more from me than anything else I've done, in ways both personal and painful. Now that it is out there, my sincerest wish is that it makes a difference.

RESOURCES FOR PARENTS, EDUCATORS, AND OTHER CAREGIVERS

THE FOLLOWING is an adapted excerpt from "Not Just a Joke: Understanding and Preventing Gender- and Sexuality-Based Bigotry," a community guide created by the Southern Poverty Law Center (SPLC) and the Polarization & Extremism Research & Innovation Lab (PERIL). The full guide is available at www.splcenter.org/peril and is intended to be a resource for the range of caregivers who surround and support young people—parents and relatives, teachers and educators, counselors and therapists, coaches and youth mentors, and more. The brief excerpt below and the resource list offer tangible guidance for readers seeking additional support for survivors and strategies to address misogyny, gender-based bigotry, or the risk of interpersonal or mass violence.

Strategies for Prevention and Resilience-Building

Just as there's no one pathway to radicalization, there is also no single method or tactic to build young people's resilience to manipulation. The most promising approaches are rooted in whole-community strategies that secure young people's overall well-being, build social engagement and inclusion, and work to counter harmful narratives and stereotypes. Below are some strategies for various caregivers—parents, educators, counselors, coaches, youth mentors, and others.

Start early. Engage young people early and often, in age-appropriate ways, about the historical foundations of contemporary discrimination and oppression. These conversations will help young people understand their own experiences and will help build empathy for those with differing lived experiences and identities.

Discuss internet safety. Young people should know not to share their personal information online, including their full name, address, phone number, social security number, and school location. They should also know that photos can live online for a long time and understand that images they share with others may end up in the public domain. Help young people build a regular practice of changing passwords every six months, setting social media accounts to private, and checking with trusted adults before they open email attachments. Beginning this dialogue when young people first start using the internet will make it easier to address problems if they arise later.

Harness the positive power of the internet. Social media is a foundational aspect of young people's lives. That time spent online isn't all bad. Online platforms can create spaces for marginalized youth to feel more comfortable exploring and expressing themselves. Have conversations with young people about what they like and dislike about social media and how it might be used for good. Help young people understand and harness positive internet usage by helping them explore online platforms and communities that engage in healthy community building.

Be a role model and take it seriously. Speak up and stand up when you see or hear harmful beliefs, attitudes, and behaviors. Since male supremacist and anti-LGBTQ bigotry often show up as "edgy humor," these harms are regularly dismissed with phrases like "boys will be boys," "it's just locker room talk," or accusing the targeted individual of being too sensitive. It's important to counter these norms by taking every incident seriously and responding to the impacted individual's needs swiftly.

Don't ignore problematic statements or behavior. Parents, caregivers, and educators may feel caught off guard and be uncertain about the right response when a young person says something harmful or discriminatory. But silence is often interpreted as indifference or even acceptance. Be careful to confront all problematic statements and behavior without ridicule or shame, separating the young person's behavior from their identity. Shame can drive youth further into online communities that convert hurt feelings into a sense of betrayal or anger.

Discuss peer to peer support. Similarly aged peers have the advantage of comparable life experiences and conditions, shared cultural knowledge, and strong emotional ties. These relationships can be some of the most effective channels for challenging harmful beliefs. When peers become aware of changing behaviors, language, and beliefs of their contemporaries, they can also alert trusted adults to the young person's need for support. It's important that young people know who they can go to when a peer has become vulnerable to harmful beliefs and rhetoric.

Promote inclusive sex education. Preventing misogynist, male supremacist, and anti-LGBTQ beliefs and actions begins with developing an understanding of and respect for all people's bodily autonomy, gender identity, and sexual orientation. Comprehensive, consent-centered, gender-expansive sexual health education is foundational to instilling young people with this respect from a young age—to help fill knowledge gaps that male supremacist and anti-LGBTQ extremists seek to exploit and manipulate.

Teach about consent versus coercion. Conversations about active consent can begin at an early age by helping young people set the boundaries they prefer with hugs, handshakes, high-fives, and other forms of contact. In age-appropriate ways, pleasure and sexual media literacy can be discussed to help prevent dating and sexual violence and to help young people stay resilient to the negative impacts of violent pornography. Young people should also discuss different forms of coercive and violent relationships that limit access to reproductive healthcare, undermine bodily autonomy, and have negative mental health outcomes for the individual being coerced.

Affirm young people's identities. It's imperative that young people's identities are affirmed and respected. Affirmative measures include asking for and respecting a young person's pronouns, honoring a person's chosen name, and helping young people research and access the resources and support they may need to understand and make decisions for their own bodies, lives, and wellbeing.

Support affinity groups. Clubs such as Gay-Straight Alliances improve student health and wellbeing and protect students from harassment by offering a safe place for LGBTQ youth to connect, share experiences, and build friendships. In communities where inclusive clubs and policies may be difficult to develop, affinity groups dedicated to specific hobbies, sports, or other topics can help young people build community and be a conduit for difficult conversations.

Reach out. If a young person seems isolated or begins to socially disengage, help them connect with a broader network of trusted adults. A continuum of care with educators, counselors, coaches, mentors, and others can alleviate stress within the home and offer young people a variety of safe spaces to have tough conversations.

Stay informed. Keep up with events in your community and stay educated on issues related to extremism. Information-sharing with other community members and practitioners can deepen supportive networks and foster conversations about community wellbeing. Discuss local and national news events with young people in age-appropriate ways. Facilitating informed conversations grounded in facts will help young people develop a sense of agency while filling knowledge gaps that can be exploited by extremists.

Advocate. In coalition with other parents, caregivers, and community members, advocate for school, sports league, after school program, local, and state policies that will ensure the inclusion and wellbeing of all young people. Such advocacy could include working to eradicate dress codes that sexualize female students, pushing for policies that respect people's pronouns, and making sure sports teams are gender-inclusive. The voices, perspectives, and leadership of parents and caregivers of diverse racial and cultural identities, as well as those of diverse gender identities and sexual orientations, should be centered in these conversations and movements.

Uncover the source. Ask the young person open-ended, exploratory questions to help understand where harmful ideas and narratives might be coming from. It is impossible to prevent young people from encountering hate-fueled rhetoric on the internet, but uncovering the source of their words and actions will help trusted adults begin developing a response and prevention plan. Questions like, "What draws you to this kind of stuff?" and "What do you like about this person?" can help get the conversation started.

Be intentional. The cyclical nature of media coverage of traumatic community harms can increase a young person's mental distress, especially when they share a social identity with the targeted individual or community. Stay mindful of the amount of trauma-related media coverage young people are consuming and ensure that exposure to such coverage is accompanied with time to reflect, discuss, and ask questions.

Develop clear, consistent reporting channels. To ensure young people have access to the support they need after experiencing a biased incident, schools should allow for various methods and platforms for reporting an incident. This could include writing a note and slipping it under a trusted teacher's door, using an online submission platform, or providing office hours with school counselors before or after the school day. Reporting channels among school staff and administrators should also be clear and consistent so incident response can be swift and transparent, and school administrators can identify patterns of harassment, bullying, and harm.

Where to Get Help: A US-based Resource List

Online and Social Media Safety

Internet Safety Tips: www.nationalcac.org/internet-safety-tips/
6 Ways to Model Responsible Social Media Use to Your Kids:
   https://www.psychologytoday.com/us/blog/mental-wealth
   /202305/6-ways-to-model-responsible-social-media-use-to
   -your-kids
Media, Digital, and News Literacy Skills:
   www.learningforjustice.org/frameworks/digital-literacy
   https://newslit.org/
   https://www.learningforjustice.org/magazine/fall-2023
      /building-resilience-against-manipulative-disinformation
The Trevor Project's Online Safety for LGBTQ+ Young People:
   https://www.thetrevorproject.org/resources/guide/online
   -safety-for-lgbtq-young-people/

Hotlines and Online Chat Support for Sexual Assault and Gender-Based Violence

National Sexual Assault Hotline: https://rainn.org/resources
National Domestic Violence Hotline: https://www.thehotline.org/
National Human Trafficking Hotline: https://polarisproject.org/
National Helpline for Male Survivors: https://supportgroup.1in6
.org/
Online National Street Harassment Hotline: https://hotline.rainn
.org/ssh-en
National Sexual Violence Resource Center: https://www.nsvrc.org
/organizations
Supporting Survivors with Intellectual/Developmental Disabilities
(IDD): https://pcar.org/sites/default/files/resource-pdfs/tab
_2019_supporting_survivors_with_idd_508.pdf

Consent, Sexual Health, and Sexuality

Advocates for Youth's Rights, Respect, Responsibility: https:/
/www.3rs.org/3rs-curric-search/
Inclusive Consent and Sexual Health Curriculum:
https://safebae.org/360-schools/consent-curriculum/
https://teachingsexualhealth.ca/teachers/sexual-health
-education/information-by-topic/consent/
https://siecus.org/contraceptive-coercion-access-and-sex
-education/
https://www.glsen.org/sexed
Gender and Sexuality Development: https://www.aacap.org
/AACAP/Member_Resources/SOGIIC/Gender_Sexuality
_Development.aspx
Transgender Map: https://www.transgendermap.com/
Gay Straight Alliance Network: https://gsanetwork.org/
Gay-Straight Alliances: Creating Safer Schools for LGBT Students
and Their Allies, GLSEN: https://www.glsen.org/sites/default
/files/2020-04/Gay-Straight%20Alliances_0.pdf

Guidance on Talking to Kids about Online and Offline Harms

Coaching Boys into Men: https://coachescorner.org/

How to talk to your kids about misogyny in school: https://pursuit
.unimelb.edu.au/articles/q-amp-a-how-to-talk-to-your-kids
-about-misogyny-in-school#:~:text=You%20might%20dis-
cuss%20the%20intersectionality,genders%20with%20re-
spect%20and%20dignity

Talking with kids about pornography and violence, Living Earth
Sex Ed: https://www.livingearthsexed.com/talking-with-kids
-about-pornography-workbook

The Good Men Project: https://goodmenproject.com/

"My Child Is Sharing Conspiracy Theories and Racist Memes.
What Do I Say?," Western States Center: https://
westernstatescenter.medium.com/my-child-is-sharing
-conspiracy-theories-and-racist-memes-what-do-i-say
-ea1c8916d064

Anti-Bullying, Speaking Up, and Standing Up

Responding to Everyday Bigotry: Speak Up!, Learning for Justice:
https://www.learningforjustice.org/sites/default/files/2021-05
/Speak-Up-2021.pdf

The Trevor Project, How to Signal You Are an Ally in a Hostile
Environment: https://www.thetrevorproject.org/resources
/guide/how-to-signal-you-are-an-ally-in-hostile-environment/

Bullying Bystanders Become Upstanders, Stomp Out Bullying:
https://www.stompoutbullying.org/bullying-bystanders
-become-upstanders

Bystander Intervention: Engaging Masculine-Identifying Folks as
Allies: https://righttobe.org/trainings/bystander-intervention
-engaging-masculine-identifying-folks-as-allies/

NOTES

Preface

1. See introduction to Simone de Beauvoir, *The Second Sex* (New York: Random House, 2011[1949]).
2. "Snatch and grab, man," a militia member told an FBI informant in July 2020. "Grab the fuckin' governor. Just grab the bitch. Because at that point, we do that, dude—it's over." Gabbatt, "How the Domestic Terror Plot."
3. Sexton, *The Man They Wanted Me to Be*, p. 220.
4. Chu, *When Boys Become Boys*, p. 174.
5. Guerrero, "Why Are Men So Lonely?"
6. Luba Kassova, "The Lethal Price of Misogyny in Security and Defense," *New Lines Magazine*, August 6, 2024, https://newlinesmag.com/argument/the-lethal-price-of-misogyny-in-security-and-defense/.
7. See reporting at PBS Newshour, "Researchers Report Stunning Surge of Misogyny After the Election." December 10, 2024. Researchers report stunning surge of misogyny after the election | PBS News. The 4600% increase is reported in Frances-Wright and Ayad, "Your body, my choice."
8. "Global Terrorism Index 2024," Institute for Economics & Peace, February 2024, https://www.visionofhumanity.org/wp-content/uploads/2024/02/GTI-2024-web-290224.pdf.
9. As articulated by McCarthy and Taylor, "Misogyny," p. 467.

Acknowledgments

1. Onuoha, "Book Review."

Introduction

1. Other women in professional settings have openly talked about avoiding elevators for this very reason. See, e.g., Ruiz, "Senator Used to 'Avoid Elevators.'"
2. Andrews, "These 10 Stories."
3. Bates, "Being a Woman Is Scary."
4. Bates, "Being a Woman Is Scary."
5. The Associated Press, "Teenager Sentenced to 25 Years"; Bosman, "A College Student."
6. See D'Angelo, "California Man"; List, "14-Year Old Shot His Teen Girlfriend."
7. 4,970 women were victims of murder and nonnegligent manslaughter in 2021, and 34% of them (1,690) were killed by an intimate partner. That adds up to 4.63 women dying every day in 2021 at the hands of a spouse or partner. Smith, "Female Murder Victims."
8. The Associated Press, "Police Investigated Michael Haight."

9. Engel, "Being Too Nice."

10. Chemaly, "Street Harassment"; also see McEwen, "#YesAllWomen."

11. Andrighetto, et al., "Lonely Hearts and Angry Minds."

12. Jensen, et al., "Profiles."

13. 93.7% of sexual abuse offenders in the United States are men, according to 2021 data from the US Sentencing Commission, available at https://www.ussc.gov/sites/default/files/pdf /research-and-publications/quick-facts/Sexual_Abuse_FY21.pdf. 97.7% of US mass shooting perpetrators from 1966 to 2019 were male, according to National Institute of Justice data, available at https://nij.ojp.gov/topics/articles/public-mass-shootings-database-amasses-details-half -century-us-mass-shootings. See reporting by Treisman, "The Wisconsin Shooting Suspect Is Female."

14. Native American and Alaska Native Women are nearly four times more likely, and Black women three times more likely, to be shot fatally by an intimate partner, compared to white women. For Black women aged 18–34 years old, this jumps to five times more likely to be shot and killed by an intimate partner, compared to white women of the same age. Similar or worse data are true for other ethnic groups. A third of Latinas have been victims of intimate partner violence, and over 40% of Latina homicides are committed by an intimate partner. Asian American and Pacific Islander women experience the highest proportion of firearm homicides (58%) by intimate partners. Everytown For Gun Safety, "Guns and Violence Against Women."

15. See "Domestic Violence Statistics," National Coalition Against Domestic Violence (NCADV), https://ncadv.org/STATISTICS.

16. Of the 263 homicides of transgender or gender-diverse people that took place between 2017 and 2023, nearly half targeted Black trans women. See Everytown for Gun Safety, "New Everytown Data on Transgender Homicides Reveals Concentration in the South," February 13, 2024. https:// www.everytown.org/press/new-everytown-data-on-transgender-homicides-reveals-concen tration-in-the-south/#:~:text=This%20violence%20is%20not%20evenly,under%20the%20 age%20of%2030; also see "Transgender People Over Four Times More Likely Than Cisgender People to Be Victims of Violent Crime," UCLA Williams Institute, March 23, 2021, https:// williamsinstitute.law.ucla.edu/press/ncvs-trans-press-release/; Emily Ledingham, Graham W. Wright, and Monika Mitra, "Sexual Violence Against Women with Disabilities: Experiences with Force and Lifetime Risk," *American Journal of Preventive Medicine* 62, no. 6 (2022): 895–902; https://doi.org/10.1016/j.amepre.2021.12.015. The term cisgender, sometimes shortened to cis, is a term for a person whose gender identity is aligned with the sex they were assigned at birth. See full definition at www.merriam-webster.com/dictionary/cisgender. The term heterosexual is sometimes shortened to het or hetero, including in this book.

17. As described in Franklin, "Inside the Mind of People Who Hate Gays," and originally excerpted from "Unassuming Motivations: Contextualizing the Narratives of Antigay Assailants," in Gregory M. Herek, ed., *Stigma and Sexual Orientation: Understanding Prejudice Against Lesbians, Gay Men, and Bisexuals* (Thousand Oaks, CA: Sage, 1998), pp. 1–20.

18. There are differing opinions on how misogyny should be defined, but in this book, I follow Manne's definition. For a critique of this approach, see Wrisley, "Feminist Theory."

19. Everytown for Gun Safety, "Guns and Violence Against Women."

20. Everytown for Gun Safety, "Guns and Violence Against Women"; also see Geller, et al., "The Role of Domestic Violence."

21. As reported in Dobash and Dobash, "Who Died?," various studies report collateral killing rates ranging from 30%—"about half" of the victims in intimate partner and domestic violence disputes.

22. Bosman, et al., "A Common Trait."

23. Marganski, "Making a Murderer."

24. The man who killed 32 people at Virginia Tech in 2007 had two prior reports of stalking against women students. See Montagne and Abramson, "Cho Was Accused of Stalking in 2005." The 2016 terrorist who killed 49 people and injured 53 others in the Florida Pulse nightclub shooting, which targeted members of the LGBTQ+ and Latinx community, had a history of domestic violence against his wife. The killer of 17 students and staff at a Parkland, Florida high school in 2018 had previously stalked and harassed an ex-girlfriend and had praised the California sorority attacker in an online post. See Srinivasan, *The Right to Sex*, p. 111. The man who attacked a Maryland newsroom in 2018 had previously harassed a former high school classmate who ignored his advances.

25. Miller-Idriss, "America's Epidemic of Hate."

26. Miller, et al., "2 Men Charged." The prior posts were reported by Williams and Annese, "Co-conspirator."

27. For a longer discussion, see Lawrence, et al., "Antisemitism and Misogyny."

28. Dale, et al., "'Men's Rights' Lawyer"; also see Reyes, "A Latina Trailblazer."

29. In 2019, a terrorist at a Poway, California, synagogue killed one and injured three others while blaming Jews for promoting feminism. A few months later, a terrorist targeted a synagogue on Yom Kippur in Halle, Germany, killing two people, having made an (English-language) video that blamed feminism and falling birth rates in the West as the source of problematic immigration (alongside Jews, who he viewed as the root of both problems). See Olson, "Antifeminismus." In February 2020, a shooter who killed nine people in a 2019 racist and xenophobic attack in Hanau, Germany, left behind a manifesto filled with misogynist ideas, including a sense of sexual entitlement and frustration with women who didn't provide it. See Jasser, et al., "Male Supremacism." The 2022 white supremacist shooter in the Buffalo grocery store that took the lives of 11 mostly Black victims referenced declining white birth rates in his manifesto. The man who killed nine worshippers at a historic Black Charleston church stated during the massacre, "I have to do this because y'all are raping our women." See Srinivasan, *The Right to Sex*, pp. 111–119.

30. Winton, et al., "Not Invited to the Dance."

31. In 2018, five women were injured and two killed in a yoga class by a 40-year-old man who was frustrated by women's rejections—after decades of reports, job firings, evictions, and a military dismissal for harassment and stalking of women. Ten people died that same year in Toronto when a 29-year-old man mowed them down with a van, motivated by hatred of women cultivated in an online network of misogynist incels (involuntary celibates). He was directly inspired by an earlier misogynist incel attack that killed six and injured fourteen others in California, when a 22-year-old gunman attacked a sorority house because he believed the students should be punished for "looking down" on him when he made sexual advances. Other documented incel attacks took the lives of ten people at an Oregon community college in 2015, two high school students in New Mexico in 2017, and five people in Plymouth, England in 2022. As I write, details are emerging about the suspect in a vicious 2022 murder of four college students in Idaho, who had repeatedly messaged one of the victims on Instagram, sending message after message even though she ignored them, and who was investigated by his university for behavior that made some women students feel uncomfortable. See The Associated Press, "Idaho Murder Suspect"; Baker and Bogel-Burroughs, "University."

32. Pascoe and Hollander, "Good Guys Don't Rape"; Connell, *Masculinities*.

33. For a heart-wrenching account of the ubiquity of violence in boys' lives, see Dubus, *Townie*.

34. For a good overview of recent mainstream discussions, see Katz, "Explaining Men."

35. Barker, et al., "State of American Men 2023." Also see Guerrero, "Why Are Men So Lonely?"

36. US Office of the Surgeon General, "Our Epidemic of Loneliness and Isolation."

37. *Neuroscience News,* "Teen Friends Shape Long-Term Wellbeing."

38. See Greene, *The Little #MeToo Book for Men,* especially chap. 5, "The Man Box."

39. Schilt and Westbrook, "Doing Gender," p. 460.

40. Mittleman, "Homophobic Bullying," p. 10.

41. For a historical analysis of American constructions of manhood and its intersections with violence, see Bederman, *Manliness and Civilization.*

42. See Piazza and O'Rourke, "Hostile Sexism." Also see Kalmoe and Mason, *Radical American Partisanship;* Johnston and True, "Misogyny and Violent Extremism"; and Rottweiler, et al., "A Common Psychology of Male Violence?"; Díaz and Valji, "Symbiosis."

43. Johnston and True, "Misogyny and Violent Extremism"; also see Hudson and Hodgson, "Sex and Terror."

44. See, e.g., Jankowicz, "How Disinformation Became a New Threat to Women."

45. Barker and Jurasz, "Online Misogyny."

46. See Johnston and True, "Misogyny and Violent Extremism," p. 4.

47. Bardall et al., "How Is Political Violence Gendered?"

48. hooks, *The Will to Change,* 43.

49. Solnit, *Men Explain Things to Me.*

50. Federal Bureau of Investigation, "A Study of Pre-Attack Behaviors." As cited in Timmons, "Here's the FBI's Warning Signs."

51. See an elaboration of this point by Alex DiBranco, "On the Anniversary of the Isla Vista Attack," Dangerousspeech.org, May 22, 2024, https://dangerousspeech.org/on-the-anniversary-of-the-isla-vista-attack/

52. See the 2023 Strategic Intelligence Assessment on Domestic Terrorism issued by the FBI and the US Department of Homeland Security (DHS) at https://www.dhs.gov/sites/default/files/2023-07/23_0724_opa_strategic-intelligence-assessment-data-domestic-terrorism.pdf; also see "Domestic Violent Extremism Poses Heightened Threat in 2021," Office of the Director of National Intelligence, March 1, 2021, https://www.dni.gov/files/ODNI/documents/assessments/UnclassSummaryofDVEAssessment-17MAR21.pdf

53. Hwang, "Examining Extremism."

54. There is progress in other countries, such as Canada, where the Canadian Security Intelligence Service named gender-driven violence as a form of ideologically motivated violent extremism starting in 2019. See discussion in Hunter and Jouenne, "All Women Belong in the Kitchen," p. 77.

55. I am indebted to Jane Palmer for this point.

56. Scrinzi, *The Racialization of Sexism.*

57. Bederman, *Manliness and Civilization.*

58. See, for example, "Shooter in Allen, Texas, Embraced Antisemitism, Misogyny and White Supremacy." Anti-Defamation League, May 8, 2023, https://www.adl.org/resources/blog/shooter-allen-texas-embraced-antisemitism-misogyny-and-white-supremacy; Silvia Foster-Frau, "Texas Mall Shooter's 'Neo-Nazi Ideation' Shocks Latino Community," *The Washington Post,* May 12, 2023, available at: https://www.washingtonpost.com/nation/2023/05/12/mauricio-garcia-latino-racism/.

59. Hamzah Firdaus, "Singaporean Teen Who Identified as White Supremacist Placed Under ISA Restrictions for Far-Right Extremism," Channel News Asia, January 24, 2024, https://www.channelnewsasia.com/singapore/singaporean-teen-16-year-old-isa-restriction-order-radicalised-far-right-extremist-ideology-white-supremacist-4069791.

60. For a concise discussion, see Tanya Hernández's analysis in "The Proud Boys' Latino Connection, Explained," *Fordham Law News,* June 13, 2022.

61. Hosang and Lowndes, *Producers, Parasites, Patriots*, p. 104.

62. For recent threat assessments and trends, see the "Strategic Intelligence Assessment and Data on Domestic Terrorism"; "U.S. Crisis Monitor," ACLED, last modified August 2024, https://acleddata.com/us-crisis-monitor/; and "Profiles of Individual Radicalization in the United States (PIRUS)," START, accessed September 11, 2024, https://www.start.umd.edu/data -tools/profiles-individual-radicalization-united-states-pirus.

63. For media coverage citing recent statistics, see for example N'Dea Yancey-Bragg, "Hate Crimes Reached Record Levels in 2023. Why 'A Perfect Storm' Could Push Them Higher," *USA Today*, January 5, 2023, https://www.usatoday.com/story/news/nation/2024/01/05/hate -crimes-hit-record-levels-in-2023-why-2024-could-be-even-worse/72118808007/; Toni Mo- rales Pinales, "How Reports of Hate Crimes in the US Were Already at Record Highs, in 4 Charts," CNN.com, December 11, 2023, https://www.cnn.com/2023/10/29/us/hate-crimes -antisemitism-anti-muslim-dg/index.html; Molly Ormsby, "Hate Crimes Reach Record High in New York," NBC5, August 29, 2024, https://www.mynbc5.com/article/hate-crimes-reach -record-high-new-york/62007721.

64. See the July 2024 press release on threats and harassment from the Bridging Divides Initiative, Princeton University, available at: "Threats and Harassment Against Local Officials Spiked in July, New Data Shows," Bridging Divides Initiative, July 2024, https://bridgingdivides .princeton.edu/updates/2024/threats-and-harassment-against-local-officials-spiked-july-new -data-shows.

65. See the Institute for Economics & Peace, "Global Terrorism Index 2024."

66. I am indebted to the excellent analysis of my research assistant Sydney Worrell for this section on trends in online misogyny.

67. US Secret Service National Threat Assessment Center (NTAC), "Hot Yoga Tallahasee."

68. Jacqueline Ryan Vickery, et al., *Mediating Misogyny* (Cham, Switzerland: Palgrave Mac- millan, 2018), pp. 11–12.

69. See discussion of 2011 start date for significantly rising online misogyny in Jane, "'Back to the Kitchen, Cunt,'" as cited in Moloney and Love, "Assessing Online Misogyny," p. 3.

70. Fontanella, et al., "How Do We Study Misogyny."

71. Farrell, et al., "Exploring Misogyny"; also see Ribeiro, et al., "Evolution."

72. Hunter and Jouenne, "All Women Belong in the Kitchen," p. 59. For a discussion of in- person misogyny in public spaces, see Bows, et al., "'It's Like a Drive by Misogyny.'"

73. Blake, et al., "Misogynistic Tweets."

74. Vickery and Everbach, "The Persistence of Misogyny," pp. 11–12.

75. Vickery and Everbach, "The Persistence of Misogyny," p. 13, citing Emma Alice Jane's research on gendered vitriol online. See Jane, "'Back to the Kitchen, Cunt.'"

76. Vogels, "The State of Online Harassment."

77. Aliche, "'You Don't Talk Like a Woman.'"

78. Blake, et al., "Misogynistic Tweets," p. 316.

79. Quoted text from Hunter and Jouenne, "All Women Belong in the Kitchen," p. 58. Also see Vickery and Everbach, "Mediating Misogyny," p. 10. On online disinhibition effects, see Azy Barak, "Sexual Harassment on the Internet," *Social Science Computer Review* 23 (2005): 77–92.

80. Hunter and Jouenne, "All Women Belong in the Kitchen," p. 58.

81. Hunter and Jouenne, "All Women Belong in the Kitchen," pp. 69–70. The analysis tested the rhetoric of both the incel movement and ISIS.

82. Cox, et al., "Generation Z."

83. Cox, "Why Young Men Are Turning Against Feminism."

84. Brenan, "Gender Disparities."

85. Cox, et al., "Generation Z." For more on survey research findings on Gen Z and politics, see Deckman, *The Politics of Gen Z*.

86. For more on the US law on unlawful paramilitaries and militias in all 50 states, see the "Fact Sheets on Unlawful Militias for All 50 States Now Available from Georgetown Law's Institute for Constitutional Advocacy and Protection | Institute for Constitutional Advocacy and Protection," Georgetown Law, September 22, 2020, https://www.law.georgetown.edu/icap/our -press-releases/fact-sheets-on-unlawful-militias-for-all-50-states-now-available-from -georgetown-laws-institute-for-constitutional-advocacy-and-protection/.

87. I am indebted to Pasha Dashtgard for his articulation of "some" men and "some" women in a guest lecture at American University on April 6, 2023. I also rely in this section on the definitions and discussions in Schuller, *The Trouble with White Women*, p. 9; and see Gilligan and Snider, *Why Does Patriarchy Persist?*, p. 6.

88. Moloney and Love, "Assessing Online Misogyny."

89. It is worth noting that the acknowledgment that "not all men" are violent has been misused by male supremacists and men's rights activists in various hashtags and discussions in ways that have slowed momentum toward change and distracted online discussions from the core issues at hand. I am grateful to Alex DiBranco for this reminder.

90. As articulated by Hunnicut, "Varieties of Patriarchy and Violence."

91. See discussion in Saini, *The Patriarchs*, p. 35.

92. See Edström, et al., "Patriarchal (Dis)orders"; also see Calarco, *Holding It Together*.

93. Saini, *The Patriarchs*.

94. Saini, *The Patriarchs*.

95. Craanen, et al., "Transmisogyny," p. 7.

96. See the 2011 PBS film "Two Spirits," directed by Linda Nibley, for an accessible overview of gender diversity among the Navajo, for example. Available at Two Spirits | Native American Gender Diversity | Independent Lens | PBS. For more on Native American matriarchal societies, see Courtney Defriend, et al., "Reawakening of Indigenous Matriarchal Systems: A Feminist Approach to Organizational Leadership." *Healthcare Management Forum* 37, no. 3 (2024):160–163, https://doi.org/10.1177/08404704231210255; for more on the histories of transgender youth in previous generations, see Gill-Peterson, *Histories of the Transgender Child*.

97. See especially the work of Niobe Way on the ways that adolescent boys increasingly lose intimate friendships as they grow up. Way, *Deep Secrets*.

98. Adichie, *We Should All Be Feminists*, p. 27.

99. See Petro, *Shame on You*, pp. 24–25, and see Crenshaw, *On Intersectionality*, and McMillan Cottom, *Thick*.

100. See hooks, *The Will to Change*, especially pp. 17–19.

101. Way, *Rebels with a Cause*.

102. Petro, *Shame on You*, p. 20.

103. Bridges and Pascoe, "Hybrid Masculinities," p. 255; also see Bridges, "A Very 'Gay' Straight?"

104. Calarco, *Holding It Together*.

105. See especially the extensive writing on this by Black feminist scholars, such as hooks, *The Will to Change*.

106. Hunnicutt, "Varieties of Patriarchy and Violence."

107. hooks, *Ain't I a Woman*; Kendall, *Hood Feminism*; Hunt and Martin, *Letters to the Future*; Lorde, *The Master's Tools*; Carruthers, *Unapologetic*.

108. Crenshaw, *On Intersectionality*.

109. Blee, et al., *Out of Hiding*, 6.

110. Rosin, "The Patriarchy Is Dead."

111. See fact-checking and sources at Hill, "Fact Check."

112. Mittleman, "Homophobic Bullying," p. 24.

113. Schilt and Westbrook, "Doing Gender, Doing Heteronormativity," p. 448.

114. Carian, et al., *Male Supremacism*, p. 23; also see Lyons, "The U.S. Far Right's Politics of Gender."

115. Saini, *Inferior*.

116. Glick and Fiske, "Hostile and Benevolent Sexism"; Jolley, et al., "Sexism and Feminist Conspiracy Beliefs"; Garg, "Russia's Sexist List"; Weir, "Rise of the Volga Boatwoman?"

117. Schuller, *The Trouble with White Women*, p. 9.

118. Schuller, *The Trouble with White Women*, pp. 9–10.

119. See for example Gomes, et al., "Are We Getting Less Sexist?"

120. Millions of women around the world, of course, do still live in places where they lack fundamental rights, including the right to go to school or university, to work, or to travel without their father's or husband's permission.

121. Orenstein, *Cinderella Ate My Daughter*.

122. Manne, *Down Girl*, p. 19. For a critique of Manne and this definition, see Wrisley, "Feminist Theory." On gender policing, see Mittleman, "Homophobic Bullying"; also see Payne and Smith, "Gender Policing."

123. See Manne, *Entitled*; Manne, *Down Girl*; Banet-Weiser, *Empowered*.

124. McCarthy and Taylor, "Misogyny and Organizational Studies," p. 462.

125. Manne, *Entitled*.

126. Banet-Weiser, *Empowered*, p. 36.

127. Loewen Walker, "Call It Misogyny."

128. Bailey, *Misogynoir Transformed*, p. 1.

129. See especially the rich discussion of these layered oppressions—and white feminists' lack of acknowledgment or commitment to combating them—in Zakaria, *Against White Feminism*; in Beck, *White Feminism*; and in Hamad, *White Tears/Brown Scars*.

130. Collins, *Black Feminist Thought*, pp. 76–77.

131. See the discussion in Givens, *The Roots of Racism*, especially in the preface.

132. See examples and fuller discussion throughout the introduction to Bailey, *Misogynoir Transformed*, pp. 1–33.

133. Onuoha, et al., "Far-Right Misogynoir."

134. There is a wide range of prevailing masculinities that coexist in any given time and place—that determine what it means to "be a man" in a particular community, racial group, immigrant diaspora, or in a particular country or an era of history—an issue I take up in greater depth throughout this book and especially in chapter 3 and in the conclusion.

135. Michael Flood, "Toxic Masculinity: What Does It Mean, Where Did It Come From— and Is the Term Useful or Harmful?" *The Conversation*, September 21, 2022. Available at: "Toxic Masculinity": What Does It Mean, Where Did It Come From—and Is the Term Useful or Harmful?, theconversation.com.

136. See especially discussion of these terms in Kelly, et al., "Misogynist Incels"; Leidig, Eviane, "Why Terrorism Studies Miss the Mark."

137. Pruitt, "The Night of Terror."

138. See discussion in Vickery and Everbach, *Mediating Misogyny*, pp. 1–27.

139. Rosario, "Iowa State University."

140. Wondwosen, "The Catt's Out of the Bag."

141. Catt was far from the only white woman who used that same logic. The well-known suffragist Elizabeth Cady Stanton openly argued that educated white women should be a priority

for voting rights, rather than "former slaves or ignorant immigrants." As quoted and cited in Saini, *The Patriarchs*, p. 51.

142. This kind of "bargaining with patriarchy" is something women around the world have done strategically for generations to optimize their choices—but in this case, white women bargained in favor of their own rights while excluding Black women from the same ones. Kandiyoti, "Bargaining with Patriarchy."

143. Text in the memorial exhibit and the museum exhibit as observed on September 13, 2024, during an in-person visit.

144. Bailey and Trudy, "On Misogynoir Citation"; Bailey, *Misogynoir Transformed*.

145. For just a few citations, see Blee, *Women of the Klan*; Blee, "Does Gender Matter"; Carian, et al., *Male Supremacism*; Cooter, *Nostalgia*; Darby, *Sisters in Hate*; Leidig, *The Women of the Far Right*; Jasser, et al., "'Welcome to #GabFam'"; Mattheis, "Shieldmaidens of Whiteness; Pearson, *Extreme Britain*; Phelan, et al., "Misogyny and Masculinity." Also see the work of the Institute for Research on Male Supremacism at Institute for Research on Male Supremacism (theirms.org).

146. The most notable exception is the excellent report by the US Secret Service National Threat Assessment Center (NTAC) on the Tallahassee Yoga studio shooting. See "Hot Yoga Tallahassee," Department of Homeland Security, March 2022, https://www.secretservice.gov /sites/default/files/reports/2022-03/NTAC%20Case%20Study%20-%20Hot%20Yoga%20 Tallahassee_0.pdf.

147. As spoken by the Santa Barbara shooter in a misogynist incel attack targeting a university sorority. See Holly Yan, et al., "Inside the Gunman's Head."

1. Gendered Gaps in Extremism and Violence

1. I rely here on the use of blind spots as a driving metaphor that relates to the part of a driver's view in the rearview mirror that is blocked by the physical car—not to a use of the term referring to physical blindness. For fuller definitions of blind spot, see www.merriam-webster .com, www.dictionary.com, and www.thesaurus.com.

2. Díaz and Valji, "Symbiosis," quote on p. 44.

3. For recent comprehensive reviews of this literature, see Phelan, "Special Issue"; Scrinzi, *The Racialization of Sexism*. Also see especially Connell, *Masculinities*; Cooter, *Nostalgia*; Ferber, "Racial Warriors and Weekend Warriors"; Floya and Yuval-Davis, *Woman-Nation-State*; Koonz, *Mothers in the Fatherland*; Köttig, et al., *Gender and Far Right Politics in Europe*; Mattheis, "Shieldmaidens of Whiteness," pp. 128–162; Nagel, "Masculinity and Nationalism"; Pearson, "Extremism"; Pilkington, et al., *Russia's Skinheads*; Yuval-Davis, *Gender and Nation*.

4. Blee, *Women of the Klan*; Blee, "Does Gender Matter," pp. 253–265; Leidig, *The Women of the Far Right*.

5. Caplan, "Militarism"; George L. Mosse, *Nationalism and Sexuality* (Madison: University of Wisconsin Press, 1985); Linke, *German Bodies*; Linke, "Gendered Difference, Violent Imagination," p. 564.

6. Miller-Idriss, *The Extreme Gone Mainstream*; Mosse, *The Image of Man*; Nagel, "Masculinity and Nationalism," pp. 242–269.

7. See especially the extensive discussion and data in Scrinzi, *The Racialization of Sexism*.

8. Anand, "Anxious Sexualities," p. 257; Waetjen, "The Limits of Gender Rhetoric"; Tumblety, *Remaking the Male Body*; Vlossak, *Marianne or Germania*.

9. Some of the arguments in this chapter were first developed and published in Miller-Idriss, "Triumph of the Women?: The Female Face of Populism and Extremism," and in Miller-Idriss, "Christian Nationalism."

10. Johnston and True, "Misogyny and Violent Extremism"; Hudson and Hodgson, "Sex and Terror," pp. 605–632; Piazza and O'Rourke, "Hostile Sexism." Manuscript under review. Also see Kalmoe and Mason, *Radical American Partisanship*; Rottweiler, et al., "A Common Psychology of Male Violence?"; Díaz and Valji, "Symbiosis."

11. Johnston and True, "Misogyny and Violent Extremism"; Hudson and Hodgson, "Sex and Terror," pp. 605–632.

12. Elin Bjanegård, et al., "The Sexism and Violence Nexis," UN Women, November 2020, https://www.unwomen.org/sites/default/files/Headquarters/Attachments/Sections/Library/Publications/2020/New-insights-on-WPS-The-sexism-and-violence-nexus-en.pdf. Also see Phelan, et al., "Misogyny."

13. Glick, "Gender," see especially p. 721.

14. Rottweiler, et al., "A Common Psychology of Male Violence?," p. 12.

15. Jolley, et al., "Sexism and Feminist Conspiracy Beliefs."

16. Christina M. Santana, et al., "Masculine Gender Roles Associated with Increased Sexual Risk and Intimate Partner Violence Perpetration among Young Adult Men," *Journal of Urban Health* 83, no. 4 (2006): 575–585; Díaz and Valji, "Symbiosis," pp. 37–57, both cited in Hunter and Joenne, "All Women Belong in the Kitchen," p. 60.

17. Vandello, et al., "Precarious Manhood," cited in Hunter and Jouenne, "All Women Belong in the Kitchen," pp. 60–61.

18. Valerie M. Hudson, et al., *Sex and World Peace* (New York: Columbia University Press, 2012), as cited in Hunter and Jouenne, "All Women Belong in the Kitchen," p. 78.

19. See Buljubasic, et al., "Women's Empowerment." See discussion of quantitative data on p. 130. Also see the range of United Nations efforts and reporting on promotion of social cohesion and reduction of violent extremism through gender equality and women's empowerment. For a recent report on these efforts, see "Empowered Women, Peaceful Communities," UN Women, 2003, https://asiapacific.unwomen.org/en/digital-library/publications/2023/03/empowered-women-peaceful-communities. Also see the 2024 PERIL-Southern Poverty Law Center guide for communities to counter and prevent bigotry based on gender, sex, and sexuality at www.splcenter.org/peril.

20. Lamphere-Englund, et al., "Pathways of Resilience."

21. Schuller, *The Trouble with White Women*, p. 9.

22. See extensive discussion of this research in Blake, et al., "Misogynistic Tweets."

23. Díaz and Valji, "Symbiosis," p. 42.

24. Hudson and Hodgson, "Sex and Terror," p. 610.

25. See Michael Smerconish's discussion with Reeves about his book on how men and boys are struggling. Reeves, *Of Boys and Men*; Richard Reeves: "Of Boys and Men" | Book Club with Michael Smerconish, simplecast.com.

26. Hunter and Jouenne, "All Women Belong in the Kitchen," pp. 69–70. The analysis tested the rhetoric of both the incel movement and ISIS.

27. Edström, et al., "Patriarchal (Dis)orders."

28. Cassino and Besen-Cassino, *Gender Threat*, p. 1.

29. Cassino and Besen-Cassino, *Gender Threat*, p. 62.

30. See Gilligan and Richards, *Darkness Now Visible*, especially pp. 13 and 49; also see Gilligan, *Violence*.

31. Rottweiler, et al., "A Common Psychology of Male Violence?" p. 14.

32. Maass, et al., "Sexual Harassment," cited in Cassino and Besen-Cassino, *Gender Threat*, p. 23.

33. See an excellent articulation of these arguments throughout Gilligan and Richards, *Darkness Now Visible*.

34. Rottweiler, et al., "A Common Psychology of Male Violence?" p. 14, citing Roose, "'Ideological Masculinity.'"

35. Glick, "Gender," p. 721.

36. Du Mez, *Jesus and John Wayne*, p. 3.

37. Du Mez, *Jesus and John Wayne*, p. 271.

38. Gilligan and Richards, *Darkness Now Visible*, p. 111; also see Rottweiler, et al., "A Common Psychology of Male Violence?," p. 4.

39. Rottweiler, et al., "A Common Psychology of Male Violence?," p. 4.

40. Rottweiler, et al., "A Common Psychology of Male Violence?," p. 14.

41. An earlier version of these ideas was first published as Miller-Idriss, "Christian nationalism is a racist, ahistorical ideology of violence."

42. Allyson F. Shortle, et al., "Americans Are Growing More Accepting of Christian Nationalism," *The Washington Post*, September 1, 2022, https://www.washingtonpost.com/politics /2022/09/01/marjorie-taylor-greene-christian-nationalist/; "Christians Against Christian Nationalism Statement," Christians Against Christian Nationalism, https://www.christiansaga instchristiannationalism.org/statement; also see Smith, "The American Right's Future"; "Christian Nationalism on the Rise," NBC, September 15, 2022, https://www.nbcnews.com/meet-the -press/video/christian-nationalism-on-the-rise-148548677936.

43. PBS News (@NewsHour), "A growing movement led by right-wing politicians is increasingly challenging a centuries-old value of America's political system: The separation of church and state. @lbarronlopez spoke with @kkdumez about the rise of this religious rhetoric. https://t.co/x2wbLMySWm," Twitter (now X), October 11, 2022, https://twitter.com/newshour /status/1579967197279322113?s=46&t=4Gbs3iv1r_9HlaGq1pM9OA. In the spring of 2022, Doug Mastriano, Pennsylvania's Republican nominee for governor, called the separation of church and state a "myth." That same month, Maryland's Republican nominee for governor, Dan Cox, told a crowd that his platform "recognizes the creator" and said "we have rights that supersede government." Rep. Lauren Boebert of Colorado argued in June 2022 that "the church is supposed to direct the government. The government is not supposed to direct the church." Greene put it more bluntly in July 2022. "I'm a Christian and I say it proudly," she said. "We should be Christian nationalists." Suliman and Bella, "GOP Rep. Lauren Boebert."

44. Rouse and Telhami, "Most Republicans."

45. Luo, "How White Christian Nationalists Seek to Transform America"; also see "Understanding White Christian Nationalism." By definition, Christian nationalism is incompatible with the Establishment Clause of the First Amendment to the US Constitution, which prohibits the government from imposing or endorsing a particular religion. The Christians Against Christian Nationalism website contends that Christian nationalism "often overlaps with and provides cover for white supremacy and racial subjugation." See https://www.christiansagainstchristian nationalism.org/statement

46. Du Mez, *Jesus and John Wayne*, pp. 188, 189.

47. Monk-Turner, "White Evangelical Activism."

48. Tucker Carlson, "The End of Men," Fox News, October 5, 2022, https://nation.foxnews .com/tucker-carlson-originals-the-end-of-men-nation/.

49. Martinez, "Man Boobs and Raw Eggs."

50. Gorski, "Why Evangelicals Voted for Trump," see especially pp. 9 and 11.

51. Cooter, *Nostalgia*, p. 92.

52. Posner, *Unholy*, p. xv.

53. Ben-Ghiat, *Strongmen*, p. 121.

54. Brown, "About 5% of Young Adults."

55. "Which Countries Offer Gender-Neutral Passports?"

56. See Riedel, "For the First Time."

57. See the June 2023 issue of *Smart Family Magazine*, including its cover, at Smart Family Magazine (@smartfamilymagazine), Instagram photos and videos.

58. Du Mez, *Jesus and John Wayne*, pp. 238, 240–241.

59. Gilligan and Richards, *Darkness Now Visible*, p. 7.

60. Vickery and Everbach, *Mediating Misogyny*, p. 18.

61. See discussion in Moloney and Love, "Assessing Online Misogyny," p. 5.

62. Du Mez, *Jesus and John Wayne*, p. 253.

63. Du Mez, *Jesus and John Wayne*, pp. 260–261.

64. Gilligan and Richards, *Darkness Now Visible*, p. 49.

65. Ben-Ghiat, *Strongmen*, p. 121. I am indebted to Joe and Tara Palmore for reminding me of this historical connection.

66. Cox, "Rise of Conspiracies."

67. Nordås and Cohen, "Conflict Related Sexual Violence," p. 195.

68. "Toward Meaningful Accountability for Sexual and Gender-Based Violence"; Asal and Nagel, "Control over Bodies and Territories."

69. One exception of scholarship looking at misogyny across both domestic and international forms of terrorism is Roose and Cook, "Supreme Men."

70. "Mission Report: Official Visit of the Office of the SRSG-SVC to Israel and the Occupied West Bank," United Nations Office of the Special Representative of the Secretary General on Sexual Violence in Conflict, March 4, 2024, 20240304-Israel-oWB-CRSV-report.pdf (un.org). United Nations Security Council CTED, November 2023; Gettleman, et al., "'Screams Without Words'"; "Under ISIS: Where Being Gay Is Punished by Death," ABC News, June 13, 2016. go.com.

71. Sella, "Israeli Rape-Crisis Group Report."

72. Rawnsley and Hughes, "Neo-Nazi Marine."

73. United Nations Security Council CTED, "Toward Meaningful Accountability for Sexual and Gender-Based Violence Linked to Terrorism." p. 31.

74. United Nations Security Council CTED, "Toward Meaningful Accountability for Sexual and Gender-Based Violence Linked to Terrorism," p. 9; also see United Nations Security Council CTED, "Member States Concerned by the Growing and Increasingly Transnational Threat of Extreme Right Wing Terrorism," April 2020, CTED XRW Trends Alert - Final_31_March. docx (un.org).

75. Blee, "Where Do We Go from Here?," quotation on p. 419.

76. Belew, *Bring the War Home*, p. 159.

77. Belew, *Bring the War Home*; Mattheis, "Shieldmaidens of Whiteness," pp. 128–162; Miller-Idriss and Pilkington, *Gender and the Radical and Extreme Right*. I am grateful to Brian Hughes for early discussions of these issues in a coauthored working paper on masculinities and extremism. For a thorough discussion of white anger and histories of violence against people of color in the United States, see Anderson, *White Rage*.

78. United Nations Security Council CTED, "Toward Meaningful Accountability for Sexual and Gender-Based Violence Linked to Terrorism," p. 6.

79. I am indebted to Jessica White for this insight.

80. Emezi, *Pet*, p. 61.

2. Containment: "Lock Her Up"

1. For more on obscene phone calls as a misogynistic tactic, see Sheffield, "The Invisible Intruder."

2. For related reading, see Criado-Perez, "'Women that Talk Too Much Need to Get Raped.'"

3. Manne, *Down Girl*, p. 33. Cited and discussed in McCarthy and Taylor, "Misogyny and Organizational Studies."

4. Quote from Karla Mantilla, "Gendertrolling: Misogyny Adapts to New Media," *Feminist Studies* 39, no. 2 (2013): 563–570, 568, as cited in Moloney and Love, "Assessing Online Misogyny," p. 5.

5. Moloney and Love, "Assessing Online Misogyny," p. 4.

6. Frances-Wright and Ayad, "'Your body, my choice'".

7. Tranchese and Sugiura, "'I don't hate all women,'" see especially the discussion of women staying "in their place" on p. 2730.

8. Cravens, "Hate Group."

9. Saini, *The Patriarchs*, p. 104.

10. Saini, *The Patriarchs*, p. 47.

11. As discussed in Moloney and Love, "Assessing Online Misogyny," Also see Know Your Meme, "But God, She Won't Even Make Me aSandwich," https://knowyourmeme.com/memes/make-me-a-sandwich.

12. Jamieson, "How 'Barefoot and Pregnant' Became a Dark American Joke."

13. Kelley, "Taylor Swift's Real NFL Screen Time."

14. Blake, "Taylor Swift AI Images"; Saner, "Inside the Taylor Swift Deepfake Scandal"; also see Davila, "'Women Turn Us into Women.'"

15. Saner, "Inside the Taylor Swift Deepfake Scandal"; also see Davila, "Women Turn Us into Women."

16. Solnit, "The Serious Side of 'Mansplaining' Has Been Lost."

17. McMillan Cottom, "Dying to Be Competent," in *Thick and Other Essays*, pp. 73–97.

18. Weintraub, et al., "How a 7-Year-Old Helped Investigators."

19. Croom, "Slurs."

20. Transcript of the 2005 recording is available in Montell, *Wordslut*, pp. 87–88.

21. Tranchese and Sugiura, "'I Don't Hate All Women'", citing Ann Russo, et al., *Pornography: The Production and Consumption of Inequality* (London: Routledge, 2013), p. 81.

22. Montell, *Wordslut*. Montell attributes this idea to the computational linguist Chi Luu on p. 37.

23. Krook, *Violence Against Women in Politics*, p. 189.

24. Montell, *Wordslut*, p. 38.

25. Downey, "It Rhymes with Gingrich," cited on p. 602; Anderson, "'Rhymes with Rich.'"

26. Ashwell, "Gendered Slurs," especially p. 235; also see Luu, "Bad Language for Nasty Women."

27. Anderson, "'Rhymes with Rich.'"

28. Gilligan and Richards, *Darkness Now Visible*, p. 1841.

29. Ashwell, "Gendered Slurs," pp. 228–239, especially p. 235; also see Luu, "Bad Language for Nasty Women."

30. Anderson, "'Rhymes with Rich,'" pp. 599–623. Quotes from this sentence and the previous one are from p. 615.

31. Sobieraj, "Bitch, Slut, Skank, Cunt."

32. See for example Taylor, *Sexy but Psycho*.

33. See Urban Dictionary, "Butterface," https://www.urbandictionary.com/define.php?term=butterface.

34. Sobieraj, "Bitch, Slut, Skank, Cunt."

35. Moloney and Love, "Assessing Online Misogyny," pp. 6–7.

36. Saucier, et al., "Slurs Against Masculinity." For a discussion of "simp" and the "stop simping" trend on social media that discourages and makes fun of men's sympathy and kindness

toward women, see Diverting Hate, "Diverting Hate: Misogynistic Extremism, The Manosphere, and Mainstream Social Media."

37. Ashwell, "Gendered Slurs."

38. Romano, "The Right's Moral Panic."

39. See especially Connell, *Masculinities*, and the longer discussion of masculinities in Miller-Idriss, *The Extreme Gone Mainstream*.

40. Phelan, et al., "Misogyny and Masculinity."

41. For more on boys' intimacy, connection, and friendships, see especially Way, "Deep Secrets"; Reeves, *Of Boys and Men*; also see Greene, "Close: The Oscar-Nominated Movie."

42. Gilligan and Richards, *Darkness Now Visible*, pp. 26–27.

43. Mittleman, "Homophobic Bullying," see especially p. 6.

44. Pascoe, *Dude, You're a Fag*; also see Mittleman, "Homophobic Bullying," p. 9.

45. See discussion throughout Diefendorf and Bridges, "On the Enduring Relationship"; also see Bridges, "A Very 'Gay' Straight?"; Mittleman, "Homophobic Bullying."

46. Pearson, "Extremism."

47. See transcript at https://www.nytimes.com/2016/10/08/us/donald-trump-tape-transcript.html.

48. Sexton, *The Man They Wanted Me to Be*, p. 8.

49. Everytown for Gun Safety, "Misogyny, Extremism, and Gun Violence."

50. "U.S. Youth Attitudes on Guns," *PERIL, SPLC, Everytown for Gun Safety*, July 2023, https://perilresearch.com/wp-content/uploads/2023/07/PERIL-Everytown-Report_U.S.-Youth-Attitudes-on-Guns_JULY-19-2023-2.pdf.

51. Everytown for Gun Safety, "Misogyny, Extremism, and Gun Violence."

52. Twitter, June 4–11, 2017.

53. Felmlee, et al., "Sexist Slurs."

54. Levey, *Sexual Harassment Online*, pp. 123–125. Cited in Krook, *Violence Against Women in Politics*, p. 29.

55. Carlson, "Misogynistic Hate Speech."

56. See, e.g., Ritchie, "Creating a Monster."

57. Anderson, "Rhymes with Rich," p. 608.

58. See discussion of the foundational nature of hostile sexism (Greene, *Remaking Manhood in the Age of Trump*; Manne, *Entitled*) as it relates to these issues.

59. Manne, *Down Girl*, p. 260.

60. Quinn, "Twitter Bomb Threats"; Also see Carlin and Winfrey, "Have You Come a Long Way, Baby?"

61. Anderson, "Rhymes with Rich."

62. Ashley Parker, et al., "Attack on Nancy Pelosi's Husband."

63. Also see, for example, Wright and Holland, "Leadership and the Media."

64. Krook, *Violence Against Women in Politics*, see especially pp. 9 and 25, citing journalist Anne Summers's account of the vilification of Australian prime minister Julia Gillard: Summer, *The Misogyny Factor*, and pp. 57–60 on backlash, gender ideology, and anti-feminism. Also see Mona Lena Krook, "Violence Against Women in Politics," *Journal of Democracy* 28, no. 1 (2017): 74–88. See discussion of attacks on "gender ideology" in Shearing, *Pink-Pilled*.

65. Krook, *Violence Against Women in Politics*, pp. 189–206.

66. Associated Press. "'She's not my type.'"

67. See, e.g., Lawless, et al., "Is It Really Just a Joke?"

68. Bates, *Everyday Sexism*, p. 3.

69. Emily Ledingham, Graham W. Wright, and Monika Mitra, "Sexual Violence Against Women with Disabilities."

70. Crenshaw, *On Intersectionality*; Bailey and Trudy, "On Misogynoir Citation"; Bailey, *Misogynoir Transformed*.

71. See Krook, *Violence Against Women in Politics*, pp. 192–193; Puwar, *Space Invaders*.

72. Chittal, "Trump's Latest Tweets."

73. Chittal, "Trump's Latest Tweets."

74. For a longer discussion of these four congresswomen and their treatment by the media and by their peers, see Oluo, *Mediocre*, pp. 208–225.

75. Flyer pictured in Feola, *The Rage of Replacement*, p. 105.

76. See the analysis of respectability narratives and respectability politics at Emily Chen and Jenny Dorsey, "Understanding . . . Respectability Politics," *Center for Food and Social Justice*, July 1, 2021, https://www.studioatao.org/respectability-politics. I am indebted to Alexandra Onuoha for this point. Also see Gay, "The Politics of Respectability," *Bad Feminist: Tenth Anniversary Edition*, pp. 257–260.

77. See discussion in Nudson, *All Made Up*, pp. 1–3, quoting McMillan Cottom, *Thick*, p. 44.

78. See especially Sabrina Strings, *Fearing the Black Body: The Racial Origins of Fat Phobia* (New York: NYU Press, 2019).

79. As argued throughout Nudson, *All Made Up*.

80. See Crenshaw, *On Intersectionality*, and Bailey and Trudy, *On Misogynoir*.

81. I thank Alexandra Onuoha for reminding me of the scholarly link to intersectionality and misogynoir here.

82. Nudson, *All Made Up*, p. 31.

83. Nudson, *All Made Up*, p. 175.

84. Ani DiFranco, "Little Plastic Castle," Track 1, *Little Plastic Castle*. Righteous Babe Records, 1998.

85. Leidig, Eviane. *The Women of the Far Right*.

86. For example, see Hetzner, "What Is Discord?"; O'Connor, "The Extreme Right on Twitch." Also see Miller-Idriss, "Misogyny Incubators."

87. Schlegel and Kowert, "Introduction: Extremism in Digital Gaming Spaces," pp. 1–8 in *Gaming and Extremism*. Also see Mariana Olaizola Rosenblat, "Gaming the System: How Extremists Exploit Gaming Sites and What Can Be Done to Counter Them," NYU STERN, May 2023, https://bhr.stern.nyu.edu/tech-gaming-report.

88. Jesse Fox and Wai Yen Tang, "Sexism in Online Video Games: The Role of Conformity to Masculine Norms and Social Dominance Orientation," *Computers in Human Behavior* 33 (2014): 314–320, https://doi.org/10.1016/j.chb.2013.07.014; Marja Leonhardt and Stian Overå, "Are There Differences in Video Gaming and Use of Social Media among Boys and Girls?—A Mixed Methods Approach," *International Journal of Environmental Research and Public Health* 18, no. 1 (2021), https://doi.org/10.3390/ijerph18116085; Vickie Chen, "Leveling Up the Gaming Gender Gap," Forbes.com, August 24, 2023. https://www.forbes.com/councils/forbesbusinesscouncil/2023/08/24/leveling-up-the-gaming-gender-gap/.

89. See media coverage and law enforcement warnings on Roblox and extremist recruitment, for example: Schultz, "Roblox Used by Extremists"; "Online Gaming Platforms Such as Roblox used as 'Trojan Horse' for Extremist Recruitment of Children, AFP Warns | Australian Police and Policing," *The Guardian*, December 2, 2023, https://www.theguardian.com/australia-news/2023/dec/03/online-gaming-platforms-such-as-roblox-used-as-trojan-horse-for-extremist-recruitment-of-children-afp-warns; Farivar, "Extremists Creep into Roblox"; also see discussions of Minecraft and Discord in Stephen Myers and Kellen Browning, "Extremism Finds Fertile Ground in Chat Rooms for Gamers," *The New York Times*, May 18, 2023, https://www.nytimes.com/2023/05/18/technology/video-games-extremism.html; and Rosenblat, "Gaming the System."

90. Beauchamp, "White Supremacists." Also see the 2023 Anti-Defamation League report on online gaming and hate, "Hate Is No Game."

91. See especially the discussion on *League of Legends* in Beauchamp, "White Supremacists."

92. Lamphere-Englund and White, "The Online Gaming Ecosystem." Also see Lamphere-Englund, "Theories of Digital Games and Radicalization," pp. 32–56, 44. Also see Kowert, et al., "Not Just a Game."

93. Koehler, et al., "From Gaming to Hating"; on toxicity and hate in online gaming, also see "2023 Toxicity in Multiplayer Games Report," Unity, 2023, https://create.unity.com/toxicity-report; Anti-Defamation League, "Hateful Usernames"; and Davey, "Gamers Who Hate"; also see Rosenblat, "Gaming the System"; "Examining the Intersection Between Gaming and Extremism"; Consalvo, "Confronting Toxic Gamer Culture."

94. UNOCT survey data analyzed in Amarasingham and Kelley, "Hate and Extremism on Gaming Platforms" pp. 110–129, 115.

95. Healey, "Proving Grounds."

96. Steinkuehler and Squire, "Introduction to Videogames," pp. 9–31, 20.

97. I am indebted to an external reviewer for the joint PERIL-SPLC Guide to Preventing Gender and Sexuality-Based Bigotry for this point.

98. GamerGate is a term used to refer to a 2014 trolling and harassment campaign from the male-dominated gaming world against Zoe Quinn, a woman game creator, which followed similar harassment against another woman creator, Anita Sarkeesian. GamerGate evolved into conspiracies that argue feminists are forcing political correctness into games, along with the collusion of corporate and government actors. For more on GamerGate, see Chess and Shaw, "A Conspiracy of Fishes."

99. MacDonald, "It's 10 Years since Gamergate"; Farokhmanesh, "The Small Company at the Center of 'Gamergate 2.0.'"

100. Prinz, "Extremist Games and Modifications," pp. 57–71, 67.

101. I am indebted to Galen Lamphere-Englund for this point and for a thoughtful review of this section of the book, as well as for references to research on the connection between violence and video games. See for example Sher and Kowert, "Episode 43—What the Research REALLY Says"; The Video Game Debate | Rachel Kowert, PhD (rkowert.com); Kowert, *The Video Game Debate 2*; along with APA task force report here: "APA Task Force Report on Violent Video Games."

102. Claudia, Wallner, Jessica White, and Petra Regeni. "Building Resilience to Extremism in Gaming: Identifying and Addressing Toxicity in Gaming Culture," European Commission Radicalization Awareness Network (RAN) Policy Support, 2023, RAN-building-resilience-extremism-gaming_en.pdf (europa.eu).

103. Steinkuehler and Squire, "Introduction to Videogames," p. 13.

104. Kingdon, "God of Race War." Also see Green, "Far Cry 5."

105. "Lock Her Up: The Trump Supremacy"; also see mention of this game in Davey, "Extremism on Gaming (-Adjacent) Platforms," pp. 95–109.

106. Bridget Johnson, "FBI, DHS Cite 'Kill Count' Gamification as Key Threat Inspiring Future Domestic Terrorism," *Government Technology and Services Coalition Homeland Security*, May 18, 2021, https://www.hstoday.us/federal-pages/dhs/fbi-dhs-cite-kill-count-gamification-as-key-threat-inspiring-future-domestic-terrorism/; also see Lakhani, "When Digital and Physical World Combine"; Lakhani and Wiedlitzka, "'Press F to Pay Respects.'"

107. Prinz, "Extremist Games," pp. 57–58.

108. For more on how like-minded gaming communities can reinforce and radicalize players' views, see Lamphere-Englund and White, "The Online Gaming Ecosystem"; Kowert and Kilmer, "Toxic Gamers"; and Kowert, et al., "You Are What You Play."

109. The phrase "alt-right" is contested. Created by the modern US far right, it is criticized for the ways that it can soften or mask the extremist ideas of the varied groups that constitute it. Despite these concerns, the term carries a specific connotation to a unique development in the far right scene in the United States since 2015, which is distinct from older factions of the American far right such as the Ku Klux Klan and the Aryan Brotherhood. I opt to deploy the term here but use single quotation marks around the phrase to signal its contested nature.

110. I discuss Pepe the Frog and other memes in greater detail in Cynthia Miller-Idriss, "What Makes a Symbol Far Right?," pp. 123–136, and in Miller-Idriss, Hate in the Homeland. Also see Serwer, "It's Not Easy Being Meme"; Roy, "How 'Pepe the Frog' Went from Harmless to Hate Symbol."

111. Daniels, "The Algorithmic Rise of the 'Alt Right'"; also see Donovan, et al., Meme Wars; Anti-Defamation League, "ADL Adds 'Pepe the Frog' Meme."

112. Woods, "Where the Hell Is Kekistan."

113. Pérez, The Souls of White Jokes.

114. Miller-Idriss, Hate in the Homeland. Also see the extensive discussion of memes and humor in Donovan, et al., Meme Wars, and Sienkiewicz and Marx, That's Not Funny.

115. See De Luna, "Creators Say Youtube Shorts Has a Transphobia Problem"; also see "You-Tube Shorts' Suggesting Banned-Andrew Tate's Content to Young Boys."

116. I am indebted to my undergraduate students in a spring 2024 American University course for this insight, based on their discussions with middle school boys they know.

117. Baker, et al., "Recommending Toxicity."

118. See one version of this meme at "Trad Girl/Tradwife," Know Your Meme, 2020, https://knowyourmeme.com/photos/1815505-trad-girl-tradwife.

119. Di Placido, "Taylor Swift's Matty Healy and Ice Spice Controversy, Explained."

120. See "Teens and Pornography," Common Sense Media, 2022, https://www.commonsensemedia.org/sites/default/files/research/report/2022-teens-and-pornography-final-web.pdf.

121. Tranchese and Sugiura, "I Don't Hate All Women."

122. As discussed in Krook, Violence Against Women in Politics, p.189, citing Kristina Horn Sheeler and Karrin Vasby Anderson, Woman President: Confronting Postfeminist Political Culture (College Station: Texas A&M University Press, 2013).

123. Tranchese, "Why We Need to Talk about Porn."

124. Tranchese and Sugiura, "I Don't Hate All Women," p. 2710.

125. As reported in Peggy Orenstein, "The Troubling Trend in Teenage Sex," The New York Times, April 12, 2024, https://www.nytimes.com/2024/04/12/opinion/choking-teen-sex-brain-damage.html. Similar findings from research in Australia are reported in Douglas, et al., "More Than Half of Australian Young People Are Using Strangulation During Sex."

126. Tranchese and Sugiura, "I Don't Hate All Women," p. 2710.

127. Tranchese, "Why We Need to Talk about Porn."

128. Cassino and Besen-Cassino, Gender Threat, p. 105.

129. Lawrence, et al., "Antisemitism and Misogyny," p. 12.

130. See Simon Usborne, "From Bone Smashing to Chin Extensions: How 'Looksmaxxing' Is Reshaping Young Men's Faces," The Guardian, February 15, 2024, https://www.theguardian.com/lifeandstyle/2024/feb/15/from-bone-smashing-to-chin-extensions-how-looksmaxxing-is-reshaping-young-mens-faces.

131. See for example Hannah Price, "Instagram Influencer Jailed for Trafficking and Slavery," BBC, July 14, 2024, https://www.bbc.com/news/articles/cydvj6951dyo.

132. Ramirez, "The Proud Boys Have Really Strict Rules"; also see Kutner, "Swiping Right."

133. This section is adapted from Miller-Idriss, "Andrew Tate's Violent, Misogynistic Teachings"; Will, "Misogynist Influencer Andrew Tate"; Also see Sung, "The Internet Can't Stop Talking about Andrew Tate."

134. Banting, "Teachers Warn"; "Children Are Mimicking a Hand Gesture."

135. Will, "Misogynist Influencer Andrew Tate"; Fazackerley, "'Vulnerable Boys Are Drawn In.'"

136. This section is adapted from Miller-Idriss, "Andrew Tate's Violent, Misogynistic Teachings"; also see Norman, "Greta Thunberg's Andrew Tate Smackdown"; The Associated Press, "Andrew Tate to Remain Detained."

137. Tolentino, "Johnny Depp Topped Google's List"; Sung, "Andrew Tate Banned"; Sung, "The Internet Can't Stop Talking about Andrew Tate."

138. Booth, "Gen Z Boys and Men"; see full report at emerging-tensions.pdf (kcl.ac.uk).

139. Barker, et al., "The State of American Men," p. 34.

140. Haslop, et al., "Mainstreaming the Manosphere's Misogyny," p. 9.

141. O'Connell, "How Did Andrew Tate Become a Role Model"; Ging, "Why Influencers Like Andrew Tate Want Your Sons' Attention"; Will, "Misogynist Influencer Andrew Tate"; Diverting Hate, "Misogynistic Extremism."

142. Sung, "The Internet Can't Stop Talking about Andrew Tate."

143. Lisa Miller, "Tate-Pilled: What a Generation of Boys Have Found in Andrew Tate's Extreme Male Gospel," New York Magazine, March 13–26, 2023, p. 112; also see Way, Rebels with a Cause; and Way, Deep Secrets.

144. Diverting Hate, "Misogynistic Extremism," especially pp. 12–13.

145. Haslop, et al., "Mainstreaming the Manosphere's Misogyny," p. 6.

146. Haslop, et al., "Mainstreaming the Manosphere's Misogyny," p. 5.

147. Al Aqueedi, "Andrew Tate"; Ali, "Andrew Tate's Muslim 'Faith Washing'"; Samuelson, "The Countries."

148. Cunliffe, "'There are thousands of Andrew Tates out there'"; Bratich and Banet-Weiser, "From Pick-Up Artists to Incels."

149. See Miller-Idriss, Hate in the Homeland; The Associated Press, "Boys' Mock Government Proposed Eliminating Women's Vote," June 26, 2019, https://apnews.com/article/b5a67ee195584bd6a0ee3afbc0a271fc; Ewens, "Young, Male, and Anti-Feminist"; Fear and Hope Reports, "Young People in the Time of Covid-19," Hope Not Hate, March 8, 2020, https://hopenothate.org.uk/2020/08/03/young-people-in-the-time-of-covid-19/.

3. Punishment: "Grab the Bitch"

1. National Threat Assessment Center, "Hot Yoga Tallahassee: A Case Study of Misogynistic Extremism."

2. "Fiscal Year 2022 Targeted Violence."

3. Observed during a personal visit to the CELL exhibit in October 2023.

4. "Domestic Violent Extremism Poses Heightened Threat in 2021."

5. See Macklin, "The Conspiracy to Kidnap Governor Gretchen Whitmer."

6. Survey data from the National Asian Pacific American Women's Forum (NAPAWF), cited in Shivaram, "One Year Later."

7. Gentry, Disordered Violence, p. 2.

8. Ebner, Going Mainstream, p. 28; also see Jasser, et al., "Male Supremacism."

9. Aguilera and Adams, "What the Buffalo Tragedy Has to Do."

10. Mattheis, et al., "The Allen, Texas, Attack."

11. While some of this increase is due to enhanced reporting requirements, the spike also occurred during a period of increased circulation of hostile misogyny online, in the manosphere and in youth spaces like in-game chats in online gaming. US Government Accountability Office, "K-12 Education."

12. With thanks to Brian Hughes for rich discussions about AI and tech-enabled misogyny, harassment, and abuse. Also see "VOX-Pol Virtual Roundtable"; "AI and Children"; Melissa Chan and Kat Tenbarge, "Little Recourse for Teens Girls Victimized by AI 'Deepfake' Nudes," NBC, November 23, 2023, https://www.nbcnews.com/news/us-news/little-recourse-teens-girls-victimized-ai-deepfake-nudes-rcna126399; Maiberg, "Andreessen Horowitz Invests in Civitai"; Samantha Cole, "Deepnude: The Horrifying App Undressing Women," VICE, June 26, 2019, https://www.vice.com/en/article/kzm59x/deepnude-app-creates-fake-nudes-of-any-woman.

13. For example, the Counterterrorism Education Learning Lab in Denver, Colorado now includes a dedicated section on male supremacism and misogynist incels.

14. For more on misogynist incels, see Bates, *Men Who Hate Women*; Sugiura, *The Incel Rebellion*; Van Brunt and Taylor, *Understanding and Treating Incels*.

15. For an empirical analysis that reinforces this claim, see especially Frounfelker, et al., "'Between the Self and the Other'."

16. Chan and Tenbarge, "Little Recourse for Teen Girls Victimized by AI 'Deepfake' Nudes." Henry Ajder, Giorgio Patrini, Francesco Cavalli, and Laurence Cullen, "The State of Deepfakes: Landscape, Threat, and Impact," Deeptrace.com, September 2019, https://regmedia.co.uk/2019/10/08/deepfake_report.pdf.

17. Haslop, et al., "Mainstreaming the Manosphere's Misogyny," p. 3.

18. Tracie Farrell, et al., "Exploring Misogyny"; also see discussion of the manosphere and harassment in Marwick and Caplan, "Drinking Male Tears." For a historical analysis of the discourse of men's rights movements, see Messner, "The Limits of 'the Male Sex Role.'"

19. It is worth noting that the term "chad" has been embraced in some parts of internet culture and is not always used in a negative way. Context is important to determine the meaning of any term, especially given ever-evolving shifts in slang, cultural meanings, and usage of any word or symbol.

20. There are many different masculinities that coexist in any given time and place—that determine what it means to "be a man" in a particular community, racial group, immigrant diaspora, or in a particular country or an era of history. But one of those types of masculinities tends to be the most influential at any given moment—this is what scholars mean when they refer to hegemonic masculinity. See hooks, *The Will to Change*; Connell, *Masculinities*; Miller-Idriss, *The Extreme Gone Mainstream*; Pascoe and Bridges, *Exploring Masculinities*; Vaccaro and Swauger, *Unleashing Manhood*. Also see Greene, *Remaking Manhood in the Age of Trump*.

21. Carian, et al., *Male Supremacism*. Also see Ging, "Alphas, Betas, and Incels."

22. I am indebted to Alex DiBranco for this point, and for pointing me to Heron Greenesmith's linking of authoritarianism and gender policing in Tina Vasquez, "You Can't Keep Good Queens Down," *Prism Reports*, July 1, 2022, https://prismreports.org/2022/07/01/you-cant-keep-good-queens-down/.

23. See "U.S. Youth Attitudes on Guns," *PERIL, SPLC, Everytown for Gun Safety*, p. 14.

24. I am indebted to Pasha Dashtgard for explaining these connections in an April 4, 2024, lecture at American University, and throughout his publications and empirical research more broadly.

25. Carian, "The Inversive Sexism Scale: Endorsement of the Belief that Women Are Privileged," in Carian, et al., *Male Supremacism in the United States*, pp. 20–47.

26. I am indebted to a colleague in the mental health field for this point and for extensive discussions about masculinity, shame, power, anger, and male violence, including ways that male

youth violence can be a way of preventing or reacting to actual or anticipated humiliation and a fear of not being strong or fierce enough.

27. Adichie, *We Should All Be Feminists*.

28. Cooter, *Nostalgia*, pp. 30, 92.

29. Feola, *The Rage of Replacement*, pp. 120–124.

30. Blais and Dupuis-Déri, "Masculinism," p. 27.

31. I am indebted to my research lab cofounder Dr. Brian Hughes for discussions on this point.

32. David Lawrence, et al., "Antisemitism and Misogyny."

33. There are endless case study examples, but for a discussion of how this manifests among veterans, for example, see discussion in Darda, *How White Men Won the Culture Wars*.

34. "Men's Rights Activists: What You Need to Know"; also see Haslop, et al., "Mainstreaming the Manosphere's Misogyny."

35. As discussed in Banet-Weiser, *Empowered*.

36. Tebaldi, "Make Women Great Again."

37. Goetz and Mayer, "Concluding Remarks."

38. O'Connell, "JD Vance Attacks Working Women As Being 'On Path to Misery' in Unearthed Audio."

39. Lawrence, et al., *Antisemitism and Misogyny*, p. 4; also see Ann-Kathrin Rothermel, "The Role of Evidence-Based Misogyny in Antifeminist Online Communities of the Manosphere," *Big Data and Society* (2023), https://doi.org/10.1177/20539517221145671.

40. Jolley, et al., "Sexism and Feminist Conspiracy Beliefs," p. 3.

41. Jolley, et al., "Sexism and Feminist Conspiracy Beliefs," p. 16.

42. Vegetti and Littvay, "Belief in Conspiracy Theories"; Rottweiler and Gill, "Conspiracy Beliefs."

43. Alex DiBranco and Megan Kelly, "Anti-Feminist Conspiracism."

44. DiBranco and Kelly, "Anti-Feminist Conspiracism," citing a 2017 post on a now-defunct Roosh V forum, previously available at Roosh V, "The Decline in Testosterone Is Destroying the Basis of Masculinity," 2017, https://www.rooshv.com/the-decline-in-testosterone-is-destroying-the-basis-of-masculinity.

45. DiBranco and Kelly, "Anti-Feminist Conspiracism."

46. Walton, "Anti-Feminism and Misogyny."

47. Kelly, et al., "Misogynist Incels," p. 166; also see Eglin and Hester, "You're All a Bunch of Feminists."

48. Nicole Hong, et al., "'Anti-Feminist' Lawyer Is Suspect in Killing of Son of Federal Judge in N.J.," *The New York Times*, July 20, 2020, https://www.nytimes.com/2020/07/20/nyregion/esther-salas.html.

49. Zuckerberg, *Not All Dead White Men*, p. 13. See @moroi, "Reddit is closing /r/TheRedPill with 419000 subscribers through Policy Update," r/WatchRedditDie, 2019, https://www.reddit.com/r/WatchRedditDie/comments/dbklnd/reddit_is_closing_rtheredpill_with_419000/ and review quarantined content at "The Red Pill," Reddit, https://www.reddit.com/r/TheRedPill/; "Pussy Pass Denied," Reddit, https://www.reddit.com/r/pussypassdenied/top/ has 593,000 members as of March 21, 2024.

50. See "Emerging Tensions?" Summary of report's findings available at: "Masculinity and Women's Equality: Study Finds Emerging Gender Divide in Young People's Attitudes," King's College London, February 1, 2024, https://www.kcl.ac.uk/news/masculinity-and-womens-equality-study-finds-emerging-gender-divide-in-young-peoples-attitudes; also see Booth, "Gen Z Boys and Men."

51. See poll results at Miller, "Racist 'Replacement' Theory Believed by Half of Americans."

52. "U.S. Youth Attitudes on Guns," *PERIL, SPLC, Everytown for Gun Safety*, p. 15.

53. Sugiura, *The Incel Rebellion*, p. 8.

54. "U.S. Youth Attitudes on Guns," *PERIL, SPLC, Everytown for Gun Safety*, p. 27; also see Jennifer Carlson, "Mourning Mayberry: Guns, Masculinity, and Socioeconomic Decline," *Gender & Society* 29, no. 3 (2015): 386–409, https://psycnet.apa.org/doi/10.1177/0891243214554799; Scaptura and Boyle, "Masculinity Threat"; Warner, et al., "To Provide or Protect?"; and Cassino and Besen-Cassino, *Gender Threat*, on issues related to "masculinity threat," the idea of protection and defense of families as part of manhood, and firearms.

55. Carlson, "Mourning Mayberry," p. 389.

56. Cooter, *Nostalgia*, p. 107.

57. Warner, et al., "To Provide or Protect?"

58. hooks, *The Will to Change*, p. 61.

59. Marganski, "Making a Murderer."

60. Among others, see especially Kathleen Blee's extensive ethnographic work on women and gender in the far right as cited throughout this book, alongside the work of Leidig, *The Women of the Far Right*; Marwick, "Morally Motivated Networked Harassment"; Mattheis, "Shieldmaidens of Whiteness"; Pearson, *Extreme Britain*.

61. Perliger, et al., "Mapping the Ideological Landscape."

62. Crenshaw, *On Intersectionality*.

63. Sections of this chapter were first developed in Miller-Idriss, "Triumph of the Women."

64. I am indebted to Lydia Bates for this point and for a close read and helpful feedback on the entire proposal and draft manuscript.

65. Arbeit, et al., "From Misogynist Incels to 'One of the Shooters'"; also see Phelan, et al., "Misogyny," citing Alexandra Krendel, "The Men and Women, Guys and Girls of the 'Manosphere': A Corpus-Assisted Discourse Approach," *Discourse & Society* 31, no. 6 (2020): 607–630, https://doi.org/10.1177/09579265209396902, p. 627.

66. See Dashtgard, *Male Supremacy and Online Radicalization*.

67. Bailey and Trudy, "On Misogynoir"; Bailey, *Misogynoir Transformed*; Onuoha, et al., "Far-Right Misogynoir."

68. Gentry, *Disordered Violence*, p. 179.

69. See DiBranco, "The Long History"; also see "Neo-Nazi website attacks female founder of institute for research on male supremacism," *Institute for Research on Male Supremacism*, October 3, 2019. Originally published at https://www.theirms.org/2019/10/03/neo-nazi-website-attacks-female-founder-of-institute-for-research-on-male-supremacism/, link inactive as of September 21, 2023.

70. Kelly, et al., "Misogynist Incels," p. 171.

71. See, e.g., Miller, et al., "2 Men Charged"; for more on the anti-trans/misogynistic statements, see comments by assistant District Attorney Bourdakos as reported in Yahoo News, Nicholas Williams, et al., "Co-Conspirator in Plot to Shoot Up NYC Synagogue Is Jewish Descendant of Holocaust Survivor, Relative Says," *Yahoo News*, November 20, 2022, https://sports.yahoo.com/co-conspirator-plot-shoot-nyc-175900616.html.

72. Manne, *Entitled*, pp. 18–19.

73. Blee, et al., *Out of Hiding*, p. 7.

74. As cited in Mills, et al., "Far-Right Violence"; also see Hoffman, et al., "Assessing the Threat of Incel Violence."

75. See for example Martin, "Online Disinhibition."

76. "The Incelosphere: Exposing Pathways into Incel Communities and the Harms They Pose to Women and Children," *Center for Countering Digital Hate Quant Lab*, 2022, 35, https://counterhate.com/wp-content/uploads/2023/08/CCDH-The-Incelosphere-FINAL.pdf. I am

indebted to Dr. Pasha Dashtgard for sharing this data in a guest lecture at American University on April 6, 2023.

77. Alex DiBranco, "Mobilizing Misogyny"; Manne, *Entitled*; Nagle, *Kill All Normies*.

78. Nagle, *Kill All Normies*.

79. Ging, "Alphas, Betas, and Incels"; also see Jennings, "Incel"; Baele, et al., "From 'Incel' to 'Saint.'"

80. I first articulated this trajectory in Miller-Idriss, *Hate in the Homeland*. For a comprehensive discussion of Gamergate, see Salter, "From Geek Masculinity to Gamergate." For discussions of Gamergate's evolution into the "alt right," see Lees, "What Gamergate Should Have Taught Us"; Urquist, "Gamergate Never Died."

81. Miller-Idriss, *Hate in the Homeland*.

82. See Dashtgard, *Male Supremacy and Online Radicalization*.

83. Di Branco, "Mobilizing Misogyny"; Gotell and Dutton, "Sexual Violence in the 'Manosphere.'"

84. Gotell and Dutton, "Sexual Violence in the 'Manosphere.'"

85. I am indebted to Pasha Dashtgard for the point about cognitive distortions.

86. Ramirez, "The Proud Boys Have Really Strict Rules."

87. I am indebted to the students in my 2024 Masterclass at Central European University (CEU) in Vienna, Austria, for reminding me of the nationalist dimensions of the manosphere in a fascinating discussion about this point on May 8, 2024.

88. DiBranco and Kelly, "Anti-Feminist Conspiracism."

89. Lamoreaux, "Why Do Neo-Nazis Keep Getting Arrested"; De Simone, "Order of Nine Angles."

90. Martynova, "Order of Nine Angles"; also see "The Order of Nine Angles," *Institute for Strategic Dialogue*, https://www.isdglobal.org/explainers/the-order-of-nine-angles-explainer/; Winston, "The Satanist Neo-Nazi Plot"; Charles P. Pierce, "Now We Have to Worry about Misogynistic Neo-Nazi Jihadist Satanists Infiltrating the Military?" *Esquire*, March 8, 2023, https://www.esquire.com/news-politics/politics/a43253018/ethan-melzer-sentenced-order-of-nine-angles/.

91. Kelly, et al., "Misogynist Incels," p. 166; Ebner, *Going Dark*, pp. 53–55; Perliger, "Mapping the Ideological Landscape."

92. Gheorghe, "'Just Be White (JBW),'" p. 67.

93. Halpin, et al., "Men Who Hate Women."

94. Kelly, et al., "Misogynist Incels," p. 167.

95. DiBranco and Kelly, "Anti-Feminist Conspiracism"; Alexander Dignam and Rohlinger, "Misogynistic Men Online."

96. Solea and Suiuram, "Mainstreaming the Blackpill."

97. Gheorghe, "'Just Be White (JBW),'" p. 61.

98. Bratich and Banet-Weiser, "From Pick-Up Artists to Incels."

99. See especially discussion of these terms in Kelly, et al., "Misogynist Incels," in Carian, et al., *Male Supremacism*, pp. 164–180; Leidig, et al., "Why Terrorism Studies Miss the Mark When It Comes to Incels."

100. See discussion of incels in Pearson, *Extreme Britain*, p. 12.

101. The number of deaths at the hands of violent misogynist incels ranges from 38 to 50, depending on the source and how the data are counted. See Ferrise, "Man Who Planned Mass Shooting"; Wilson, "Nostalgia."

102. Halpin, et al., "Men Who Hate Women."

103. Sugiura, *The Incel Rebellion*, p. 5.

104. Whittaker, et al., "Predicting Harm among Incels," p. 7; also see data analysis in Ribeiro, et al., "Evolution."

105. See especially the glossary of incel terms and concepts in Sugiura, *The Incel Rebellion*, pp. xvii–xxi.

106. Kelly, et al., "Misogynist Incels," p. 171.

107. See post at @RoastieBeef, "Has anyone heard of the 'fresh and fit' podcast?," *Incels.is - Involuntary Celibate Forum*, July 8, 2021, https://incels.is/threads/has-anyone-heard-of-the-fresh -and-fit-podcast.305329/.

108. See the recent call for submissions to a special issue of *Critical Discourse Studies* on the language of the manosphere, which specifically seeks to broaden the focus of linguistic research beyond English, at https://think.taylorandfrancis.com/special_issues/language-manosphere -global-perspectives/.

109. DeCook and Kelly, "Interrogating the 'Incel Menace'"; Jasser, Kelly, and Rothermel, "Male Supremacism and the Hanau Terrorist Attack." Also see Ebner, *Going Mainstream*, p. 28; and see Jasser, et al., "Male Supremacism."

110. Diverting Hate, "Misogynistic Extremism," September 2024, especially pp. 27–46.

111. For an analysis of mental health among misogynist incels, see Whittaker, et al., "Predicting Harm among Incels"; for discussion of autism and misogynist incels, see Gheorghe and Clement, "Weaponized Autism."

112. Whittaker, et al., "Predicting Harm among Incels," pp. 21–23; on male sexual entitlement and misogyny as foundational to the victimhood of male supremacists and incels, see Kelly, et al., "Victim, Violent, Vulnerable."

113. See Gheorghe and Clement, "Weaponized Autism."

114. Czerwinsky, "Misogynist Incels Gone Mainstream."

115. Broyd, et al., "Incels, Violence, and Mental Disorder," p. 257.

116. See extensive discussion in Gheorghe and Clement, "Weaponized Autism"; also see the discussion of weaponized autism in Christie Welch, et al., "Understanding the Use of the Term 'Weaponized Autism' in An Alt-Right Social Media Platform," *Journal of Autism and Developmental Disorders* 53, no. 10 (2023): 4035–4046. https://doi.org/10.1007/s10803-022-05701-0; for a discussion of autism and risk of violent extremism, see Cécile Janique Johnson-Lafleur Rousseau, et al., "Social and Individual Grievances and Attraction to Extremist Ideologies in Individuals with Autism: Insights from a Clinical Sample," *Research in Autism Spectrum Disorders* 105, 2023, https://doi.org/10.1016/j.rasd.2023.102171.

117. In addition to the literature already cited in this chapter, see for example Gheorghe, "Just Be White (JBW)"; Jonanssen, "Reconsidering Trauma"; Solea and Sugiura, "Mainstreaming the Blackpill."

118. Phil Helsel, "Ohio 'Incel' Who Plotted to Kill Women"; "Southern District of Ohio | Highland County Man Sentenced to More Than 6 Years in Prison for Attempting Hate Crime," US Department of Justice, February 29, 2024, https://www.justice.gov/usao-sdoh/pr/highland -county-man-sentenced-more-6-years-prison-attempting-hate-crime; Ferrise, "Man Who Planned Mass Shooting."

119. *Dobbs, State Health Officer of the Mississippi Department of Health, et. al, v. Jackson Women's Health Organization et al,"* no. 19–1392 (2021).

120. See the explanation in "Dobbs v. Jackson Women's Health Organization," *Center for Reproductive Rights*, March 19, 2018, https://reproductiverights.org/case/scotus-mississippi -abortion-ban/.

121. As already argued in Miller-Idriss, "How the Loss of *Roe* Directly Serves White Supremacists' Horrifying Plot"; also see Fieldstadt, "Former Marine Is Accused"; Rawnsley and Hughes, "Neo-Nazi Marine Plotted Mass Murder."

122. See Miller-Idriss, "Tucker Carlson Is the No.1 Champion of This Leading Far-Right Conspiracy."

123. Aguilera and Adams, "What the Buffalo Tragedy Has to Do."

124. "White Supremacists' Mixed Reactions."

125. Odette Yousef, "Supremacy Movements Unite."

126. Mattheis, "Shieldmaidens of Whiteness."

127. Stanley, *How Fascism Works*, pp. 128–129.

128. Stern, "Alt-Right Women and the 'White Baby Challenge.'"

129. A. Kheyfets, S. Dhaurali, P. Feyock, F. Khan, A. Lockley, B. Miller, and N. Amutah-Onukagha, "The Impact of Hostile Abortion Legislation on the United States Maternal Mortality Crisis: A Call for Increased Abortion Education," *Front Public Health* (2023), https://doi.org/10.3389/fpubh.2023.1291668; also see Kelly Baden, Joerg Dreweke, and Candace Gibson, "Clear and Growing Evidence That Dobbs Is Harming Reproductive Health and Freedom," *Guttmacher Institute*, May 2024, www.guttmacher.org/2024/05/clear-and-growing-evidence-dobbs-harming-reproductive-health-and-freedom.

130. Lithwick, "The Horrifying Implications."

131. Blakemore, "How U.S. Abortion Laws."

132. Samuels and Potts, "How the Fight to Ban Abortion."

133. DiBranco, "The Long History."

134. Aguilera and Adams, "What the Buffalo Tragedy Has to Do."

135. Lamoureux, "New York Cop Bought Rifle."

136. Leidig, "'We Are Worth Fighting For.'"

4. Exploitation: #SaveTheChildren

1. See Kang, "Fake News Onslaught"; Helm, "Pizzagate Nearly Destroyed My Restaurant."

2. "The Nexus Between Terrorism and Human Trafficking"; "Trafficking in Human Beings and Terrorism," *Organization for Security and Co-operation in Europe*, 2021, CTHB_Nexus Terrorism_210708.indd (osce.org).

3. See, e.g., John Feffer, "The Global Right Wing's Bizarre Obsession with Pedophilia," *Institute for Policy Studies*, July 28, 2021, The Global Right Wing's Bizarre Obsession with Pedophilia - Institute for Policy Studies (ips-dc.org).

4. Feffer, "The Global Right Wing's Bizarre Obsession."

5. Tait, "How the Alt-Right Wields and Weaponises Accusations of Paedophilia."

6. "The QAnon Conspiracy"; Robb, "Anatomy of a Fake News Scandal"; "Train Operator"; Ling, "Gun-Wielding QAnon Advocate"; "Texas Butterfly Centre Closes."

7. Jensen and Kane, "QAnon-Inspired Violence."

8. Contrera, "A QAnon Con."

9. Anjana Rajan, et al., "Countering QAnon," *Polaris*, February 2021, https://polarisproject.org/wp-content/uploads/2021/02/Polaris-Report-Countering-QAnon.pdf, p. 2.

10. Rajan, et al., "Countering QAnon," p. 9.

11. Barrón-López and Lane, "How Some Evangelical Leaders." Also see Rogers, "Why QAnon Has Attracted So Many White Evangelicals."

12. "What You Need to Know about QAnon"; Katrin Bennhold and Erika Solomon, "Fringe Group Suspected in German Plot Got a Lift from QAnon," *The New York Times*, December 8, 2022, https://www.nytimes.com/2022/12/08/world/europe/germany-plot-qanon.html.

13. Coster van Voorhout, "How Human Trafficking Fuels Erosion."

14. Cook, *The Quiet Damage*.

15. Feffer, "The Global Right Wing's Bizarre Obsession."

16. As noted by sociologist Robert Bartholomew in Tait, "How the Alt-Right Wields and Weaponises Accusations of Paedophilia."

17. Crawford and Argentino, "QAnon Women in Politics Part One."

18. Russonello, "QAnon Now As Popular in U.S. as Some Major Religions."

19. Jackman, et al., "A Quarter of Americans Believe."

20. Rajan, et al., "Countering QAnon," 13, citing Michael Barbaro and Sheera Frenkel, "Is More Violence Coming?," *The New York Times*, January 13, 2021, https://www.nytimes.com /2021/01/13/podcasts/the-daily/capitol-attack-social-media-parler-twitter-facebook.html.

21. See the meta-analysis in Kim and Royle, "Domestic Violence."

22. See for example the meta-analysis at Karbasi, et al., "The Silent Crisis."

23. See 30-year statistics at "Reported Forcible Rape Rate in the United States from 1990 to 2022," Statista, July 5, 2024, https://www.statista.com/statistics/191226/reported-forcible-rape -rate-in-the-us-since-990/#:~:text=In%202022%2C%20the%20rate%20of,forcible%20 rapes%20per%20100%2C000%20inhabitants.; see the revised FBI definition at "Rape," FBI, https://ucr.fbi.gov/crime-in-the-u.s/2017/crime-in-the-u.s.-2017/topic-pages/rape. On the underreporting of rape and sexual assault, see "Statistics About Sexual Violence."

24. Data from "How Does Gun Violence Impact the Communities You Care About?" Everytown for Gun Safety, with statistics updated as of August 20, 2024, EveryStat - EveryStat.org.

25. See a full-length book discussion in Esman, *Rage*; also see Geller, et al., "The Role of Domestic Violence."

26. Rottweiler, et al., "A Common Psychology of Male Violence?"

27. Hudson and Hodgson, "Sex and Terror," p. 611; Marganski, "Making a Murderers."

28. See "Ending Domestic Violence Requires Us All to Work Together," Office on Violence Against Women, October 31, 2023, https://www.justice.gov/ovw/blog/dvam-2023-ending -domestic-violence-requires-us-all-work-together#:~:text=Data%20from%20the%20last%20 National,intimate%20partner%20violence%2Drelated%20impact.

29. See Fast Facts: "About Sexual Violence," Centers for Disease Control (CDC), January 23, 2024, https://www.cdc.gov/sexual-violence/about/?CDC_AAref_Val=https://www.cdc.gov /violenceprevention/sexualviolence/fastfact.html.

30. See "Domestic Violence Statistics," National Domestic Violence Hotline, https://www .thehotline.org/stakeholders/domestic-violence-statistics/. Also see Lyons and Brewer, "Experiences of Intimate Partner Violence."

31. See the most recent data in "Reports and Publications," National Intimate Partner and Sexual Violence (NIPSV), May 16, 2024, https://www.cdc.gov/nisvs/documentation/index. html.

32. See "Home, the Most Dangerous Place for Women, with Majority of Female Homicide Victims Worldwide Killed by Partners or Family, UNODC Study Says," *Global Study on Homicide, United Nations*, November 25, 2018, https://www.unodc.org/unodc/en/frontpage/2018 /November/home-the-most-dangerous-place-for-women-with-majority-of-female-homicide -victims-worldwide-killed-by-partners-or-family--unodc-study-says.html.

33. Hudson and Hodgson, "Sex and Terror," p. 611.

34. Hudson and Hodgson, "Sex and Terror," p. 624.

35. Hudson and Hodgson, "Sex and Terror," p. 624.

36. Johnston and True, "Misogyny and Violent Extremism," p. 1.

37. "Trauma as Precursor to Violent Extremism."

38. Pollak, "An Intergenerational Model of Domestic Violence."

39. For more on this argument, see Cynthia Miller-Idriss, "Stop Calling Far-Right Terrorists 'Crazy'," *Politico*, February 20, 2020, https://www.politico.eu/article/stop-calling-far-right -terrorists-crazy/.

40. Gentry, *Disordered Violence*, p. 169.

41. Esman, *Rage*, p. 133.

42. For a longer discussion, see Issa, "'A Profoundly Masculine Act.'"

43. Rottweiler, et al., "A Common Psychology of Male Violence?".

44. See the Duluth Model on the Domestic Abuse Interventions Program website at "Understanding the Power and Control Wheel," Domestic Abuse Intervention Programs, https://www.theduluthmodel.org/wheels/

45. I am indebted to the investigative journalist Jordan Green for discussions about this case. See *United States of America v. Lawrence Powell Earhart*, II. Plea Agreement. District Court, Eastern District of Tennessee at Greeneville. Nr. 2:18-CR-17 Judge Jordan.

46. Personal correspondence and conversations with Jordan Green, February 2024.

47. Forget, "Violent Drug Organizations."

48. "Leader of White Supremist Gang"; "Drug Ring Tied to Aryan Prison Gang"; Hernandez, "Operation"; Valazquez, "57 Member/Associates"; Bote, "21 Alleged White Supremacists"; Sinha, "Drug Ring"; Andy Rose, "Prosecutors in Utah."

49. Brownmiller, *Against Our Will*, pp. 126–131.

50. Phelan, et al., "Misogyny," p. 14.

51. Brownmiller, *Against Our Will*, pp. 49–56.

52. "Part 4B: Women's Camps and Brothels."

53. Tsoutsoumpis, "The Far Right in Greece."

54. Reported in Tsoutsoumpis, "The Far Right in Greece."

55. AFP, "Germany Opens Files."

56. "Aryan Brotherhood."

57. Personal correspondence with Jordan Green, February 2024.

58. McMurtry, "Police Arrest 14 Members."

59. Reuters, "Austrian Neo-Nazi Group Members."

60. Roos, "Backlash against Prostitutes' Rights."

61. Tagliabue, "The Dresden Scene."

62. AFP, "Russian Neo-Nazi Jailed."

63. Diverting Hate, "Misogynistic Extremism," especially pp. 14–15; Tahsin and Shea, "Andrew Tate: Chats in 'War Room' Suggest Dozens of Women Groomed."

64. Carpenter and Gates, "The Nature and Extent of Gang Involvement."

65. See, e.g., Henry, "Theorizing Wartime Rape."

66. See discussion in Pascoe and Hollander, "Good Guys Don't Rape"; also see the discussion of violent porn and its impact on unwanted sexual choking and asphyxiation behaviors in Orenstein, "The Troubling Trend in Teenage Sex."

67. Hayes, et al., "Are Honor Killings Unique?"

68. Lamoreaux, "Why Do Neo-Nazis Keep Getting Arrested?"

69. Weiner, "Accused Former Atomwaffen Division Leader."

70. Annie Todd, "Cult Member Accused of Embezzling from US Government," Organized Crime and Corruption Reporting Center, June 26, 2019, https://www.occrp.org/en/daily/10064-mormon-man-accused-of-embezzling-from-us-government; Stephen Lemons, "Blood Cult," Southern Poverty Law Center, August 18, 2017, https://www.splcenter.org/fighting-hate/intelligence-report/2017/blood-cult.

71. On Andrew Tate's views on younger women, see for example "Andrew Tate: 'The reason 18 and 19-year-olds are more attractive than 25-year-olds is because they've been through less dick. I'll say this right here on the fucking Internet. I don't give a shit,'" r/Nelk (reddit.com), https://www.reddit.com/r/Nelk/comments/wb6n9g/andrew_tate_the_reason_18_and_19yearolds_are_more/. For a longer analysis of "hitting the wall" and the sexualization of younger women and girls, see Diverting Hate, "Diverting Hate: Misogynistic Extremism," pp. 22–23.

72. Whittier, "Where Are the Children?"

73. Roxane Gay, "The Careless Language of Sexual Violence," in *Bad Feminist: Tenth Anniversary Edition*, p. 129.

74. See, e.g., "Prevention of Child Recruitment and Exploitation."

75. See FBI Public Service Announcement Alert Number I-091223-PSA, "Violent Online Groups Extort Minors to Self-Harm and Produce Child Sexual Abuse Material," Federal Bureau of Investigation, September 12, 2023, https://www.ic3.gov/Media/Y2023/PSA230912.

76. CTEC, "Dangerous Organizations and Bad Actors: Order of Nine Angles," *Middlebury Institute of International Studies at Monterey*, September 29, 2023, https://www.middlebury.edu/institute/academics/centers-initiatives/ctec/publications/dangerous-organizations-and-bad-actors-order-nine.

77. "Southern District of New York | Former U.S. Army Soldier Sentenced to 45 Years in Prison for Attempting to Murder Fellow Service Members in Deadly Ambush," US Department of Justice, March 3, 2023, https://www.justice.gov/usao-sdny/pr/former-us-army-soldier-sentenced-45-years-prison-attempting-murder-fellow-service.

78. See the extensive discussion in Argentino, et al., "764: The Intersection of Terrorism."

79. See August 27, 2024, news release from the Royal Canadian Mounted Police at "RCMP Reminds Canadians About Violent Online Groups Targeting Youth," Royal Canadian Mounted Police, August 27, 2024, https://www.rcmp-grc.gc.ca/en/news/2024/rcmp-reminds-canadians-violent-online-groups-targeting-youth.

80. Lamoreaux, "The Vile Sextortion and Torture Ring Where Kids Target Kids."

81. Argentino, et al., "764: The Intersection of Terrorism"; also see Lamoreaux, "Police Arrest Alleged Leader"; Tangalakis-Lippert, "FBI Busts Neo-Nazi Cult"; Anugrah Kumar, "FBI Warns About Global Satanic Pedophile Cult Seeking to Destroy Judeo-Christian Western Society," *Christian Post*, October 2, 2023, https://www.christianpost.com/news/fbi-warns-about-global-satanic-pedophile-cult.html (businessinsider.com); https://www.christianpost.com/news/fbi-warns-about-global-satanic-pedophile-cult.html.

82. Argentino, et al., "764: The Intersection of Terrorism."

83. See August 27, 2024 news release from the Royal Canadian Mounted Police, "RCMP Reminds Canadians About Violent Online Groups Targeting Youth."

84. See Kilmer and Kowert, "Grooming for Violence."

85. See Iselin Frydenlund and Eviane Leidig, "Introduction: 'Love Jihad': Sexuality, Reproduction and the Construction of the Predatory Muslim Male," *Religions* 13, no. 3 (2022): 201, https://doi.org/10.3390/rel13030201

86. Wilson, "Nostalgia," p. 1813.

87. Feola, *The Rage of Replacement*, p. 22.

88. Feola, *The Rage of Replacement*, p. 115.

89. Burnett and Richardson, "'Breeders for Race and Nation.'"

90. See, e.g., St-Esprit, "Targeted by a White Supremacist."

91. Wilson, "Nostalgia," p. 1814.

92. Feola, *The Rage of Replacement*, p. 117.

93. Feola, *The Rage of Replacement*, pp. 117–118.

94. Feola, *The Rage of Replacement*, pp. 118.

95. "Day of the Rope."

96. "Towards Meaningful Accountability."

97. Feola, *The Rage of Replacement*, pp. 119–120.

98. Basu, "The Metaverse Has a Groping Problem Already"; for more on the metaverse and violent extremism, see Lakhani, "When Digital and Physical World Combine."

99. Burgess, "The AI-Generated Child Abuse Nightmare Is Here"; U.K. Home Office and the Right Honorable Suella Braverman KC MP, "UK and US Pledge to Combat AI-Generated Images of Child Abuse," Gov.uk, September 27, 2023, https://www.gov.uk/government/news /uk-and-us-pledge-to-combat-ai-generated-images-of-child-abuse.

100. "Sextortion: A Growing Threat Targeting Minors."

101. Atwood, *Second Words*, p. 413.

5. Erasure: "Don't Say Gay"

1. Accettulla and Sloan, "WATCH."

2. Ian King, "Disney Caught in Crossfire of 'Don't Say Gay' Row," *Sky News*, April 21, 2022, https://news.sky.com/story/disney-caught-in-crossfire-of-dont-say-gay-row-12595241; "Statement from Walt Disney Company on Signing of Florida Legislation."

3. McShane, "Neo-Nazi Groups Spew Hate"; Faiza Saqib, "Nazi Protesters Wave Swastika Flags Outside Disney World," *Sky News*, June 13, 2023, https://news.sky.com/story/absolutely -disgusting-nazi-protesters-wave-swastika-flags-outside-disney-world-12901495.

4. "2023 Anti-Trans Bills: Trans Legislation Tracker."

5. "Mapping Attacks on LGBTQ Rights."

6. See the full text of President Trump's executive order dated January 20, 2025, "Defending Women from Gender Ideology Extremism and Restoring Biological Truth to the Federal Government," at https://www.whitehouse.gov/presidential-actions/2025/01/defending-women -from-gender-ideology-extremism-and-restoring-biological-truth-to-the-federal-government.

7. Jamie Ballard, "One-third of Americans Say Their Ideal Relationship Is Non-Monogamous," YouGov, January 31, 2020, https://today.yougov.com/society/articles/27639 -millennials-monogamy-poly-poll-survey-data.

8. Namaste, *Invisible Lives*; Rose, "Land Rights and Deep Colonising"; Zongrone, et al., "Erasure and Resilience"; Gray, "Addressing LGBTQ Erasure; Lugg and Tooms, "A Shadow of Ourselves"; Andrews, et al., "#SaytheWord"; Klein, *The History of Forgetting*; Ruefle, "On Erasure."

9. Bailey and Trudy, "On Misogynoir."

10. Morrison, ed. *Burn This Book*, pp. 3–4.

11. Bauer, et al., "'I Don't Think This Is Theoretical.'"

12. Encarnacion, "Florida's 'Don't Say Gay' Bill."

13. Aja Romano, "The Right's Moral Panic Over "Grooming" Invokes Age-Old Homophobia," Vox, April 21, 2022, https://www.vox.com/culture/23025505/leftist-groomers -homophobia-satanic-panic-explained.

14. Jenkins, *Moral Panic*, pp. 61–63.

15. Jenkins, *Moral Panic*, p. 227.

16. I am indebted to an anonymous reviewer at Princeton University Press for this point. For an analysis of homophobia as a political and nationalist project, see K. Slootmaeckers, "Nationalism as Competing Masculinities: Homophobia as a Technology of Othering for Hetero- and Homonationalism," *Theory and Society* 48 (2019): 239–265, https://doi.org/10.1007/s11186-019-09346-4.

17. "Challenging Christian Nationalism."

18. PBS News (@NewsHour), "A growing movement led by right-wing politicians is increasingly challenging a centuries-old value of America's political system."

19. See my fuller argument about Christian nationalism in Miller-Idriss, "Christian Nationalism."

20. The following section relies on the extensive timeline detailed here: "Timeline: Building a Pseudoscience Network."

21. See the discussion of the Obama administration guidance and the Trump administration's formal rescinding of that guidance at Casey, "After Trump Rescinds Title IX Guidance."

22. See the extensive discussion in Butler, *Who's Afraid of Gender?*

23. Posner, "The Christian Nationalist Boot Camp."

24. HRC Staff, "For the First Time Ever."

25. Feola, *The Rage of Replacement*, p. 118.

26. Squirrell and Davey, "A Year of Hate"; also see Correa, "Gender Ideology"; Corredor, "Unpacking 'Gender Ideology'".

27. As articulated by Angela Saini, "Confronting the Anti-Gender Movement," *The Lancet*, March 23, 2024, https://doi.org/10.1016/S0140-6736(24)00540-3, written as a review of Butler, *Who's Afraid of Gender?*

28. Posner, "The Christian Nationalist Boot Camp."

29. Daviess and Berger, "Lawful Extremism," p. 9.

30. Butler, *Who's Afraid of Gender?*, pp. 43–46. For a discussion of the term "feminazi," see Zoe Williams, "Feminazi: The Go-To Term for Trolls Out to Silence Women," *The Guardian*, September 15, 2015.

31. Butler, *Who's Afraid of Gender?*, pp. 50–51.

32. See the bills Arizona HB1700 and Arizona SB1001, discussed at http://translegislation.com.

33. Posner, "The Christian Nationalist Boot Camp."

34. McCann and Walker, "Abortion Bans Across the Country"; "State Legislation Tracker."

35. Bendix, "Three Alabama Clinics Pause IVF."

36. Karin Brulliard, "Fears of Witch Hunts Over Utah Ban on Trans Athletes in Girls' Sports," *The Washington Post*, February 26, 2024, https://www.washingtonpost.com/nation/2024/02/26/utah-transgender-students-sports-ban/; Whitehurst, "Transgender Athlete Ban Challenged in Utah Lawsuit."

37. Brulliard, "Fears of Witch Hunts Over Utah Ban on Trans Athletes in Girls' Sports."

38. Stern, "A New Witch-Hunt"; "#Outlawed: 'The Love That Dare Not Speak Its Name,'" Human Rights Watch, https://features.hrw.org/features/features/lgbt_laws/.

39. Anti-Defamation League, "Online Hate and Harassment."

40. Anti-Defamation League, "Online Hate and Harassment."

41. Westbrook, *Unlivable Lives.*

42. Levengood and Hadland, "Hostile Laws and Hospitalization."

43. Goldberg, "Impact of HB 1557."

44. Goldberg, et al., "Perceived Impact."

45. Rios, "Idaho Librarian Resigns"; Kingkade, "Conservative Activists."

46. Holmes, "Book Burning and Banning."

47. Elizabeth A. Harris and Alexandra Alta, "With Rising Book Bans, Librarians Have Come Under Attack," *The New York Times*, July 6, 2022, https://www.nytimes.com/2022/07/06/books/book-ban-librarians.html.

48. Baptiste, "Florida's 'Don't Say Gay' Law."

49. Nittle, "Florida Faces Teacher Shortage."

50. Prieur, "In Florida, Teachers Are Quitting."

51. Trudell, *Doing Sex Education.*

52. Squirrell and Davey, "A Year of Hate."

53. Waxman, "Why Toni Morrison Books Are Frequent Targets of Book Bans"; Kasakove, "The Fight Over 'Maus.'"

54. "Banned Book List"; also see PEN America's report, "Spineless Shelves: Two Years of Book Banning," *PEN America*, December 14, 2023, https://pen.org/spineless-shelves/.

55. Natanson, "Virginia Mom Challenges One School Book a Week." Investigations by *The Washington Post* found that the same 11 people were responsible for 60% of schoolbook challenges in 2021–22: see McDaniel and Natanson, "Dictionaries."

56. Smith, "School Book Bans."

57. McDaniel and Natanson, "Dictionaries."

58. Yurcaba, "Missouri Republican Candidate."

59. Posner, *Unholy*, p. 156; also see Miller-Idriss, *Hate in the Homeland*.

60. McGee, "Lawmakers Advance Bill."

61. Confessore, "'America Is Under Attack.'"

62. Luscombe, "Ron DeSantis Condemned"; "Board of Governors Adds Factual History Course."

63. Paul, "Cultural Marxism."

64. Posner, *Unholy*, p. 156.

65. Phillips-Fein, "How the Right Learned to Loathe Higher Education."

66. The Anti-Defamation League reported that, in March 2018, Yiannopoulos announced that the charity administering the grant had closed. Anti-Defamation League, "Milo Yiannopoulos: Five Things to Know," *ADL*, n.d., accessed February 27, 2020, https://www.adl.org/resources/backgrounders/milo-yiannopoulos-five-things-to-know.

67. Patricia Mezzai, "DeSantis Targeted New College of Florida. Here's What's Changed," *The New York Times*, September 22, 2023, https://www.nytimes.com/2023/09/22/us/new-college-florida-desantis.html.

68. Jim DeLa, "New College Students Begin Exodus After Conservative Control."

69. Rose Horowitch, "Florida's 'Stop WOKE' Law"; Katie Reilly, "What Florida's Stop Woke Act Means for Schools, Businesses," *TIME*, April 22, 2022, https://time.com/6168753/florida-stop-woke-law/; "Stop Woke Handout."

70. Benjamin Krämer and Magdalena Klingler. "A Bad Political Climate."

71. Krämer and Klingler, "A Bad Political Climate," p. 258.

72. Stanley, *How Fascism Works*.

73. Thomas Nichols, *The Death of Expertise: The Campaign against Established Knowledge and Why It Matters* (London: Oxford University Press, 2017). Also see the discussion in Frank, "Why Expertise Matters."

74. Miller-Idriss, *Hate in the Homeland*; Russell Muirhead and Nancy L. Rosenblum, *A Lot of People Are Saying: The New Conspiracism and the Assault on Democracy* (Princeton, NJ: Princeton University Press, 2019), pp. 5–7.

75. Brubaker, "Why Populism?"; Berezin, "Facism and Populism"; Miller-Idriss, "The Global Dimensions of National Populism"; Woods, et al., "COVID-19 and Nationalism."

76. Jones, "Trans Bans Expand."

77. Odette Yousef, "Patriot Front Members Arrested Near a Pride Event in Coeur d'Alene, Idaho," NPR, June 12, 2022, https://www.npr.org/2022/06/11/1104405804/patriot-front-white-supremacist-arrested-near-idaho-pride.

78. There are dozens of media reports easily accessible online. To name a few examples: Brandon Tensley, "Proud Boys Crashed Drag Queen Story Hour at a Local Library. It Was Part of a Wider Movement," CNN, July 22, 2022, https://www.cnn.com/2022/07/21/us/drag-lgbtq-rights-race-deconstructed-newsletter-reaj/index.html; Emily Mikkelsen and Nexstar Media Wire, "Proud Boys 'Came to Fight' at North Carolina Drag Brunch," *The Hill*, November 4, 2022, https://thehill.com/homenews/3718909-proud-boys-came-to-fight-at-north-carolina-drag-brunch/; Christopher Wiggins, "Drag Producer Cancels Shows After Armed Proud Boys Threaten Event," *The Advocate*, January 26, 2023, https://www.advocate.com/news/proud-boys-drag-suspend-show; WTOL Newsroom, "Neo-Nazis Harass Attendees at Equality

Toledo's Love Fest Celebration," WTOL.com, July 17, 2023, https://www.wtol.com/article/news/local/neo-nazis-harass-attendees-equality-toledo-love-fest-celebration/512-3df9c50c-3c0d-4133-b032-dc13f804190c.

79. Cited in Harris and Alta, "With Rising Book Bans, Librarians Have Come Under Attack."

80. Grant, "How to Stop Neo-Nazis from Crashing Pride Month."

81. Suarez, "Protesters."

82. Johnston and True, "Misogyny and Violent Extremism," p. 4.

83. Evidence later suggested that the attacker, who was motivated by Islamist extremist ideology, may not have known the Pulse nightclub was a gay nightclub, but the impact of the shooting was still terrorizing to gay people nationwide, as researchers have demonstrated. See Relihan, et al., "Shared Social Identity." See Coaston, "New evidence Shows the Pulse Nightclub Shooting Wasn't About Anti-LGBTQ Hate."

84. Grant, "How to Stop Neo-Nazis from Crashing Pride Month."

85. Anti-Defamation League, "Anti-Defamation League, White Supremacist Propaganda Incidents Soar to Record High in 2023," ADL, March 26, 2023, https://www.adl.org/resources/report/white-supremacist-propaganda-incidents-soar-record-high-2023.

86. "ADL and GLAAD Report."

87. GLAAD, "GLAAD, UPDATED Report."

88. Wiggins, "FBI Says Anti-LGBTQ+ Hate Crimes Are Way Up."

89. Bennett, et al., "How the Rise of Anti-LGBTQ+ Hate and Violence Is Impacting the Community"; "Store Owner Shot to Death"; Espadas and Leal, "Two Soldiers Arrested in Virginia."

90. WTOL11, "Neo-Nazis Harass Attendees"; Lavietes, "Pride Flag Burned Outside a City Hall in Arizona"; Myers, "Pride Flags Stolen"; Schuba, "Gay-Owned Restaurant."

91. Craanen, et al., "Transmisogyny," p. 5 and pp. 15–16.

92. "An Epidemic of Violence: Fatal Violence against the Transgender and Gender-Expansive Community in 2021," Human Rights Campaign, https://reports.hrc.org/an-epidemic-of-violence-fatal-violence-against-transgender-and-gender-non-confirming-people-in-the-united-states-in-2021; "Fatal Violence Against the Transgender and Gender-Expansive Community in 2022," Human Rights Campaign, https://www.hrc.org/resources/fatal-violence-against-the-transgender-and-gender-expansive-community-in-2022.

93. Data from Everytown for Gun Safety, with statistics updated as of August 20, 2024. See https://everystat.org/#transgender.

94. Craanen, et al., "Transmisogyny," p. 9.

95. "2024 U.S. National Survey on the Mental Health of LGBTQ+ Young People," The Trevor Project, https://www.thetrevorproject.org/survey-2024/.

96. Craanen, et al., "Transmisogyny." pp. 6 and 10; also see Jones, "Trans Bans Expand"; Schilt and Westbrook, "Doing Gender."

97. Jones, "Trans Bans Expand."

98. Wareham, "Beaten, Stabbed and Shot"; "Fatal Violence against the Transgender and Gender-Expansive Community in 2023," Human Rights Campaign, November 13, 2023, https://www.hrc.org/resources/fatal-violence-against-the-transgender-and-gender-expansive-community-in-2023; "Report Says At Least 32 Transgender People Were Killed in the U.S. in 2022," PBS NewsHour, November 16, 2022, https://www.pbs.org/newshour/nation/report-says-at-least-32-transgender-people-were-killed-in-the-u-s-in-2022; also see data cited in "U.S. National Plan to End Gender-Based Violence." Banks and Kyckelhahn, "Characteristics of Suspected Trafficking Incidents."

99. "ADL and GLAAD Report."

100. Bennet, et al., "How the Rise of Anti-LGBTQ Hate and Violence Is Impacting the Community"; Tebor, "Suspect in O'Shae Sibley Killing Charged with Murder."

101. See "Uganda: Court Upholds Anti-Homosexuality Act," Human Rights Watch, April 4, 2024, https://www.hrw.org/news/2024/04/04/uganda-court-upholds-anti-homosexuality-act; Daniel Anthony, "Uganda's Anti-Gay Bill Leads a Terrifying Domino Effect Across Africa," *The Daily Beast*, August 19, 2023, https://www.thedailybeast.com/ugandas-anti-gay-bill-leads-a-terrifying-domino-effect-across-africa; Caleb Okehere, "How U.S. Evangelicals Helped Homophobia Flourish in Africa," *Foreign Policy*, March 19, 2023, https://foreignpolicy.com/2023/03/19/africa-uganda-evangelicals-homophobia-antigay-bill/.

102. Squirrel and Davey, "A Year in Hate."

103. Adamczeski, "Children's Hospital in D.C."; Morse, "Hospital and Physicians Groups"; Media Matters, "Libs of TikTok Targets Phoenix Children's Hospital," Libs of TikTok Targets Phoenix Children's Hospital | Media Matters for America; Webster, "Critics attack UPMC Children's"; Lin-Fisher, "Right-Wing Social Media Attack"; Gluck, "Vanderbilt Transgender Clinic."

104. "Children's Hospitals Harassed Over Transgender Care Programs."

105. Sana Sinha, Nicolas Zerbino, Jon Valant, and Rachel M. Perera, "Moms for Liberty: Where Are They, and Are They Winning?" *Brookings Institution*, October 10, 2023; Smythe, "I'm Credited with Having Coined the Word 'Terf.'"

106. Gill-Peterson, *A Short History of Trans Misogyny*.

107. Butler, *Who's Afraid of Gender?*, p. 144.

108. Aja Romano, "Is J. K. Rowling Transphobic? Let's Let Her Speak for Herself," Vox, August 2, 2024, J. K. Rowling's Transphobia: A History—Vox; Gardner, "A Complete Breakdown."

109. "Transgender People Over Four Times More Likely Than Cisgender People to Be Victims of Violent Crime," UCLA School of Law Williams Institute, March 23, 2021.

6. Enabling: The White Baby Challenge

1. The Ruby Ridge standoff, together with the siege at the Branch Davidian compound in Waco, Texas, the following year, would together inspire the terrorist attack on Oklahoma City. See Belew, *Bring the War Home*, p. 198; Pitcavage, "Twenty Years Later"; "Ruby Ridge," Brittanica.com, https://www.britannica.com/event/Ruby-Ridge.

2. I am indebted to Lydia Bates for this point.

3. See the US Department of Justice redacted report on Ruby Ridge at https://www.justice.gov/sites/default/files/opr/legacy/2006/11/09/rubyreport40_84.pdf

4. As cited in Belew, *Bring the War Home*, p. 184; also see the description of the Ruby Ridge siege and the killing of Vicki Weaver on pp. 187–188.

5. Darby, *Sisters in Hate*, p. 238.

6. For US figures (women represent 5.8% of violent far-right extremists and terrorists in the US) see the National Consortium for the Study of Terrorism and Responses to Terrorism (START). "Profiles of Individual Radicalization in the United States (PIRUS)." Research Brief, May 2020, https://www.start.umd.edu/pubs/START_PIRUS_ResearchBrief_May2020.pdf.

7. See the US Department of Justice report of the investigation of Ashli Babbitt's death at: https://www.justice.gov/usao-dc/pr/department-justice-closes-investigation-death-ashli-babbitt. Also see Paul Schwartzman and Josh Dawsey, "How Ashli Babbitt Went from Capitol Rioter to Trump-embraced 'Martyr,'" *The Washington Post*, July 30, 2021.

8. See Anti Defamation League, "Far-Right Extremists Memorialize 'Martyr' Ashli Babbitt," January 15, 2021, https://www.adl.org/blog/far-right-extremists-memorialize-martyr-ashli-babbitt.

9. See Russonello, "QAnon Now as Popular in U.S. as Some Major Religions"; and Kelly, "Mothers for QAnon."

10. "Ashli Babbitt: The US Veteran Shot Dead Breaking into the Capitol"; Ellen Barry, Nicholas Bogel-Burroughs, and Dave Philipps, "Woman Killed in Capitol Embraced Trump and Qanon," *The New York Times*, January 7, 2021, https://www.nytimes.com/2021/01/08/us/who-was-ashli-babbitt.html

11. Santucci, et al., "Gender and Right-Wing Extremism in America."

12. See GWU Program on Extremism's Capitol Siege database at https://extremism.gwu.edu/Capitol-Hill-Siege.

13. As argued in Miller-Idriss, "Women among the Jan. 6 Attackers." See historical data in the START PIRUS dataset at the University of Maryland at https://www.start.umd.edu/profiles-individual-radicalization-united-states-pirus-keshif. Some of the arguments articulated in this section of this chapter were first published in Miller-Idriss, "Triumph of the Women."

14. Blee, *Women of the Klan*; McRae, "The Women Behind White Power."

15. See especially Blee, *Women of the Klan*.

16. See Matfess and Margolin, "The Women of January 6th"; also see Miller-Idriss, *Hate in the Homeland*.

17. Several polls estimated that a majority of Tea Party supporters were women. See, e.g., Vogel, Kenneth P. "Face of the Tea Party Is Female." At its peak in 2010, nearly one-third of Americans supported the Tea Party, and 24% supported it in 2014. See Gallup polling data at Tea Party Support Holds at 24% (gallup.com).

18. Deckman, *Tea Party Women*, p. 1.

19. For a fuller review of these arguments, see Deckman, *Tea Party Women*, pp. 3–4 and 17.

20. Deckman, *Tea Party Women*, pp. 19–21.

21. Amélie Ribieras, "'I want to thank my husband Fred for letting me come here,' or Phyllis Schlafly's opportunistic defense of gender hierarchy," pp. 68–93 in Carian, et al., *Male Supremacism*; Kennedy, "How Phyllis Schlafly Derailed the Equal Rights Amendment."

22. Farris, *In the Name of Women's Rights*.

23. Indelicato and Lopes, "Understanding Populist Far-Right Anti-Immigration."

24. For a fuller discussion of the range of women's roles in white supremacist movements, see Latif, et al., "Do White Supremacist Women Adopt Movement Archetypes of Mother, Whore, and Fighter?"

25. Belew, *Bring the War Home*, p. 160.

26. See Darby, *Sisters in Hate*; Mattheis, "Shieldmaidens of Whiteness."

27. See Echtermann, et al., "Kein Filter fuer Rechts."

28. See especially Leidig, *The Women of the Far Right*.

29. Stern, "Alt-right women and the 'white baby challenge.'"

30. Leidig, "'We Are Worth Fighting For'"; Burns, "'The Matrix Resurrections.'"

31. Darby, *Sisters in Hate*; Hunt, "What Is a 'Tradwife'."

32. Diverting Hate, "Misogynistic Extremism," pp. 20–25.

33. Tebaldi, "Tradwives and Truth Warriors," p. 26.

34. Christou, "#TradWives."

35. See Williams, "Women's Engagement with the Far Right," see especially p. 5. Also see Leidig, *The Women of the Far Right*.

36. Darby, *Sisters in Hate*, p. 156. Also see Leidig, *The Women of the Far Right*.

37. Katie Couric Media, "The Real Tradwives of 2022: Why More Young Moms Are Becoming Traditional Housewives." *Katie Couric Media*, April 8, 2022. https://katiecouric.com/culture/what-is-a-tradwife/

38. Matfess and Margolin, "The Women of January 6th"; also see Mattheis, "Shieldmaidens of Whiteness."

39. As detailed in Linder, "The Ruby Ridge (Randy Weaver) Trial."

40. Matfess and Margolin, "The Women of January 6th."

41. Kahney, "'Mommy Liberty' Packs a Gun."

42. Leidig, *Women of the Far Right*, p. 108.

43. As argued by Kristy Campion, quoted in Katie Couric Media, "The Real Tradwives of 2022"; the "softer face" quote is from Mattheis, "Shieldmaidens of Whiteness," p. 143.

44. Kelly, "The Housewives of White Supremacy."

45. Darby, *Sisters in Hate*, p. 136; Mattheis, "Shieldmaidens of Whiteness," p. 128.

46. Darby, *Sisters in Hate*, p. 143. To read the original post by Garland, "What Role for Women in Our Movement?," dated October 17, 2017, see the American Renaissance website at https://www.amren.com/commentary/2017/10/role-women-movement/.

47. Stern, "Alt-Right Women and the 'White Baby Challenge.'"

48. Green, "The Re-Birth of America's Pro-Natalist Movement."

49. See discussion in Farris, *In the Name of Women's Rights*, p. 35.

50. "The QAnon Conspiracy"; Robb, "Anatomy of a Fake News Scandal."

51. "What You Need to Know about QAnon."

52. Russonello, Giovanni. "QAnon Now As Popular in U.S. As Some Major Religions."

53. Araujo-Hawkins, "QAnon Moms"; Beckett, "QAnon."

54. Dickson, "The Birth of QAnon."

55. Argentino, and Crawford, "The Women of QAnon."

56. Cecile Guerin, "The Yoga World Is Riddled with Anti-Vaxxers and Qanon Believers," *WIRED*, January 28, 2021, https://www.wired.co.uk/article/yoga-disinformation-qanon-conspiracy-wellness

57. Dickson, "The Birth of QAmom."

58. Rahman, "Some of the Signs."

59. See image in BBC coverage here: "Stay at Home Protesters: 'We Want Our Lives Back,'" April 23, 2020, https://www.bbc.com/news/av/world-us-canada-52406515

60. I am indebted to Alex DiBranco for this point.

61. Reilly, "Women Put 'Friendly Face' on Jan. 6 Attack." Also see Matfess and Margolin, "The Women of Jan 6th."

62. Miller-Idriss and Pilkington, "Women Are Joining the Far Right."

63. Belew, *Bring the War Home*.

64. Hill Collins, "Toward a New Vision."

65. Gershon, "White Women's Role in School Segregation"; Bonds, "Race and Ethnicity II"; McRae, "White Women," drawing on her book, *Mothers of Massive Resistance*. Talk delivered at the Center for Study of the American South, November 25, 2018, Available for Viewing, "White Women and the Politics of Racial Inequality" with Dr. Elizabeth McRae—The Center for the Study of the American South (unc.edu).

66. Blee, *Inside Organized Racism*, p. 148; also see Llanera, "The Misogyny Paradox and the Alt-Right." Also see the definition of "oi toy" at Urban Dictionary.

67. Llanera, "The Misogyny Paradox and the Alt-Right."

Conclusion. Centering Gender: What Can We Do?

1. See the unclassified report, "Domestic Violent Extremism Poses Heightened Threat in 2021," US Office of the Director of National Intelligence, March 1, 2021, https://www.dni.gov/files/ODNI/documents/assessments/UnclassSummaryofDVEAssessment-17MAR21.pdf

2. See Johnston and True, "Misogyny and Violent Extremism."

3. Aslam, "Islamism and Masculinity," quotation on p. 145; the quote was cited in Hudson and Hodgson, "Sex and Terror," p. 608.

4. Swann, "Helping Boys Deal With Loneliness."

5. Sanders and Young, "A Black Mother Reflects"; Anderson, et al., "'The Talk' and Parenting While Black in America."

6. United Nations Security Council Counter-Terrorism Security Directorate (UN CTED). "Toward Meaningful Accountability for Sexual- and Gender-based Violence Linked to Terrorism," p. 42.

7. Kendi, *How to Be an Anti-Racist*. Also see the discussion of Ordinary White Supremacy (OWS) and Extremist White Supremacy (EWS) in Blee, et al., *Out of Hiding*.

8. Kendi, *How to Be an Antiracist*.

9. Manne *Down Girl*, p. 101.

10. Manne, *Down Girl*, p. 27.

11. Manne, *Down Girl*, p. 24, emphasis added.

12. DiMaggio, "Culture and Cognition," quotation on p. 269.

13. The United States elected its first woman vice president in 2020. Women hold nearly a third of CEO and executive leadership roles across industries as of 2021. A third of all universities in the US are now led by women presidents—by far the highest percentage in US higher education history. See Gilligan, "States with the Highest Percentage of Female Top Executives"; Zernicke, "The Campus Wars." Data on US presidents available in "The American College President: 2023 edition," The American Council on Education, April 14, 2023, https://www.acenet.edu/Research-Insights/Pages/American-College-President-Study-2023.aspx.

14. hooks, *The Will to Change*, p. 117.

15. hooks, *The Will to Change*, pp. 126–127.

16. On the normative and expected nature of online harassment and misogynistic shaming, see Banet-Weiser, *Empowered*, especially pp. 83–91. On the impact of cyberhate on women's economic wellbeing, see Jane, "Gendered Cyberhate."

17. Ebner, *Going Mainstream*, p. ix.

18. Mattheis, "Shieldmaidens of Whiteness," p. 130. Also see Belew, *Bring the War Home*; Davis, *Woman, Race, and Class*; Hill Collins, "Toward a New Vision"; hooks, *Ain't I a Woman*; hooks, *The Will to Change*; Lorde, *The Master's Tools*.

19. Wilson, "Nostalgia," p. 1821.

20. For evidence on the preventative tools created by the Polarization and Extremism Research and Innovation Lab (PERIL), see www.perilresearch.com.

21. Fazackerley, "'Vulnerable Boys Are Drawn In'"; also see Miller-Idriss, "Andrew Tate's Violent, Misogynistic Teachings," which articulates an early version of some of the analyses on Tate in this chapter.

22. Valerie M. Hudson, et al., *Sex and World Peace* (New York: Columbia University Press, 2012), as cited in Hunter and Jouenne, "All Women Belong in the Kitchen," p. 78.

23. See Buljubasic, et al., "Women's Empowerment." See discussion of quantitative data on p. 130. Also see the range of United Nations efforts and reporting on promotion of social cohesion and reduction of violent extremism through gender equality and women's empowerment. For a recent report on these efforts, see UN Women, *Empowered Women, Peaceful Communities*, 2003. Published by the United Nations Entity for Gender Equality and the Empowerment of Women (UN Women). Available at: Empowered Women, Peaceful Communities | Publications | UN Women—Asia-Pacific. Also see the 2024 PERIL-SPLC guide for communities to counter and prevent bigotry based on gender, sex, and sexuality at www.splcenter.org/peril.

24. For examples, see The Good Men Project at https://goodmenproject.com, Warrior Compassion at https://www.warriorcompassion.com, Walking Talking Men at https://walkingtalkingmen.org, and A Call to Men at https://www.acalltomen.org.

25. Jon Roozenbeek, Sander van der Linden, and Thomas Nygren, "Prebunking Interventions Based on 'Inoculation' Theory Can Reduce Susceptibility to Misinformation Across Cultures," *Misinformation Review.* Harvard Kennedy School Shorenstein Center on Media, Politics, and Public Policy, (2020), https://misinforeview.hks.harvard.edu/article/global-vaccination-badnews/.

26. See this argument as articulated in Rottweiler, et al., "A Common Psychology of Male Violence?"

27. See Anderson, "Rhymes with Rich," p. 614, on statements about this by several women including Jo Freeman, known as Joreen, the author of *The Bitch Manifesto*, a classic second-wave feminist text written sometime between 1968 and 1970 that urged women to reclaim the slur "bitch." Original text scan available at https://repository.duke.edu/dc/wlmpc/wlmms01012. See the description of the essay in the Johns Hopkins University archives at https://aspace.library.jhu.edu/repositories/3/resources/1388.

28. See Cepollaro and López de Sa, "Who Reclaims Slurs?"; also see Bianchi, "Slurs and Appropriation."

29. Montell, *Wordslut*, p. 43.

30. See the original essay by Jo Freeman (Joreen) at https://aspace.library.jhu.edu/repositories/3/resources/1388.

31. Tweet from Hillary Clinton, November 9, 2022, available at https://x.com/HillaryClinton/status/1590358280458899459.

32. Media Matters Staff, "Fox News Host Says 'we need these ladies to get married' following Republicans weak performance with single women." *Media Matters*, November 9, 2022.

33. PBS News Hour, "Researchers Report Stunning Surge of Misogyny After the Election."

34. Natalie Wynn, YouTuber on the channel Contrapoints, as quoted in Lisa Miller, "Tate-Pilled: What a Generation of Boys have Found in Andrew Tate's Extreme Male Gospel," *New York Magazine*, March 13–26, 2023, quotation on p. 57.

35. Anonymous, "What Happened After My 13-Year-Old Son Joined the Alt-Right," *Washingtonian*, May 5, 2019.

36. "Why Andrew Tate and Internet's Nastiest Men Keep Mentioning 'The Matrix,'" *The Daily Beast*, January 18, 2023 (thedailybeast.com).

37. Will, "Misogynist Influencer Andrew Tate."

38. Will, "Misogynist Influencer Andrew Tate."

39. "Violent Online Groups Extort Minors to Self-Harm and Produce Child Sexual Abuse Material." FBI Public Service Announcement Alert Number I-091223-PSA, September 12, 2023, Violent Online Groups Extort Minors to Self-Harm and Produce Child Sexual Abuse Material (ic3.gov).

40. Sharman, Fitzgerald, and Douglas, "Prevalence of Sexual Strangulation/Choking among Australian 18–35 Year Olds"; Herbenick, et al., "Prevalence and Characteristics of Choking/Strangulation During Sex."

41. Will Worley, "Stockbroker Accused of Rape 'Thought Woman Was Crying Due to the Size of His Penis,'" *The Independent*, September 8, 2016, https://www.independent.co.uk/news/uk/home-news/stockbroker-accused-rape-penis-size-woman-crying-daniel-green-sexual-assault-a7231426.html; David Sanderson, "Boy Rapists Expect Girls to Cry During Sex, Says Activist Laura Bates," *The Times*, August 13, 2018, https://www.thetimes.com/uk/crime/article/boy-rapists-expect-girls-to-cry-during-sex-says-activist-7z7r06lqr.

42. Roberts, "How to Respond to Boys Inspired by Andrew Tate."

43. See the work of Coaching Boys into Men at their website, available at: https://coachescorner.org/.

44. See the guide for communities created by the Southern Poverty Law Center (SPLC) and the Polarization and Extremism Research and Innovation Lab (PERIL) at https://www.splcenter.org/peril-community-guide.

45. See recommendations for prevention in Diverting Hate's September 2024 biannual report, "Misogynistic Extremism, The Manosphere, and Mainstream Social Media."

46. I am indebted to Pasha Dashtgard for this point.

47. Chisholm, "Racism and Anti-Feminism."

48. See the extensive discussion in Way, *Rebels With a Cause*.

49. Messner, "Bad Men, Good Men, Bystanders."

50. See *Diverting Hate*, Vol. 3 (2024), especially pp. 48–49.

51. hooks, *The Will to Change*, p. 121.

52. See especially the discussion throughout Manley, *The New Masculinity*.

53. "A Longitudinal Impact Study of the Parents and Caregivers Guide: Final Report." Polarization and Extremism Research and Innovation Lab (PERIL) in partnership with the Southern Poverty Law Center (SPLC). Available at www.perilresearch.com.

54. "LGBT-Owned Kilt Maker Denounces Kilt-Clad Proud Boys."

55. I am indebted to Alexandra Onuoha for this reminder.

56. Helen Catt and Charlotte Rose, "Misogyny to Be Treated as Extremism by UK Government," BBC.com, August 18, 2024. Available at https://www.bbc.com/news/articles /c15gn0lq7p5o; Lukas Coch, "Should Misogyny Be Treated as a Form of Extremism?" *The Conversation*, August 27, 2024. Available at: https://theconversation.com/should-misogyny-be -treated-as-a-form-of-extremism-237229.

57. "Shedding Light on Online Misogyny: New Research Reveals Its Links to Violent Extremism." New Zealand Classification Office, May 13, 2024, https://www.classificationoffice .govt.nz/news/news-items/shedding-light-on-online-misogyny-new-research-reveals-its-links -to-violent-extremism/.

58. See "Public Safety Canada Implementation Plan for Canada's National Action Plan on Women, Peace and Security—2023 to 2029," Government of Canada, https://www.international .gc.ca/transparency-transparence/women-peace-security-femmes-paix-securite/2023-2029 -implementation-plans-mise-ceuvre-ps-sp.aspx?lang=eng#a4_1.

59. Rottweiler, et al., "A Common Psychology of Male Violence?," p. 15.

60. Johnston and True, "Misogyny and Violent Extremism."

61. Jessica White, *Gender Mainstreaming in Counter Terrorism Policy: Building Transformative Strategies to Counter Violent Extremism* (London: Routledge, 2023).

62. This recommendation is included in the first US national plan to end gender-based violence, released in 2023 by the Biden administration. See "U.S. National Plan to End Gender-Based Violence: Strategies for Action" (May 2023): 53, https://www.whitehouse.gov/wp -content/uploads/2023/05/National-Plan-to-End-GBV.pdf.

63. Trevor Hoppe, "Punishing Sex: Sex Offenders and the Missing Punitive Turn in Sexuality Studies," *Law and Social Inquiry* 41, no. 3 (2016): 573–594, https://doi.org/:10.1111/lsi.12189; also see Daniel Filler, "Silence and the Racial Dimension of Megan's Law," *Iowa Law Review* 89 (2004): 1535–1594. I am indebted to Sahar Fathi for this point and for directing me toward these sources.

64. United Nations Security Council Counter-Terrorism Security Directorate (UN CTED), "Toward Meaningful Accountability for Sexual- and Gender-based Violence Linked to Terrorism," pp. 54–55.

65. Levengood and Hadland, "Hostile Laws," p. 4.

66. For a review of social media policies related to gender and misogyny as of September 2024, see Diverting Hate's September 2024 biannual report, "Misogynistic Extremism, The Manosphere, and Mainstream Social Media."

67. See Ermyas, et al., "Meta Oversight Board Co-Chair Responds to Company's Decision to End Fact-Checking."

68. See these and other recommendations as elaborated in Craanen, et al., "Transmisogyny," pp. 21–22.

69. As argued in Lamphere-Englund, et al., "Pathways of Resilience," p. 13.

70. In part this is likely due to the gendered biases of all research and policy work, in which man is "normal" and woman is "other." I am indebted to Lydia Bates for this point. See also Simone de Beauvoir, "Introduction: Woman as Other" in *The Second Sex* (1949).

71. Wolfe, *You Can't Go Home Again*, p. 335.

72. See Manne, *Down Girl*, pp. 84–86.

Epilogue

1. Laura Killingbeck, "A Woman Who Left Society to Live With Bears Weighs in on Man vs. Bear," Bikepacking.com, May 24, 2024.

2. A. J. Willingham, "Man or Bear? A Viral Tiktok Question Has Revealed Some Uncomfortable Truths," CNN, May 6, 2024.

3. See World Health Organization statistics on sexual and gender-based violence at Violence against women (who.int).

4. Rios-Gonzalez, et al., "Not All Men."

5. Lucy Clarke-Billings, "Man Accused of Recruiting Strangers to Rape His Wife," BBC.com, September 2, 2024.

6. For just one example, see the critique of Harris's laugh at David Masciotra, "The Weird and Sexist Criticism of Kamala's 'Cackle': Decoding How Harris Got the Last Laugh," August 10, 2024, Salon.com.

7. As articulated by Hearn and Parkin, *Gender, Sexuality and Violence in Organizations*, p. 9, cited in McCarthy and Taylor, "Misogyny and Organizational Studies," p. 463.

REFERENCES

"2023 Anti-Trans Bills." *Trans Legislation Tracker*. https://translegislation.com/bills/2023.

Accettulla, Kevin, and Kaycee Sloan. "WATCH: Protesters Wave Nazi Flags Outside Disney World Entrance." *WFLA*, June 12, 2023. https://www.wfla.com/news/florida/watch-protesters-wave-nazi-flags-outside-disney-world-entrance/.

Adamczeski, Ryan. "Children's Hospital in D.C. Under Attack Over Gender-Affirming Care." *Advocate.com*, September 1, 2022. https://www.advocate.com/news/2022/9/01/childrens-hospital-dc-under-attack-over-gender-affirming-care.

Adichie, Chimamanda Ngozi. *We Should All Be Feminists*. New York: Random House, 2012.

"ADL Adds 'Pepe the Frog' Meme, Used by Anti-Semites and Racists, to Online Hate Symbols Database." *ADL*, September 27, 2016. https://www.adl.org/resources/press-release/adl-adds-pepe-frog-meme-used-anti-semites-and-racists-online-hate-symbols.

"ADL and GLAAD Report: More than 350 Anti-LGBTQ+ Hate and Extremism Incidents Recorded as Anti-LGBTQ+ Rhetoric Soared." *ADL*, June 22, 2023. https://www.adl.org/resources/press-release/adl-and-glaad-report-more-350-anti-lgbtq-hate-and-extremism-incidents.

AFP. "Germany Opens Files on Chile Sect Run by Nazi Pedophile." *The Times of Israel*, April 26, 2016. https://www.timesofisrael.com/germany-opens-files-on-chile-sect-run-by-nazi-pedophile/.

AFP. "Russian Neo-Nazi Jailed for Forcing Prostitutes to March Naked Down Street." *The Times of Israel*, March 20, 2018. https://www.timesofisrael.com/russian-neo-nazi-jailed-for-forcing-prostitutes-to-march-naked-down-street/.

Aguilera, Jasmine, and Abigail Adams. "What the Buffalo Tragedy Has to Do with the Effort to Overturn Roe." *Time*, May 21, 2022. https://time.com/6178135/buffalo-shooting-abortion-replacement-theory/.

"AI and Children: Risks and Opportunities of the Enhanced Internet." *Children and Screens*, December 6, 2023. https://www.childrenandscreens.org/event/ai-and-children-risks-and-opportunities-of-the-enhanced-internet/.

Al Aqueedi, Rasha. "Andrew Tate and the Moral Bankruptcy of Muslim Proselytization." *New Lines Magazine*, January 26, 2023. https://newlinesmag.com/argument/andrew-tate-and-the-moral-bankruptcy-of-muslim-proselytization/.

Ali, Wajahat. "Andrew Tate's Muslim 'Faith Washing' Can't Hide His Misogynistic Sins." *MSNBC*, January 8, 2023. https://www.msnbc.com/opinion/msnbc-opinion/andrew-tates-muslim-conversion-cant-hide-misogyny-rcna64707.

Aliche, Bridget O. "'You Don't Talk Like a Woman': The Influence of Gender Identity in the Constructions of Online Misogyny." *Feminist Media Studies* 23, no. 4 (2023): 1409–1428. https://doi.org/10.1080/14680777.2022.2032253.

Alter, Alexandra. "With Rising Book Bans, Librarians Have Come Under Attack." *The New York Times*, July 6, 2022. https://www.nytimes.com/2022/07/06/books/book-ban-librarians.html.

Amarasingham, Amarnath, and Daniel Kelley. "Hate and Extremism on Gaming Platforms: Insights from Surveys with the Gaming Community." In *Gaming and Extremism: The Radicalization of Digital Playgrounds*, ed. Linda Schlagel and Rachel Kowert. New York: Taylor & Francis, 2024, 110–129.

American Academy of Pediatrics, et al. "DOJ Letter Final." October 3, 2022. https://downloads .aap.org/DOFA/DOJ%20Letter%20Final.pdf.

Anand, Dibyesh. "Anxious Sexualities: Masculinity, Nationalism, and Violence." *British Journal of Political and International Relations* 9 (2007): 257–269.

Anderson, Carol. *White Rage: The Unspoken Truth about Our Racial Divide*. London: Bloomsbury, 2016.

Anderson, Karrin Vasby. "'Rhymes with Rich': "Bitch" as a Tool of Containment in Contemporary American Politics." *Rhetoric & Public Affairs* 2, no. 4 (1999): 599–623.

Anderson, Leslie, et al. "'The Talk' and Parenting While Black in America: Centering Race, Resistance, and Refuge." *Journal of Black Psychology* 48, nos. 2–4 (2022): 475–506. https:// doi.org/10.1177/00957984211034294.

Andrews, E. E., et al. "#SaytheWord: A Disability Culture Commentary on the Erasure of 'Disability.'" *Rehabilitation Psychology* 64, no. 2 (2019): 111–118. https://doi.org/10.1037/ rep0000258.

Andrews, Taylor. "These 10 Stories Show How Crazy-Aggressive Men Can Get When They Are Rejected." *Cosmopolitan*, February 6, 2019. https://www.cosmopolitan.com/sex-love /a26198244/why-do-males-reject-to-rejection-aggressively/.

Andrighetto, Luca, et al. "Lonely Hearts and Angry Minds: Online Dating Rejection Increases Male (But Not Female) Hostility." *Aggressive Behavior* 45, no. 5 (2019): 571–581. https://doi .org/10.1002/ab.21852.

Anti-Defamation League. "Hate Is No Game: Hate and Harassment in Online Games 2023." *ADL*, February 6, 2024. https://www.adl.org/resources/report/hate-no-game-hate-and -harassment-online-games-2023.

Anti-Defamation League. "Hateful Usernames in Online Multiplayer Games." *ADL*, July 24, 2023. https://www.adl.org/resources/blog/hateful-usernames-online-multiplayer -games.

Anti-Defamation League. "Men's Rights Activists: What You Need to Know." *ADL*, January 24, 2024. https://www.adl.org/resources/blog/mens-rights-activists-what-you-need-know.

Anti-Defamation League. "Milo Yiannopoulos: Five Things to Know." *ADL*, April 11, 2018. https://www.adl.org/resources/backgrounder/milo-yiannopoulos-five-things-know

Anti-Defamation League. "Online Hate and Harassment: The American Experience 2022." *ADL Center for Technology and Society (CTS)*, 2022. https://www.adl.org/sites/default/files/pdfs /2022-09/Online-Hate-and-Harassment-Survey-2022.pdf.

Anti-Defamation League. "White Supremacists' Mixed Reactions to Alabama Abortion Law Reflect Divide on Issue." Anti Defamation League, May 28, 2019. https://www.adl.org/blog/white -supremacists-mixed-reactions-to-alabama-abortion-law-reflect-divide-on-issue.

"APA Task Force Report on Violent Video Games." *American Psychological Association*, March 1, 2020. https://www.apa.org/science/leadership/bsa/report-violent-video-games.pdf.

Araujo-Hawkins, Dawn. "QAnon Moms." *The Christian Century*, April 19, 2022. https://www .christiancentury.org/article/features/qanon-moms.

Arbeit, Miriam R., et al. "From Misogynist Incels to 'One of the Shooters': What Can Help College Sexual Violence Prevention Confront Male Supremacism?" *Journal of Women and Gender in Higher Education* 15, no. 4 (2022): 309–331. https://doi.org/10.1080/26379112 .2022.2132951.

Argentino, Marc, and Blyth Crawford. "The WQmen of QAnon—GNET." *Global Network on Extremism and Technology*, March 12, 2021. https://gnet-research.org/2021/03/12/the-wqmen-of-qanon/.

Argentino, Marc, et al. "764: The Intersection of Terrorism, Violent Extremism, and Child Sexual Exploitation—GNET." *Global Network on Extremism and Technology*, January 19, 2024. https://gnet-research.org/2024/01/19/764-the-intersection-of-terrorism-violent-extremism-and-child-sexual-exploitation/.

"Aryan Brotherhood." *Southern Poverty Law Center.* https://www.splcenter.org/fighting-hate/extremist-files/group/aryan-brotherhood.

Asal, Victor, and Robert U. Nagel. "Control over Bodies and Territories: Insurgent Territorial Control and Sexual Violence." *Security Studies* 30, no. 1 (2021): 136–158. https://doi.org/10.1080/09636412.2021.1885726.

"Ashli Babbitt: The US Veteran Shot Dead Breaking into the Capitol." *BBC*, January 8, 2021. https://www.bbc.com/news/world-us-canada-55581206.

Ashwell, Lauren. "Gendered Slurs." *Social Theory and Practice* 42, no. 2 (2016): 228–239. https://www.jstor.org/stable/24871341.

Aslam, Maleeha. "Islamism and Masculinity: Case Study Pakistan." *Historical Social Research* 39, no. 3 (2014): 135–149. https://doi.org/10.12759/hsr.39.2014.3.135-149.

Atwood, Margaret. *Second Words: Selected Critical Prose, 1960–1982.* Toronto: House of Anansi Press, 2018.

Baele, Stephanie J., et al. "From 'Incel' to 'Saint': Analyzing the Violent Worldview behind the 2018 Toronto Attack." *Terrorism and Political Violence* 33, no. 8 (2019): 1667–1691. https://doi.org/10.1080/09546553.2019.1638256.

Bailey, Moya. *Misogynoir Transformed: Black Women's Digital Resistance.* New York: New York University Press, 2021, 1.

Bailey, Moya, and Trudy. "On Misogynoir Citation, Erasure, and Plagiarism." *Feminist Media Studies* 18, no. 4 (2018): 762–768. https://doi.org/10.1080/14680777.2018.1447395.

Baker, Catherine, Debbie Ging and Maja Brandt Anderson. "Recommending Toxicity The role of algorithmic recommender functions on YouTube Shorts and TikTok in promoting male supremacist influencers." Dublin City University Anti-Bullying Center. April 2024. DCU-Toxicity-Full-Report.pdf

Baker, Mike, and Nicholas Bogel-Burroughs. "University Investigated Idaho Murder Suspect's Behavior Around Time of Killings." *The New York Times*, February 10, 2023. https://www.nytimes.com/2023/02/10/us/idaho-murders-kohberger-fired-wsu.html?smid=nytcore-ios-share&referringSource=articleShare.

Ballard, Jamie. "One-Third of Americans Say Their Ideal Relationship Is Non-Monogamous." *YouGov*, January 31, 2020. https://today.yougov.com/society/articles/27639-millennials-monogamy-poly-poll-survey-data.

Banet-Weiser, Sarah. *Empowered: Popular Feminism and Popular Misogyny.* Durham, NC: Duke University Press, 2018.

Banks, Duren, and Tracey Kyckelhahn. "Characteristics of Suspected Human Trafficking Incidents, 2008–10." U.S. Department of Justice, Office of Justice Programs, Bureau of Justice Statistics. April 2011. https://bjs.ojp.gov/content/pub/pdf/cshti0810.pdf

"Banned Book List: 3,362 Books Banned in 2022–2023." *PEN America*, September 21, 2023. https://pen.org/2023-banned-book-list/.

Banting, Rodlyn-mae. "Teachers Warn That Misogynist Andrew Tate Has 'Radicalized' School-Age Boys." *Jezebel*, August 23, 2022. https://jezebel.com/andrew-tate-influence-boys-teachers-1849447030.

Baptiste, Nathalie. "Florida's 'Don't Say Gay' Law Is Driving Teachers to Quit." *HuffPost*, June 2, 2023. https://www.huffpost.com/entry/florida-teacher-resigns-lgbtq_n_647a19d1e4 b0a7554f444ac6.

Barbaro, Michael, and Sheera Frenkel. "Is More Violence Coming?" *The New York Times*, January 13, 2021. https://www.nytimes.com/2021/01/13/podcasts/the-daily/capitol-attack -social-media-parler-twitter-facebook.html.

Bardall, Gabrielle, et al. "How Is Political Violence Gendered? Disentangling Motives, Forms, and Impacts." *Political Studies* 68, no. 4 (2019): 916–935. https://doi.org/10.1177/0032321719881812.

Barker, Gary, Caroline Hayes, Brian Heilman, and Michael Reichert. "The State of American Men: From Crisis and Confusion to Hope." Washington, DC: Equimundo, 2023. https://www .equimundo.org/wp-content/uploads/2023/05/STATE-OF-AMERICAN-MEN-2023.pdf

Barker, Kim, and Olga Jurasz. "Online Misogyny." *Journal of International Affairs* 72, no. 2 (2019): 95–114. https://www.jstor.org/stable/26760834.

Barrón-López, Laura, and Sam Lane. "How Some Evangelical Leaders Are Combating Political Radicalization in Their Congregations." *PBS*, December 14, 2023. https://www.pbs.org /newshour/show/how-some-evangelical-leaders-are-combating-political-radicalization-in -their-congregations.

Basu, Tanya. "The Metaverse Has a Groping Problem Already." *MIT Technology Review*, December 16, 2021. https://www.technologyreview.com/2021/12/16/1042516/the-metaverse-has -a-groping-problem/.

Bates, Laura. "'Being a Woman Is Scary': The Unspoken Danger of Declining a Man's Advances." *The Guardian*, March 25, 2019. https://www.theguardian.com/world/shortcuts/2019/mar /25/being-a-woman-is-scary-the-unspoken-danger-of-declining-a-mans-advances.

Bates, Laura. *Everyday Sexism: The Project That Inspired a Worldwide Movement.* New York: St. Martin's Griffin, 2012.

Bates, Laura. *Men Who Hate Women: From Incels to Pickup Artists: The Truth about Extreme Misogyny and How It Affects Us All.* Naperville, IL: Sourcebooks, 2021.

Bauer, Greta R., et al. "'I Don't Think This Is Theoretical; This Is Our Lives': How Erasure Impacts Health Care for Transgender People." *Journal of the Association of Nurses in AIDS Care* 20, no. 5 (2009): 348–361. https://doi.org/10.1016/j.jana.2009.07.004.

Beauchamp, Zack. "White Supremacists Are Trying to Recruit American Teens Through Video Games." Vox, April 9, 2019. https://www.vox.com/policy-and-politics/2019/4/9/18296864 /gamer-gaming-white-supremacist-recruit.

Beck, Koa. *White Feminism: From the Suffragettes to Influencers and Who They Leave Behind.* New York: Atria Books, 2021.

Beckett, Lois. "Qanon: A Timeline of Violence Linked to the Conspiracy Theory." *The Guardian*, October 16, 2020. https://www.theguardian.com/us-news/2020/oct/15/qanon-violence -crimes-timeline.

Bederman, Gail. *Manliness and Civilization: A Cultural History of Gender and Race in the United States, 1880–1917.* Chicago: University of Chicago Press, 1995.

Belew, Kathleen. *Bring the War Home: The White Power Movement and Paramilitary America.* Cambridge, MA: Harvard University Press, 2018.

Bendix, Aria. "Three Alabama Clinics Pause IVF After Court Rules Embryos Are Children." *NBC News*, February 22, 2024. https://www.nbcnews.com/health/health-news/university -alabama-pauses-ivf-services-court-rules-embryos-are-childre-rcna139846.

Ben-Ghiat, Ruth. *Strongmen: Mussolini to the Present.* New York: W. W. Norton, 2020.

Bennett, Geoff, et al. "How the Rise of Anti-LGBTQ+ Hate and Violence Is Impacting the Community." *PBS*, August 31, 2023. https://www.pbs.org/newshour/show/how-the-rise-of -anti-lgbtq-hate-and-violence-is-impacting-the-community.

Berezin, Mabel. "Fascism and Populism: Are They Useful Categories for Comparative Socio-logical Analysis?" *Annual Review of Sociology* 45 (2019): 345–361. https://doi.org/10.1146/annurev-soc-073018-022351.

Bianchi, Claudia. "Slurs and Appropriation: An Echoic Account." *Journal of Pragmatics* 66 (2014): 35–44. https://doi.org/10.1016/j.pragma.2014.02.009.

Bjanegård, Elin, et al. "Women, Peace and Security: The Sexism and Violence Nexus." *Joint Brief Series: New Insights on Women, Peace and Security (WPS) for the Next Decade.* Stockholm: Folke Bernadotte Academy, PRIO and UN Women. November 2020. https://www.unwomen.org/sites/default/files/Headquarters/Attachments/Sections/Library/Publications/2020/New-insights-on-WPS-The-sexism-and-violence-nexus-en.pdf.

Blais, Melissa, and Francis Dupuis-Déri. "Masculinism and the Antifeminist Countermove-ment." *Social Movement Studies* 11, no. 1 (2012): 21–39. https://doi.org/10.1080/14742837.2012.640532.

Blake, Khandis R., et al. "Misogynistic Tweets Correlate with Violence Against Women." *Psychological Science* 32, no. 3 (2021): 315–325. https://doi.org/10.1177/0956797620968529.

Blake, Montgomery. "Taylor Swift AI Images Prompt US Bill to Tackle Nonconsensual, Sexual Deepfakes." *The Guardian*, January 30, 2024. https://www.theguardian.com/technology/2024/jan/30/taylor-swift-ai-deepfake-nonconsensual-sexual-images-bill.

Blakemore, Erin. "How U.S. Abortion Laws Went from Nonexistent to Acrimonious." *National Geographic*, May 17, 2022. https://www.nationalgeographic.com/history/article/the-complex-early-history-of-abortion-in-the-united-states.

Blee, Kathleen. "Does Gender Matter in the United States Far Right?" *Politics, Religion & Ideology* 13, no. 2 (2012): 253–265. https://doi.org/10.1080/21567689.2012.675705.

Blee, Kathleen. *Inside Organized Racism: Women in the Hate Movement.* Berkeley: University of California Press, 2003.

Blee, Kathleen. "Where Do We Go from Here? Positioning Gender in Studies of the Far Right." *Politics, Religion and Ideology* 21, no. 4 (2020): 416–431. https://doi.org/10.1080/21567689.2020.1851870.

Blee, Kathleen. *Women of the Klan: Racism and Gender in the 1920s.* Berkeley: University of California Press, 2008.

Blee, Kathleen, et al. *Out of Hiding: Extremist White Supremacy and How It Can Be Stopped.* London: Taylor & Francis, 2024.

"Board of Governors Adds Factual History Course as Option for Requirements for Social Sciences Core." *State University System of Florida*, January 24, 2024. https://www.flbog.edu/2024/01/24/board-of-governors-adds-factual-history-course-as-option-for-requirements-for-social-sciences-core/.

Bonds, Anne. "Race and Ethnicity II: White Women and the Possessive Geographies of White Supremacy." *Progress in Human Geography* 44, no. 4 (2020): 778–788. https://doi.org/10.1177/0309132519863479.

Booth, Robert. "Gen Z Boys and Men More Likely than Baby Boomers to Believe Feminism Harmful, Says Poll." *The Guardian*, February 1, 2024. https://www.theguardian.com/news/2024/feb/01/gen-z-boys-and-men-more-likely-than-baby-boomers-to-believe-feminism-harmful-says-poll?CMP=oth_b-aplnews_d-1.

Bosman, Julie. "A College Student Was Killed by a Man Whose Catcalls She Tried to Ignore, Prosecutors Say." *The New York Times*, November 27, 2019. https://www.nytimes.com/2019/11/27/us/chicago-college-student-killed-catcall.html.

Bosman, Julie, et al. "A Common Trait Among Mass Killers: Hatred Toward Women." *The New York Times*, August 10, 2019. https://www.nytimes.com/2019/08/10/us/mass-shootings-misogyny-dayton.html.

Bote, Joshua. "21 Alleged White Supremacists in Utah Charged in Drug Trafficking." *USA Today*, October 17, 2020. https://www.usatoday.com/story/news/nation/2020/10/17/alleged -white-supremacists-utah-charged-drug-trafficking/3694031001/.

Bows, Hannah, et al. "'It's Like a Drive-by Misogyny': Sexual Violence at UK Music Festivals." *Violence Against Women* 30, no. 2 (2024): 372–393. https://doi.org/10.1177/10778012 221120443.

"Boys' Mock Government Proposed Eliminating Women's Vote." *Associated Press*, June 26, 2019. https://apnews.com/article/b5a67ee195584bd6a0ee3afbc0a271fc.

Bratich, Jack, and Sarah Banet-Weiser. "From Pick-Up Artists to Incels: Con(fidence) Games, Networked Misogyny, and the Failure of Neoliberalism." *International Journal of Communication* 13 (2019): Feature 5003–5027. https://ijoc.org/index.php/ijoc/article/view /13216.

Brenan, Megan. "Gender Disparities in Views of Women's Equality Persist." *Gallup*, October 15, 2021. https://news.gallup.com/poll/355958/gender-disparities-views-women-equality -persist.aspx.

Bridges, Tristan. "A Very 'Gay' Straight?: Hybrid Masculinities, Sexual Aesthetics, and the Changing Relationship Between Masculinity and Homophobia." *Gender and Society* 28, no. 1 (2014): 58–62. https://doi.org/10.1177/0891243213503901.

Bridges, Tristan, and C. J. Pascoe. "Hybrid Masculinities: New Directions in the Sociology of Men and Masculinities." *Sociology Compass* 8, no. 3 (2014): 246–258. http://dx.doi.org/10 .1111/soc4.12134.

Brown, Anna. "About 5% of Young Adults in the U.S. Say Their Gender Is Different from Their Sex Assigned at Birth." *Pew Research Center*, June 7, 2022. https://www.pewresearch.org/fact -tank/2022/06/07/about-5-of-young-adults-in-the-u-s-say-their-gender-is-different-from -their-sex-assigned-at-birth/.

Browning, Kellen. "Extremism Finds Fertile Ground in Chat Rooms for Gamers." *The New York Times*, May 18, 2023. https://www.nytimes.com/2023/05/18/technology/video-games -extremism.html.

Brownmiller, Susan. *Against Our Will: Men, Women, and Rape*. New York: Fawcett Books, 1975.

Broyd, Josephine, et al. "Incels, Violence, and Mental Disorder: A Narrative Review with Recommendations for Best Practice in Risk Assessment and Clinical Intervention." *BJPsych Advances* 29, no. 4 (2023): 254–264. https://doi.org/10.1192/bja.2022.15.

Brubaker, Rogers. "Why Populism?" *Theory and Society* 46, no. 5 (2017): 357–385. https://www .jstor.org/stable/44981871.

Brulliard, Karin. "Utah Official's Post Suggesting a Student Is Transgender Causes a Furor." *The Washington Post*, February 26, 2024. https://www.washingtonpost.com/nation/2024/02 /26/utah-transgender-students-sports-ban/.

Buljubasic, Mirza, et al. "Women's Empowerment and Resilience to Violent Extremism in Bosnia and Herzegovina: A Subnational Qualitative Assessment." *Democracy and Security in Southeastern Europe* 7, no. 1 (2020): 130–152.

Burgess, Matt. "The AI-Generated Child Abuse Nightmare Is Here." *WIRED*, October 24, 2023. https://www.wired.com/story/generative-ai-images-child-sexual-abuse/.

Burnett, Scott, and John E. Richardson. "'Breeders for Race and Nation': Gender, Sexuality and Fecundity in Post-War British Fascist Discourse." *Patterns of Prejudice* 55, no. 4 (2021): 331–356. https://doi.org/10.1080/0031322X.2021.2011088.

Burns, Katelyn. "'The Matrix Resurrections' Makes More Room for Trans Identity in Corporate Hollywood." *MSNBC*, December 22, 2021. https://www.msnbc.com/opinion/matrix -resurrections-makes-more-room-trans-identity-corporate-hollywood-n1286408.

Butler, Judith. *Who's Afraid of Gender?* New York: Farrar, Straus and Giroux, 2024.

Calarco, Jessica. *Holding It Together: How Women Became America's Safety Net.* New York: Portfolio, 2024.

"Capitol Hill Siege | Program on Extremism | The George Washington University." *Program on Extremism.* https://extremism.gwu.edu/Capitol-Hill-Siege.

Caplan, Gregory A. "Militarism and Masculinity as Keys to the 'Jewish Question' in Germany." In *Military Masculinities: Identity and the State.* Westport, CT: Praeger, 2003.

Carian, Emily. "The Inversive Sexism Scale: Endorsement of the Belief that Women Are Privileged." In *Male Supremacism in the United States: From Patriarchal Traditionalism to Misogynist Incels and the Alt-Right.* New York: Routledge, 2022.

Carian, Emily K., et al. *Male Supremacism in the United States: From Patriarchal Traditionalism to Misogynist Incels and the Alt-Right.* New York: Routledge, 2022.

Carlin, Diana B., and Kelly L. Winfrey. "Have You Come a Long Way, Baby? Hillary Clinton, Sarah Palin, and Sexism in 2008 Campaign Coverage." *Communication Studies* 60, no. 4 (2009): 326–343. https://doi.org/10.1080/10510970903109904.

Carlson, C. R. "Misogynistic Hate Speech and Its Chilling Effect on Women's Free Expression during the 2016 U.S. Presidential Campaign." *Journal of Hate Studies* 14, no. 1 (2018): 97–111. https://jhs.press.gonzaga.edu/articles/10.33972/jhs.126.

Carpenter, Ami, and Jamie Gates. "The Nature and Extent of Gang Involvement in Sex Trafficking in San Diego County." *Office of Justice Programs,* 2016. https://www.ojp.gov/pdffiles1/nij/grants/249857.pdf.

Carruthers, Charlene. *Unapologetic: A Black, Queer, and Feminist Mandate for Radical Movements.* Boston: Beacon Press, 2019.

Casey, Logan. "After Trump Rescinds Title IX Guidance, What's Next for Transgender Students' Rights?" *Brookings Institution,* March 1, 2017. https://www.brookings.edu/articles/after-trump-rescinds-title-ix-guidance-whats-next-for-transgender-students-rights/.

Cassino, Dan, and Yasemin Besen-Cassino. *Gender Threat: American Masculinity in the Face of Change.* Stanford, CA: Stanford University Press, 2022.

"Celebrating Inclusivity in Nepal." *Smart Family: Issue 71,* June 2023, https://www.smartfamily.com.np/magazine/issue-71.

Cepollaro, Bianca, and Dan López de Sa. "Who Reclaims Slurs?" *Pacific Philosophical Quarterly* 103, no. 3 (2022): 606–619. https://doi.org/10.1111/papq.12403.

"Challenging Christian Nationalism." *Interfaith Alliance.* https://interfaithalliance.org/initiatives/challenging-christian-nationalism/.

Chemaly, Soraya. "Street Harassment: Is a Man Running Over a 14-Year-Old Girl for Refusing Sex Serious Enough?" *HuffPost,* November 27, 2013. https://www.huffpost.com/entry/street-harassment-is-runn_b_4004394.

Chess, Shira, and Adrienne Shaw. "A Conspiracy of Fishes, or, Howe We Learned to Stop Worrying about #GamerGate and Embrace Hegemonic Masculinity." *Journal of Broadcasting and Electronic Media* 59, no. 1 (2015): 208–220. https://doi.org/10.1080/08838151.2014.999917.

"Children Are Mimicking a Hand Gesture Linked to Misogynist Influencer Andrew Tate." *ISD,* Mary 26, 2020. https://www.isdglobal.org/isd-in-the-news/children-are-mimicking-a-hand-gesture-linked-to-misogynist-influencer-andrew-tate/.

"Children's Hospitals Harassed Over Transgender Care Programs." *AP News,* August 17, 2022. https://apnews.com/article/health-social-media-boston-7a6bed81a86fe5576ca0145d893ad153.

Chisholm, Shirley. "Racism and Anti-Feminism." *The Black Scholar* 1, nos. 3–4 (1970): 40–45. https://www.jstor.org/stable/41163421.

Chittal, Nisha. "Trump's Latest Tweets Are About Silencing Women of Color in Congress." *Vox,* July 15, 2019. https://www.vox.com/policy-and-politics/2019/4/8/18272072/ilhan-omar -rashida-tlaib-alexandria-ocasio-cortez-racism-sexism.

"Christian Nationalism on the Rise." *NBC News,* September 15, 2022. https://www.nbcnews.com /meet-the-press/video/christian-nationalism-on-the-rise-148548677936.

Christou, Miranda. 2020. "#TradWives: Sexism as Gateway to White Supremacy." *OpenDemocracy,* March 17, 2020. https://www.opendemocracy.net/en/countering-radical-right /tradwives-sexism-gateway-white-supremacy/

Chu, Judy. *When Boys Become Boys: Development, Relationships, and Masculinity.* New York: New York University Press, 2014.

"Cisgender Definition & Meaning." *Merriam-Webster.* https://www.merriam-webster.com /dictionary/cisgender.

Coaston, Jane. "New Evidence Shows the Pulse Nightclub Shooting Wasn't About Anti-LGBTQ Hate." *Vox,* April 5, 2018. https://www.vox.com/policy-and-politics/2018/4/5/17202026 /pulse-shooting-lgbtq-trump-terror-hate.

Cole, Samantha. "This Horrifying App Undresses a Photo of Any Woman with a Single Click." *Vice,* June 26, 2019. https://www.vice.com/en/article/kzm59x/deepnude-app-creates-fake -nudes-of-any-woman.

Collins, Patricia Hill. *Black Feminist Thought.* New York: Routledge, 2000.

Confessore, Nicholas. "'America Is Under Attack': Inside the Anti-D.E.I. Crusade." *The New York Times,* January 20, 2024. https://www.nytimes.com/interactive/2024/01/20/us/dei -woke-claremont-institute.html.

Connell, R. W. *Masculinities.* Berkeley: University of California Press, 1995.

Consalvo, Mia. "Confronting Toxic Gamer Culture: A Challenge for Feminist Game Studies Scholars." *Scholars' Bank,* 2012. https://scholarsbank.uoregon.edu/xmlui/handle/1794/26289.

Contrera, Jessica. "A QAnon Con: How the Viral Wayfair Sex Trafficking Lie Hurt Real Kids." *The Washington Post,* December 16, 2021. https://www.washingtonpost.com/dc-md-va /interactive/2021/wayfair-qanon-sex-trafficking-conspiracy/.

Cook, Jesselyn. *The Quiet Damage: QAnon and the Destruction of the American Family.* New York: Crown, 2024.

Cooter, Amy. *Nostalgia, Nationalism, and the U.S. Militia Movement.* New York: Routledge, 2024.

Corrêa, Sonia. "Gender Ideology: Tracking Its Origins and Meanings in Current Gender Politics." *London School of Economics (LSE) Blogs,* December 12, 2017. https://blogs.lse.ac.uk /gender/2017/12/11/gender-ideology-tracking-its-origins-and-meanings-in-current -gender-politics/

Corredor, Elizabeth S. "Unpacking 'Gender Ideology' and the Global Right's Antigender Countermovement." *Signs* 44, no. 3 (2019): 613–638. https://doi.org/10.1086/701171.

Coster van Voorhout, Jill E. B. "How Human Trafficking Fuels Erosion of Liberal Democracies—In Fiction and Fact, and from Within and Without." *Social Sciences* 11, no. 12 (2022): 560. https://doi.org/10.3390/socsci11120560.

"Countering QAnon." *Polaris Project,* February 2021. https://polarisproject.org/wp-content /uploads/2021/02/Polaris-Report-Countering-QAnon.pdf.

Counter-Terrorism Committee Executive Directorate. "Member States Concerned by the Growing and Increasingly Transnational Threat of Extreme Right Wing Terrorism." *United Nations Security Council,* April 2020. /https://www.un.org/securitycouncil/ctc/sites/www .un.org.securitycouncil.ctc/files/files/documents/2021/Jan/cted_trends_alert_extreme _right-wing_terrorism.pdf.

Cox, Daniel. "Why Young Men Are Turning Against Feminism." Survey Center on American Life, December 14, 2023. https://www.americansurveycenter.org/newsletter/why-young -men-are-turning-against-feminism/

Cox, Daniel, et al. "Generation Z and the Transformation of American Adolescence: How Gen Z's Formative Experiences Shape Its Politics, Priorities, and Future." Survey Center on American Life, November 9, 2023. https://www.americansurveycenter.org/research /generation-z-and-the-transformation-of-american-adolescence-how-gen-zs-formative -experiences-shape-its-politics-priorities-and-future/

Cox, Daniel A. "Rise of Conspiracies Reveals an Evangelical Divide in the GOP." Survey Center on American Life, February 12, 2021. https://www.americansurveycenter.org/rise-of -conspiracies-reveal-an-evangelical-divide-in-the-gop/.

Craanen, Anne, et al. "Transmisogyny, Colonialism and Anti-Trans Activism Following Violent Extremist Attacks in the US and EU." *Global Network on Extremism & Technology (GNET)*, May 24, 2024. https://gnet-research.org/2024/05/24/transmisogyny-colonialism-and -online-anti%E2%80%90trans-activism-following-violent-extremist-attacks-in-the-us-and -eu/.

Cravens, R. G. "Hate Group Documents Dozens of Attacks on LGBTQ+ Affirming Churches, Claims Trans Rights Motivates Attacks on Christians." Southern Poverty Law Center, February 29, 2024. https://www.splcenter.org/hatewatch/2024/02/29/hate-group-documents -dozens-attacks-lgbtq-affirming-churches-claims-trans-rights-motivates.

Crawford, Blyth, and Marc Argentino. "QAnon Women in Politics Part One: The QAnon Candidates—GNET." *Global Network on Extremism and Technology (GNET)*, April 28, 2021. https://gnet-research.org/2021/04/28/qanon-women-in-politics-part-one-the-qanon -candidates/.

Crenshaw, Kimberlé. *On Intersectionality: Essential Writings.* New York: New Press, 2014.

Criado-Perez, Caroline. "'Women that Talk Too Much Need to Get Raped': What Men Are Really Saying When They Abuse Women Online." *Countering Online Abuse of Female Journalists,* 2016. https://www.osce.org/files/f/documents/c/3/220411.pdf.

Croom, Adam M. "Slurs." *Language Sciences* 33, no. 3 (2011): 343–358.

CTED. "Towards Meaningful Accountability for Sexual and Gender-Based Violence Linked to Terrorism." *The United Nations,* November 2023. https://www.un.org/securitycouncil/ctc /sites/www.un.org.securitycouncil.ctc/files/cted_report-_sgbv_linked_to_terrorism _final.pdf.

Cunliffe, Rachel. "'There Are Thousands of Andrew Tates Out There': The Battle Against Online Extremism." *The New Statesman,* January 23, 2023. https://www.newstatesman.com /culture/social-media/2023/01/andrew-tates-battle-against-online-extremism-social -media-hate-speech.

Czerwinsky, Alyssa. "Misogynist Incels Gone Mainstream: A Critical Review of the Current Directions in Incel-Focused Research." *Crime Media Culture* 20, no. 2 (2024): 196–217. https://doi.org/10.1177/17416590231196125.

Dale, Maryclaire, et al. "Men's Rights' Lawyer Suspected in Shooting of New Jersey Judge's Family." *Associated Press,* July 20, 2020. https://www.pbs.org/newshour/nation/mens-rights -lawyer-suspected-in-shooting-of-new-jersey-judges-family.

D'Angelo, Bob. "California Man Going Through Divorce Allegedly Crashes Dump Truck into Wife's Home." *KIRO 7,* January 18, 2023. https://www.kiro7.com/news/trending/california -man-going-through-divorce-allegedly-crashes-dump-truck-into-wifes-home/GAHGN UXG45BMRLATAKP7NVM7YQ/.

"Dangerous Organizations and Bad Actors: Order of Nine Angles." *Middlebury Institute of International Studies at Monterey,* September 29, 2023. https://www.middlebury.edu/institute /academics/centers-initiatives/ctec/publications/dangerous-organizations-and-bad-actors -order-nine.

Daniels, Jessie. "The Algorithmic Rise of the 'Alt Right.'" *Contexts* 17, no. 3 (2018): 60–65. https:// doi.org/10.1177/1536504218766547.

Darby, Seyward. *Sisters in Hate: American Women on the Front Lines of White Nationalism.* New York: Little, Brown, 2020.

Darda, Joseph. *How White Men Won the Culture Wars: A History of Veteran America.* Berkeley: University of California Press, 2021.

Dashtgard, Pasha. *Male Supremacy and Online Radicalization: An Open-Source Ideology.* PhD dissertation, University of California-Irvine, 2022. https://escholarship.org/uc/item/6937c98h.

Davey, Jacob. "Extremism on Gaming (-Adjacent) Platforms." In *Gaming and Extremism: The Radicalization of Digital Playgrounds,* ed. Linda Schlagel and Rachel Kowert. New York: Taylor & Francis, 2024.

Davey, Jacob. "Gamers Who Hate: An Introduction to ISD's Gaming and Extremism Series." *ISD,* August 12, 2021. https://www.isdglobal.org/isd-publications/gamers-who-hate-an-introduction-to-isds-gaming-and-extremism-series/.

Daviess, Beth and J.M. Berger. "Lawful Extremism: Florida's Anti-Trans Laws." Middlebury Institute of International Studies at Monterey, Center on Terrorism, Extremism, and Counterterrorism (CTEC). December 2024. https://www.middlebury.edu/institute/academics/centers-initiatives/ctec/ctec-publications/lawful-extremism-floridas-anti-trans-laws

Davila, Devon. "'Women Turn Us into Women': How Taylor Swift's Presence at Football Games Unleashed an Onslaught of Misogyny and Reveals Society's Fear of Powerful Women." *Hercampus.com,* February 11, 2024. https://www.hercampus.com/school/st-andrews/women-turn-us-into-women-how-taylor-swifts-presence-at-football-games-unleashed-an-onslaught-of-misogyny-and-reveals-societys-fear-of-powerful-women/.

Davis, Angela. *Women, Race and Class.* First edition. New York: Vintage Books, 1983.

"Day of the Rope." *ADL.* https://www.adl.org/resources/hate-symbol/day-rope.

Deckman, Melissa. *The Politics of Gen Z: How the Youngest Voters Will Shape our Democracy.* New York: Columbia University Press, 2024.

Deckman, Melissa. *Tea Party Women: Mama Grizzlies, Grassroots Leaders, and the Changing Face of the American Right.* New York: New York University Press, 2016.

DeLa, Jim. "New College Students Begin Exodus after Conservative Control." *Bradenton Herald,* August 18, 2023. https://www.bradenton.com/news/local/education/article278368274.html.

de Luna, Elizabeth. "Creators Say YouTube Shorts Has a Transphobia Problem." *Mashable,* October 25, 2022. https://mashable.com/article/youtube-shorts-transphobic.

"Department of Justice Closes Investigation into the Death of Ashli Babbitt." *Department of Justice,* April 14, 2021. https://www.justice.gov/usao-dc/pr/department-justice-closes-investigation-death-ashli-babbitt.

De Cook, Julia and Megan Kelly. "Interrogating the 'incel menace': assessing the threat of male supremacy in terrorism studies." *Critical Studies on Terrorism* 15, no. 3 (2021): 706–726. https://doi.org/10.1080/17539153.2021.2005099

De Simone, Daniel. "Order of Nine Angles: What Is This Obscure Nazi Satanist Group?" *BBC,* June 23, 2020. https://www.bbc.com/news/world-53141759.

Díaz, Pablo Castillo, and Nahla Valji. "Symbiosis of Misogyny and Violent Extremism: New Understandings and Policy Implications." *Journal of International Affairs* 72, no. 2 (2019): 37–56. https://www.jstor.org/stable/26760831.

DiBranco, Alex. "The Long History of the Anti-Abortion Movement's Links to White Supremacy." *The Nation,* February 3, 2020. https://www.thenation.com/article/politics/anti-abortion-white-supremacy/.

DiBranco, Alex. "Mobilizing Misogyny." *Political Research Associates*, March 8, 2017. https://
politicalresearch.org/2017/03/08/mobilizing-misogyny

DiBranco, Alex, and Megan Kelly. "Anti-Feminist Conspiracism." In *Conspiracy as Genre: Narrative, Power and Circulation*, ed. Catherine,Tebaldi, Tommaso Milani, Alistair Plum, and Christoph Purschke. London: Bloomsbury Publishing, 2025.

Dickson, E. J. "The Birth of QAmom." *Rolling Stone*, September 2, 2020. https://www
.rollingstone.com/culture/culture-features/qanon-mom-conspiracy-theory-parents-sex
-trafficking-qamom-1048921/.

Diefendorf, Sarah, and Tristan Bridges. "On the Enduring Relationship Between Masculinity and Homophobia." *Sexualities* 23, no. 7 (2020): 1264–1284. https://doi.org/10.1177/136346
0719876843.

Dignam, Pierce Alexander, and Deana A. Rohlinger. "Misogynistic Men Online: How the Red Pill Helped Elect Trump." *Signs: Journal of Women in Culture and Society* 44, no. 3 (2019): 589–613. https://doi.org/10.1086/701155.

DiMaggio, Paul. "Culture and Cognition." *Annual Review of Sociology* 23 (1997): 263–287. https://doi.org/10.1146/annurev.soc.23.1.263.

Dines, Gail, Bob Jensen, and A. Russo. *Pornography: The Production and Consumption of Inequality*. London: Routledge, 2013.

Di Placido, Dani. "Taylor Swift's Matty Healy And Ice Spice Controversy, Explained." *Forbes*, May 24, 2023. https://www.forbes.com/sites/danidiplacido/2023/05/24/taylor-swifts
-matty-healy-controversy-explained/?sh=5829dd4026bc

Diverting Hate. "Diverting Hate: Misogynistic Extremism, The Manosphere, and Mainstream Social Media." A Bi-Annual Report from Diverting Hate. March 2024, vol. 3.

Diverting Hate. "Diverting Hate: Misogynistic Extremism, The Manosphere, and Mainstream Social Media." A Bi-Annual Report from Diverting Hate. September 2024, vol. 4.

Dobash, R. P., and Dobash, R. E. "Who Died? The Murder of Collaterals Related to Intimate Partner Conflict." *Violence Against Women* 18, no. 6 (2012): 662–671. https://doi.org/10.1177
/1077801212453984.

"Domestic Violent Extremism Poses Heightened Threat in 2021." Office of the Director of National Intelligence, March 1, 2021. https://www.dni.gov/files/ODNI/documents
/assessments/UnclassSummaryofDVEAssessment-17MAR21.pdf.

"Domestic Violence Statistics—The Hotline." National Domestic Violence Hotline. https://
www.thehotline.org/stakeholders/domestic-violence-statistics/.

Donovan, Joan, Emily Dreyfuss, and Brian Friedberg. *Meme Wars: The Untold Story of the Online Battles Upending Democracy in America*. New York: Bloomsbury Publishing, 2022.

Douglas, Heather, Leah Sharman, and Robin Fitzgerald. "More than half of Australian young people are using strangulation during sex: new research." *The Conversation*, July 1, 2024. https://findanexpert.unimelb.edu.au/news/88534-more-than-half-of-australian-young
-people-are-using-strangulation-during-sex--new-research

Downey, Maureen. "It Rhymes with Gingrich: Remark by Mother of the House Speaker Sparks Debate on Use of 'Bitch' to Describe Women with Power." *Atlanta Journal and Constitution*, January 5, 1995.

"Drug Ring Tied to Aryan Prison Gang Indicted with 24 Federal Arrests." Department of Justice, March 27, 2023. https://www.justice.gov/usao-wdwa/pr/drug-ring-tied-aryan-prison
-gang-indicted-24-federal-arrests.

du Mez, Kristin Kobes. *Jesus and John Wayne: How White Evangelicals Corrupted a Faith and Fractured a Nation*. New York: Liveright, 2020.

Dubus III, Andre. *Townie: A Memoir*. New York: W.W. Norton, 2012.

Ebner, Julia. *Going Dark: The Secret Social Lives of Extremists*. London: Bloomsbury, 2020.

Ebner, Julia. *Going Mainstream: How Extremists Are Taking Over*. London: Ithaka, 2023.

Echtermann, Alice, et al. "Kein Filter für Rechts: Wie die rechte Szene Instagram benutzt, um junge Menschen zu rekruitieren." *Correctiv*, October 7, 2020. https://correctiv.org/top-stories/2020/10/06/kein-filter-fuer-rechts-instagram-rechtsextremismus-frauen-der-rechten-szene/

Edström, Jerker, et al. "Patriarchal (Dis)orders: Backlash as Crisis Management." *Signs: Journal of Women in Culture and Society* 49, no. 2 (2024): 277–309. https://doi.org/10.1086/726744.

Eglin, P., and S. Hester. "'You're All a Bunch of Feminists': Categorization and the Politics of Terror in the Montreal Massacre." *Human Studies* 22 (1999): 253–272. https://doi.org/10.1023/A:1005444602547.

Elkins, Ansel. "Autobiography of Eve." *Blue Yodel*. New Haven, CT: Yale University Press, 10.

"Emerging Tensions? How Younger Generations Are Dividing on Masculinity and Gender Equality." *King's College London*, February 1, 2024. https://www.kcl.ac.uk/policy-institute/assets/emerging-tensions.pdf.

Emezi, Akwaeke. *Pet*. New York: Make Me a World/Random House, 2019.

Encarnación, Omar G. "Florida's 'Don't Say Gay' Bill Is Part of the State's Long, Shameful History." *Time*, May 12, 2022. https://time.com/6176224/florida-dont-say-gay-history-lgbtq-rights/.

Engel, Beverly. "How Being Too Nice Can Be Dangerous for Women." *Psychology Today*, August 8, 2019. https://www.psychologytoday.com/us/blog/the-compassion-chronicles/201908/how-being-too-nice-can-be-dangerous-women.

Ermyas, Tinbete, Jason Fuller, and Mary Louise Kelly. "Meta Oversight Board co-chair responds to company's decision to end fact-checking." *National Public Radio*, January 10, 2025, https://www.wunc.org/2025-01-10/meta-oversight-board-co-chair-responds-to-companys-decision-to-end-fact-checking.

Esman, Abigail. *Rage: Narcissism, Patriarchy, and the Culture of Terrorism*. Lincoln, NE: Potomac Books, 2020.

Espadas, Isabela, and Barros Leal. "Two Soldiers Arrested on Charges of Stealing Pride Flags from a Queer Couple's Virginia Home." *NBC News*, February 7, 2024. https://www.nbcnews.com/nbc-out/out-news/two-arrested-charges-stealing-pride-flags-lesbian-couples-virginia-hom-rcna137351.

Everytown for Gun Safety. "Guns and Violence Against Women: America's Uniquely Lethal Intimate Partner Violence Problem." December 16, 2022. https://everytownresearch.org/report/guns-and-violence-against-women-americas-uniquely-lethal-intimate-partner-violence-problem/.

Everytown for Gun Safety. "Misogyny, Extremism, and Gun Violence." January 13, 2022. https://everytownresearch.org/report/misogyny-extremism-and-gun-violence/.

Ewens, Hannah. "Young, Male, and Anti-Feminist—The Gen Z Boys Who Hate Women." *Vice*, May 28, 2021. https://www.vice.com/en/article/dyv7by/anti-feminist-gen-z-boys-who-hate-women.

"Examining the Intersection Between Gaming and Extremism." *The United Nations*, October 5, 2022. https://www.un.org/counterterrorism/sites/www.un.org.counterterrorism/files/221005_research_launch_on_gaming_ve.pdf.

Farivar, Cyrus. "Extremists Creep into Roblox, an Online Game Popular with Children." *NBC News*, August 21, 2019. https://www.nbcnews.com/tech/tech-news/extremists-creep-roblox-online-game-popular-children-n1045056.

Farokhmanesh, Megan. "The Small Company at the Center of 'Gamergate 2.0.'" *WIRED*, March 14, 2024. https://www.wired.com/story/sweet-baby-video-games-harassment-gamergate/.

"Far-Right Extremists Memorialize 'Martyr' Ashli Babbitt." *ADL*, January 15, 2021. https://www.adl.org/resources/blog/far-right-extremists-memorialize-martyr-ashli-babbitt.

Farrell, Tracie, et al. "Exploring Misogyny across the Manosphere in Reddit." In *11th ACM Conference on Web Science* (*WebSci '19*), June 30–July 3, 2019. https://doi.org/10.1145/3292522.3326045.

Farris, Sara R. *In the Name of Women's Rights: The Rise of Femonationalism*. Durham, NC: Duke University Press, 2017.

"Fast Facts: Preventing Sexual Violence | Violence Prevention | Injury Center | CDC." Centers for Disease Control and Prevention. https://www.cdc.gov/violenceprevention/sexualviolence/fastfact.html.

"Fatal Violence Against the Transgender and Gender Expansive Community in 2021." Human Rights Campaign. https://www.hrc.org/resources/fatal-violence-against-the-transgender-and-gender-expansive-community-in-2021.

"Fatal Violence Against the Transgender and Gender-Expansive Community in 2023." Human Rights Campaign. https://www.hrc.org/resources/fatal-violence-against-the-transgender-and-gender-expansive-community-in-2023.

Fazackerley, Anna. "'Vulnerable Boys Are Drawn In': Schools Fear Spread of Andrew Tate's Misogyny." *The Guardian*, January 7, 2023. https://www.theguardian.com/society/2023/jan/07/andrew-tate-misogyny-schools-vulnerable-boys.

"FBI—Rape." *Crime/Law Enforcement Stats* (*Uniform Crime Reporting Program*). https://ucr.fbi.gov/crime-in-the-u.s/2017/crime-in-the-u.s.-2017/topic-pages/rape.

Federal Bureau of Investigation. "A Study of Pre-Attack Behaviors of Active Shooters in the United States Between 2000 and 2013." June 2018. https://www.fbi.gov/file-repository/pre-attack-behaviors-of-active-shooters-in-us-2000-2013.pdf/view.

Feffer, John. "The Global Right Wing's Bizarre Obsession with Pedophilia." *Institute for Policy Studies*, July 28, 2021. https://ips-dc.org/the-global-right-wings-bizarre-obsession-with-pedophilia/.

Felmlee, Diane, et al. "Sexist Slurs: Reinforcing Feminine Stereotypes Online." *Sex Roles* 83 (2020): 16–28. https://doi.org/10.1007/s11199-019-01095-z.

Feola, Michael. *The Rage of Replacement: Far-Right Politics and Demographic Fear*. Minneapolis: University of Minnesota Press, 2024.

Ferber, Abby. "Racial Warriors and Weekend Warriors." *Men and Masculinities* 3, no. 1 (2000): 30–56. https://doi.org/10.1093/oso/9780199267248.003.0018.

Ferrise, Adam. "Man Who Planned Mass Shooting of Women at Ohio State Is First 'Incel' Convicted of Federal Hate Crime." *Cleveland.com*, February 24, 2024. https://www.cleveland.com/court-justice/2024/02/man-who-planned-mass-shooting-of-women-at-ohio-state-is-first-incel-convicted-of-federal-hate-crime.html.

Fieldstadt, Elisha. "Former Marine Is Accused of Leading Neo-Nazi Group and Planning to Attack a New York Synagogue." NBC News, July 27, 2022. https://www.nbcnews.com/news/us-news/former-marine-accused-leading-neo-nazi-group-planning-attack-new-york-rcna40295.

"Fiscal Year 2022 Targeted Violence and Terrorism Prevention Grantee Abstracts." Homeland Security, September 6, 2023. https://www.dhs.gov/fiscal-year-2022-targeted-violence-and-terrorism-prevention-grantee-abstracts.

Flores, Andrew R., et al. "Transgender People Over Four Times More Likely Than Cisgender People to Be Victims of Violent Crime." *Williams Institute*, March 23, 2021. https://williamsinstitute.law.ucla.edu/press/ncvs-trans-press-release/.

Floya, Anthias, and Nira Yuval-Davis. *Woman-Nation-State*. New York: Springer, 1989.

Fontanella, Lara, et al. "How Do We Study Misogyny in the Digital Age? A Systematic Literature Review Using a Computational Linguistic Approach." *Humanities and Social Science Communications* 11 (2024): 478. https://doi.org/10.1057/s41599-024-02978-7.

Forget, Jarod. "Violent Drug Organizations Use Human Trafficking to Expand Profits." DEA .gov, January 28, 2021. https://www.dea.gov/stories/2021/2021-01/2021-01-28/violent -drug-organizations-use-human-trafficking-expand-profits.

"Former U.S. Army Soldier Sentenced to 45 Years in Prison for Attempting to Murder Fellow Service Members in Deadly Ambush." Department of Justice, March 3, 2023. https://www .justice.gov/usao-sdny/pr/former-us-army-soldier-sentenced-45-years-prison-attempting -murder-fellow-service.

"Fox News Host Says 'We Need These Ladies to Get Married' Following Republicans' Weak Performance with Single Women." *Media Matters for America*, November 9, 2022. https:// www.mediamatters.org/jesse-watters/fox-news-host-says-we-need-these-ladies-get -married-following-republicans-weak.

Frances-Wright, Isabelle, and Moustafa Ayad. "'Your body, my choice': Hate and Harassment Towards Women Spreads Online." *Institute for Strategic Dialogue*, November 8, 2024. https:// www.isdglobal.org/digital_dispatches/your-body-my-choice-hate-and-harassment -towards-women-spreads-online/.

Frank, Adam. "Why Expertise Matters." *NPR*, April 7, 2017. https://www.npr.org/sections/13 .7/2017/04/07/522992390/why-expertise-matters.

Franklin, Karen. "Inside the Mind of People Who Hate Gays." *PBS Frontline: Roots of Homophobia*, https://www.pbs.org/wgbh/pages/frontline/shows/assault/roots/franklin.html.

Franklin, Karen. "Unassuming Motivations: Contextualizing the Narratives of Antigay Assailants." *APA Psycinfo* (1998): 1–23. https://psycnet.apa.org/doi/10.4135/9781452243818.n1.

Frounfelker, Rochelle, Janique Johnson-Lafleur, Catherine Montmagny Grenier, et al. "'Between the Self and the Other': Clinical Presentation of Male Supremacy in Violent Extremists." *Behavioral Sciences of Terrorism and Political Aggression* (2023): 1–21. https://doi.org/10 .1080/19434472.2023.2185277.

Gabbatt, Adam. "How the Domestic Terror Plot to Kidnap Michigan's Governor Unravelled." *The Guardian*, October 9, 2020. https://www.theguardian.com/us-news/2020/oct/08 /michigan-governor-gretchen-whitmer-kidnap-plot.

"Gaming the System: How Extremists Exploit Gaming Sites and What Can Be Done to Counter Them—NYU Stern Center for Business and Human Rights." NYU Stern Center for Business and Human Rights, May 2023. https://bhr.stern.nyu.edu/tech-gaming-report.

Gardner, Abby. "A Complete Breakdown of the J. K. Rowling Transgender-Comments Controversy." *Glamour*, April 11, 2024. https://www.glamour.com/story/a-complete-breakdown-of -the-jk-rowling-transgender-comments-controversy.

Garg, Rahul. "Russia's Sexist List of Banned Professions for Women Must End." *LSE Blogs*, January 18, 2021. https://blogs.lse.ac.uk/socialpolicy/2021/01/18/russias-sexist-list-of -banned-professions-for-women-must-end/.

Garland, Victoria. "What Role for Women in Our Movement?" *American Renaissance*, October 17, 2017. https://www.amren.com/commentary/2017/10/role-women-movement/.

Gay, Roxane. *Bad Feminist: Tenth Anniversary Edition*. New York: Harper Perennial, 2024.

Geller, Lisa B., Marisa Booty, and Cassandra K. Crifasi. "The Role of Domestic Violence in Fatal Mass Shootings in the United States, 2014–2019." *Injury Epidemiology* 8 (2021): 38–38. https://doi.org/10.1186/s40621-021-00330-0.

Gentry, Caron E. *Disordered Violence: How Gender, Race and Heteronormativity Structure Terrorism*. Edinburgh, Scotland: Edinburgh University Press, 2020.

Gershon, Livia. "White Women's Role in School Segregation." *JSTOR Daily*, January 4, 2019. https://daily.jstor.org/white-womens-role-in-school-segregation/.

"Get the 2023 Toxicity in Multiplayer Games Report." *Unity*, 2023. https://create.unity.com/toxicity-report.

Gettleman, Jeffrey, et al. "'Screams Without Words': How Hamas Weaponized Sexual Violence on October 7." *The New York Times*, December 28, 2023. https://www.nytimes.com/2023/12/28/world/middleeast/oct-7-attacks-hamas-israel-sexual-violence.html.

Gheorghe, Ruxandra M. "'Just Be White (JBW)': Incels, Race and the Violence of Whiteness." *Affilia: Feminist Inquiry in Social Work* 39, no. 1 (2024): 59–77. https://doi.org/10.1177/08861099221144275.

Gheorghe, Ruxandra M., and David Yuzva Clement. "Weaponized Autism: Making Sense of Violent Internalized Ableism in Online Incel Communities." *Deviant Behavior* 45, no. 6 (2023): 896–910. https://doi.org/10.1080/01639625.2023.2268253

Gill-Peterson, Jules. *A Short History of Trans Misogyny*. New York: Verso, 2024.

Gill-Peterson, Jules. *Histories of the Transgender Child*. Minneapolis: University of Minnesota Press, 2018.

Gilligan, Carol, and David A. J. Richards. *Darkness Now Visible: Patriarchy's Resurgence and Feminist Resistance*. Cambridge, UK: Cambridge University Press, 2018.

Gilligan, Carol, and Naomi Snider. *Why Does Patriarchy Persist?* New York: Polity Press, 2018.

Gilligan, Chris."States with the Highest Percentage of Women in Business Leadership Roles | Best States | U.S. News." *USNews.com*, March 6, 2023. https://www.usnews.com/news/best-states/articles/2023-03-06/states-with-the-highest-percentage-of-women-in-business-leadership-roles.

Gilligan, James. *Violence: Reflections on a National Epidemic*. New York: Knopf Doubleday Publishing Group, 1997.

Ging, Debbie. "Alphas, Betas, and Incels: Theorizing the Masculinities of the Manosphere." *Men and Masculinities* 11, no. 4 (2019): 638–657. http://dx.doi.org/10.1177/1097184X17706401.

Ging, Debbie. "Why Influencers Like Andrew Tate Want Your Sons' Attention." *The Irish Times*, January 24, 2023. https://www.irishtimes.com/opinion/2023/01/24/why-influencers-like-andrew-tate-want-your-sons-attention/.

Givens, Terri. *The Roots of Racism: The Politics of White Supremacy in the U.S. and Europe*. Bristol: Bristol University Press, 2022.

GLAAD. "UPDATED Report: Drag Events Faced More than 160 Protests and Significant Threats Since Early 2022." *GLAAD*, April 25, 2023. https://glaad.org/anti-drag-report/.

Glick, Peter. "Gender, Sexism, and the Election: Did Sexism Help Trump More Than It Hurt Clinton?" *Politics, Groups, and Identities* 7, no. 3 (2019): 713–723. https://doi.org/10.1080/21565503.2019.1633931

Glick, Peter, and Susan Fiske. "Hostile and Benevolent Sexism." *Psychology of Women Quarterly* 21, no. 1 (1996): 119–135. https://doi.org/10.1111/j.1471-6402.1997.tb00104.x

Gluck, Frank. "Vanderbilt Transgender Clinic Faces GOP Criticism, Investigation." *The Tennessean*, September 21, 2022. https://www.tennessean.com/story/news/health/2022/09/21/vanderbilt-transgender-clinic-faces-gop-criticism-investigation-republican/69508530007/.

Goetz, Judith, and Stephanie Mayer. "Concluding Remarks: Global Articulations of Antifeminism." In *Global Perspectives on Anti-feminism: Far-Right and Religious Attacks on Equality and Diversity*, ed. Judith Goetz and Stefanie Mayer. Edinburgh: Edinburgh University Press, 2023.

Goldberg, Abbie E. "Impact of HB 1557 (Florida's Don't Say Gay Bill) on LGBTQ+ Parents in Florida." *Williams Institute*, January 2023. https://williamsinstitute.law.ucla.edu/publications/impact-dont-say-gay-parents/.

Goldberg, Abbie E., Roberto Abreu, and Andrew Flores. "Perceived Impact of the Parental Rights in Education Act ('Don't Say Gay') on LGBTQ+ Parents in Florida." *The Counseling Psychologist* 52, no. 2 (2024): 224–266. https://doi.org/10.1177/00110000231219767.

Gomes, Alexandra, et al. "Are We Getting Less Sexist? A Ten-Year Gap Comparison Analysis of Sexism in a Portuguese Sample." *Psychological Reports* 125, no. 4 (2022): 2160–2177. https://doi.org/10.1177/00332941211011073.

Gorski, Paul C. *Reaching and Teaching Students in Poverty: Strategies for Erasing the Opportunity Gap*. New York: Teachers College Press, 2013.

Gorski, Phil. 2017. "Why Evangelicals Voted for Trump: A Critical Cultural Sociology." *American Journal of Cultural Sociology* 5 (2017): 338–354. https://doi.org/10.1057/s41290-017-0043-9.

Gotell, Lise, and Emily Dutton. "Sexual Violence in the 'Manosphere': Antifeminist Men's Rights Discourses on Rape." *International Journal for Crime, Justice and Social Democracy* 5, no. 2 (2016): 65–80. https://doi.org/10.5204/ijcjsd.v5i2.310.

Graham, Dave. "New Book Reveals Horror of Nazi Camp Brothels." *Reuters*, August 17, 2009. https://www.reuters.com/article/us-germany-nazis-brothels/new-book-reveals-horror-of-nazi-camp-brothels-idINTRE57G45X20090817/.

Grant, Melissa Gira. "How to Stop Neo-Nazis from Crashing Pride Month." *The New Republic*, May 31, 2023. https://newrepublic.com/article/173096/stop-neo-nazis-crashing-pride-month.

Gray, John. "Addressing LGBTQ Erasure through Literature in the ELT Classroom." *ELT Journal* 75, no. 1 (2021): 142–151. https://doi.org/10.1093/elt/ccaa079.

Green, Amy M. "Far Cry 5, American Right-Wing Terrorism, and Doomsday Prepper Culture." *Games and Culture* 17, nos. 7–8 (2022): 1015–1035. https://doi.org/10.1177/15554120211073379.

Green, Emma. "The Re-Birth of America's Pro-Natalist Movement." *The Atlantic*, December 6, 2017. https://www.theatlantic.com/politics/archive/2017/12/pro-natalism/547493/.

Greene, Mark. *Remaking Manhood in the Age of Trump: Collected Writings in the Battle against Dominance-Based Masculinity*. New York: ThinkPlay Partners, 2021.

Greene, Mark. *The Little #MeToo Book for Men*. New York: ThinkPlay Partners, 2018.

Greene, Mark, et al. "'Close': The Oscar-Nominated Movie that Names the Threat in Our Sons' Lives." *Ms. Magazine*, February 8, 2023. https://msmagazine.com/2023/02/08/close-lukas-dhont-masculinity/.

Guerin, Cecile. "The Yoga World Is Riddled with Anti-Vaxxers and Qanon Believers." *WIRED*, January 28, 2021. https://www.wired.co.uk/article/yoga-disinformation-qanon-conspiracy-wellness.

Guerrero, Jean. "Why Are Men So Lonely?" *Los Angeles Times*, January 15, 2024. https://www.latimes.com/opinion/story/2024-01-15/men-friendship-gen-z-loneliness.

Halpin, Michael, Norann Richard, Kayla Preston, et al. 2023. "Men Who Hate Women: The Misogyny of Involuntarily Celibate Men." *New Media and Society* (2023): 1–19. https://doi.org/10.1177/14614448231176777.

Hamad, Ruby. *White Tears/Brown Scars: How White Feminism Betrays Women of Color*. London: Trapeze, 2020.

Haslop, Craig, Jessica Ringrose, Idil Cambazoglu, et al. "Mainstreaming the Manosphere's Misogyny through Affective Homosocial Currencies: Exploring How Teen Boys Navigate the Andrew Tate Effect." *Social Media and Society* (2024): 1–11. https://doi.org/10.1177/20563051241228811.

Hayes, Brittany E., Colleen E. Mills, Joshua D. Freilich, et al. "Are Honor Killings Unique? A Comparison of Honor Killings, Domestic Violence Homicides, and Hate Homicides by Far-Right Extremists." *Homicide Studies* 22, no. 1 (2018): 70–93. http://journals.sagepub.com/doi/abs/10.1177/1088767917736796.

Healey, Gareth. "Proving Grounds: Performing Masculine Identities in Call of Duty: Black Ops." *Game Studies* 16, no. 2 (2016). https://www.researchgate.net/publication/313574951_Proving_grounds_Performing_masculine_identities_in_call_of_duty_Black_ops.

Hearn, Jeff, and Wendy Parkin. *Gender, Sexuality and Violence in Organizations: The Unspoken Forces of Organizational Violations*. London: Sage, 2001.

Helm, Burt. "Pizzagate Nearly Destroyed My Restaurant. Then My Customers Helped Me Fight Back." *Inc. Magazine*, July/August 2017. https://www.inc.com/magazine/201707/burt-helm /how-i-did-it-james-alefantis-comet-ping-pong.html.

Helsel, Phil. "Ohio 'Incel' Who Plotted to Kill Women at College Is Sentenced to 6 Years in Prison." *NBC News*, March 1, 2024. https://www.nbcnews.com/news/us-news/ohio-incel -plotted-kill-women-college-sentenced-6-years-prison-rcna141473.

Henry, Nicola. "Theorizing Wartime Rape: Deconstructing Gender, Sexuality, and Violence." *Gender & Society* 30, no. 1 (2016): 44–56. https://www.jstor.org/stable/24756163.

Herbenick, D., T. C. Fu, C. Patterson, Y. R. Rosenstock Gonzalez, M. Luetke, D. Svetina Valdivia, H. Eastman-Mueller, L. Guerra-Reyes, and M. Rosenberg. "Prevalence and Characteristics of Choking/Strangulation During Sex: Findings from a Probability Survey of Undergraduate Students." *Journal of American College Health* 71, no. 4 (2023): 1059–1073. doi: 10.1080/07448481.2021.1920599. Epub 2021 Jul 9. PMID: 34242530.

Hernandez, David. "Operation Takes Down Suspected San Diego Criminal Network with Ties to White Supremacist Groups." *San Diego Union-Tribune*, January 24, 2023. https://www .sandiegouniontribune.com/news/public-safety/story/2023-01-24/san-diego-police -operation-takes-down-criminal-network-with-ties-to-white-supremacist-groups.

Hetzner, Christiaan. "What Is Discord? App at the Centre of Investigation for Its Role in the Deadly Buffalo Supermarket Shooting." *Fortune.com*, May 19, 2022. https://fortune.com /2022/05/19/buffalo-shooting-video-what-is-twitch-discord-new-york-inquiry-social -media/.

Hidalgo, Rosie. "DVAM 2023: Ending Domestic Violence Requires Us All to Work Together." *Department of Justice*, October 31, 2023. https://www.justice.gov/ovw/blog/dvam-2023 -ending-domestic-violence-requires-us-all-work-together.

"Highland County Man Sentenced to More than 6 Years in Prison for Attempting Hate Crime." *Department of Justice*, February 29, 2024. https://www.justice.gov/usao-sdoh/pr/highland -county-man-sentenced-more-6-years-prison-attempting-hate-crime.

Hill, Jessica. "Fact Check: Post Detailing 9 Things Women Couldn't Do Before 1971 Is Mostly Right." *USA Today*, October 20, 2020. https://www.usatoday.com/story/news /factcheck/2020/10/28/fact-check-9-things-women-couldnt-do-1971-mostly-right /3677101001/.

Hill Collins, Patricia. "Toward a New Vision Race, Class, and Gender as Categories of Analysis and Connection." *Race, Sex & Class* 1, no. 1 (1993): 25–43. https://www.jstor.org/stable /41680038.

Hoffman, Bruce, et al. "Assessing the Threat of Incel Violence." *Studies in Conflict & Terrorism* 43, no. 7 (2020): 565–587. https://doi.org/10.1080/1057610X.2020.1751459.

Holmes, Helen. "Book Burning and Banning Is Increasing Across the Political Spectrum." *Observer*, February 9, 2022. https://observer.com/2022/02/book-banning-is-increasing-across -the-united-states-a-book-burning-in-tennessee/.

"Home | What Is CBIM." *Coaching Boys Into Men (CBIM)*. https://coachescorner.org/.

"Home, the Most Dangerous Place for Women, with Majority of Female Homicide Victims Worldwide Killed by Partners or Family, UNODC Study Says." *United Nations Office on Drugs and Crime*, November 26, 2018. https://www.unodc.org/unodc/en/frontpage/2018 /November/home-the-most-dangerous-place-for-women-with-majority-of-female -homicide-victims-worldwide-killed-by-partners-or-family--unodc-study-says.html.

hooks, bell. *Ain't I a Woman: Black Women and Feminism*. New York: Routledge, 2014.

hooks, bell. *The Will to Change*. New York: Atria Books, 2004.

Horowitch, Rose. "Florida's 'Stop WOKE' Law to Remain Blocked in Colleges, Appeals Court Rules." *NBC News*, March 17, 2023. https://www.nbcnews.com/politics/politics-news/floridas-stop-woke-law-remain-blocked-colleges-appeals-court-rules-rcna75455.

Hosang, Daniel Martinez, and Joseph E. Lowndes. *Producers, Parasites, Patriots: Race and the New Right-Wing Politics of Precarity*. Minneapolis: University of Minnesota Press, 2019.

HRC Staff. "For the First Time Ever, Human Rights Campaign Officially Declares 'State of Emergency' for LGBTQ+ Americans; Issues National Warning and Guidebook to Ensure Safety for LGBTQ+ Residents and Travelers." *Human Rights Campaign*, June 6, 2023. https://www.hrc.org/press-releases/for-the-first-time-ever-human-rights-campaign-officially-declares-state-of-emergency-for-lgbtq-americans-issues-national-warning-and-guidebook-to-ensure-safety-for-lgbtq-residents-and-travelers.

Hudson, Valerie, and Kaylee Hodgson. "Sex and Terror: Is the Subordination of Women Associated with the Use of Terror?" *Terrorism and Political Violence* 34, no. 3 (2022): 605–632. https://doi.org/10.1080/09546553.2020.1724968.

Hunnicut, Gwen. "Varieties of Patriarchy and Violence Against Women: Resurrecting 'Patriarchy' as a Theoretical Tool." *Violence Against Women* 15, no. 5 (2009): 553–573. https://doi.org/10.1177/1077801208331246.

Hunt, Amy. "What Is a 'Tradwife'—And Why Is the Idea Proving So Controversial?" *Woman & Home*, January 24, 2020. https://www.womanandhome.com/life/tradwife-definition-alena-petitt-346861/

Hunt, Erica, and Dawn Lundy Martin. *Letters to the Future: Black Women/Radical Writing*. Tucson, AZ: Kore Press, 2018.

Hunter, Kyleanne, and Emma Jouenne. "All Women Belong in the Kitchen, and Other Dangerous Tropes: Online Misogyny as a National Security Threat." *Journal of Advanced Military Studies* 12, no. 1 (2021): 57–85. https://doi.org/10.21140/mcuj.20211201003.

Hwang, Grace. "Examining Extremism: Violent Animal Rights Extremists." *Center for Strategic and International Studies (CSIS)*, August 20, 2021. https://www.csis.org/blogs/examining-extremism/examining-extremism-violent-animal-rights-extremists.

Indelicato, Maria Elena, and Maira Magalhaes Lopes. "Understanding Populist Far-Right Anti-Immigration and Anti-Gender Stances Beyond the Paradigm of Gender as a 'Symbolic Glue': Giorgia Meloni's Modern Motherhood, Neo-Catholicism, and Reproductive Racism." *European Journal of Women's Studies* 31, no. 1 (2024): 1–15. https://doi.org/10.1177/13505068241230819.

Institute for Economics and Peace. "Global Terrorism Index 2024." February 2024. http://visionofhumanity.org/resources.

Issa, Yasmine. "'A Profoundly Masculine Act': Mass Shootings, Violence Against Women, and the Amendment That Could Forge a Path Forward." *California Law Review*, April 2019. https://www.californialawreview.org/print/a-profoundly-masculine-act-mass-shootings-violence-against-women-and-the-amendment-that-could-forge-a-path-forward.

Jackman, Tom, Scott Clement, Emily Guskin, et al. "A Quarter of Americans Believe FBI Instigated Jan. 6, Post-UMD Poll Finds." *The Washington Post*, January 4, 2024. https://www.washingtonpost.com/dc-md-va/2024/01/04/fbi-conspiracy-jan-6-attack-misinformation/.

Jamieson, Katherine. "How 'Barefoot and Pregnant' Became a Dark American Joke." *Slate*, October 22, 2022. https://slate.com/human-interest/2022/10/barefoot-and-pregnant-history-origin-of-saying.html.

Jane, Emma A. "'Back to the Kitchen, Cunt': Speaking the Unspeakable About Online Misogyny." *Continuum* 28, no. 4 (2014): 558–570. https://doi.org/10.1080/10304312.2014.924479

Jane, Emma A. "Gendered Cyberhate as Workplace Harassment and Economic Vandalism." *Feminist Media Studies* 18, no. 4 (2018): 575–591. https://doi.org/10.1080/14680777.2018.1447344.

Jankowicz, Nina. "How Disinformation Became a New Threat to Women." *Coda Story*, December 11, 2017. https://www.codastory.com/disinformation/how-disinformation-became-a-new-threat-to-women/.

Jasser, Greta, Megan Kelly, and Ann-Kathrin Rothermel. "Male Supremacism and the Hanau Terrorist Attack: Between Online Misogyny and Far-Right Violence." International Centre for Counter-Terrorism (ICCT), May 20, 2020. https://icct.nl/publication/male-supremacism-and-the-hanau-terrorist-attack-between-online-misogyny-and-far-right-violence/.

Jasser, Greta, Jordan McSwiney, and Savvas Zannetou. "'Welcome to #GabFam': Far-Right Virtual Community on Gab." *New Media & Society* 25, no. 7 (2023): 1728–1745. https://doi.org/10.1177/14614448211024546.

Jasser, Greta, Megan Kelly, and Ann-Kathrin Rothermel. "Male Supremacism and the Hanau Terrorist Attack: Between Online Misogyny and Far-Right Violence." International Centre for Counter-Terrorism (ICCT), May 20, 2020. https://icct.nl/publication/male-supremacism-and-hanau-terrorist-attack-between-online-misogyny-and-far-right.

Jenkins, Philip. *Moral Panic: Changing Concepts of the Child Molester in Modern America.* New Haven, CT: Yale University Press, 1998.

Jenkins, Philip. "Ruby Ridge | History, Facts, Aftermath, & Map." *Britannica*, April 11, 2024. https://www.britannica.com/event/Ruby-Ridge.

Jennings, Rebecca. "Incel: What Are Chads, Stacys, and Beckys?" *Vox*, April 28, 2018. https://www.vox.com/2018/4/28/17290256/incel-chad-stacy-becky.

Jensen, Michael, and Sheehan Kane. "QAnon-Inspired Violence in the United States: An Empirical Assessment of a Misunderstood Threat." *Behavioral Sciences of Terrorism and Political Aggression* 16, no. 1 (2024): 65–83. https://www.tandfonline.com/doi/abs/10.1080/19434472.2021.2013292?journalCode=rirt20.

Jensen, Michael, Sheehan Kane, and Elena Akers. "Profiles of Individual Radicalization in the United States (PIRUS)." START, 2019. https://www.start.umd.edu/publication/profiles-individual-radicalization-united-states-pirus-1.

Johnston, Melissa, and Jacqui True. "Misogyny and Violent Extremism: Implications for Preventing Violent Extremism." *Monash University Gender, Peace and Security and UN Women*, 2019. https://giwps.georgetown.edu/resource/misogyny-and-violent-extremism-implications-for-preventing-violent-extremsim/.

Jolley, Daniel, Sylvia Mari, Tanya Schrader, et al. "Sexism and Feminist Conspiracy Beliefs: Hostile Sexism Moderates the Link Between Feminist Conspiracy Beliefs and Rape Myth Acceptance." *Violence Against Women*, 2024. https://doi.org/10.1177/10778012241234892.

Jonanssen, Jacob. "Reconsidering Trauma and Symbolic Wounds in Times of Online Misogyny and Platforms." *Media, Culture and Society* 45, no. 1 (2023): 191–201. https://doi.org/10.1177/01634437221127362.

Jones, Tiffany. "Trans Bans Expand: Anti-LGBTQ+ Lawfare and New-fascism." *Sexuality Research and Social Policy*, 2024. https://doi.org/10.1007/s13178-024-00948-x

Kahney, Leander. "'Mommy Liberty' Packs a Gun." *WIRED*, September 26, 2001. https://www.wired.com/2001/09/mommy-liberty-packs-a-gun/.

Kalmoe, Nathan P., and Liliana Mason. *Radical American Partisanship: Mapping Violent Hostility, Its Causes, and the Consequences for Democracy.* Chicago: University of Chicago Press, 2022.

Kandiyoti, Deniz. "Bargaining with Patriarchy." *Gender & Society* 2, no. 3 (1988): 274–290. https://www.jstor.org/stable/190357.

Kang, Cecilia. "Fake News Onslaught Targets Pizzeria as Nest of Child-Trafficking." *The New York Times*, November 21, 2016. https://www.nytimes.com/2016/11/21/technology/fact-check-this-pizzeria-is-not-a-child-trafficking-site.html.

Karbasi, Zahra, et al. "The Silent Crisis of Child Abuse in the COVID-19 Pandemic: A Scoping Review." *Health Science Reports* 5, no. 5 (2022): e790. https://doi.org/10.1002/hsr2.790.

Kasakove, Sophie. "The Fight Over 'Maus' Is Part of a Bigger Cultural Battle in Tennessee." *The New York Times*, March 4, 2022. https://www.nytimes.com/2022/03/04/us/maus-banned-books-tennessee.html.

Katz, Jackson. 2024. "Explaining Men." *Ms. Magazine* (Spring 2024): 24–27.

Kelley, Jeanna. "Taylor Swift's Real NFL Screen Time Is So Much Lower Than You Think." *SB Nation*, February 11, 2024." https://www.sbnation.com/nfl/2024/2/7/24056297/taylor-swift-travis-kelce-super-bowl-2024-broadcast-screen-time-chiefs-niners.

Kelly, Annie. "The Housewives of White Supremacy." *The New York Times*, June 1, 2018. https://www.nytimes.com/2018/06/01/opinion/sunday/tradwives-women-alt-right.html.

Kelly, Annie. "Opinion | Mothers for QAnon." *The New York Times*, September 10, 2020. https://www.nytimes.com/2020/09/10/opinion/qanon-women-conspiracy.html.

Kelly, Megan, Alex DiBranco, and Julia R. DeCook. "Misogynist Incels and Male Supremacist Violence." In *Male Supremacism in the United States: From Patriarchal Traditionalism to Misogynist Incels and the Alt-Right*, ed. Emily K. Carian, Alex DiBranco, and Chelsea Ebin. New York: Routledge, 2022.

Kelly, Megan, Ann-Kathrin Rothermel, and Lisa Sugiura. "Victim, Violent, Vulnerable." *Perspectives on Terrorism* 18, no. 1 (2024): 91–119. https://researchportal.port.ac.uk/files/88274913/Victim_violent_vulnerable.pdf.

Kendall, Mikki. *Hood Feminism: Notes from the Women that a Movement Forgot*. New York: Viking, 2020.

Kendi, Ibram X. *How to Be an Anti-Racist*. New York: Random House, 2019.

Kennedy, Lesley. "How Phyllis Schlafly Derailed the Equal Rights Amendment." *History*, March 19, 2020. https://www.history.com/news/equal-rights-amendment-failure-phyllis-schlafly.

Kilmer, Elizabeth D., and Rachel Kowert. "Grooming for Violence: Similarities Between Radicalisation and Grooming Processes in Gaming Spaces—GNET." *Global Network on Extremism and Technology*, February 8, 2024. https://gnet-research.org/2024/02/08/grooming-for-violence-similarities-between-radicalisation-and-grooming-processes-in-gaming-spaces/.

Kim, Bitna, and Meghan Royle. "Domestic Violence in the Context of the COVID-19 Pandemic: A Synthesis of Systematic Reviews." *Trauma, Violence and Abuse* 25, no. 1 (2023): 476–493. https://doi.org/10.1177%2F15248380231155530.

Kingdon, Ashton. "God of Race War: The Utilisation of Viking-Themed Video Games in Far-Right Propaganda—GNET." *Global Network on Extremism and Technology*, February 6, 2023. https://gnet-research.org/2023/02/06/god-of-race-war-the-utilisation-of-viking-themed-video-games-in-far-right-propaganda/.

Kingkade, Tyler. "Conservative Activists Want to Ban 400 Books from a Library—But They Aren't Even on Shelves." *NBC News*, August 23, 2022. https://www.nbcnews.com/news/us-news/conservative-activists-want-ban-400-books-library-arent-even-shelves-rcna44026.

Klein, Norman M. *The History of Forgetting: Los Angeles and the Erasure of Memory*. New York: Verso, 1997.

Koehler, Daniel, et al. "From Gaming to Hating: Extreme Right Indoctrination and Mobilization for Violence of Children in Gaming Platforms." *Political Psychology* 44, no. 2 (2022): 419–434. https://doi.org/10.1111/pops.12855.

Koonz, Claudia. *Mothers in the Fatherland: Women, the Family, and Nazi Politics*. New York: Routledge, 2014.

Köttig, Michaela, Bitzan, Renate, and Petö, Andrea, eds. *Gender and Far Right Politics in Europe*. Basingstoke: Palgrave Macmillan, 2017.

Kowert, Rachel. *The Video Game Debate 2*. London: Routledge, 2020.

Kowert, Rachel, et al. "Not Just a Game: Identity Fusion and Extremism in Gaming Cultures." *Frontiers in Communication* 7 (2022): 1–16. https://doi.org/10.3389/fcomm.2022.1007128.

Kowert, Rachel, and Elizabeth Kilmer. "Toxic Gamers Are Alienating Your Core Demographic." *Take This*. https://www.takethis.org/wp-content/uploads/2023/08/ToxicGamersBottom LineReport_TakeThis.pdf.

Kowert, Rachel, Alexi Martel, William B. Swann, William B. Swann, et al. "You Are What You Play: The Risks of Identity Fusion in Toxic Gamer Cultures." *Games: Research and Practice* 1, no. 2 (2023): 1–3. https://doi.org/10.1145/3604402.

Kramer, Benjamin, and Magdalena Klingler. "A Bad Political Climate for Climate Research and Trouble for Gender Studies: Right-wing Populism as a Challenge to Science Communication." *Perspectives on Populism and the Media* 7 (2020): 253–272. https://doi.org/10.5771/9783845297392.

Krook, Mona Lena. *Violence against Women in Politics*. Oxford, UK: Oxford University Press, 2020.

Kutner, Samantha. "Swiping Right: The Allure of Hyper Masculinity and Cryptofascism for Men Who Join the Proud Boys." International Center for Counter-Terrorism (ICCT), May 26, 2020. www.icct.nl/publication/swiping-right-allure-hyper-masculinity-and-cryptofascism-men-who-join-proud-boys.

Lakhani, Suraj. "When Digital and Physical World Combine." *Perspectives on Terrorism* 17, no. 2 (2023): 108–125. https://www.jstor.org/stable/27255595.

Lakhani, Suraj, and Susann Wiedlitzka. "'Press F to Pay Respects': An Empirical Exploration of the Mechanics of Gamification in Relation to the Christchurch Attack." *Terrorism and Political Violence* 35, no. 7 (2023): 1586–1603. https://doi.org/10.1080/09546553.2022.2064746.

Lamoureux, Mack. "New York Cop Bought Rifle for Neo-Nazi 'Rapekrieg' Marine who Planned Synagogue Attack: Feds." *VICE News*, July 27, 2022. https://www.vice.com/en/article/akeewg/nypd-officer-bought-marine-rapekrieg-neo-nazi-gun.

Lamoureux, Mack. "Police Arrest Alleged Leader of Horrific Child Sextortion Ring." *VICE*, December 19, 2023. https://www.vice.com/en/article/wxjkxm/police-arrest-kalana-limkin-alleged-leader-of-horrific-child-sextortion-ring.

Lamoureux, Mack. "The Vile Sextortion and Torture Ring Where Kids Target Kids." *VICE*, February 20, 2024. https://www.vice.com/en/article/7kxjnz/the-vile-sextortion-and-torture-ring-where-kids-target-kids.

Lamoureux, Mack. "Why Do Neo-Nazis Keep Getting Arrested for Child Sexual Abuse Material?" *VICE*, July 20, 2023. https://www.vice.com/en/article/3akvbw/why-do-neo-nazis-keep-getting-arrested-for-child-porn.

Lamphere-Englund, Galen. "Theories of Digital Games and Radicalization." In *Gaming and Extremism: The Radicalization of Digital Playgrounds* ed. Linda Schlagel and Rachel Kowert. New York: Taylor & Francis, 2024.

Lamphere-Englund, Galen, Amores Hamonangan, Farah Putri, et al. "Pathways of Resilience to Violent Extremism in Indonesian Higher Education: A Mixed Method Study Using the Building Resilience Against Violence Extremism (BRAVE) Approach." *USAID Harmoni*, 2022. https://www.crisconsortium.org/research-reports-pathways-to-resilience.

Lamphere-Englund, Galen, and Jessica White. "The Online Gaming Ecosystem: Assessing Digital Socialisation, Extremism Risks and Harms Mitigation Efforts." *Global Network on Extremism and Technology*, May 2023. https://gnet-research.org/wp-content/uploads/2023/05/GNET-37-Extremism-and-Gaming_web.pdf.

Latif, Mehr, et al. "Do White Supremacist Women Adopt Movement Archetypes of Mother, Whore, and Fighter?" *Studies in Conflict & Terrorism* 46, no. 4 (2023): 415–432. https://doi.org/10.1080/1057610X.2020.1759264.

Lavietes, Matt. "Pride Flag Burned Outside a City Hall in Arizona." *NBC News*, June 7, 2023. https://www.nbcnews.com/nbc-out/out-politics-and-policy/pride-flag-burned-city-hall-arizona-rcna88112.

Lawless, Tiffany J., et al. "Is It Really Just a Joke? Gender Differences in Perceptions of Sexist Humor." *HUMOR* 33, no. 2 (2020): 291–315. https://psycnet.apa.org/doi/10.1515/humor-2019-0033.

Lawrence, David, Limor Simhony-Philpott, and Danny Stone. "Antisemitism and Misogyny: Overlap and Interplay." *Hope not Hate* and the *Antisemitism Policy Trust*, September 2021. https://antisemitism.org.uk/wp-content/uploads/2021/09/Antisemitism-and-Misogyny-Overlap-and-Interplay.pdf.

"Leader of White Supremist Gang Receives 25 Years in Federal Prison for Armed Drug Trafficking and Assaulting an Officer." *Department of Justice*, July 26, 2023. https://www.justice.gov/usao-ednc/pr/leader-white-supremist-gang-receives-25-years-federal-prison-armed-drug-trafficking.

Lees, Matt. "What Gamergate Should Have Taught Us about the 'Alt-Right.'" *The Guardian*, December 1, 2016. https://www.theguardian.com/technology/2016/dec/01/gamergate-alt-right-hate-trump.

Leidig, Eviane. "From Love Jihad to Grooming Gangs: Tracing Flows of the Hypersexual Muslim Male through Far-Right Female Influencers." *Religions* 12, no. 12 (2021): 1083. https://doi.org/10.3390/rel12121083.

Leidig, Eviane. *The Women of the Far Right: Social Media Influencers and Online Radicalization.* New York: Columbia University Press, 2023.

Leidig, Eviane. "'We Are Worth Fighting For': Women in Far-Right Extremism." International Centre for Counter-Terrorism (ICCT), October 26, 2021. https://icct.nl/publication/women-far-right-extremism/.

Leidig, Eviane. "Why Terrorism Studies Miss the Mark When It Comes to Incels." International Centre for Counter-Terrorism (ICCT), August 31, 2021. www.icct.nl/publication/why-terrorism-studies-miss-mark-when-it-comes-incels.

Levengood, Timothy, and Scott Hadland. "Hostile Laws and Hospitalization: Why Anti-LGBTQ+ Legislation Threatens Adolescent Lives." *Journal of Hospital Medicine* 18, no. 5 (2023): 449–445. https://doi.org/10.1002/jhm.13038.

Levey, Tania G. *Sexual Harassment Online: Shaming and Silencing Women in the Digital Age.* Boulder, CO: Lynne Rienner, 2018.

Levine, Phillip. "Moms for Liberty: Where Are They, and Are They Winning?" Brookings Institution, October 10, 2023. https://www.brookings.edu/articles/moms-for-liberty-where-are-they-and-are-they-winning/.

"LGBT-Owned Kilt Maker Denounces Kilt-Clad Proud Boys." *BBC*, December 15, 2020. https://www.bbc.com/news/world-us-canada-55326451.

@libsoftiktok. ".@PHXChildrens Hospital Boasts About Doing Medical Transitions on Kids. They Also Follow WPATH Guidelines Which Allows 'Gender Affirming' Surgeries for Minors." *Twitter*, August 16, 2022, 6:33 pm. https://www.mediamatters.org/media/3992530.

Linder, Douglas O. "The Ruby Ridge (Randy Weaver) Trial: An Account." *Famous Trials,* hosted by the University of Missouri-Kansas City School of Law. https://www.famous-trials.com /rubyridge/1152-home.

Lin-Fisher, Betty. "Right-Wing Social Media Attack Targets Akron Children's Hospital." *Akron Beacon Journal,* September 2, 2022. https://www.beaconjournal.com/story/news/local /2022/09/22/social-media-attack-targets-akron-childrens-hospital-transgender-program -gender-affirming/69511217007/.

Ling, Justin. "Gun-Wielding QAnon Advocate Targets Justin Trudeau as Conspiracy Spreads." *Foreign Policy,* July 13, 2020. https://foreignpolicy.com/2020/07/13/qanon-canada-trudeau -conspiracy-theory/.

Linke, Uli. "Gendered Difference, Violent Imagination: Blood, Race, Nation." *American Anthropologist* 99, no. 3 (1997): 559–573. https://www.jstor.org/stable/681743.

Linke, Uli. *German Bodies: Race and Representation after Hitler.* New York: Routledge, 1999.

List, Madeline. "14-Year Old Shot His Teen Girlfriend in 'Fit Of Rage' Over Breakup, Wisconsin Cops Say." *Idaho Statesman,* January 11, 2023. https://www.idahostatesman.com/news /nation-world/national/article271071592.html.

Lithwick, Dahlia. "The Horrifying Implications of Alito's Most Alarming Footnote." *Slate,* May 10, 2022. https://slate.com/news-and-politics/2022/05/the-alarming-implications-of -alitos-domestic-supply-of-infants-footnote.html.

Llanera, Tracy. "The Misogyny Paradox and the Alt-Right." *Hypatia* 38, no. 1 (2023): 157–176. https://doi.org/10.1017/hyp.2023.4.

"Lock Her Up: The Trump Supremacy on Steam." *Steam,* April 27, 2018. https://store .steampowered.com/app/769980/Lock_Her_Up_The_Trump_Supremacy/.

Loewen Walker, Rachel. "Call It Misogyny." *Feminist Theory* 25, no. 1 (2024): 64–82. https://doi .org/10.1177/14647001221119995.

Lorde, Audre. *The Master's Tools Will Never Dismantle the Master's House.* New York: Penguin, 2018.

Lugg, Catherine A., and Autumn K. Tooms. "A Shadow of Ourselves: Identity Erasure and the Politics of Queer Leadership." *School Leadership and Management* 30, no. 1 (2010): 77–91. https://doi.org/10.1080/13632430903509790.

Luo, Michael. "How White Christian Nationalists Seek to Transform America." *The New Yorker,* July 21, 2022. https://www.newyorker.com/podcast/politics-and-more/how-white -christian-nationalists-seek-to-transform-america.

Luscombe, Richard. "Ron DeSantis Condemned as Florida Removes Sociology as Core College Class." *The Guardian,* January 26, 2024. https://www.theguardian.com/us-news/2024 /jan/26/florida-sociology-classes-ron-desantis-condemned.

Luu, Chi. "Bad Language for Nasty Women (and Other Gendered Insults)." *Lingua Obscura,* November 9, 2016. https://daily.jstor.org/the-language-of-nasty-women-and-other -gendered-insults/.

Lyons, Matthew. "The U.S. Far Right's Politics of Gender." In *Male Supremacism in the United States: From Patriarchal Traditionalism to Misogynist Incels and the Alt-Right,* ed. Emily K. Carian, Alex DiBranco, and Chelsea Ebin. New York: Routledge, 2022.

Lyons, Minna, and Gayle Brewer. "Experiences of Intimate Partner Violence During Lockdown and the COVID-19 Pandemic." *Journal of Family Violence* 37, no. 6 (2022): 969–977. https:// doi.org/10.1007/s10896-021-00260-x.

Maass, Anne, Mara Cadinu, Gaia Guarnieri, et al. "Sexual Harassment under Social Identity Threat: The Computer Harassment Paradigm." *Journal of Personality and Social Psychology* 85, no. 5 (2003): 853–870. https://psycnet.apa.org/doi/10.1037/0022-3514.85.5.853.

MacDonald, Keza. "It's 10 Years Since Gamergate—The Industry Must Now Stand Up to Far-Right Trolls." *The Guardian*, March 8, 2024. https://www.theguardian.com/games/2024/mar/08/gamergate-trolls-woke-game-consultants.

Macklin, Graham. "The Conspiracy to Kidnap Governor Gretchen Whitmer—Combating Terrorism Center at West Point." *Combating Terrorism Center* 14, no. 6 (2023): 1–15. https://ctc.westpoint.edu/the-conspiracy-to-kidnap-governor-gretchen-whitmer/.

Maiberg, Emanuel. "Andreessen Horowitz Invests in Civitai, Which Profits from Nonconsensual AI Porn." *404 Media*, March 5, 2024. https://www.404media.co/andreessen-horowitz-invests-in-civitai-key-platform-for-deepfake-porn/.

Manley, Alex. *The New Masculinity: A Roadmap for a 21st Century Definition of Manhood*. Toronto: ECW Press, 2023.

Manne, Kate. *Down Girl*. London: Penguin Books, 2019.

Manne, Kate. *Entitled: How Male Privilege Hurts Women*. New York: Random House, 2020.

"Mapping Attacks on LGBTQ Rights in U.S. State Legislatures in 2024." *American Civil Liberties Union*. https://www.aclu.org/legislative-attacks-on-lgbtq-rights-2024.

"Maps of Anti-LGBT Laws Country by Country." *Human Rights Watch*, https://features.hrw.org/features/features/lgbt_laws/.

Marganski, Alison. "Making a Murderer: The Importance of Gender and Violence Against Women in Mass Murder Events." *Sociology Compass* 13, no. 9 (2019): 1–15. http://dx.doi.org/10.1111/soc4.12730.

Martin, Alan. "Online Disinhibition and the Psychology of Trolling." *WIRED*, May 30, 2013. https://www.wired.com/story/online-aggression/.

Martinez, Nikki McCann. "Man Boobs and Raw Eggs: The Most Absurd Moments from Tucker Carlson's Ball-Tanning Special." *Rolling Stone*, October 5, 2022. https://www.rollingstone.com/politics/politics-news/tucker-carlson-end-of-men-most-absurd-moments-1234606090/.

Martynova, Elena. "Order of the Nine Angles." *Insight Monitor*, May 30, 2023. https://newsletter.insightthreatintel.com/p/order-of-nine-angles.

Marwick, Alice. "Morally Motivated Networked Harassment as Normative Reinforcement." *Social Media and Society* 7, no. 2 (2021). https://doi.org/10.1177/20563051211021378.

Marwick, Alice, and Robyn Caplan. "Drinking Male Tears: Language, the Manosphere, and Networked Harassment." *Feminist Media Studies* 18, no. 4 (2018): 543–559. https://doi.org/10.1080/14680777.2018.1450568.

Matfess, Hilary, and Devorah Margolin. "The Women of January 6th: A Gendered Analysis of the 21st Century American Far Right." *GWU Program on Extremism*, April 2022. Women-of-Jan6_Matfess-and-Margolin.pdf (gwu.edu).

Mattheis, Ashley. "Shieldmaidens of Whiteness: (Alt)Maternalism and Women Recruiting for the Far/Alt-Right." *Journal for Deradicalization* no. 17 (2018): 128–162. https://www.researchgate.net/publication/330093800_Shieldmaidens_of_Whiteness_Alt_Maternalism_and_Women_Recruiting_for_the_FarAlt-Right.

Mattheis, Ashley, et al. "The Allen, Texas, Attack: Ideological Fuzziness and the Contemporary Nature of Far-Right Violence." *Combating Terrorism Center* 16, no. 6 (2023): 16–22. https://ctc.westpoint.edu/the-allen-texas-attack-ideological-fuzziness-and-the-contemporary-nature-of-far-right-violence/.

Mazzei, Patricia. "DeSantis Targeted New College of Florida. Here's What's Changed." *The New York Times*, September 23, 2023. https://www.nytimes.com/2023/09/22/us/new-college-florida-desantis.html.

McCann, Allison, and Amy Schoenfield Walker. "Abortion Bans Across the Country: Tracking Restrictions by State." *The New York Times*, https://www.nytimes.com/interactive/2022/us/abortion-laws-roe-v-wade.html

McCarthy, Lauren, and Scott Taylor. "Misogyny and Organization Studies." *Organization Studies* 45, no. 3 (2024): 457–473. https://doi.org/10.1177/01708406231213964.

McCormick, Patricia. "Spineless Shelves: Two Years of Book Banning." *PEN America*, December 13, 2023. https://pen.org/spineless-shelves/.

McDaniel, Justine, and Hannah Natanson. "Dictionaries Among Books Removed from Shelves of Florida School District." *The Washington Post*, January 11, 2024. https://www.washingtonpost.com/education/2024/01/11/escambia-dictionaries-removed/.

McEwen, Lauren. "#YesAllWomen: A Short Fuse Between Rejection and Violence." *The Washington Post*, May 27, 2014. https://www.washingtonpost.com/blogs/she-the-people/wp/2014/05/27/yesallwomen-a-short-fuse-between-rejection-and-violence/.

McGee, Kate. "Lawmakers Advance Bill to Ban College Diversity, Equity, Inclusion Offices." *The Texas Tribune*, May 27, 2023. https://www.texastribune.org/2023/05/27/texas-university-diversity-equity-inclusion-dei-bill-conference/.

McMillan Cottom, Tressie. *Thick and Other Essays*. New York: New Press, 2019.

McMurtry, Alyssa. "Police Arrest 14 Members of Notorious Barcelona Hooligan Gang." *AA*, November 25, 2021. https://www.aa.com.tr/en/europe/police-arrest-14-members-of-notorious-barcelona-hooligan-gang/2430841.

McRae, Elizabeth Gillespie. "The Women Behind White Power." *The New York Times*, February 2, 2018. https://www.nytimes.com/2018/02/02/opinion/sunday/white-supremacy-forgot-women.html.

McRae, Elizabeth Gillespie. "'White Women and the Politics of Racial Inequality' with Dr. Elizabeth McRae." *The Center for the Study of the American South*, November 25, 2018. https://south.unc.edu/2018/11/25/available-for-viewing-white-women-and-the-politics-of-racial-inequality-with-dr-elizabeth-mcrae/.

McShane, Julianne. "Neo-Nazi Groups Spew Hate Outside Disney World and Near Orlando, Officials Say." *NBC News*, September 5, 2023. https://www.nbcnews.com/news/us-news/neo-nazi-groups-spew-hate-disney-world-orlando-officials-say-rcna103186.

Meger, Sara. "When Is Terrorism Not Terrorism." *The Gender and War Project*, April 26, 2018. http://www.genderandwar.com/2018/04/26/when-is-terrorism-not-terrorism.

Messner, Michael. "Bad Men, Good Men, Bystanders: Who Is the Rapist?" *Gender and Society* 30, no. 1 (2016): 57–66. https://doi.org/10.1177/0891243215608781.

Messner, Michael. "The Limits of 'the Male Sex Role': An Analysis of the Men's Liberation and Men's Rights Movements' Discourse." *Gender and Society* 12, no. 3 (1998): 255–276. https://www.jstor.org/stable/190285.

Miller, Cassie. "Racist 'Replacement' Theory Believed by Half of Americans." *Southern Poverty Law Center*, June 1, 2022. https://www.splcenter.org/news/2022/06/01/poll-finds-support-great-replacement-hard-right-ideas#gender.

Miller-Idriss, Cynthia. "America's Epidemic of Hate: Stopping Mass Shootings Requires Combating Online Extremism." *Foreign Affairs*, July 8, 2022. https://www.foreignaffairs.com/articles/united-states/2022-07-08/americas-epidemic-hate.

Miller-Idriss, Cynthia. "Andrew Tate's Violent, Misogynistic Teachings Are Seeping into Classrooms." *MSNBC*, February 7, 2023. https://www.msnbc.com/opinion/msnbc-opinion/counter-andrew-tates-growing-subculture-violent-toxic-masculinity-rcna69411.

Miller-Idriss, Cynthia. "Christian Nationalism Is a Racist, Ahistorical Ideology of Violence." *MSNBC.com*, October 23, 2022. https://www.msnbc.com/opinion/msnbc-opinion/these-midterms-republicans-run-against-first-amendment-n1299932

Miller-Idriss, Cynthia. *The Extreme Gone Mainstream: Commercialization and Far Right Youth Culture in Germany*. Princeton, NJ: Princeton University Press, 2018.

Miller-Idriss, Cynthia. "The Global Dimensions of Nationalist Populism." *International Spectator* 54, no. 2 (2019): 17–34. https:/doi.org/full/10.1080/03932729.2019.1592870.

Miller-Idriss, Cynthia. *Hate in the Homeland: The New Global Far Right.* Princeton, NJ: Princeton University Press, 2020.

Miller-Idriss, Cynthia. "How the Loss of Roe Directly Serves White Supremacists' Horrifying Plot." MSNBC, August 14, 2022. https://www.msnbc.com/opinion/msnbc-opinion/how-anti-abortion-rights-white-supremacist-extremism-overlap-n1297896.

Miller-Idriss, Cynthia. "Misogyny Incubators: How Gaming Helps Channel Everyday Sexism into Violent Extremism." Unpublished manuscript currently being revised for resubmission, last modified November 30, 2024. Microsoft Word file.

Miller-Idriss, Cynthia. 2020. "Triumph of the Women?: The Female Face of Populism and Extremism." Case Study 03: United States of America. *Friedrich Ebert Stiftung,* 2020. 17096.pdf (fes.de).

Miller-Idriss, Cynthia. "Tucker Carlson Is the No.1 Champion of This Leading Far-Right Conspiracy." MSNBC, May 7, 2022. https://www.msnbc.com/opinion/msnbc-opinion/fox-s-tucker-carlson-s-biggest-racist-conspiracy-theory-n1295212.

Miller-Idriss, Cynthia. "What Makes a Symbol Far Right? Co-Opted and Missed Meanings in Far Right Iconography." *Post-Digital Cultures of the Far-Right: Online Actions and Offline Consequences in Europe and the US.* New York: Transcript International Academic Publishing/ Columbia University Press, 2018, 123–136.

Miller-Idriss, Cynthia. "Women Among the Jan. 6 Attackers Are the New Normal of Right-Wing Extremism." MSNBC, January 8, 2022. https://www.msnbc.com/opinion/women-among-jan-6-attackers-are-new-normal-right-wing-n1287163.

Miller-Idriss, Cynthia, and Hilary Pilkington, eds. *Gender and the Radical and Extreme Right: Mechanisms of Transmission and the Role of Educational Interventions.* New York: Routledge, 2018.

Miller-Idriss, Cynthia, and Hilary Pilkington. "Women Are Joining the Far Right—We Need to Understand Why." *The Guardian,* January 24, 2019. https://www.theguardian.com /commentisfree/2019/jan/24/women-far-right-gender-roles-radical-right-migrant-muslim.

Miller, John, Brynn Gingras, Samantha Beech, et al. "2 Men Charged, 1 with Nazi Arm-Band, in Connection with Threats to Attack New York Synagogue." CNN, November 20, 2022. https://www.cnn.com/2022/11/19/us/nyc-jewish-threat-community-arrest.

Mills, Colleen E., Margaret Schmuhl, and Joel A. Capellan. "Far-Right Violence As Backlash Against Gender Equality: A County-Level Analysis of Structural and Ideological Gender Inequality and Homicides Committed by Far-Right Extremists." *Journal of Crime and Justice* 43, no. 5 (2020): 568–584. https://doi.org/10.1080/0735648X.2020.1738261.

Mittleman, Joel. "Homophobic Bullying As Gender Policing: Population-Based Evidence." *Gender and Society* 37, no. 1 (2023): 5–31. https://doi.org/10.1177/08912432221138091.

Moloney, Mairead Eastin, and Tony P. Love. "Assessing Online Misogyny: Perspectives from Sociology and Feminist Media Studies." *Sociology Compass* 12, no. 5 (2018): 1–12. https://doi .org/10.1111/soc4.12577.

Monk-Turner, Elizabeth. "White Evangelical Activism and the Gender Divide in the 2016 Presidential Election." *Society* 57, no. 1 (2020): 30–40. https://doi.org/10.1007/s12115-019 -00438-6.

Montagne, Renee, and Larry Abramson. "Cho Was Accused of Stalking in 2005." NPR Morning Edition, April 18, 2007. https://www.npr.org/templates/story/story.php?storyId=9645423

Montell, Amanda. *Wordslut: A Feminist Guide to Taking Back the English Language.* New York: Harper, 2019.

Morrison, Toni, ed. *Burn This Book.* New York: Harper Collins, 2009.

Morse, Susan. "Hospital and Physician Groups Ask DOJ to Investigate Threats to Gender-Affirming Care." *Healthcare Finance,* October 10, 2022. https://www.healthcarefinancenews

.com/news/hospital-and-physician-groups-ask-doj-investigate-threats-gender-affirming -care.

Mosse, George. *The Image of Man: The Creation of Modern Masculinity*. New York: Oxford University Press, 1998.

Myers, Amanda Lee. "Pride Flags Stolen, Burned Across US Amid Surge in Online Hate." *USA Today*, June 8, 2023. https://www.usatoday.com/story/news/nation/2023/06/08/gay -pride-flag-attacks-online-challenge/70304213007/.

Nagel, Joane. "Masculinity and Nationalism: Gender and Sexuality in the Making of Nations." *Ethnic and Racial Studies* 21, no. 2 (1998): 242–269. https://doi.org/10.1080 /014198798330007.

Nagle, Angela. "Kill All Normies: Online Culture Wars from 4chan and Tumblr to Trump and the Alt-Right." *Czech Journal of Political Science* 25, no. 3 (2018): 270–272. https://doi.org/10 .5817/PC2018-3-270.

Namaste, Viviane. *Invisible Lives: The Erasure of Transsexual and Transgendered People*. Chicago: University of Chicago Press, 2000.

Natanson, Hannah. "Virginia Mom Challenges One School Book a Week. She's Had Dozens Removed." *The Washington Post*, September 28, 2023. https://www.washingtonpost.com /education/2023/09/28/virginia-frequent-school-book-challenger-spotsylvania/.

"National Statistics." *National Coalition Against Domestic Violence*. https://ncadv.org /STATISTICS/.

National Threat Assessment Center. "Hot Yoga Tallahassee: A Case Study of Misogynistic Extremism." United States Secret Service, March 2022. https://www.secretservice.gov/sites /default/files/reports/2022-03/NTAC%20Case%20Study%20-%20Hot%20Yoga%20 Tallahassee_0.pdf.

"Neo-Nazi Website Attacks Female Founder of Institute for Research on Male Supremacism." Institute for Research on Male Supremacism, October 3, 2019. https://web.archive.org/web /20230202081856/https://www.malesupremacism.org/2019/10/03/neo-nazi-website -attacks-female-founder-of-institute-for-research-on-male-supremacism/. Link defunct as of September 26, 2024.

(@NewsHour). "A Growing Movement Led by Right-Wing Politicians Is Increasingly Challenging a Centuries-Old Value of America's Political System: The Separation of Church and State. @lbarronlopez Spoke with @kkdumez about the Rise of This Religious Rhetoric. https://t.co/x2wbLMySWm." Twitter (now X), October 11, 2022. https://twitter .com/newshour/status/1579967197279322113?s=46&t=4Gbs3iv1r_9HlaGq1pM9OA.

Newport, Frank. "Tea Party Support Holds at 24%." *Gallup News*, October 1, 2014. https://news .gallup.com/poll/177788/tea-party-support-holds.aspx.

Neuroscience News. "Teen Friends Shape Long-Term Wellbeing." October 13, 2024. https:// neurosciencenews.com/teen-friendships-wellbeing-27851/.

Nittle, Nadra. "Florida Faces Teacher Shortage in Wake of 'Don't Say Gay' and the Stop WOKE Act." *The 19th News*, July 21, 2022. https://19thnews.org/2022/07/national-school-teacher -shortage-florida-controversial-laws/.

Nordås, Ragnhild, and Dara Kay Cohen. "Conflict Related Sexual Violence." *Annual Review of Political Science* 24 (2021): 191–211. https://doi.org/10.1146/annurev-polisci-041719 -102620.

Norman, Noor. "Greta Thunberg's Andrew Tate Smackdown Is Just the Tip of a Disgusting Iceberg." MSNBC, December 30, 2022. https://www.msnbc.com/opinion/msnbc-opinion /andrew-tate-vs-greta-thunberg-twitter-fight-tip-iceberg-rcna63769.

Nudson, Rae. *All Made Up: The Power and Pitfalls of Beauty Culture, from Cleopatra to Kim Kardashian*. Boston, MA: Beacon Press, 2021.

O'Connell, Jennifer. "How Did Andrew Tate Become a Role Model for a Generation of Lost Boys?" *The Irish Times*, January 14, 2023. https://www.irishtimes.com/opinion/2023/01/14/jennifer-oconnell-how-did-andrew-tate-become-a-role-model-for-a-generation-of-lost-boys/.

O'Connell, Oliver. "JD Vance attacks working women as being 'on path to misery' in unearthed audio." *The Independent*, August 31, 2024. JD Vance attacks working women as being 'on path to misery' in unearthed audio | The Independent.

O'Connor, Ciaran. "The Extreme Right on Twitch." *London: Institute for Strategic Dialogue*, 2021. 05-gaming-report-twitch.pdf (isdglobal.org).

Office of the Director of National Intelligence. "Domestic Violent Extremism Poses Heightened Threat in 2021." March 1, 2021. https://www.dni.gov/files/ODNI/documents/assessments/UnclassSummaryofDVEAssessment-17MAR21.pdf.

Office of the Special Representative of the Secretary-General. "Sexual Violence in Conflict." United Nations, March 4, 2024. /https://www.un.org/sexualviolenceinconflict/wp-content/uploads/2024/03/report/mission-report-official-visit-of-the-office-of-the-srsg-svc-to-israel-and-the-occupied-west-bank-29-january-14-february-2024/20240304-Israel-oWB-CRSV-report.pdf.

Office of the US Surgeon General. "The Surgeon General's Advisory on the Healing Effects of Social Connection and Community." 2023. https://www.hhs.gov/sites/default/files/surgeon-general-social-connection-advisory.pdf

O'Flynn, Erin. "Why Andrew Tate and Internet's Nastiest Men Keep Mentioning 'The Matrix.'" *The Daily Beast*, January 18, 2023. https://www.thedailybeast.com/why-andrew-tate-and-internets-nastiest-men-keep-mentioning-the-matrix.

Olson, Greta. "Antifeminismus und die bedrohte Männlichkeit der Rechten." *Frankfurter Rundschau*, October 22, 2019. https://www.fr.de/meinung/halle-antifeminismus-bedrohte-maennlichkeit-rechten-13139748.html

Oluo, Ijeoma. *Mediocre: The Dangerous Legacy of White Male America*. New York: Seal, 2020.

"Online Gaming Platforms Such as Roblox Used as 'Trojan Horse' for Extremist Recruitment of Children, AFP Warns." *The Guardian*, December 2, 2023. https://www.theguardian.com/australia-news/2023/dec/03/online-gaming-platforms-such-as-roblox-used-as-trojan-horse-for-extremist-recruitment-of-children-afp-warns.

Onuoha, Alexandra C. "Book Review: Hate in the Homeland: The New Global Far Right." *Sociology of Race and Ethnicity* 9, no. 2 (2023): 239–240. https://doi.org/10.1177/2332649 2221120670

Onuoha, Alexandra C., Miriam R. Arbeit, and Seanna Leath. "Far-Right Misogynoir: A Critical Thematic Analysis of Black College Women's Experiences with White Male Supremacist Influences." *Psychology of Women Quarterly* 47, no. 2 (2023): 180–196. https://doi.org/10.1177/03616843231156872.

Orenstein, Peggy. *Cinderella Ate My Daughter: Dispatches from the Front Lines of the New Girlie-Girl Culture*. New York: Harper Paperbacks, 2012.

Orwell, George. *1984*. New York: HarperCollins Publishers Deluxe Edition, 2020.

Parker, Ashley, Hannah Allam, and Marianna Sotomayor. "Attack on Nancy Pelosi's Husband Follows Years of GOP Demonizing Her." *The Washington Post*, October 29, 2022. https://www.washingtonpost.com/politics/2022/10/29/paul-pelosi-attack-republicans-target/.

"Part 4B: Women's Camps and Brothels—The Concentration Camps." In the exhibit, *The Concentration Camps: Inside the Nazi System of Incarceration and Genocide*, 2022. Kupferberg Holocaust Center, Queensborough Community College, CUNY. https://khc.qcc.cuny.edu/camps/part-4b-womens-camps/.

Pascoe, C. J. *Dude, You're a Fag: Masculinity and Sexuality in High School*. Berkeley: University of California Press, 2011.

Pascoe, C. J., and Tristan Bridges. *Exploring Masculinities: Identity, Inequality, Continuity, and Change*. New York: Oxford University Press, 2016.

Pascoe, C. J., and Jocelyn A. Hollander. "Good Guys Don't Rape: Gender, Domination, and Mobilizing Rape." *Gender & Society* 30, no. 1 (2016): 67–79. https://doi.org/10.1177/0891243215612707.

Paul, Ari. "'Cultural Marxism': The Mainstreaming of a Nazi Trope." FAIR.org, June 4, 2019. https://fair.org/home/cultural-marxism-the-mainstreaming-of-a-nazi-trope/.

Payne, Elizabethe, and Melissa J. Smith. "Gender Policing." In *Critical Concepts in Queer Studies and Education: An International Guide for the Twenty-First Century*, ed. Nelson Rodriguez, Wayne Martino, Jennifer Ingrey, and Edward Brockenbrough. New York: Palgrave Macmillan, 2016.

Pearson, Elizabeth. *Extreme Britain: Gender, Masculinity, and Radicalisation*. London: Hearst & Company, 2023.

Pearson, Elizabeth. "Extremism and Toxic Masculinity." *International Affairs* 95, no. 6 (2019): 1251–1270. https://doi.org/10.1093/ia/iiz177.

Pérez, Raúl. *The Souls of White Jokes: How Racist Humor Fuels White Supremacy*. Stanford, CA: Stanford University Press, 2022.

Perliger, Arie, Catherine Stephens, and Eviane Leidig. "Mapping the Ideological Landscape of Extreme Misogyny." International Centre for Counter-Terrorism (ICCT), January 26, 2023. https://www.icct.nl/publication/mapping-ideological-landscape-extreme-misogyny.

Petro, Melissa. *Shame on You: How to Be a Woman in the Age of Mortification*. New York: G.P. Putnam's Sons, 2004.

Phelan, Alexandra. "Special Issue Introduction for Terrorism, Gender, and Women: Toward an Integrated Research Agenda." *Studies in Conflict and Terrorism* 46, no. 4 (2023): 353–361. https://doi.org/10.1080/1057610X.2020.1759252.

Phelan, Alexandra, Jacqui True, Emily Winterbotham, et al. "Misogyny, Hostile Beliefs and the Transmission of Extremism: A Comparison of the Far-Right in the U.K. and Australia." Centre for Research and Evidence on Security Threats (CREST), May 2023. www.crestresearch.ac.uk/projects/misogyny-hostile-beliefs-and-transmission-of-extremism.

Phelan, Alexandra, Jessica White, James Paterson, et al. "Misogyny and Masculinity: Toward a Typology of Gendered Narratives Amongst the Far-Right," Monash University, 2023. https://crestresearch.ac.uk/download/4479/36_37_csr16_phelan.pdf.

Philipps, Dave. "Who Was Ashli Babbitt? Woman Killed in Capitol Embraced Trump, QAnon." *The New York Times*, December 11, 2023. https://www.nytimes.com/2021/01/08/us/who-was-ashli-babbitt.html.

Phillips-Fein, Kim. "How the Right Learned to Loathe Higher Education." *Chronicle of Higher Education*, January 31, 2019. https://www.chronicle.com/article/how-the-right-learned-to-loathe-higher-education/.

Piazza, James, and Lauren O'Rourke. "Hostile Sexism, Social Dominance Orientation, Political Illiberalism and Support for Political Violence in the United States." (2024): 1–25. doi:10.1017/S1743923X24000400

Pierce, Charles P. "Ex-Army Private Gets 45 Years for Passing Sensitive Info to Misogynist Neo-Nazi Satanists." *Esquire*, March 8, 2023. https://www.esquire.com/news-politics/politics/a43253018/ethan-melzer-sentenced-order-of-nine-angles/.

Pilkington, Hilary, Al'bina Garifzianova, and Elena Omel'chenko. *Russia's Skinheads*. New York: Routledge, 2010.

Pitcavage, Mark. "20 Years Later, Shadows of Ruby Ridge Standoff Still Linger." *ADL*, August 27, 2012. https://www.adl.org/resources/news/20-years-later-shadows-ruby-ridge-standoff-still-linger.

Pollak, Robert. "An Intergenerational Model of Domestic Violence." *Journal of Population Economics* 17, no. 2 (2004): 311–329. http://dx.doi.org/10.1007/s00148-003-0177-7.

Posner, Sarah. "The Christian Nationalist Boot Camp Pushing Anti-Trans Laws Across America." *Business Insider*, September 21, 2022. https://www.businessinsider.com/christian-nationalist-trans-statesmen-academy-alabama-ohio-missouri-laws-2022-8.

Posner, Sarah. *Unholy: Why White Evangelicals Worship at the Altar of Donald Trump*. New York: Random House, 2020.

"Prevention of Child Recruitment and Exploitation by Terrorist and Violent Extremist Groups: The Role of the Justice." United Nations Office of Drugs and Crime (UNODC), 2019. https://www.unodc.org/documents/justice-and-prison-reform/Child-Victims/Handbook_on_Children_Recruited_and_Exploited_by_Terrorist_and_Violent_Extremist_Groups_the_Role_of_the_Justice_System.E.pdf.

Prieur, Danielle. "In Florida, Teachers Are Quitting Over Anti-LGBTQ Laws." *WUSF*, June 30, 2023. https://www.wusf.org/education/2023-06-30/florida-teachers-quitting-anti-lgbtq-laws.

Prinz, Mick. "Extremist Games and Modifications: The 'Metapolitics' of Anti-Democratic Forces." In *Gaming and Extremism: The Radicalization of Digital Playgrounds*, ed. Linda Schlagel and Rachel Kowert. New York: Taylor & Francis, 2024.

"Profiles of Individual Radicalization in the United States (PIRUS)," *START*, May 2020. https://www.start.umd.edu/pubs/START_PIRUS_ResearchBrief_May2020.pdf.

Pruitt, Sarah. "The Night of Terror: When Suffragists Were Imprisoned and Tortured in 1917." History.com, April 17, 2019. https://www.history.com/news/night-terror-brutality-suffragists-19th-amendment.

Puwar, Nirmal. *Space Invaders*. New York: Berg, 2004.

Quinn, Ben. "Twitter Bomb Threats Made Against More Women in Public Eye." *The Guardian*, August 5, 2013. https://www.theguardian.com/technology/2013/aug/05/twitter-bomb-threats-women

Rahman, Khaleda. "Some of the Signs Held By Protesters Calling for End to Coronavirus Lockdown Raise Eyebrows: 'I Need a Haircut.'" *Newsweek*, April 20, 2020. https://www.newsweek.com/protesters-wave-signs-branded-dumb-ignorant-1498873.

Ramirez, Nikki McCann. "The Proud Boys Have Really Strict Rules about Jerking Off." *Rolling Stone*, January 23, 2023. https://www.rollingstone.com/politics/politics-news/proud-boys-trial-rule-book-masturbation-ban-1234666317/.

Rawnsley, Adam, and Seamus Hughes. "Neo-Nazi Marine Plotted Mass Murder, Rape Campaigns with Group—Feds." *Rolling Stone*, July 26, 2022. https://www.rollingstone.com/politics/politics-news/marine-murder-rape-plot-rapekrieg-1388238/.

"Reddit Is Closing /r/TheRedPill with 419000 Subscribers through Policy Update." Reddit. https://www.reddit.com/r/WatchRedditDie/comments/dbklnd/reddit_is_closing_rtheredpill_with_419000/.

Reeves, Richard V. *Of Boys and Men: Why the Modern Male Is Struggling, Why It Matters, and What to Do About It*. London: Swift Press, 2023.

Reilly, Katie. "Florida's Governor Just Signed the 'Stop Woke Act.' Here's What It Means for Schools." *Time*, April 22, 2022. https://time.com/6168753/florida-stop-woke-law/.

Reilly, Ryan J. "Women Put 'Friendly Face' on Jan. 6 Attack, Extremism Research Argues in New Study." NBC News, April 26, 2022. https://www.nbcnews.com/politics/national-security/women-put-friendly-face-jan-6-attack-extremism-research-argues-new-stu-rcna25831.

Relihan, Dan, Nickolas M. Jones, E. Alison Holman et al. "Shared Social Identity and Media Transmission of Trauma." *Scientific Reports* 13 (2023): 11609. https://doi.org/10.1038/s41598-023-33898-2.

"Report of Ruby Ridge Task Force; June 10, 1994—Page 40–84." Department of Justice, November 9, 2006. https://www.justice.gov/sites/default/files/opr/legacy/2006/11/09/rubyreport40_84.pdf.

Reuters. "Austrian Neo-Nazi Group Members Get Up to Six Years' Prison." Reuters, November 5, 2013. https://www.reuters.com/article/idUSBRE9A40D8/.

Reyes, Raul A. "A Latina Trailblazer: Esther Salas, Federal Judge Whose Son Was Killed, Described As 'Mentor.'" NBC News, July 20, 2020. https://www.nbcnews.com/news/latino/latina-trailblazer-esther-salas-federal-judge-whose-son-was-killed-n1234361

Ribeiro, Manoel, Jeremy Blackburn, Barry Bradlyn, et al. "The Evolution of the Manosphere Across the Web." Paper presented at the 15th International Conference on Web and Social Media (ICWSM), 2021. https://ojs.aaai.org/index.php/ICWSM/article/view/18053.

Riedel, Samantha. "For the First Time, the U.S. Census May Start Asking About Gender Identity." Them.us, September 21, 2023. https://www.them.us/story/sexual-orientation-gender-identity-census.

Rios-Gonzalez, Oriol, Torres, Analia, Aiello, Emilia, et al. "Not All Men: The Debates in Social Networks on Masculinities and Consent." *Humanities and Social Sciences Communications* 11, no. 67 (2024). https://doi.org/10.1057/s41599-023-02569-y.

Rios, Edwin. "Idaho Librarian Resigns Over 'Atmosphere of Extremism' and 'Intimidation Tactics.'" *The Guardian*, August 24, 2022. https://www.theguardian.com/world/2022/aug/24/idaho-librarian-resigns-ban-books-lgbtq.

Ritchie, Jessica. "Creating a Monster: Online Media Constructions of Hillary Clinton During the Democratic Primary Campaign." *Feminist Media Studies* 13, no. 1 (2013): 102–119. https://doi.org/10.1080/14680777.2011.647973.

Robb, Amanda. "Anatomy of a Fake News Scandal." *Rolling Stone*, November 16, 2017. https://www.rollingstone.com/feature/anatomy-of-a-fake-news-scandal-125877/.

Robb, Michael B., and Supreet Mann. "2022 Teens and Pornography." *Common Sense Media*, January 5, 2023. https://www.commonsensemedia.org/sites/default/files/research/report/2022-teens-and-pornography-final-web.pdf.

Roberts, Mark. "How to Respond to Boys Inspired by Andrew Tate." *Tes*, January 9, 2023. https://www.tes.com/magazine/teaching-learning/secondary/andrew-tate-how-schools-tackle-misogyny.

Rogers, Kaleigh. "Why QAnon Has Attracted So Many White Evangelicals." *FiveThirtyEight*, March 4, 2021. https://fivethirtyeight.com/features/why-qanon-has-attracted-so-many-white-evangelicals,

Romano, Aja. "J. K. Rowling's Transphobia: A History." Vox, April 1, 2024. https://www.vox.com/culture/23622610/jk-rowling-transphobic-statements-timeline-history-controversy.

Romano, Aja. "The Right's Moral Panic Over 'Grooming' Invokes Age-Old Homophobia." Vox, April 21, 2022. https://www.vox.com/culture/23025505/leftist-groomers-homophobia-satanic-panic-explained.

Roos, Julia. "Backlash against Prostitutes' Rights: Origins and Dynamics of Nazi Prostitution Policies." *Journal of the History of Sexuality* 11, nos. 1–2 (2002): 67–94. https://dx.doi.org/10.1353/sex.2002.0012.

Roose, Joshua. "'Ideological Masculinity' that Drives Violence Against Women Is a Form of Violent Extremism." *The Conversation* (2018). https://theconversation.com/ideological-masculinity-that-drives-violence-against-women-is-a-form-of-violent-extremism-99603.

Roose, Joshua M., and Joana Cook. "Supreme Men, Subjected Women: Gender Inequality and Violence in Jihadist, Far Right and Male Supremacist Ideologies." *Studies in Conflict & Terrorism* (2022): 1–29. https://doi.org/10.1080/1057610X.2022.2104681.

Rosario, Isabella. "Iowa State University Could Rename Catt Hall. Here's Why the Name Is Controversial." *Ames Tribune*, August 22, 2021. https://www.amestrib.com/story/news/2021/08/22/carrie-chapman-catt-legacy-controversial-iowa-state-university-isu-womens-suffrag-racism-voting/8197034002/.

Rose, Andy. "Prosecutors in Utah File Drug Trafficking Charges Against Alleged 'White Supremacist Gang' Members." CNN, October 17, 2020. https://www.cnn.com/2020/10/17/us/white-supremacist-gang-drugs-utah/index.html.

Rose, Deborah Bird. "Land Rights and Deep Colonising: The Erasure of Women." *Aboriginal Law Bulletin* 3, no. 5 (2024): 6–13. https://classic.austlii.edu.au/au/journals/AboriginalLawB/1996/69.html.

Rosenblum, Nancy L., and Russell Muirhead. *A Lot of People Are Saying: The New Conspiracism and the Assault on Democracy*. Princeton, NJ: Princeton University Press, 2020.

Rosin, Hanna. "The Patriarchy Is Dead." *Slate*, September 11, 2013. https://slate.com/human-interest/2013/09/the-end-of-men-why-feminists-wont-accept-that-things-are-looking-up-for-women.html.

Rottweiler, Bettina, Caitlin Clemmow, and Paul Gill. "A Common Psychology of Male Violence? Assessing the Effects of Misogyny on Intentions to Engage in Violent Extremism, Interpersonal Violence and Support for Violence Against Women." *Terrorism and Political Violence* (2024). https://www.tandfonline.com/doi/full/10.1080/09546553.2023.2292723

Rottweiler, Bettina, and Paul Gill. "Conspiracy Beliefs and Violent Extremist Intentions: The Contingent Effects of Self-efficacy, Self-control and Law-related Morality." *Terrorism and Political Violence* 34, no. 7 (2022): 1485–1504. https://doi.org/10.1080/09546553.2020.1803288.

Rouse, Stella, and Shibley Telhami. "Most Republicans Support Declaring the United States a Christian Nation." *Politico*, September 21, 2022. https://www.politico.com/news/magazine/2022/09/21/most-republicans-support-declaring-the-united-states-a-christian-nation-00057736.

Roy, Jessica. "How 'Pepe the Frog' Went from Harmless to Hate Symbol." *Los Angeles Times*, October 11, 2016. https://www.latimes.com/politics/la-na-pol-pepe-the-frog-hate-symbol-20161011-snap-htmlstory.html.

Ruefle, Mary. "On Erasure." *Quarter After Eight: A Journal of Innovative Writing* 16: 1 (2010). https://ia.eferrit.com/ea/dcf81aca20f61e00.pdf.

Ruiz, Sarah. "Senator Used to 'Avoid Elevators' as Congressional Intern for Fear of Sexual Harassment." *Huffington Post*, November 14, 2017. https://huffpost.netblogpro.com/entry/mccaskill-sexual-harassment-congress_n_5a0b8018e4b0b17ffce11e6f/amp.

Russonello, Giovanni. "QAnon Now As Popular in U.S. As Some Major Religions." *The New York Times*, May 27, 2021. https://www.nytimes.com/2021/05/27/us/politics/qanon-republicans-trump.html.

Saini, Angela. *Inferior: How Science Got Women Wrong and the New Research That's Rewriting the Story*. Boston, MA: Beacon Press, 2017.

Saini, Angela. *The Patriarchs: The Origins of Inequality*. Boston, MA: Beacon Press, 2023.

Salter, Michael. "From Geek Masculinity to Gamergate: The Technological Rationality of Online Abuse." *Crime, Media, Culture* 14, no. 2 (2018): 247–264. https://doi.org/10.1177/1741659017690893

Samuels, Alex, and Monica Potts. "How the Fight to Ban Abortion Is Rooted in the 'Great Replacement' Theory." *FiveThirtyEight*, July 25, 2022. https://fivethirtyeight.com/features/how-the-fight-to-ban-abortion-is-rooted-in-the-great-replacement-theory/.

Samuelson, Kate. "The Countries Where Men and Women Can Be Stoned to Death." *The Week*, July 14, 2022. https://www.theweek.co.uk/news/crime/957354/the-countries-where-men -women-can-be-stoned-to-death.

Sanders, Sam, and Kenya Young. "A Black Mother Reflects on Giving Her 3 Sons 'The Talk' . . . Again and Again." NPR, June 28, 2020. https://www.npr.org/2020/06/28/882383372/a -black-mother-reflects-on-giving-her-3-sons-the-talk-again-and-again.

Saner, Emine. "Inside the Taylor Swift Deepfake Scandal: 'It's Men Telling a Powerful Woman to Get Back in Her Box.'" *The Guardian*, January 31, 2024. https://www.theguardian.com /technology/2024/jan/31/inside-the-taylor-swift-deepfake-scandal-its-men-telling-a -powerful-woman-to-get-back-in-her-box.

Santucci, Julia, Regina Waugh, and Hallie Schneir. "Gender and Right-Wing Extremism in America: Why Understanding Women's Roles Is Key to Preventing Future Acts of Domestic Terrorism." *Just Security*, March 5, 2021. https://www.justsecurity.org/75068/gender-and -right-wing-extremism-in-america-why-understanding-womens-roles-is-key-to-preventing -future-acts-of-domestic-terrorism/.

Saucier, Donald A., Derrick F. Till, Stuart S. Miller, et al. "Slurs against Masculinity: Masculine Honor Beliefs and Men's Reactions to Slurs." *Language Sciences* 52 (2015): 108–120. https:// doi.org/10.1016/j.langsci.2014.09.006.

Scaptura, Maria N., and Kaitlin M. Boyle. "Masculinity Threat, 'Incel' Traits, and Violent Fantasies Among Heterosexual Men in the United States." *Division on Women and Crime of the American Society of Criminology* 15, no. 3 (2019): 278–298. https://doi.org/10.1177 /1557085119896415.

Schilt, Kristen, and Laurel Westbrook. "Doing Gender, Doing Heteronormativity: 'Gender Normals,' Transgender People, and the Social Maintenance of Heterosexuality." *Gender and Society* 23, no. 4 (2009): 440–464. https://psycnet.apa.org/doi/10.1177 /0891243209340034.

Schlegel, Linda, and Rachel Kowert. *Gaming and Extremism: The Radicalization of Digital Playgrounds*. New York: Routledge, 2024.

Schoenbaum, Hannah, and Associated Press. "Report Says at Least 32 Transgender People Were Killed in the U.S. in 2022." PBS, November 16, 2022. https://www.pbs.org/newshour/nation /report-says-at-least-32-transgender-people-were-killed-in-the-u-s-in-2022.

Schuba, Tom. "Gay-Owned Restaurant in Rogers Park Targeted in Suspected Homophobic Attack." *Chicago Sun-Times*, January 16, 2023. https://chicago.suntimes.com/crime/2023/1 /16/23558371/gay-owned-restaurant-in-rogers-park-targeted-in-suspected-homophobic -attack.

Schuller, Kyla. *The Trouble with White Women: A Counterhistory of Feminism*. New York: Bold Type Books, 2023.

Schultz, Amber. "Roblox Used by Extremists to Recruit Children, Police Warn." *The Sydney Morning Herald*, December 3, 2023. https://www.smh.com.au/technology/video-games /roblox-used-by-extremists-to-recruit-children-police-warn-20231202-p5eohy.html.

Scrinzi, Francesca. *The Racialization of Sexism: Men, Women, and Gender in the Populist Radical Right*. New York: Routledge, 2024.

Sella, Adam. "Israeli Rape-Crisis Group Report Finds 'Systematic' Sexual Violence on and After Oct. 7." *The New York Times*, February 21, 2024. https://www.nytimes.com/2024/02 /21/world/middleeast/israel-hamas-sexual-violence-report.html?smid=nytcore-ios -share&referringSource=articleShare.

Serwer, Adam. "It's Not Easy Being Meme: The Creator of Pepe the Frog Talks about the Alt-Right." *The Atlantic*, September 13, 2016. https://www.theatlantic.com/politics/archive /2016/09/its-not-easy-being-green/499892/.

Sexton, Jared Yates. *The Man They Wanted Me to Be: Toxic Masculinity and a Crisis of Our Own Making*. Berkeley, CA: Counterpoint, 2019.

"Sextortion: A Growing Threat Targeting Minors." FBI, January 16, 2024. https://www.fbi.gov/news/press-releases/sextortion-a-growing-threat-targeting-minors.

Sharman, Leah, Robin Fitzgerald, and Heather Douglas. "Prevalence of Sexual Strangulation/Choking among Australian 18–35 Year Olds." *Archives of Sexual Behavior*, 2024. https://doi.org/10.1007/s10508-024-02937-y

Shearing, Lois. *Pink-Pilled: Women and the Far Right*. Manchester, UK: Manchester University Press, 2025.

Sheffield, Carole J. "The Invisible Intruder: Women's Experiences of Obscene Phone Calls." *Gender and Society* 3, no. 4 (1989): 483–488. https://psycnet.apa.org/doi/10.1177/089124389003004006.

Sher, Schlomo. "Episode 43—What the Research REALLY Says About the Connection Between Video Games + Violence, Addiction, and Sexism! (with Rachel Kowert)—Ethics and Video Games." *Ethics and Video Games*, May 17, 2022. https://ethicsandvideogames.com/?p=890.

Shivaram, Deepa. "One Year Later, Atlanta Remembers Victims of Spa Shootings." NPR, March 12, 2022. https://www.npr.org/2022/03/12/1086306008/atlanta-spa-shootings-anniversary-anti-asian-racism.

Shortle, Allyson F., Eric L. McDaniel, and Irfan Nooruddin. "How Do Americans Feel About Christian Nationalism?" *The Washington Post*, September 1, 2022. https://www.washingtonpost.com/politics/2022/09/01/marjorie-taylor-greene-christian-nationalist/.

Sienkiewicz, Matt, and Nick Marx. *That's Not Funny: How the Right Makes Comedy Work for Them*. Berkeley: University of California Press, 2022.

Sinha, Urja. "Drug Ring Tied to White Supremacist Prison Gang, 24 Arrested." *NewsNation*, March 28, 2023. https://www.newsnationnow.com/crime/drug-ring-aryan-family-gang-bust/.

Smith, Allan. "The American Right's Future Involves Waging a 'Religious Battle' Against the Left, Leaders Say at a Conservative Conference." NBC News, September 23, 2022. https://www.nbcnews.com/politics/2022-election/american-rights-future-involves-waging-religious-battle-left-leaders-s-rcna48961.

Smith, Erica L. "Female Murder Victims and Victim-Offender Relationship, 2021." US Department of Justice, Bureau of Justice Statistics, December 2022. https://bjs.ojp.gov/sites/g/files/xyckuh236/files/media/document/fmvvor21.pdf.

Smith, Tovia. "School Book Bans Show No Signs of Slowing, New PEN America Report Finds." NPR, September 21, 2023. https://www.npr.org/2023/09/21/1200725104/book-bans-school-pen-america.

Smythe, Viv. "I'm Credited with Having Coined the Word 'Terf'. Here's How It Happened." *The Guardian*, November 28, 2018. https://www.theguardian.com/commentisfree/2018/nov/29/im-credited-with-having-coined-the-acronym-terf-heres-how-it-happened.

Sobieraj, Sarah. "Bitch, Slut, Skank, Cunt: Patterned Resistance to Women's Visibility in Digital Publics." *Information, Communication & Society* 21, no. 11 (2018): 1700–1714. https://doi.org/10.1080/1369118X.2017.1348535.

Solea, Anda, and Lisa Suiura. "Mainstreaming the Blackpill: Understanding the Incel Community on TikTok." *European Journal on Criminal Policy and Research* 29 (2023): 311–336. http://dx.doi.org/10.1007/s10610-023-09559-5.

Solnit, Rebecca. *Men Explain Things to Me*. Chicago: Haymarket Books, 2014.

Solnit, Rebecca. "The Serious Side of 'Mansplaining' Has Been Lost. That's Where the Harm Begins." *The Guardian*, February 9, 2023. https://www.theguardian.com/commentisfree/2023/feb/09/mansplaining-word-problem-rebecca-solnit?CMP=oth_b-aplnews_d-1.

Solomon, Erika, and Katrin Bennhold. "Fringe Group Suspected in German Plot Got a Lift from QAnon." *The New York Times*, December 9, 2022. https://www.nytimes.com/2022/12 /08/world/europe/germany-plot-qanon.html.

Squirrell, Tom, and Jacob Davey. "A Year of Hate: Understanding Threats and Harassment Targeting Drag Shows and the LGBTQ+ Community." *ISD*, June 22, 2023. https://www .isdglobal.org/isd-publications/a-year-of-hate-understanding-threats-and-harassment -targeting-drag-shows-and-the-lgbtq-community/.

Srinivasan, Amia. *The Right to Sex: Feminism in the Twenty-First Century.* New York: Picador, 2021.

Stanley, Jason. *How Fascism Works.* New York: Random House, 2018.

"Statement from Christians Against Christian Nationalism—Christians Against Christian Nationalism." *Christians Against Christian Nationalism.* https://www.christiansagainstchristia nnationalism.org/statement.

"Statement from the Walt Disney Company on Signing of Florida Legislation." The Walt Disney Company, March 28, 2022. https://thewaltdisneycompany.com/statement-from-the-walt -disney-company-on-signing-of-florida-legislation/.

"State Legislation Tracker." Guttmacher Institute. https://www.guttmacher.org/state-legislation -tracker. Updated as of December 15, 2024.

"Statistics about Sexual Violence." National Sexual Violence Resource Center (NSVRC). 2015. https://www.nsvrc.org/sites/default/files/publications_nsvrc_factsheet_media-packet _statistics-about-sexual-violence_0.pdf.

"Stay-at-Home Protesters: 'We Want Our Lives Back.'" BBC, April 23, 2020. https://www.bbc .com/news/av/world-us-canada-52406515.

Steinkuehler, Constance, and Kurt Squire. "Introduction to Videogames and the Extremist Ecosystem." In *Gaming and Extremism: The Radicalization of Digital Playgrounds*, ed. Linda Schlagel and Rachel Kowert. New York: Taylor & Francis, 2024.

Stern, Alexandra Minna. "Alt-Right Women and the 'White Baby Challenge.'" *Salon*, July 14, 2019. https://www.salon.com/2019/07/14/alt-right-handmaidens-and-the-white-baby -challenge/.

Stern, Fabio L. "A New Witch-Hunt: LGBTQIA+ State Persecution by Brazil's Christian Far-Right." *International Journal of Latin American Religions* 8, no. 1 (2024): 1–18. http://dx.doi .org/10.1007/s41603-023-00228-3.

St-Esprit, Meg. "Targeted by a White Supremacist in Pittsburgh for Being a 'Race Traitor.'" *PublicSource*, January 29, 2018. https://www.publicsource.org/targeted-by-a-white -supremacist-in-pittsburgh-for-being-a-race-traitor/.

Stop Woke Handout. 2021. https://www.flgov.com/eog/sites/default/files/press/Stop-Woke -Handout.pdf

"Store Owner Shot to Death by Man Who Made 'Disparaging Remarks' About Pride Flag, Authorities Say." CBS News, August 21, 2023. https://www.cbsnews.com/news/storeowner -shot-dead-dispute-lgbtq-pride-flag/.

Suarez, Ken. "Protesters Wearing Nazi Gear Show Up Outside Lakeland Charity Event that Included Drag Performers." FOX 13 Tampa Bay, December 5, 2022. https://www.fox13news .com/news/demonstrators-wearing-nazi-gear-show-up-outside-lakeland-charity-event-that -included-drag-performers.

Sugiura, Lisa. *The Incel Rebellion: The Rise of the Manosphere and the Virtual War Against Women.* Bingley: Emerald Publishing, 2021.

Suliman, Adela, and Timothy Bella. "GOP Rep. Boebert: 'I'm Tired of This Separation of Church and State Junk.'" *The Washington Post*, June 28, 2022. https://www.washingtonpost .com/politics/2022/06/28/lauren-boebert-church-state-colorado/.

Summer, Anne. *The Misogyny Factor.* Sydney: NewSouth, 2013.

Sung, Morgan. "Andrew Tate Banned from YouTube, TikTok, Facebook, and Instagram." NBC News, August 19, 2022. https://www.nbcnews.com/pop-culture/viral/andrew-tate-facebook-instagram-ban-meta-rcna43998.

Sung, Morgan. "The Internet Can't Stop Talking about Andrew Tate." NBC News, August 16, 2022. https://www.nbcnews.com/pop-culture/viral/internet-cant-stop-talking-andrew-tate-tiktok-rcna42744.

"Supreme Court Case: Dobbs v. Jackson Women's Health Organization." Center for Reproductive Rights. March 19, 2018. https://reproductiverights.org/case/scotus-mississippi-abortion-ban/.

Swann, Ray. "Helping Boys Deal With Loneliness." *Psychology Today*, January 29, 2024. https://www.psychologytoday.com/us/blog/raising-healthy-boys/202401/helping-boys-deal-with-loneliness.

Tagliabue, John. "The Dresden Scene: Sex Shops and Neo-Nazis." *The New York Times*, June 13, 1991. https://www.nytimes.com/1991/06/13/world/the-dresden-scene-sex-shops-and-neo-nazis.html.

Tahsin, Jamie, and Matt Shea. "Andrew Tate: Chats in 'War Room' Suggest Dozens of Women Groomed." *BBC News*, August 31, 2023. https://www.bbc.com/news/world-europe-66604827

Tait, Amelia. "How the Alt-Right Wields and Weaponises Accusations of Paedophilia." *New Statesman*, January 4, 2018. https://www.newstatesman.com/science-tech/2018/01/how-alt-right-wields-and-weaponises-accusations-paedophilia.

Tangalakis-Lippert, Katherine. "FBI Busts Neo-Nazi Cult that Used Discord to Groom and Exploit Kids." *Business Insider*, December 18, 2023. https://www.businessinsider.com/feds-bust-nazi-cult-telegram-discord-grooming-exploit-children-2023-12.

Taylor, Jessica. *Sexy but Psycho: How the Patriarchy Uses Women's Trauma Against Them.* London: Constable, 2022.

Tebaldi, Catherine. "Make Women Great Again: Women, Misogyny and Anti-Capitalism on the Right." *Fast Capitalism*, January 12, 2021. fastcapitalism.journal.library.uta.edu/index.php/fastcapitalism/article/view/421.

Tebaldi, Catherine. "Tradwives and Truth Warriors: Gender and Nationalism in US White Nationalist Women's Blogs." *Gender and Language* 17, no. 1 (2022): 14–38. https://doi.org/10.1558/genl.18551.

Tebor, Celina. "Suspect in O'Shae Sibley Killing Charged with Murder." CNN, August 5, 2023. https://www.cnn.com/2023/08/05/us/oshae-sibley-suspect-charged/index.html.

"Texas Butterfly Centre Closes after Qanon Threats." BBC, February 3, 2022. https://www.bbc.com/news/world-us-canada-60254327.

The Associated Press. "Andrew Tate to Remain Detained in Romania on Charges of Human Trafficking and Rape, Judge Rules." NBC News, January 10, 2023. https://www.nbcnews.com/tech/internet/andrew-tate-remain-detained-romania-charges-human-trafficking-rape-jud-rcna65180.

The Associated Press. "Idaho Murder Suspect Repeatedly Dmed Victim on Instagram." *Oregon Live*, January 18, 2023. https://www.oregonlive.com/nation/2023/01/idaho-murder-suspected-repeatedly-dmed-victim-on-instagram.html.

The Associated Press. "Police Investigated Michael Haight for Abuse Before the Enoch Murder-Suicide." *Kuer90.1*, January 17, 2023. https://www.kuer.org/news/2023-01-17/police-investigated-michael-haight-for-abuse-before-the-enoch-murder-suicide.

The Associated Press. "'She's Not My Type,' Trump Says of E. Jean Carroll, Who Accused Him of Sexual Assault." NBC News, June 25, 2019. https://www.nbcnews.com/politics/donald-trump/she-s-not-my-type-trump-says-e-jean-carroll-n1021331.

The Associated Press. "Teenager Sentenced to 25 Years for Killing Girl Who Said No to the Prom." *The New York Times*, June 6, 2016. https://www.nytimes.com/2016/06/07/nyregion /teenager-sentenced-to-25-years-for-killing-girl-who-said-no-to-the-prom.html.

"The 'Liberated' Feminist vs Tradwife | Trad Girl / Tradwife." *Know Your Meme*, 2020. https:// knowyourmeme.com/photos/1815505-trad-girl-tradwife.

"The Nexus Between Terrorism and Human Trafficking." *ACAMS Today*, January 17, 2023. https://www.acamstoday.org/the-nexus-between-terrorism-and-human-trafficking/.

"The QAnon Conspiracy: Destroying Families, Dividing Communities, Undermining Democracy." Network Contagion Research Institute, Rutgers, PERIL, December 2020. https:// networkcontagion.us/wp-content/uploads/NCRI-%E2%80%93-The-QAnon-Conspiracy -FINAL.pdf.

"The Real Tradwives of 2022: Why More Young Moms Are Becoming Traditional Housewives." Katie Couric Media, April 8, 2022. https://katiecouric.com/culture/what-is-a-tradwife/.

"Timeline: Building a Pseudoscience Network." Southern Poverty Law Center, December 12, 2023. https://www.splcenter.org/captain/timeline-building-pseudoscience-network.

Timmons, Heather. "Here's the FBI's Warning Signs of a Mass Shooter." *Defense One*, November 13, 2018. https://www.defenseone.com/threats/2018/11/heres-fbis-warning-signs-mass -shooter/152786/

Tolentino, Daysia. "Johnny Depp Topped Google's List of Trending People and Actors in 2022." NBC News, December 7, 2022. https://www.nbcnews.com/pop-culture/google-search -trending-topics-2022-johnny-depp-rcna60255.

"Toward Meaningful Accountability for Sexual and Gender-Based Violence Linked to Terrorism." United Nations Security Council, Counter-Terrorism Committee Executive Directorate (CTED), November 2023. https://www.un.org/securitycouncil/ctc/sites/www.un.org .securitycouncil.ctc/files/cted_report-_sgbv_linked_to_terrorism_final.pdf.

Townsend, Mark. "Experts Fear Rising Global 'Incel' Culture Could Provoke Terrorism." *The Guardian*, October 30, 2022. https://www.theguardian.com/society/2022/oct/30/global -incel-culture-terrorism-misogyny-violent-action-forums.

"Train Operator at Port of Los Angeles Charged with Derailing Locomotive Near U.S. Navy's Hospital Ship *Mercy*." Department of Justice, April 1, 2020. https://www.justice.gov/usao -cdca/pr/train-operator-port-los-angeles-charged-derailing-locomotive-near-us-navy-s -hospital.

Tranchese, Alessia. "Why We Need to Talk About Porn When We Talk about Andrew Tate." *The Conversation*, April 28, 2023. https://theconversation.com/why-we-need-to-talk-about -porn-when-we-talk-about-andrew-tate-201059.

Tranchese, Alessia, and Lisa Sugiura. "'I don't hate all women, just those stuck-up bitches': How Incels and Mainstream Pornography Speak the Same Extreme Language of Misogyny." *Violence Against Women* 27, no. 14 (2021): 2709–2734. https://doi.org/10.1177/1077801 221996453.

"Transcript: Donald Trump's Taped Comments About Women." *The New York Times*, October 8, 2016. https://www.nytimes.com/2016/10/08/us/donald-trump-tape-transcript. html.

"Trauma as a Precursor to Violent Extremism." *START*, April 2015. https://www.start.umd.edu /pubs/START_CSTAB_TraumaAsPrecursortoViolentExtremism_April2015.pdf.

Treisman, Rachel. "The Wisconsin Shooting Suspect Is Female. That's Rare, Data Says." NPR, December 17, 2024. https://www.npr.org/2024/12/17/nx-s1-5231532/wisconsin-school -shooting-suspect-female

Trudell, Bonnie Nelson. *Doing Sex Education: Gender Politics and Schooling*. New York: Routledge, 1993.

Tsoutsoumpis, Spyridon. "The Far Right in Greece. Paramilitarism, Organized Crime and the Rise of 'Golden Dawn.'" *Comparative Southeast European Studies* 66, no. 4 (2018): 503–531. https://doi.org/10.1515/soeu-2018-0039.

Tumblety, Joan. *Remaking the Male Body: Masculinity and the Uses of Physical Culture in Interwar and Vichy France.* Cambridge: Oxford University Press, 2012.

"Under ISIS: Where Being Gay Is Punished by Death." ABC News, June 13, 2016. https://abcnews.go.com/International/isis-gay-punished-death/story?id=39826182.

"Understanding White Christian Nationalism." Institution for Social and Policy Studies, October 4, 2022. https://isps.yale.edu/news/blog/2022/10/understanding-white-christian-nationalism.

Urquist, Evan. "Gamergate Never Died," *Slate,* August 23, 2019. https://slate.com/technology/2019/08/gamergate-video-games-five-years-later.html

"USA—Reported Forcible Rape Rate 2022." *Statista,* October 20, 2023. https://www.statista.com/statistics/191226/reported-forcible-rape-rate-in-the-us-since-1990/.

US Government Accountability Office. "K-12 Education: DOD Has Taken Steps to Support Students Affected by Problematic Sexual Behaviors, but Challenges Remain." *GAO Report 24-106182,* February 13, 2024. https://www.gao.gov/products/gao-24-106182.

"US National Plan to End Gender Based Violence: Strategies for Action." The White House, May 2023. https://www.whitehouse.gov/wp-content/uploads/2023/05/National-Plan-to-End-GBV.pdf.

"U.S. Youth Attitudes on Guns Report." Southern Poverty Law Center, February 6, 2024. https://www.splcenter.org/peril-youth-attitudes-guns-report.

Vaccaro, Christian, and Melissa Swauger. *Unleashing Manhood in the Cage: Masculinity and Mixed Martial Arts.* London: Lexington Books, 2016.

Van Brunt, Brian, and Chris Taylor. *Understanding and Treating Incels: Case Studies, Guidance, and Treatment of Violence Risk in the Involuntary Celibate Community.* New York: Routledge, 2021.

Vandello, Joseph A., Jennifer K. Bosson, Dov Cohen, et al. "Precarious Manhood." *Journal of Personality and Social Psychology* 95, no. 6 (2008): 1325–1339. https://psycnet.apa.org/doi/10.1037/a0012453.

Vegetti, Federico, and Levente Littvay. "Belief in Conspiracy Theories and Attitudes Toward Political Violence." *Italian Political Science Review* 52, no. 1 (2022): 18–32. https://doi.org/10.1017/ipo.2021.17.

Velazquez, Cynthia M. "57 Member/Associates of Various White Supremacist Gangs Charged in Kidnapping and Drug Conspiracies." DEA, May 1, 2018. https://www.dea.gov/press-releases/2018/05/01/57-memberassociates-various-white-supremacists-gangs-charged-kidnapping.

Vickery, Jacqueline Ryan, and Tracy Everbach. "The Persistence of Misogyny: From the Streets, to Our Screens, to the White House." In *Mediating Misogyny: Gender, Technology, and Harassment.* Cham, Switzerland: Palgraeve Macmillan, 2018.

"Violent Online Groups Extort Minors to Self-Harm and Produce Child Sexual Abuse Material." Internet Crime Complaint Center (IC3), September 12, 2023. https://www.ic3.gov/Media/Y2023/PSA230912.

Vlossak, Elizabeth. *Marianne or Germania? Nationalizing Women in Alsace, 1870–1946.* Cambridge: Oxford University Press, 2010.

Vogel, Kenneth P. "Face of the Tea Party Is Female." *Politico,* March 26, 2010. https://www.politico.com/story/2010/03/face-of-the-tea-party-is-female-035094.

Vogels, Emily. "The State of Online Harassment." Pew Research Center, January 20, 2021. https://www.pewresearch.org/internet/2021/01/13/the-state-of-online-harassment/.

"VOX-Pol Virtual Roundtable: Artificial Intelligence and Extremism." *VOX - Pol*, December 13, 2023. https://voxpol.eu/events/vox-pol-virtual-roundtable-artificial-intelligence-and-extremism/.

Waetjen, Thembisa. "The Limits of Gender Rhetoric for Nationalism: A Case Study from Southern Africa." *Theory and Society* 30, no. 1 (2001): 121–152. https://doi.org/10.1023/A:1011099627847.

Walton, Stephen J. "Anti-Feminism and Misogyny in Breivik's 'Manifesto.'" *NORA-Nordic Journal of Feminist and Gender Research* 20, no. 1 (2012): 4–11. https://doi.org/10.1080/08038740.2011.650707.

Wareham, Jamie. "Beaten, Stabbed and Shot: 320 Trans People Killed in 2023—New Monitoring Report." *Forbes*, November 13, 2023. https://www.forbes.com/sites/jamiewareham/2023/11/13/beaten-stabbed-and-shot-320-trans-people-murdered-in-2023/?sh=471f5d251646.

Warner, Tara, Tara Leigh Tober, and David F. Warner. "To Provide or Protect? Masculinity, Economic Precarity, and Protective Gun Ownership in the United States." *Sociological Perspectives* 65, no. 1 (2022): 97–118. https://doi.org/10.1177/0731121421998406.

"Watch Tucker Carlson Originals: The End of Men." Fox Nation, October 5, 2022. https://nation.foxnews.com/tucker-carlson-originals-the-end-of-men-nation/.

Waxman, Olivia B. "Why Toni Morrison Books Are Frequent Targets of Book Bans." *Time*, January 31, 2022. https://time.com/6143127/toni-morrison-book-bans/.

Way, Niobe. *Deep Secrets: Boys' Friendships and the Crisis of Connection.* Cambridge, MA: Harvard University Press, 2011.

Way, Niobe. *Rebels with a Cause: Reimagining Boys, Ourselves, and Our Culture.* New York: Dutton, 2024.

Webster, Hanna. "Critics Attack UPMC Children's Over Transgender Care." *Pittsburgh Post-Gazette*, August 28, 2022. https://www.post-gazette.com/news/health/2022/08/27/upmc-children-transgender-care-pittsburgh-lgbtq-alt-right-threats-hospital-patients-puberty-social-medical/stories/202208250133.

Weiner, Rachel. "Accused Former Atomwaffen Division Leader Shared Child Pornography, Prosecutors Allege in Va. Court." *The Washington Post*, March 13, 2020. https://www.washingtonpost.com/local/public-safety/alleged-former-atomwaffen-division-leader-shared-child-pornography-prosecutors-allege-in-va-court/2020/03/13/ea6ced0c-6544-11ea-acca-80c22bbee96f_story.html.

Weiner, Rachel, and Ryan Fleming. "The Order of Nine Angles." ISD, September 16, 2022. https://www.isdglobal.org/explainers/the-order-of-nine-angles-explainer/.

Weintraub, Allie, Abbey Levine, Taigi Smith, et al. "How a 7-Year Old Helped Investigators Solve Her Mom's Murder." ABC News, January 20, 2023. https://abcnews.go.com/US/7-year-helped-investigators-solve-moms-murder/story?id=96239725.

Weir, Fred. "Rise of the Volga Boatwoman? Russia Ending Gender Bar on Many Jobs." *Christian Science Monitor*, January 3, 2020. https://www.csmonitor.com/World/Europe/2020/0103/Rise-of-the-Volga-boatwomen-Russia-ending-gender-bar-on-many-jobs.

Westbrook, Laurel. *Unlivable Lives: Violence and Identity in Transgender Activism.* Berkeley: University of California Press, 2021.

"What You Need to Know about QAnon." *Southern Poverty Law Center Hatewatch*, October 27, 2020. https://www.splcenter.org/hatewatch/2020/10/27/what-you-need-know-about-qanon.

"Wheels." Domestic Abuse Intervention Programs, https://www.theduluthmodel.org/wheels/.

"Which Countries Offer Gender-Neutral Passports?" *The Economist*, April 11, 2022. https://www.economist.com/graphic-detail/2022/04/11/which-countries-offer-gender-neutral-passports.

Whitehurst, Lindsay. "Transgender Athlete Ban Challenged in Utah Lawsuit." *AP News*, June 1, 2022. https://apnews.com/article/sports-lawsuits-utah-state-courts-government-and-politics-9be50d460cae6e1a0f3154a39c23e66c.

Whittaker, Joe, William Costello, and Andrew G. Thomas. "Predicting Harm among Incels (Involuntary Celibates): The Roles of Mental Health, Ideological Belief and Social Networking." *U.K. Commission for Countering Extremism. Rethinking Extremism.* https://assets.publishing.service.gov.uk/media/65cdf458130549000c867a83/140224+SISNET+Incel+Report.pdf.

Whittier, Nancy. "Where Are the Children? Theorizing the Missing Piece in Gendered Sexual Violence." *Gender and Society* 30, no. 1 (2016): 95–108. https://scholarworks.smith.edu/soc_facpubs/3?utm_source=scholarworks.smith.edu%2Fsoc_facpubs%2F3&utm_medium=PDF&utm_campaign=PDFCoverPages.

Wiggins, Christopher. "FBI Says Anti-LGBTQ+ Hate Crimes Are Way Up." Advocate.com, October 18, 2023. https://www.advocate.com/news/fbi-increase-lgbtq-hate-crimes.

Will, Madeline. "Misogynist Influencer Andrew Tate Has Captured Boys' Attention. What Teachers Need to Know." *Education Week*, February 2, 2023. https://www.edweek.org/leadership/misogynist-influencer-andrew-tate-has-captured-boys-attention-what-teachers-need-to-know/2023/02.

Williams, Katherine. "Women's Engagement with the Far Right: A Quest for a More Holistic Understanding." *Religion Compass* 18, no. 5 (2024): 1–12. https://doi.org/10.1111/rec3.12495.

Williams, Nicholas, and John Annese. "Co-Conspirator in Plot to Shoot Up NYC Synagogue Is Jewish Descendent of Holocaust Survivor, Relative Says." *New York Daily News*, November 20, 2022. https://www.nydailynews.com/2022/11/20/co-conspirator-in-plot-to-shoot-up-nyc-synagogue-is-jewish-descendant-of-holocaust-survivor-relative-says/.

Wilson, Chris. "Nostalgia, Entitlement and Victimhood: The Synergy of White Genocide and Misogyny." *Terrorism and Political Violence* 34, no. 8 (2022): 1810–1825. https://doi.org/10.1080/09546553.2020.1839428.

Winston, Ali. "The Satanist Neo-Nazi Plot to Murder U.S. Soldiers." *Rolling Stone*, June 5, 2022. https://www.rollingstone.com/culture/culture-features/the-satanist-neo-nazi-plot-to-murder-u-s-soldiers-1352629/.

Winton, Richard, Hannah Fry, Alene Tchekmedyian, et al. "Not Invited to the Dance: A Possible Motive for Monterey Park Shooting." *LA Times*, January 23, 2023. https://www.latimes.com/california/story/2023-01-23/jealousy-possible-motives-in-monterey-park-shooting.

Wolfe, Thomas. *You Can't Go Home Again.* First Perennial Classics Edition. New York: Harper & Row, 1998 [1934].

Wondwosen, Meron. "The Catt's Out of the Bag: Was She Racist? Racism in the Suffrage Movement." *UHURU*, October 1995. https://www.929movement.org/19951996.

Woods, Baynard. "Where the Hell Is Kekistan?: How Pepe-Posting Meme Warriors Responded to Real Violence of the Alt-Right." *The Baltimore Sun*, September 27, 2017. https://www.baltimoresun.com/2017/09/26/where-the-hell-is-kekistan-how-pepe-posting-meme-warriors-responded-to-real-violence-of-the-alt-right/.

Woods, Eric Taylor, Robert Schertzer, Leah Greenfeld, et al. "COVID-19 and Nationalism: A Scholarly Exchange." *Nations and Nationalism* 26, no. 4 (2020): 807–825. https://doi.org/10.1111/nana.12644.

Wright, Katherine, and Jack Holland. "Leadership and the Media: Gendered Framings of Julia Gillard's 'Sexism and Misogyny' Speech." *Australian Journal of Political Science* 49, no. 3 (2014): 455–468. https://doi.org/10.1080/10361146.2014.929089.

Wrisley, Samantha. "Feminist Theory and the Problem of Misogyny." *Feminist Theory* 24, no. 2 (2023): 188–207. https://doi.org/10.1177/14647001211039365.

WTOL11. "Neo-Nazis Harass Attendees at Equality Toledo's Love Fest Celebration." YouTube, July 17, 2023. https://www.youtube.com/watch?v=tvzUqbVp_EA.

Yan, Holly, Ben Brumfield, and Chelsea Carter. "Inside the Gunman's Head: Rejection, Jealousy, Vow to Kill." CNN, May 24, 2014. https://www.cnn.com/2014/05/24/us/california-shooting-suspect/index.html.

"Young People in the Time of COVID." *Hope Not Hate*, March 8, 2020. https://hopenothate.org.uk/2020/08/03/young-people-in-the-time-of-covid-19/.

Yousef, Odette. "Supremacy Movements Unite Over Abortion Restriction, Though for Different Reasons." NPR, May 12, 2022. https://www.kunr.org/u-s-headlines/u-s-headlines/2022-05-12/supremacy-movements-unite-over-abortion-restriction-though-for-different-reasons.

Yousef, Odette. "31 Members of the White Nationalist Patriot Front Arrested Near an Idaho Pride Event." NPR, June 11, 2022. https://www.npr.org/2022/06/11/1104405804/patriot-front-white-supremacist-arrested-near-idaho-pride.

"YouTube Shorts' Suggesting Banned-Andrew Tate's Content to Young Boys." *ISD*, April 6, 2023. https://www.isdglobal.org/isd-in-the-news/youtube-shorts-suggesting-banned-andrew-tates-content-to-young-boys/.

Yurcaba, Jo. "Missouri Republican Candidate Torches LGBTQ-Inclusive Books in Viral Video." NBC News, February 7, 2024. https://www.nbcnews.com/nbc-out/out-politics-and-policy/missouri-republican-candidate-torches-lgbtq-inclusive-books-viral-vide-rcna137715.

Yuval-Davis, Nira. *Gender and Nation*. London: Sage, 1997.

Zakaria, Rafia. *Against White Feminism: Notes on Disruption*. New York: W.W. Norton, 2021.

Zaveri, Mihir. "Son of N.J. Judge Is Killed: Roy Den Hollander, a Lawyer, Is Identified as Suspect." *The New York Times*, July 22, 2020. https://www.nytimes.com/2020/07/20/nyregion/esther-salas.html.

Zernike, Kate. "The Campus Wars Aren't About Gender . . . Are They?" *The New York Times*, January 31, 2024. https://www.nytimes.com/2024/01/28/us/colleges-antisemitism-gender.html.

Zongrone, Adrian D., Nhan L. Truong, and Joseph G. Kosciw. "Erasure and Resilience: The Experiences of LGBTQ Students of Color. Latinx LGBTQ Youth in U.S. Schools." *ERIC*, 2020. https://eric.ed.gov/?id=ED603848.

Zuckerberg, Donna. *Not All Dead White Men: Classics and Misogyny in the Digital Age*. Cambridge, MA: Harvard University Press, 2018.

INDEX

abortion: antisemitic conspiracy theory
and, 118; *Dobbs* decision and, 26, 115,
116, 117, 119; male supremacy and, 97;
memes conveying opposition to, 82;
new restrictions on, 146, 149, 151; penal-
izing travel for, 26; white supremacism
and, 116, 118, 140, 141, 149. *See also*
reproductive rights
accelerationism, violent, 78, 137
Adichie, Chimamanda Ngozi, 22, 72,
97
AI (artificial intelligence), 142. *See also*
deepfake sexualized images
al Aqeedi, Rasha, 88
Alito, Samuel, 117
alpha males, 96, 102, 108, 111, 112, 114
Al-Shabaab, 51, 121
alt-right, 13, 80, 108, 240n109
Anglin, Andrew, 105, 107
antidemocratic beliefs, xiii, 142–43; of
Christian nationalism, 148; fears about
exploitation of children and, 120;
gender-based attacks and, 158; male
supremacy and, 97; women's rising
engagement with, 173. *See also* democracy
antifeminism: conspiracy theories based
on, 40, 98, 99–101; extreme rage of incels
and, 114; mainstreaming of, 50, 101–2;
male supremacy and, 93, 109; memes
conveying, 82; of misogynist influencers,
88–89; of Phyllis Schlafly, 170; racism
and, 102; social media and, 96–97; violent,
93, 101; white women and, 172–73; women's

political participation and, 68; young
boys' online content and, 81. *See also*
feminism
antigovernment movements, 143; COVID-19
pandemic and, 175, 178–79; motherhood
and, 169–70; QAnon and, 178; Ruby
Ridge standoff and, 165–66; Sarah Palin
and, 169
antisemitic conspiracy theories, 84, 88, 89,
98, 100, 116, 118, 125, 141; QAnon and, 176
antisemitism: across the political spectrum,
19; in emails and voicemails, 58; intersectionality with other hate, 161–62; Pepe
the Frog and, 80; in reactions to war in
Gaza, 14; scientific racism and, 89;
violence against women associated with,
6, 105; white Christian values and, 148;
white women's social media and, 173
anti-vax communities, 177–78
apocalyptic end times, 45, 47,
124
artificial intelligence (AI), 142. *See also*
deepfake sexualized images
Aryan Brotherhood, 132
Asian American and Pacific Islander
women, and COVID-19, 7, 106
Asian women: slurs against, 64; tropes
about, 7; violently attacked, 105–6
Atomwaffen, 118, 124
Atwood, Margaret, 143
authoritarian trends in US, 47, 97, 158,
173
autism, among incels, 114

A NOTE ON THE TYPE

This book has been composed in Arno, an Old-style serif typeface in the classic Venetian tradition, designed by Robert Slimbach at Adobe.